The *Past & Present* Book Series

General Editor
ALEXANDRA WALSHAM

The Foundations of Gentry Life

The Foundations of Gentry Life

The Multons of Frampton and their World, 1270–1370

PETER COSS

OXFORD
UNIVERSITY PRESS

OXFORD

UNIVERSITY PRESS

Great Clarendon Street, Oxford OX2 6DP

Oxford University Press is a department of the University of Oxford.
It furthers the University's objective of excellence in research, scholarship,
and education by publishing worldwide in

Oxford New York

Auckland Cape Town Dar es Salaam Hong Kong Karachi
Kuala Lumpur Madrid Melbourne Mexico City Nairobi
New Delhi Shanghai Taipei Toronto

With offices in

Argentina Austria Brazil Chile Czech Republic France Greece
Guatemala Hungary Italy Japan Poland Portugal Singapore
South Korea Switzerland Thailand Turkey Ukraine Vietnam

Oxford is a registered trade mark of Oxford University Press
in the UK and in certain other countries

Published in the United States
by Oxford University Press Inc., New York

© Peter Coss 2010

British Library Cataloguing in Publication Data
Data available

Library of Congress Cataloging in Publication Data
Data available

Typeset by Laserwords Private Limited, Chennai, India
Printed in Great Britain
on acid-free paper by the
MPG Books Group, Bodmin and King's Lynn

ISBN 978-0-19-956000-4

3 5 7 9 10 8 6 4 2

To Barbara Harvey, whose friendship
I value and whose scholarship
I greatly admire

Contents

List of Illustrations

List of Illustrations

Acknowledgements

The completion of this book was made possible by a grant from the Arts and Humanities Research Board (now the Arts and Humanities Research Council) under their Research Leave Scheme, which I gratefully acknowledge. I also wish to thank Cardiff University for its generosity in granting me study leave for the academic year 2005–6. My research in Oxford was greatly aided by the award of two visiting fellowships, from the President and Fellows of Magdalen College and the Rector and Fellows of Exeter College, during Michaelmas Term 2005 and Hillary Term 2006 respectively. The warmth and fellowship that I enjoyed at both colleges made my stay in Oxford an extremely enjoyable as well as a productive one. Thanks are also due to Magdalen's archivist, Robin Darwell-Smith, for his help and advice during my extensive use of the Magdalen Archives in the stimulating atmosphere of the McFarlane Room, and to Laurence Brockliss, history fellow at Magdalen, for his support. Needless to say I am indebted to staff at the various other record repositories I have visited during the course of my researches, especially Duke Humphrey in the Bodleian Library, Lincoln Record Office, Norwich Record Office, the National Monuments Record at Swindon, the manuscript room at the British Library and The National Archives at Kew.

    I have accrued many other debts during the writing and preparation of this work. To Barbara Harvey fell the unenviable task of reading and commenting on the first draft, not least because it was at that point over-burdened with detail. I profited greatly from her guidance, observations, and corrections. The final product owes a very great deal to her. A second draft was read by Chris Wickham and by three other readers commissioned by *Past and Present* and by Oxford University Press. I am most grateful to them all for their trenchant criticisms. Chris Wickham, moreover, has been a constant source of help and encouragement throughout the preparation of the book. I am most grateful to Michael Clanchy for reading and commenting on Chapters 11 and 12 and for his generosity in sharing his knowledge and expertise. I am grateful too to Barrie Dobson and Christopher Harper-Bill for reading the draft that lay behind Chapters 8 and 9. Sincere thanks are due to a group of scholars who gave generously of their own work and advice: Alen Aberg, Andrew Ayton, Jean Birrell, Christopher Knusel, Richard Gorski, and David Simpkin. I would also like to thank my colleagues at Cardiff University, especially Bill Aird, Lloyd Bowen, Peter Edbury, John Hines, Helen Nicholson and David Wyatt for discussing various issues and points of interest with me. Bill Aird, in particular, has spent more time than friendship necessarily warrants in discussing the Multons of Frampton. My colleague Howard Mason is responsible for drawing the excellent maps (2.2 and 4.1). Dr David Morgan not only produced the splendid photographs for the cover, Figure 2.6, and Figures 9.1–9.6 but also gave up two weekends to accompany me on location. Carol Bestley, production editor at Oxford University Press has guided the book through the publication process with skill and kindness. I would also like to thank Rose James, the copy editor, and Joy Mellor, the proof reader. Finally, there is no way that I can express the debt that the book owes, at all stages, to the wisdom and the selfless input of my wife, Angela. Needless to say, any remaining faults or flaws are entirely my own.

List of Abbreviations

AgHR	*Agricultural History Review*
BL	British Library
CAD	*Calendar of Ancient Deeds*
CBA	Council for British Archaeology
CChR	*Calendar of Charter Rolls*
CCR	*Calendar of Close Rolls*
CFR	*Calendar of Fine Rolls*
CIM	*Calendar of Inquisitions Miscellaneous*
CIPM	*Calendar of Inquisitions Post Mortem*
CPR	*Calendar of Patent Rolls*
EcHR	*Economic History Review*
EHR	*English Historical Review*
EETS	Early English Text Society
Ex. e Rot. Fin.	*Excerpta e Rotulis Finium*
Multon	Multon Hall Archives, Magdalen College, Oxford
Oxford DNB	*Oxford Dictionary of National Biography*
Rot. Hund.	*Rotuli Hundredorum*
TNA	The National Archives, Kew
TRHS	*Transactions of the Royal Historical Society*
VCH	*Victoria Country History*

Permissions

Figure 2.3 has been reproduced by permission of *Ordnance Survey*.

Figure 2.4 Aerial photograph reproduced by permission of the National Monuments Record.

Figures 3.1, 3.2, 5.1, 7.1, 8.1 and 12.2: The British Library has granted permission for the reproduction of images from the following: Add. MS 42131 (fos. 163r, 163v, 172r, 173r, 186v, 206v, 207r, 207v, 208r, 215r), and Add. MS 49999 (fo. 95r).

Figures 10.2, 11.1, 11.2 and 13.1: Photographs reproduced by permission of the fellows of Magdalen College, Oxford.

Figure 12.1: The Bodleian Library, University of Oxford, has granted permission for the reproduction of images from the following: MS Digby 86 (fos. 4v, 34v, 84r, 102v, 205v).

1

Introduction

In *The Origins of the English Gentry* (Cambridge, 2003) I set out to show how the English gentry was formed in an accelerating process from the latter half of the thirteenth century to the middle decades of the fourteenth. In doing so I placed most of my emphasis upon two analytically separated but interconnected phenomena: the development of a partnership in governance between the state and the lesser nobility on the one hand and on the other the internal dynamics within the lesser nobility itself which led to the crystallization of a graded and relatively stable gentry. The gentry possessed a powerful elite culture around knighthood and chivalry and a substantial landed base which gave a strong territorial dimension to the exercise of its power and the expression of its interests. Gradation became a mechanism by which the gentry could combine its sense of social and cultural superiority with a degree of porosity which allowed it to accommodate lawyers, administrators, and other aspirants to gentility within its ranks.

This study provided me with a framework for understanding the basic evolution of the gentry. Yet it could only take me so far along the way towards explaining the most enduring characteristic of the gentry: its capacity for survival as a ruling class. True, this longevity can be explained by recourse to another feature: adaptability. Whether we are talking about the changes wrought by the post-plague economy, the opportunities and threats emanating from the price rise of the sixteenth century, the shifts in religious belief associated with the Reformation, the changes in educational and intellectual endeavour and civil purpose encapsulated within the term humanism, or whether we are discussing the spectacular expansion of external commerce in the era of the slave trade, the advantages brought by developments in transport, in industrialization and in financial institutions, the outlets for energy and profit-making afforded by empire, or the changes within political institutions in the nineteenth and early twentieth centuries, we find the gentry exhibiting an extraordinary capacity to go with the grain and to maintain a lifestyle, a status and a level of wealth commensurate with its function as a social elite. But to emphasize adaptability is almost tautological. Since its adaptability is unlikely to be a product of external factors alone or of pure chance, to talk of adaptability is to do little more than restate the question. This adaptability must itself derive from features that were characteristic of the gentry from the period of its formation. We need therefore to look more deeply into the gentry's way of life—its economy, its social relationships, its culture and its assumptions—during the time in which it came into being.

When we examine the characteristics of the gentry over the longer term we begin to notice a tension, a paradox even, at the heart of gentry life. Consider the following which appeared in the *Manchester Guardian* on 11 August 1906:

There is all the difference in the world between the Squire of the past and the Esquire of the present. In the days that have passed away the Squire of the village was, in sentiment at least, one of the gentlemen of England; he was a man with an ancient pedigree, taking pride in his name, his ancestors, his estate, his horses and his tenantry. But today if we cast an eye from village to village and parish to parish we shall find that in the majority of instances the county family is known no longer. The [Squire's] estate has another lord, his traditions have vanished, and his name alone remains—not, indeed, in the memory or hearts of the people, but deeply graven on the tombs erected in the churchyard, recognised only by the antiquary or the curious. The pedigree of the Squire was as pure as that of the Plantagenet; his wife was a scion of a house as noble and as proud as his own. He was a leader in all great county movements without being too intimately versed in the details of county work. He was patron of all local organisations. He was a member for his county or for some insignificant borough, the keys of which he held in his pocket. He made the most of his opportunities, believing in the divine right of his position and in the superiority of his class. His sons were carefully trained, the oldest to succeed him, the younger to take their place in the army or the navy, to cure the souls of the people in the parish in which he lived. He rode to hounds and dispensed hospitality with a free hand; his rents were moderate and punctually paid by the tenantry, who sometimes while trembling at his frown, were ready to touch the buckle of the shoes upon his feet. In the days not long passed away his park was stocked with deer and his cellars with port; he kept a family coach. The Squire's wife received the curtseys of the women of the village with smiling grace. Her sons were her pride, her daughters her difficulty—this owing chiefly to the importance of their marriage with men of her own selection and of her own rank. She was not forgetful of the claims of the village women, the sick and the poor and the troubled, but her presence in their tiny homes was not frequent, nor was much consideration affected by the family as to the substantial character, suitability, or sanitary conditions of the hovels within which many of the people lived or—shall I say—existed.

Leaving side the question as to whether the gentry really was on its knees by 1906 and give or take some of the more doubtful assumptions it contains, this journalistic piece, reprinted in the *Guardian* on 11 August 2006, pinpoints many of the gentry's most enduring characteristics. Its members enjoyed a status that was largely hereditary, that was predicated upon ancestry, upon pedigree, upon all that was invested in the continuance of a specific family name. It was equally predicated upon a pre-eminence sustained by the possession of land. These two factors—pedigree and possession—tended to combine to produce the easy sense of social superiority that the gentry projected. The *Guardian* writer reminds us, in his allusions to county office and to parliament, that there were provincial and national dimensions to gentry status. Moreover, neither nobility nor gentility could ever be sustained for long without broad social consensus and recognition. And yet, for the most part, the writer highlights the most local aspects of gentry life: the village, the estate, the parish. It is primarily neighbours and tenants who are both impressed and overawed by the gentry's God-given sense of superiority. The life is a life of quality framed locally with plenteous food and drink, hospitality, and vigorous outdoor pursuits. This dialectic between nationally and provincially sustained values and status on the one hand and a lifestyle that is highly dependent upon local factors and heavily embedded within the locality on the other must lie at the heart of the exploration we are required to make.

The respect to which they were 'entitled' came not only from their own tenantry, but also from the broader populace. This entitlement was local and parochial, but it also had county, regional, and national dimensions. This was partly due to the exercise of office, but it was also due to a national system of social gradation and a national consensus on elite recognition and behaviour. Gentry status was therefore as much a collective as an individual or family one, and it was sustained in both abstract and concrete ways, that is to say both in the world of ideas and imagination and by actual social interaction. Gentry families shared their position, elite standing and self-assurance with many others in mutually supportive ways, through social intercourse and through institutions.

This was the site of a major paradox in gentry life. There was a dual dependence upon local sustenance and national support, and a consequent need to pay regard to both. In consequence the gentry was moulded by both. This, however, was not the only paradox within gentry life. The *Guardian* writer highlights two further features of great significance. One is the capacity of 'the Squire' to make the most of his opportunities, which means quite explicitly cashing in on the social advantages and social accomplishments which his birth has given him. The other is the fact that members of the gentry belonged to a class not a caste. An easy route through life was never guaranteed for the totality of its members. The eldest son, as the writer puts it, is 'groomed' to succeed his father, but the others need to be trained for *acceptable* professions both in the family's interests and in their own. Daughters, of course, were required to sustain themselves and their family's status by another but equally vital means: marriage.

This brings us squarely to the issue of the professions. The gentry was far from being impervious to upward mobility from below. This was partly the product of biological failure and the need to replenish gentry families as surnames died with their last male holders. Replacement came to some degree from traditional sub-knightly and upper freeholding stock, as well as from those younger sons and nephews of landowners who founded cadet branches of their families. But upward movement had a structural component. The role and position of the professions in English society itself facilitated a process of social advancement. This gives rise to another deep paradox. While the gentry shared an outlook which placed a high premium on antiquity of lineage, their ranks remained porous to the influx of newcomers with the necessary wealth, even if position and influence, or even membership, was rarely conceded in full measure within a single generation. Gentility was derived from the concept of nobility as fashioned, or perhaps re-fashioned, in the high middle ages, but in England it was barely reflected, and certainly not enshrined, in law. Hence there was relatively little in the way of formal barriers to social progress into the elite. It is doubtful whether legal considerations should be seen in themselves as determinant, however. The openness of the gentry to certain of the professions reflects, as we shall see, some discernible currents within the evolution of English medieval society itself. It came to be matched, moreover, by an increasing tendency for younger, and hence largely non-inheriting, sons of the gentry to seek an outlet and an income from favoured professions. Porosity, like adaptability, is a characteristic of the gentry which can certainly be traced to the period of origin. However, the manner of its working requires clearer elucidation. It is therefore one of the themes of this book.

The quest for social recognition on the part of the sub-knightly and the aspirant professionals led directly to the crystallization of the graded gentry. The manpower needs of the state during the time of the three Edwards, both in the civilian and military spheres and in the need for a representative tax-yielding parliament, certainly played a major part. But we ought not to put too much emphasis on this side of the equation. The gentry crystallized as much through the internal dynamics of English society. The graded gentry was in fact a compromise solution to a serious social situation. It would be a mistake to assume that this crystallization occurred mechanistically, through structural changes devoid of human agency. In fact, this compromise of the graded gentry was undoubtedly the outcome of considerable social tension. It was forged in a particular cultural context, one that was dominated by chivalric knighthood. This had for long constituted a powerfully exclusive culture that was not going to widen its membership easily.[1] It was a culture moreover within which ladies as well as lords fully participated.[2] The fact that this exclusivity gave way to allow heraldic recognition to the esquires—a sure barometer of social acceptance in the cultural climate of the time—does not mean that it did so without pain. That heraldic recognition was a slow process during the early decades of the fourteenth century is in itself indicative of this.

The tensions involved can also be glimpsed through the contemporary obsession with display to which historians have recently devoted much attention. Display was necessary in order to express superiority over those below one in

---

[1] On this issue see my 'Knighthood, Heraldry and Social Exclusion in Edwardian England', in Peter Coss and Maurice Keen, *Heraldry, Pageantry and Social Display in Medieval England* (Woodbridge, 2002).

[2] This is one of the themes of my book *The Lady in Medieval England 1000–1500* (Stroud, 1998).

the hierarchy but also to assert membership with those on a par or even above. It was therefore imperative both for the solidly based and for the aspirant to declare their worth in palpable terms, by buildings and furnishings, for example, by dress and personal adornment, by means of heraldic statement, by sepulchral monuments and so on. Furthermore, display contains more subtle statements of superiority over others, in terms of lineage and affinity for example, which are often only dimly discernible by us. We might not see the underlying social tensions easily but they were certainly there. Sometimes they are revealed to us in disguised form. Moralists might point for example to extravagance in dress. That this had connotations of social competition is shown by the appearance of the first sumptuary law in 1337 restricting rich dress to knights and those above them in the social order. Gentility, then, could be hard to confine.

Fashion became a key feature in this culture of display. Though it is not so easily detected in all spheres, there can be little doubt that clothing, household furnishings and secular building, for example, were all subject to shifts in fashion. This was a culture of emulation, aspiration and competition; indeed it was upon these foundations that social display largely rested. All the landholding elite were caught up in this culture, even royalty.[3] But it was not only 'rank' itself that was displayed thereby but also an acute sense of belonging, belonging not only among those regarded as *gentils* in general terms but also more specifically belonging with particular members of the higher nobility. One thinks immediately of service connotations and of the noble retinue, in peace, in the tournament and in war. One thinks of the indentures which specify *bouche à court*, that is dining with the lord or, at the very least, at his expense. But there were also affiliations by blood and family connection.

There was a sense of belonging with one's own peers. There was often also a striving to be considered acceptable to those of higher rank. All of this was no doubt tinged with an element of competition. These factors must have provided considerable stimulus to downward cultural diffusion. The display of wealth and possessions constitutes the more materially enduring feature of medieval aspiration. However, it is hardly to be doubted that manners were of equal significance and, indeed, we can see some direct evidence of this. There were certainly norms to abide by. Most obviously, there was the capacity to speak French. 'For unless a man knows French, he is thought of little account', wrote Robert of Gloucester late in the thirteenth century.[4] Then there is the issue of table manners and other aspects of domestic behaviour.

This book does not deal directly with the content of chivalric culture nor indeed with the relationship of the gentry to the crown and to the higher nobility. These subjects have been well studied by historians and can safely be taken as

---

[3] See, for example, the remarks by Paul Binski in *Westminster Abbey and the Plantagenets; Kingship and the Representation of Power 1200–1400* (New Haven and London, 1995), 110–13.

[4] W. A. Wright (ed.), *The Metrical Chronicle of Robert of Gloucester*, 2 vols (Rolls Ser., lxxvi, London, 1887), ii. 544, l. 7542.

given within gentry life. They have figured in the previous book from which this one partly derives and have also been explored elsewhere by the present historian. However, they cannot and should not be left entirely out of the picture; indeed they will intermittently and necessarily intrude. In the final chapter, moreover, I will turn to the interaction between influences from those directions and the essentially local worlds that are the prime concerns of this work, in an attempt to comprehend the overall cultural horizons of the gentry. The emphasis for the most part, however, will be placed firmly where our *Guardian* writer placed it and for reasons that we have already explained.

Inevitably one must deal with questions of definition. The word *foundations*, as employed in the title of the book, is to be understood in two senses. In its primary sense it comprises the features of gentry culture that were present in the period of its formation and which informed, underpinned, and sustained it thereafter. Naturally, some of its characteristics had their roots in earlier ages as did the most basic institutions. As we shall see, however, many of the most enduring features of gentry culture either arose or intensified and became more visible during this period. The second sense in which I am using the word *foundations* is that what is being studied here is the true bedrock of gentry life. Whether we look at their material culture, at getting and spending, at family and estate protection, at the basic belief system, in both its religious and secular dimensions, at the capacity to record and recall, or at the connections between the rural and urban dimensions to life, gentry culture is revealed as overwhelmingly local. Moreover, many of the attitudes and assumptions that the gentry carried with them must have been conditioned, in large measure, by these all-important aspects of life.[5] This is true not only of the institutions around which life revolved—the household and the estate for instance—but also of the relationships which lay at the heart of social life. As a result there was an upward as well as a downward dimension to gentry culture. Although, inevitably, its effects are hard to discern, the historian of the gentry must be aware of this dimension. The porosity of the gentry from below allows us at least some insight into the cultural effects that newcomers must have had upon the gentry's established members. These effects took place, in large measure, locally, where they mixed with basic cultural ingredients as well as those *extra local* influences from outside to which I have already alluded. The numerous dimensions to gentry life and the social relations that dominated them constantly interacted, moulding and forming/re-forming beliefs, assumptions, and attitudes. At the same time, however, these wider cultural parameters could not exist were it not for the material, nutritional, and social underpinning provided by the household, estate, and locality. We might also suppose, with good reason, that on the ground gentility is likely to have encompassed not only

---

[5] Conditioned but not determined. One must avoid being drawn back into the discredited concepts of base and superstructure. Moreover, there were other sources of conditioning. One was the influence of chivalric culture. As E. P. Thompson said of law, so we must say of culture: it is not confined to one level, but is present at every level.

those items drawn from romance, mixing martial values and courtly courtesy, but also more basic traits, as it were, such as trust and honesty in one's dealings, and dignity and lack of arrogance in bearing and demeanour: the sorts of qualities that Philippa Maddern was able to identify in the comparatively source-rich fifteenth century.[6]

It will have become apparent to the reader that although I refer as appropriate to gentry culture, this book is not an exercise in cultural history as the term is currently understood. The 'new cultural history' has its own conceptual underpinning, dealing explicitly and as a matter of course with representations, rituals, bodies, discourse analysis, semiotics, textuality, contextuality and similar issues.[7] Much of this operates at the cutting edge of historical research, and I do not in any way question its validity. However, it is not what is on offer here. This is partly because the available sources do not readily lend themselves to it but, more importantly, because this approach is not the most appropriate in terms of what this particular book is attempting to do. What my exploration requires is a mixture of social history per se and sociocultural history. Let me explain.

Social history has traditionally centred upon structures and processes, on causes and on explanation of continuity and change. The study of culture, and hence the study of cultural history, by contrast is essentially the study of meaning, on how meaning may be discerned and interpreted.[8] Social and cultural history, or rather sociocultural and the new cultural history, are in my view complementary and overlapping perspectives. For the purpose of the current work it is the sociocultural perspective that is deemed the more appropriate. Few are likely to suggest today that society and culture are separate entities or that they operate on separate planes, and I have no intention of doing so. I start, however, from the position that humans are naturally social animals. Social practice is not just steeped in culture; it is itself constitutive of culture. When we shake hands we perform at once a social and a cultural act, and we do so in time, in place, in a material world. We can, if we wish, disembody cultural practices in order to discern their meaning. We can do so imaginatively and with empathy. We can do so with fascinating and instructive results. If, however, we are concerned to understand the causes and the origin of things, and if our concern is to understand why change occurs, or indeed does not occur, then we must study culture as embedded in social practice. In this sense I give primacy to social relations. My stance is therefore broadly the one taken in the foreword to the

---

[6] P. Maddern, 'Honour Among the Pastons: Gender and Integrity in Fifteenth-Century Provincial Society', *Journal of Medieval History*, 14 (1998), 357–71.

[7] For the 'new cultural history' see William H. Sewell, 'The Concept(s) of Culture', in Victoria E. Bonnell and Lynn Hunt (eds.), *Beyond the Cultural Turn: New Directions in the Study of Society and Culture* (Berkeley, 1999), 35–61; and Lynn Hunt (ed.), *The New Cultural History* (Berkeley, 1999). See also Miri Rubin, 'What is Cultural History Now?', in David Cannadine (ed.), *What is History Now?* (London, 2002), 80–94

[8] The fundamental differences and their underpinnings are brought out especially well in Carla Hesse, 'The New Empiricism', in *Cultural and Social History*, vol. 1, no. 2 (2004), 2001–7.

new journal, *Cultural and Social History,* in 2004. Its editorial board explained
the choice of title, partly to maintain a dialogue between the two approaches and
partly to unite them:

We . . . assume that 'the cultural' and 'the social' are mutually constitutive and inextricably
linked. We believe that an appreciation of the constellation of cultural forces that confer
meaning on the lives of historical actors is necessary if we are to understand more fully
the social experience of individuals and groups in the past. Thus 'culture' is understood
not as an entity distinct from 'society' but as a product of social practice, and therefore at
the heart of society itself.[9]

Two senses in which the term culture itself has been used are significant in
the context of the present work. The first sense is that of high culture, meaning
the art to which only the cultivated and/or initiated could properly respond, and
to which could be contrasted popular or mass culture which was more easily
comprehended by the bulk of the population. The latter was deemed to be less
demanding, even though it might contain elements that were derived from high
culture as well as elements that were formed in isolation from, or in opposition
to, it. One might also talk of minority cultures, of subcultures and so on. Culture,
in the sense of high culture, in the words of Adam Kuper, is 'the gift of educated
taste that marks off a lady or a gentleman from the upstart'.[10] The second sense
is that used by social anthropologists, meaning a way of life in its entirety. It
encompasses the manner in which people relate to the natural world and the
manner in which they relate to their fellows. I will be using the term culture
essentially in the second sense, albeit in a way that incorporates something of
the first given that the gentry were by definition an elite and self-consciously
differentiated some of their life experience from that of others. To avoid any
ambiguity in terms of content or in terms of my overall purpose, method or
approach, I have avoided the word culture in the title of the book, calling it more
accurately, I believe, *The Foundations of Gentry Life: The Multons of Frampton
and their World.* It is a contribution towards the social and sociocultural history
of the gentry.

---

[9] 'Editorial', *Cultural and Social History: The Journal of the Social History Society,* vol. 1, no. 1
(2004), 1–2.
[10] Adam Kuper, *Culture: The Anthropologists' Account* (Cambridge, Mass., and London,
1999), 4.

2

The Multons and Frampton

We are now at the point where we need to briefly review the range of sources
that are available for the study of gentry history and to introduce the families
with which we will be primarily concerned. Those who study the early history
of the gentry have, in very general terms, two main categories of sources at their
disposal, that is to say those emanating from the central government and those
of private provenance. As is often the case, the nature of the sources has tended
to determine the questions asked. Thus the evidence provided by the records of
the royal chancery, the exchequer and the law courts have favoured the study of
lesser landowners as royal commissioners and as agents of the state, as political
actors within the counties, as litigants and as stakeholders who had obligations,
both directly and indirectly, to the crown. The same sources also provide very
considerable genealogical evidence and evidence of tenurial relationships. They
are an aid, too, in understanding the political relationships between members
of the various social strata. In addition, considerable insight is also provided
into the structure of gentry estates through government surveys, particularly the
Hundred Rolls of 1279–80, and through inquisitions post-mortem, inquiries
that is on the deaths of tenants-in-chief of the crown.

On the private side of the equation, the great bulk of surviving evidence
consists of titles to property of various kinds, either as original documents or
(less often) as copies within cartularies, that is to say books comprising charters
and similar evidences. Hence much attention has been devoted to understanding
the accumulation of estates and some to their dispersal. Not surprisingly, then,
we tend to know a great deal about the gentry as property owners. We are
considerably less well off, however, when it comes to sources that tell us about
the actual economy of the gentry estates—manorial accounts, extents, court
rolls, and the like—and even worse off when it comes to records stemming from
gentry households. As we shall see, however, examples of all of these do exist,
even though they are exiguous in comparison with those emanating from other
varieties of landowner.

There are a few sources—wills for example—that provide more direct insight
into contemporary modes of thought and feeling. For the period under discussion
here, however, we lack sources like the Paston, Stonor and other letters from the
fifteenth century that would allow the historian to enter the inner world of the
gentry. This being so we neglect at our peril sources which shed indirect light

on how people thought. Visual sources are especially valuable in this respect. In addition to the close study of manuscripts, including illuminated ones such as the Luttrell Psalter, there is also the evidence provided by sepulchral monuments which are especially revealing. In short, the sociocultural historian of the gentry does not lack source material but one has to be prepared to work hard to penetrate beyond and behind the more accessible areas of gentry life.

As all historians of the medieval gentry find, it is never possible to discover a family whose memorials, written and visual, cover the whole spectrum of life. With this constraint, and bearing the above observations in mind, the present historian was prepared to approach the foundations of gentry culture by means of a series of synoptic studies, each dealing with a particular area of life. Something of this approach necessarily remains, and the surviving evidence for aspects of the lives of numerous families will be drawn upon. We will encounter, for example, the family of Le Strange of Hunstanton in Norfolk, those of Luttrell and Willoughby of Eresby from Lincolnshire, the de la Beches of Aldworth, Berkshire, and many others. However, a timely discovery enabled me to centre much of my study around the archive of one particular gentry family: the Multons of Frampton.[1] This archive survives at Magdalen College, Oxford, the manor of Frampton in Lincolnshire being one of the estates with which Bishop Wayneflete endowed the college which he founded in 1458.[2] As was normal fifteenth-century practice, he passed on its archive to the new owners. Principally, it contained the evidences accumulated by the Multons from around 1240 until their demise in the late fourteenth century, together with those of the Graa family who succeeded them.

At the heart of the Multon archive, as is so often the case, is an extensive deed collection, in this instance devoted chiefly to Frampton and parts near in Holland in South Lincolnshire.[3] Invaluable though these deeds are in allowing us to trace family and estate history over a long period, their value is further increased when the archive opens out to include estate and household records from the 1320s.[4] They include manorial account rolls from the years 1324–5 and 1325–6, an extent of the manor at Frampton from 1326, a collector's account for the years 1330–1, and a series of manor court rolls covering the period from June 1330

[1] I was alerted to this archive through the publication of the Multon household accounts in C. M. Woolgar, *Household Accounts of Medieval England*, British Academy Records of Social and Economic History, new ser. xviii, 2 vols (Oxford, 1993), i. 229–45. Woolgar subsequently made use of these in *The Great Household in Late Medieval England* (New Haven and London, 1999).

[2] For the foundation see Gerald Harriss, 'William Wayneflete and the Foundation of the College, 1448–1486', in L. W. B. Brockliss (ed.), *Magdalen College: A History* (Oxford, 2008). Strictly speaking, what Wayneflete purchased was the reversion of the manors of Multon Hall and Saltfleetby which finally came into his hands on the death of the widow of Sir John Graa in 1475.

[3] The deeds are catalogued by W. D. Macray: *Catalogue of Magdalen College Deeds, Lincolnshire*, vol. III (typescript in Magdalen College, n.d.).

[4] The estate records are listed by C. M. Woolgar in *A Catalogue of the Estate Archives of St Mary Magdalen College, Oxford*, vol. V (typescript, 1981).

to January 1332.[5] All of these belong to the early years of Thomas de Multon of Frampton III, who inherited his estates in the year 1324 after a long wardship. A second set of surviving documents is derived from the time of his son, John de Multon I. They include two sets of household accounts from the years 1343–4 and 1347–8. These were published by C. M. Woolgar in his edition of medieval household accounts for the British Academy in 1993.[6] There is also a rental belonging to the year 1343.[7] It was one of a number of estate documents produced at the beginning of John de Multon's tenure. We know this because the archive contains material from the succeeding Graa family. Belonging to the late fourteenth and early fifteenth centuries, it preserves evidence from the later Multon period. An unbound booklet comprising sixteen leaves of paper consists in large part of rentals of the mid-fourteenth century together with an 'arrentation' of the services due from the Multon serfs dating from around 1340.[8] While these records are not extensive in the sense of surviving in series, they do include examples of many of the major documents produced on gentry estates and in gentry households, enabling us to construct a composite picture. The Multon archive also contains single manorial accounts, dating from the 1320s, from two neighbouring manors, a fact which takes us, most interestingly, into a world of documentary exchange between families. There are also occasional letters, pride of place going to the one written by Sir John de Multon to his wife in November 1367 on the eve of his departure on a military expedition to Prussia.[9] In short, the nature of the Multon archive allows us to use it as a central point of reference within a broader study of gentry life and culture.

Who, then, were the Multons of Frampton? They stemmed ultimately from the Multons of Moulton by Spalding, and were distantly related thereby to several families of the higher nobility. The key figure in the genealogy of the Multons of Moulton was Thomas de Multon who died in 1240. Thomas was immensely successful as the father of dynasties. Three sons, by two wives, came to hold the baronies of Egremont, Cockermouth, and Burgh by Sands.[10] The Multons of Frampton, however, were not a direct offshoot of any these but were a junior branch of the original stock from Moulton near Spalding. They became, in contrast to their elevated relatives, solid members of the Lincolnshire gentry. The first of the Frampton line revealed by the Magdalen College archive is Sir Alan de Multon who died in 1240. He is a shadowy figure but he was very probably a younger brother of Thomas de Multon of Moulton, and the Frampton line appears to have originated with him. We learn more of Alan's widow, Margery,

[5] Multon Adds 9–13 and 84/2.
[6] The account rolls are Multon 160 and Estate Papers 85/2.   [7] Multon Add 7.
[8] Multon 165/30. There are also some parts of a cartulary: Adds 36 and 140/19.
[9] See below pp. 199–202, 207–8.
[10] I. J. Sanders, *English Baronies: A Study of their Origin and Descent 1086–1327* (Oxford, 1960), 24, 115, 135. Yet another line, the Multons of Gilsland, was an offshoot of the Egremont line. It died out in the early fourteenth century: *Complete Peerage*, ix. 405–7.

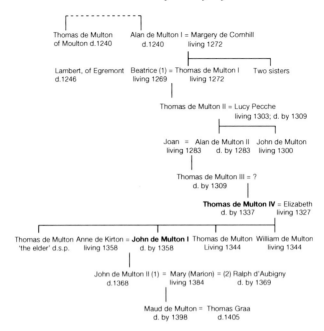

Figure 2.1. The Multons of Frampton.

and their son Thomas; especially in relation to the foundation of their chantry chapel at Frampton and to their property interests in Boston. As a result of the socially advantageous marriage of Lambert, son of Thomas de Multon, the Multons of Frampton were to hold their estates as tenants of the more elevated Multons of Egremont. It is not too difficult to trace the male descent of the Multons of Frampton, although it has to be pieced together from rather disparate material. As was quite often the case in gentry families, the Christian names chosen for the Multon males were taken from a restricted pool, so that Alan was succeeded by his son Thomas, and he in turn by his son, another Thomas. The next generation was represented by Alan, who was succeeded by his son and then by his grandson, both named Thomas. The Multon males tended to die as relatively young men, a feature which was to create intermittent difficulties for the family. They seem to have been married young, too, probably before the legal age of succession (twenty-one), and perhaps to avoid their partners being chosen for them in the event of feudal wardship. We will hear more of these men and their wives during the course of this book. It is with the last-mentioned Thomas, direct descendant of Sir Alan de Multon, the probable founder of this branch of the Multons, that the sequence of estate and household records emanating from Frampton begins.

The fourteenth-century records reveal an entrenched Lincolnshire family, with several concentrations of property: in and around Frampton and Boston in the south-east of the county; further up the coast at Saltfleetby and Somercotes; in South Lindsey at Miningsby, Coningsby and Wood Enderby; and between Gainsborough and Lincoln, where they held manors at Heapham, Sturton by Stow, Stow and Ingleby.

The family, or at least its lord, was to some degree itinerant, as we shall see later. However, the centre of their lives and their operation was at Frampton. This settlement was located in Kirton hundred, south of Boston, in Holland, the south-eastern division of Lincolnshire. Before proceeding further with a study of the Multons we need to understand the characteristics of this area. This is fenland.[11] More specifically it is siltland, and highly fertile.[12] H. E. Hallam, an economic historian who specialized on eastern England, estimated that the Lincolnshire siltland, on the seaward side of the fens, experienced something between a six and a tenfold expansion in cultivated area uring the first two centuries after Domesday Book.[13] Between them the peasantry and the 'great lords of the Wash basin' reclaimed more than one hundred square miles of the siltlands of Lincolnshire during the tenth to thirteenth centuries.[14] This had depended upon the construction of sea-dykes and fen-dykes. Although it is not recorded by name until 1178, the Sea Bank around the Wash, which protected the siltland from flooding, undoubtedly belonged to the late Saxon period. In the late twelfth century it was already regarded as 'old'.[15] The siltland was also in danger of flooding, however, from the fen-land side, as the sea level rose. Long straight banks were constructed between Lynn and Wainfleet. These were great engineering feats. Some of them sur-vive today, with roads on top and drains at their sides.[16] Kirton wapentake, between the rivers Welland and Witham, was protected by the Old Fen-dyke and the New Dyke or New Fen-dyke, the latter built, it seems, well before 1170.[17]

The siltland was distinctive in the Middle Ages, as indeed it remains today. The road system is complex, with tracks around medieval fields. There are nucleated villages, often late Saxon, with more dispersed settlement along the old droves. Remains of its saltmaking industry can still be seen, especially in Bicker Haven. However, this was only one of the many occupations that were characteristic of the area. The nearby fenland and marshland encouraged the cutting of turves, reeds and rushes, fishing and fowling, as well as grazing. Boston was a saltland port, as indeed were Wisbech and King's Lynn to the south, at a greater distance from Kirton and Frampton.

---

[11] For the fenland in general see H. C. Darby, *The Medieval Fenland* (Cambridge, 1940; repr. 1974).

[12] See especially H. C. Darby, *The Changing Fenland* (Cambridge, 1983); and D. Hall and J. Coles, *Fenland Survey: An Essay in Landscape and Persistence* (London, 1994).

[13] H. E. Hallam, 'Population Movements in England, 1086–1350 (Eastern England)' in idem (ed.), *The Agrarian History of England and Wales Volume II 1042–1350* (Cambridge, 1988), 510.

[14] Ibid.151.   [15] Hall and Coles, *Fenland Survey*, 127.

[16] Hallam, 'Population Movements', 151.   [17] Ibid. 152.

Figure 2.2. The Multon interests in Lincolnshire. Sites of Multon manors and properties are underlined.

Not surprisingly, given the richness of the soil and the scope for a variety of occupations, the siltland was an area that was teeming with people before the Black Death. The twelfth and thirteenth centuries, in particular, saw an enormous rise in population. Lincolnshire was a county where lordship had traditionally been weak and where there were high numbers of free men.[18] Nonetheless, in the siltland there were many customary or unfree tenants. Labour services varied considerably from manor to manor but tended to be moderate or light. Traditional villein holdings were normally a standard bovate or a half bovate. By the early fourteenth century, however, smallholdings had proliferated and many unfree peasants held much less than this.[19] Free men, too, often had tiny holdings, many of them no doubt practising crafts or commerce. Others were much involved in grazing. The availability of pasture meant that arable cultivation was not the main source of livelihood for many. By the early fourteenth century, and perhaps before, there was increasing penetration of land holding by townsmen, especially from Boston.[20] In short, this area, as Hallam said, was a very favourable environment in which to live. However, he also pointed to the thousands of poor cottagers who were doing no more than eking out a living by the second half of the thirteenth century: 'it is very difficult to imagine that these teeming villages, several of which were as large as thirteenth-century Coventry, could live with ease in difficult times'.[21]

This last point not withstanding, the taxation records of 1327–34 show siltland settlements to have been generally wealthy and of high tax value. Some, like Kirton, were among the very highest valued vills in the land.[22] If we take the evidence of the 1332 lay subsidy which taxed the rural communities at the rate of 1/15th of moveable goods and examine the three communities over which the Multon manor of Frampton extended, that is to say Frampton itself, Kirton, and Wyberton, we find that a total of 102 taxpayers at Frampton paid a recorded total of £15 5s, while a smaller number (77) paid the slightly higher sum of £15 11s 11¼d at Wyberton. Kirton, with its market, was the richest of the three in terms of tax yield with 148 tenants paying £25 6s 6¼d.[23]

Everything suggests a favourable environment, however, for the manorial lords. The land was both rich and populous. Although demesnes might be small, they tended to be of high unit value.[24] Both arable and pastoral farming on the one hand, and rents on the other are equally likely to have yielded high returns. Another indication of the prosperity of the area from the twelfth century through

[18] For what follows, see H. E. Hallam, *Settlement and Society: A Study of the Early Agrarian History of South Lincolnshire* (Cambridge, 1965), esp. 197–222.
[19] Christopher Dyer, *Making a Living in the Middle Ages: The People of Britain 850–1520* (New Haven and London, 2002), 160–3.
[20] See below 132.   [21] Hallam, *Agrarian History*, 595.
[22] Bruce M. S. Campbell and Ken Bartley, *England on the Eve of the Black Death: An Atlas of Lay Lordship, Land and Wealth, 1300–49* (Manchester, 2006), 323.
[23] TNA E179/135/14
[24] Campbell and Bartley, *England on the Eve of the Black Death*, 175.

to the fourteenth is the fine Norman and Early English churches that stand in the area. One of these is St Mary's, Frampton.[25]

Who, then, were the landowners in this area? At Frampton three lords are given in the 1332 subsidy. They are Sir Thomas de Multon, Sir Roger de Huntingfield and the earl of Richmond.[26] At Wyberton the lords were Sir Alexander de Cobeldyke and Sir Adam de Welle.[27] At Kirton the manorial situation is less clear. Sir John de Kirton certainly held a manor here.[28] The other highest taxpayers were Sir Thomas de Multon, Master John de Cobeldyke, Robert de Sykyston and Roger de Multon. All of these must have had residences, although in the case of Thomas de Multon at least there was no separate manor. The Multon tenants of all three settlements belonged to Frampton manor.

The Kirtons and the Cobeldykes figure in the Multon archives. One of the manorial accounts from neighbouring manors contained in the archive is that of the Cobeldyke estate centred on Wyberton for the year 1327–8, while there are strong indications that at least one of the Kirton family's manorial court rolls was once in the Multons' possession. Both families were close to the Multons socially. The other family whose account roll (for 1330–1) is found in the Multon archive is that of Huntingfield. Roger de Huntingfield held a considerable estate across Lincolnshire, East Anglia, Cambridgeshire, and elsewhere. Huntingfield itself is in Suffolk and the fact that their greater interests lay elsewhere probably explains their relative lack of social contact with the Multons. In broad terms they belonged to the same social bracket as the Multons of Frampton, although they may have been somewhat wealthier.[29] On a different social level was the third Frampton lord, no less a personage than the Earl of Richmond, who held an estate there broadly similar to that of the Huntingfields and Multons.

To broaden the picture of the secular landowning world in this area we should note that the Richmond manor at Frampton represents only one dimension of the earl's considerable lordship here. An inquisition of 1280 lists his interests more generally in Holland. In addition to the manors of Frampton and Wykes in Donington, there is his considerable income from the borough and market of Boston, the list of knights' fees held of him, and a summary of the land held by his free tenants over thirteen settlements. It amounts to over 67 carucates, rendering a total of £69 8s together with the perquisites of the soke which amounted to a further £18.[30] The greater part of this land was undoubtedly held by those free tenants known as sokemen. In 1274–5 the jurors of Kirton hundred reported that on the estates of the Earl of Richmond free sokemen were too numerous to

---

[25] Other particularly fine examples are at Sutterton, Algarkirk, and Pinchbeck.
[26] Paying £1, 17s 4d and £1 6s 8d respectively. Contributing at the same level was Amabel, widow of William de Cobeldyke, who paid £1 4d.
[27] Paying 13s 4¾d and 18s 2d respectively. There were two other wealthy payers: Walter de Ker' paying 12s 10¾d and Martin the Baker paying 10s 7¾d. The Hospitallers also held an estate here.
[28] He paid 16s 5½d.
[29] For more on the Huntingfield interests in the area see below 81, 187–9.
[30] The National Archives (TNA) C133/26/6; *CIPM* ii. no. 381.

number.[31] They were characteristic of the Richmond estate as a whole and of the region, but not in fact of Frampton.

To complete a brief survey of the landholding interests and the social structure of the area it should noted that, in addition to manors like the three Frampton estates held by the earl, the Huntingfields and the Multons, there were also some very small manors. An inquisition into the lands held by rebels in the wapentake of Kirton after the battle of Evesham in 1265 includes three of these. One of them was held by Walter Malreward in Wyberton and Frampton.[32] It comprised only 60 acres of arable, 9 acres of meadow and rent from free men. Its total value came to only £4 0s ½d. It was later amalgamated with the interest in Frampton and Kirton of the once comparatively lowly Cobeldykes.

The families that we have been discussing lived very largely in rural settings. Their dwellings, which historians tend to refer to as manor houses, were the *sine qua non* of aristocratic life in England. However, the term 'manor house' is not strictly accurate in that aristocratic dwellings comprised more than the single hall that this term implies. Rather, the hall or manor house was one of a complex of buildings. For this reason I prefer to use the Latin word *curia*, which—with its twin meanings of 'court' and 'courtyard' or enclosure—better conveys the contemporary scene.

It so happens that the site of the Multon *curia* can be precisely located. It lay at Sandholme, about a mile from Frampton village. Sandholme Lane travels south eastwards from Frampton church and then southwards before turning east at right angles and then again south east to meet the sea bank (Figure 2.3). Beyond the bank lies Frampton Marsh. The Multon *curia* lay within a moated site situated in the angle between the southward and eastward section of the lane; it was well away from the lane and equidistant from it to the east and to the north. A tiny lane runs southwards from near the south-east corner of the site to hit Sandholme Lane. Two houses now stand there and this would seem the most likely site for the Multon house described in the accounts 'at the lane end'. Multon Hall was located some way, therefore, from the main Frampton settlement. So much is shown by modern maps. The moated site is shown very clearly, too, on the Ordnance Survey maps of 1889 and 1905 (1:2500). The main entrance is unmistakeable on the western side. A beacon is marked at the south east corner, surrounded by trees and on slightly raised ground. Alongside this, on its west side, lay another feature, later marked as a pond. The moated site was still shown by the Ordnance Survey in the 1990s (1:10000) where we see a breach near the south east corner, above the site where the beacon had been. This may represent a second entrance to the Multon site, although it is not shown on the earlier maps. Apart from the disturbances at this corner, the

---

[31] *Rotuli Hundredorum* (*Rot. Hund.*), ed. W. Illingworth, 2 vols, Record Commission (London, 1812–18) ii. 305.

[32] The others were held by Sir Richard de Casterton in Wigtoft, and no less a person than Sir Roger de Huntingfield in Bicker and Wibtoft.

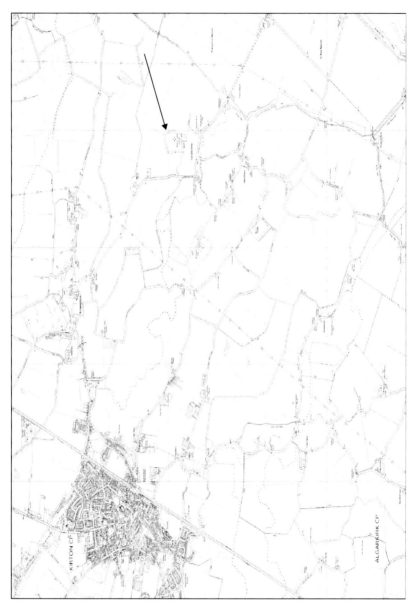

Figure 2.3. Frampton and Sandholme, Ordnance Survey 1:10000 (1990s). The map shows the Multon curia at Sandholme, south-east of Frampton village. Note also the site of Coupledyke Hall. The thirteenth-century parish church lies at the west side of the entrance to Sandholme Lane, opposite the Manor House with Frampton Hall beyond. Both of these are eighteenth-century structures. (The village of Wyberton lies off the map to the north of Frampton.)

Figure 2.4. Aerial photograph of the Multon *curia* at Sandholme.

site was then apparently intact. Aerial photography of the 1960s also shows it clearly, with both the main entrance and the south east 'breach' clearly visible (Figure 2.4).[33] By 1993, however, it had clearly been ploughed out, as revealed again by aerial photography.[34] Even so, the contours remain visible from the

---

[33] National Monuments Record MAL_62558_ 106175 (1962) and OS_68059_ 179 (1968). The NMR Report on the site (TF33NW9) indicates that it could well be the site of the moated Multon Hall 'as indicated by the building materials on the island, but [that] the earthworks are now of the fen drainage system, so it is not certain'. This follows field investigators' comments of May 1965. It was also noted, however, that 'the presence of masonry structures may be indicated by building materials on the central island'. There can be little real doubt that the drainage system follows the contours of the moated site.

[34] NMR 17879/17 (oblique aerial photograph of the site).

air.[35] Some further details of the site can be gleaned. An early twentieth-century map in the Magdalen College archive, probably based on the Ordnance Survey, notes Mill Ridge beyond the north west corner of the moated site, suggesting that the Multons' mill may have been situated here. To the south of the site lay Lady's Garth, locating the position of Lady Hall, which, like the mill, features in the Multon accounts.[36]

Although we can no longer see the Multon residence, it can be reconstructed in large measure by means of the account rolls of 1324–6. In order to make sense of these, however, it is necessary to begin with a brief survey of what is known in general terms about the evolution of aristocratic residences up to the time of the fourteenth-century Multons. The hall was, of course, the most significant component, the centre of the estate and its public face. This was by long tradition where the household and its guests dined, where communal entertainment and ceremony took place and where justice was administered. The hall contained a central hearth for heating and a roof vent (louvre or louver) to allow the smoke to escape. A striking fifteenth-century example of a louvre survives at Gainsborough Old Hall not far from the Multon manor of Heapham. It had long been the case that a hall was accompanied by a private room, a *camera* or chamber. Whereas the hall was single-storeyed, the chamber was located on an upper floor, with service or storage rooms below. These rooms were often referred to as the solar and the cellar respectively. During the thirteenth century a cross-passage was often created at the lower end of the hall, separating the hall from the services. In the same period the chamber tended to be relocated for privacy and convenience at the upper end of the hall, beyond the high table, which was sometimes placed on a dais. Although there was now access to the hall from the chamber, the main entrance to it was still located at the side towards the service end. A variety of arrangements developed from this basic pattern, with an additional wing or wings, for example, at right angles to the hall. This could produce a T plan of hall and cross-wing often leading in time to the famous H plan, with a central hall and two cross-wings, which became widespread during the first half of the fourteenth century in midland and southern England.[37]

The resulting complex could be described as a manor house. However, it is important to remember that additional buildings were also required, including

[35] i.e. by Google Earth.

[36] There is also a map surviving from around 1810. However, it reveals nothing more, except to mark the general disturbance on the southern side of the site: Lincoln Record Office, Frampton Parish 23/2–3.

[37] The standard, monumental, work, on elite fourteenth- and fifteenth-century residences is now Anthony Emery, *Greater Medieval Houses of England and Wales: 1300–1500*, 3 vols (Cambridge, 1996–2006). Vol. 2, on East Anglia, Central England, and Wales, contains discussions of Gainsborough Hall (242–50), Haddon Hall (383–90) and Stokesay Hall (574–6) which are briefly mentioned here. The same author has provided an excellent précis in his *Discovering Medieval Houses* (Princes Risborough, 2007). For an older, socially broader, discussion see also the classic Margaret Wood, *The English Medieval House* (London, 1965).

the vital kitchen and stables. These might be arranged around an enclosed courtyard with a gatehouse. Within the enclosure a variety of buildings could be attached to one another. More often, however, the subsidiary buildings were detached from the main one(s). Sometimes they were in stone, but often they were timber framed. From the mid twelfth-century onwards there had been increasing building in stone. But this was not readily available in all areas, and building in timber continued. Needless to say, timber-framed buildings, notwithstanding some major developments in technique, were less durable than those in stone. Where residences were constructed in a mixture of materials, the stone buildings might survive alone, as is the case with the chamber block at Boothby Pagnall in Lincolnshire which gave rise to a long-standing but erroneous assumption that it had been a first-floor hall.[38] Manor houses have a greater tendency to survive from the fifteenth and sixteenth centuries, sometimes as a mixture of timber and stone (or brick). On other occasions earlier features remain more or less intact but incorporated within a later, revised and expanded structure. A good example here is Haddon Hall in Derbyshire which preserves a hall, service wing with screen passage and kitchen beyond from the second quarter of the fourteenth century, roughly contemporary with the Multon *curia* revealed in the accounts (Figure 2.5). [Plate 2]. The kitchen, originally detached but in line with the service rooms was later connected, as was often the case, by an enclosed passage in place of an open courtyard. Earlier arrangements can sometimes be seen from excavation.[39]

One arrangement that does survive in its late thirteenth-century form, is the so-called Stokesay Castle in Shropshire. In many respects it is indicative of the sort of complex that existed throughout the country. However, it is important to be aware of the variables that tended to determine the characteristics of particular residences. Much depended upon geographical location. Physical factors, as well as defence and status, helped to determine whether or not the *curia* would be moated, as was the case at Sandholme and at Stokesay. Status as much as defence also determined whether a house would be crenellated. This required a royal licence and was as much a mark of distinction and recognition as anything else. These licences, which had to be purchased, became increasingly popular from the mid-thirteenth century and reached their peak in the second quarter of the fourteenth. Stokesay, the home of the Ludlows, Shropshire wool merchants turned gentry, was in many respects state of the art at the end of the thirteenth

[38] Older interpretations have been superseded, thanks initially to the work of John Blair on Boothby Pagnall in Lincolnshire. See his 'Hall and Chamber: English Domestic Planning 1000–1250', in G. Meirion-Jones and M. Jones (eds), *Manorial Domestic Buildings in England and Northern France* (London, 1993), 1–21.

[39] See, for example, Guy Beresford, 'The Medieval Manor of Penhallam, Jacobstow, Cornwall', *Medieval Archaeology* 18 (1974), 90–145, and the discussion and pictorial representations in Colin Platt, *Medieval England: A Social History and Archaeology from the Conquest to 1600* (London, 1978), 57–60.

Figure 2.5. Haddon Hall. Note the screen passage and the entrances to the services beyond.

century, with its tower and crenellations, reflecting the great wealth of a family of nouveau riche.[40] Although many (and probably most) gentry homes were not crenellated, nor indeed built wholly, or even partly, in stone, Stokesay can still demonstrate on the ground many of the features that were widely shared. At Stokesay, within the enclosure, lay, in addition to the great hall and private apartments, service buildings of various kinds. The timber-framed kitchen, although demolished, is known from its relatively late survival (Figure 2.6). Other service buildings, their structure and precise location within the enclosure, can only be surmised. The majority of gentry residences of the late-thirteenth to mid-fourteenth centuries would have been less extravagant and less opulent than Stokesay, but the general principles in terms of both structure and internal features remain the same.[41]

With these observations in mind let us turn to the account rolls emanating from the Frampton estate of the Multons in 1324–6. They show, in fact, that a

---

[40] For Lawrence de Ludlow, see below 266–7.
[41] For the variety of arrangements within moated sites see, for example, S. E. Rigold, 'Structures Within English Moated Sites' in F. A. Aberg (ed.), *CBA Research Report No. 17: Medieval Moated Sites* (London, 1978), 29–36.

Figure 2.6. Stokesay 'Castle'. Note the entrance to the hall between the buttresses. Beyond this lay the timber-framed kitchen, at right-angles to the main structure.

major rebuilding was being undertaken in these years and the details they supply enable us to visualize the *curia*. The relevant section of the 1325–6 account, called domestic costs or *custus domorum*, begins with the kitchens. It tells us that in that year money was paid out for making the oven and a *midilhild* (which was probably an area of shelving or storage),[42] for four furnaces or kilns for lead vessels (three in the said [bake]house and one in the kitchen), for tiles for the oven and furnaces, for timber for laths for *le midilhild* within the bakehouse and for three hundred spike nails in order to carry this work out. Wages were paid to a carpenter for fitting the laths in the two *midilhild* between the bakehouse and the brewhouse and beyond the [main] oven (*ultra furnum*). In addition to the main kitchen, then, there were a series of structures including a bakehouse and a brewhouse. There were also storage facilities, primarily perhaps for kitchen, baking, and brewing utensils.

The location of the bakehouse and brewhouse *beyond* the kitchen suggests the probability of a linear structure such as that found at Old Gainsborough

---

[42] My interpretation here is supposition from the context in which it occurs. The word does not appear in either the Middle English Dictionary or the Oxford English Dictionary. Perhaps it is cognate with 'hold'.

and commonly elsewhere, with the kitchen detached from the service end but in alignment with it and the bakehouse and brewhouse, still in line, beyond. Alternatively, as at Stokesay, the kitchen, and ancillary buildings, could have been constructed at right angles to the hall range. There was often, initially at least, a space between the main range and the kitchen, as a fire precaution. That there were storage facilities between the bakehouse and the brewhouse suggests that they were either very close to one another or that in practice they were two parts of a single structure, a situation that was not unusual.[43]

The same carpenter who was responsible for the shelving was paid for mending a window in the solar, the door of the lady's bower (i.e. chamber),[44] the door of the bakehouse, two divisions in the horses' stable, a manger in the palfreys' stable, and a crib in the byre as well as the door of the sheepcote by the sea. The account also shows him mending the table dormant in the hall (that is a 'sleeping' or fixed table that could be used as a sideboard), and another in the knights' chambers (*in cameris militum*). One thinks inevitably of Chaucer's epicurean Franklin, whose:

> . . . table dormant in his halle alway
> Stood redy covered al the longe day

These details reveal the complex of buildings that one would expect, with the knights' chambers almost certainly constituting a separate range from the hall and solar. It may well have been a cross-wing, perhaps at the dais end of the hall, in which case the solar is likely to have been a first floor chamber at the service end of the hall, producing an H plan. Alternatively, if the solar were at the dais end, the knights' chambers would likely have been a separate structure. We have also the lady's bower to accommodate within the complex. Whatever the precise disposition of buildings, a picture of the *curia* is beginning to build up, complete with hall, accommodation, kitchen, bakehouse, brewhouse, and stables.

The account then turns from the kitchen and the carpentry to the roofing. Money was paid after Christmas for roofing 'the house beyond the oven', perhaps signifying the bakehouse/brewhouse and for roofing the sheepcote by the sea. Work then began on roofing the hall itself, which was followed by the roofing of the lady's bower. Large quantities of rushes were bought for the purpose.

Locks and keys came next. These were bought for the door of the pantry and for the door of the garderobe or privy. Locks and keys were mended for the bakehouse and for the doors of the knights' chambers. Hinges and crooks were bought for windows in the garderobe and in the hall while hinges and hooks were bought for the door of the pantry. At this point the service wing at the

[43] Peter Brears, *Cooking and Dining in Medieval England* (Totnes, 2008), 87: 'From at least the thirteenth century through to the late Victorian period, the brewing of ale and the baking of bread were virtually inseparable activities in major households, usually being carried out either in the same or adjacent rooms.'

[44] The account reads *bouar' domine*. An alternative reading would be the lady's byre.

lower end of the hall is beginning to be revealed. As we shall see in a moment, the pantry's twin storage room, the buttery, is also in evidence. These twin storage rooms evolved essentially because of the differing requirements of ale and wine on the one hand and bread and table linen on the other. Whereas the former needed a cool temperature, the latter needed the atmosphere to be dry. Ideally, the buttery would be to the north, the pantry to the south.[45] In the pantry were likely to be stored such items as towels and tablecloths, baskets, knives, salt cellars, candlesticks, dishes, and saucers. In the buttery one would find, apart from casks and tuns, pitchers, ewers and basins, cups and spoons. Both rooms would need to be equipped for storage.

Considerable expenditure is recorded at this point for rushes, some of it explicitly for wattling. There was also the cost of daubing the solar. Two thousand three hundred cords of rushes (using cord here as a measure) were also bought for *sewingrope*. The barn was roofed and a carpenter paid for making two *wyndeskaithes* on the barn as well as a piece of furniture for storage in the buttery. Money was also spent on a long list of items which were accounted for under the section entitled minor necessities or *minute necessarie*. These ranged from a trivet or tripod, a brass pot and a ladle for the kitchen, through bars for gates, to 200 corfs of turves dug in the marsh, no doubt for fuel.

There were, however, additional labour costs included. Hugh the Carpenter was very active trimming wood from trees for sawing, making and erecting boards in the hall, making a *maldyngbord* for the bakehouse (that is to say a moulding board used in baking) and a bench and other necessities over a period of ten-and-a-half days. Over a further nineteen days he worked at a variety of tasks including making the gates next to the kitchen, the gates to the vineyard garden, the door of the chapel, the door of the pantry, and two windows in the garderobe.[46]

These items reveal further details of the *curia*. In terms of buildings we should note in particular the existence of a chapel. Its foundation will be discussed later. Externally there is a vineyard garden, kept under lock.[47] The gates next to the kitchen probably represent a side entrance rather than the main gate, perhaps that indicated on maps by the small breach at the south-east. The hall itself, including its service end, was undoubtedly of timber. Considerable use was made of wattle and the walls daubed.

[45] Brears, *Cooking and Dining*, 383. There was also an element of tradition in this arrangement. On this, see Mark Gardiner, 'Buttery and Pantry and Their Antecedents: Idea and Architecture in the English Medieval House', in M. Kowaleski and P. J. P. Goldberg (eds), *Medieval Domesticity: Home, Housing and Household in Medieval England* (Cambridge, 2008), 37–65. For the hall see also Michael Thompson, *The Medieval Hall: The Basis of Secular Domestic Life, 600–1600 AD* (Aldershot, 1995).
[46] Further labour costs were incurred in felling and trimming willows and in sawing. Also in evidence was Andrew the Smith. He was paid for various ironwork, including a pan, a pair of tongs, the bases of two jars, a *furgon* (a long-handled oven fork), and two additional forks.
[47] This may have been external to the enclosure.

The rebuilding of much of the *curia* was evidently costly and required careful itemization. However, it was not only the buildings that needed attention. A separate item covered the 'close' or enclosure (*clausura*). The costs were itemized:

- 17s 6d was spent on 31 rods of ditch dug around the manor beginning at the gates and going up to *le Coninghill*, at 1s 6d per rod
- £1 3s on 21 rods dug on the other side of the gates, at 1s 4d per rod[48]
- £3 13s 6d on 67 rods and 16 feet dug on the eastern and northern sides of the manor, at 1s 1d per rod.

In other words we are dealing here with the digging of the moat. On the face of it, at least, we have the length of the perimeter of the enclosure, i.e. 119 rods 16 feet, or, assuming the rod to be the statutory perch of $16\frac{1}{2}$ feet, a total of $1,979\frac{1}{2}$ feet. The eastern side of the enclosure is shown on the maps as longer than the other three. The main gate, as we have seen, is on the west. *Coninghill* may be the slightly raised, and later disturbed, ground that we have noted at the south-east corner. Was this, however, a restoration or the first making of the moat?[49] That the latter may have been the case is suggested by the fact that the word repair is not used, while the next item moves on to note a further 11s spent in *repairing* the Frampton and Kirton section of the Fendyke. Whether the moat was entirely new or not, it was clearly an expensive matter. Moreover it was not the only work that was required on the perimeter. Additional work involved 3 rods, 4 feet of wall between the hall and the kitchen, 1 rod between the kitchen and the gates, 5 rods between the barn and the knights' chamber, 5 rods between the barn and the sheepcote, and $6\frac{1}{2}$ rods between the solar and the ditch next to the bakehouse, at a cost of 9s 9d.

The total cost of work itemized under the 'close' came to £8 13s 1d, and the total cost of building, restoring and refurbishing at the Multon *curia* in the year 1325–6 to £14 8s $4\frac{3}{4}$d.[50] It was normal practice for manorial account rolls to contain expenses for repairs to the buildings and allied matters. The account roll for the neighbouring Huntingfield manor at Frampton for the year 1330–1 itemizes £1 1s $7\frac{1}{2}$d in *custus domorum*, plus £ 2 9s 9d on necessaries and £1 18s 1d on walls. The account for the Cobeldyke manor at nearby Wyberton for 1327–8 included £1 3s 7d on repairs to buildings, 2s $1\frac{1}{2}$d on walls, 16s $1\frac{1}{4}$d on minor necessities and 13s 6d on repairs to the mill.[51] The expenditure on the Multon manor in 1325–6 was therefore exceptional. Why was this so?

The explanation is not in fact hard to find. Thomas de Multon had been a ward in the king's hands since June 1311, and his estates held by the crown in

---

[48] This and the previous total are those given in the account. When the cost per rod is multiplied by the number of rods they should read £2 6s 6d and £1 8s respectively.

[49] For the effort involved in digging a moat see C. C. Dyer, *Standards of Living in the Later Middle Ages: Social Change in England c.1200–1520* (Cambridge, 1989), 106–7.

[50] One further item in the account which is relevant here is the 11s $4\frac{1}{2}$d for canvas for the sails of the windmill.

[51] For these account rolls see below 95–9, 102–4.

wardship. The wardship was a long one. In June 1322 the manor of Frampton is said to have been lately in the king's hands. However, the estates were not yet held by Thomas but had passed to Hugh le Despenser the Younger who had asked for a special commission of oyer and terminer 'to examine his complaint that a group of men had entered the manor of Frampton and carried away goods from there'.[52] These words are formulaic. Nonetheless Thomas de Multon had been three times unfortunate: in suffering a long wardship, in having the disreputable Hugh le Despenser in charge of his lands, and in suffering an attack on his property towards the end of the wardship. One way or another the manor is likely to have been pillaged, and Thomas to have received it back in a fairly run-down state. Thomas was only just in possession by the time of the surviving accounts. Indeed 1324–5 was his first full accounting year. We know this because in 1325 the reeve accounted for £1 cash given to the lady of Moulton for the entry (*introitum*) of the lord into his land at Frampton. This was presumably payment of, or towards, a feudal relief. By June 1324 he was in possession of his other estates and, presumably, of Frampton too.[53]

Although the account roll for 1325–6 indicates that the bulk of the repairs to the Multon *curia* were carried out in that year, the accounts for 1324–5 show that the process had begun in the previous year. Roofing was the most urgent matter. Attention was paid to roofing the hall of the house next to the gates, of the byre, stable and barn, as well as the houses of William son of Cecily, the house 'at the lane end', the sheepcote at the sea and the house called *Pecchecot(e)*. Money was spent on daubing the walls of the hall, byre, stable, and hencoop. Moreover the hall, barn and stable were roofed at the feast of St Margaret (20 July), and the byre again in the autumn. Some vital improvements were made internally. A board for the louvre, the vital device for allowing the escape of smoke from the central hearth in the hall, was bought and a carpenter was paid for mending it and, at the same time, for propping up the house 'at the lane end'. Spike nails were bought for this job, for repairing windows in the hall, and for repairing the mill. Finally money was spent on partly daubing the stable walls after the raising of the timber. There were also labour costs involved in all of this. Moreover, once again there were also small necessities that were accounted for separately. Some of these were in fact of considerable importance, such as a lock and key bought for the great gates, a key for the door of the chamber beyond (or perhaps above) the gates[54] and the mending of its lock, and the mending of the lock for the door of the porterhouse. In the context this term probably means the lodging of the porter or gatehouse keeper. Clearly, the buildings had been left insecure.

[52] *Calendar of Fine Rolls* (*CFR*) ii. 94; *Calendar of Patent Rolls* (*CPR*) *1321–4*, 169, 372, 378.

[53] In November 1324 he is found as Thomas son of Thomas de Multon of Frampton, leasing a plot of land in Boston: Multon Hall, 78a, 96a.

[54] *Ultra portas*.

In addition, the garden had to be planted. Garlic, onion seed, large onions, and leek seed were all purchased. There was also a cleaning operation. The cesspit in the vineyard garden, those next to the byre and in the garden in front of the gates all had to be dealt with, involving the hiring of labour. There were various minor purchases of equipment and some agricultural costs.[55] A costly item was the turf bought in the marsh on May Day,[56] no doubt for fuel, and again in the autumn.[57] The door of the house called *le Cerehous* (that is the wax house) was repaired and its walls daubed. Money was spent on repairing Newlands channel against the inundation of the sea in the autumn. Two baskets were bought for winnowing, as were a seed basket, riddles, a fork and spades, and a bronze jar, while salt was bought for salting eels at the end of autumn. In this first year then, the most basic and urgent repairs were made. Roofing was undertaken both at the manor house and at other buildings, and the place was generally made habitable, serviceable, and secure. A garden was planted, the mill was made operable and basic equipment for house and table was purchased. A total of £2 14s 6d had been paid out, and the foundations were laid for the further developments that took place the following year.

What then can we say in summary of the Multon *curia* at Michaelmas 1326? The manorial site can be visualized, at least in general terms. It was moated and walled. It was well off in terms of domestic buildings. In addition to the hall with its solar and service rooms, there were the knights' chambers, the lady's bower, a chapel and a garderobe. These last may have been attached to the hall and solar, but are quite likely to have been separated from them. There was, of course, a kitchen and ovens, as well as a bakehouse and a brewhouse. There was a barn, a byre, and stables. There was also a hencoop. There were great gates and a chamber above the gates. There was also a porterhouse. There was an additional gate next to the kitchen and another to the vineyard garden. The garden or orchard seems to have been fairly extensive and to have included a green (*viridarium*) as well as vegetable garden and fruit trees. The gates and doors were well-fitted with locks. The windows of the hall and the garderobe were fitted with shutters. The hall had a louvre for the escape of smoke. The buildings were mostly, if not all, of timber and thatch, and the walls were wattled and daubed. Beyond the close lay the sheepcote near the sea, which was roofed, and a windmill. There is no mention of two other manorial appurtenances, a *vivarium* or fishpond, and a dovecote, although their absence from the records does not of course prove that they were not there. There is no mention of buildings in

---

[55] A millstone for the lord's mill cost 1s 10d, and 3d was spent in making a piece of iron bought from Miningsby into bills for the mill, presumably bills for dressing mill stones. A gift of 2s was made to the shepherds, Alexander and Alan, sons of Robert and Alice Knight, for moving the fold onto the lord's land for twelve weeks in the summer. This seems to refer to pasture in the fields after harvest, privileging the demesne. See Hallam, 'Farming Techniques (Eastern England)', in idem (ed.), *Agrarian History*, 273.

[56] Sixty corfs bought for £2 16s 8d.   [57] Sixty corfs for 7s 6d.

stone, although it is possible that the chamber block may have been. Everything suggests that the Multon residence was a sizeable but fairly standard gentry home of the early fourteenth century. It was not avant-garde nor even state of the art, but it possessed the range of facilities that the family's status required.

With the Multon *curia* envisaged we can turn to a closer examination of the gentry household. The next chapter will concentrate on the material culture of the Multons and of other representatives of the medieval gentry. Chapter 4 will then examine the household in terms of the social relationships it involved, looking at both its internal life and its relationship to local society. The medieval household is by no means a new subject for historians. However, the provenance of surviving sources has meant that scholars have necessarily concentrated on the households of royalty, the higher nobility and their ecclesiastical equals.[58] There are relatively few household records for the gentry, and very few before the late fourteenth and fifteenth centuries. We will concentrate on these. Naturally, many of the issues will be the same or similar to those discussed in earlier works. At the very least, however, we can expect to encounter differences in scale; these are bound to have created qualitative distinctions. First, then, the material culture of the gentry household.

---

[58] See, especially, Woolgar, *The Great Household*; and Kate Mertes, *The English Noble Household 1250–1600: Good Governance and Politic Rule* (Oxford, 1988). An older work is Margaret Wade Labarge, *A Baronial Household in the Thirteenth Century* (London, 1965). For published sources in addition to those in Woolgar see, for example, M. S. Giuseppi, 'The Wardrobe and Household Accounts of Bogo de Clare, A.D. 1284–6', *Archaeologia*, 70 (1918–20), 1–56; J. A. Robinson, 'Household Roll of Bishop Ralph of Shrewsbury (1337–8)' in T. E. Palmer (ed.), *Collectanea I, Somerset Record Society*, 39 (1924), 72–174. For a discussion of household accounts as historical sources, see Woolgar, *Household Accounts*, ii. 10–65.

3

The Gentry Household
The Locus of Consumption

The study of material culture has been defined as 'the investigation of the relationship between people and things' and as the study of 'the use and meaning of artefacts'.[1] As far as the gentry is concerned, where better to observe their material culture than in the household, the primary locus of their consumption? This is where members of the gentry ate, dressed, and learned to relate to family members and others. This is the environment into which they were born and where they experienced their earliest cultural influences. People have an impact on their material environment throughout their lives, but they are also from the outset moulded by it. With these observations in mind let us return to the Multons of Frampton.

The manorial accounts of 1324–6, as we have seen, tell us a great deal about the rebuilding and repairs at Frampton following the long wardship of Thomas de Multon IV. They tell us that some basic refurbishing had to be undertaken. The fact that in the very first year the Multons had to buy basic tableware—twelve dishes, twelve plates, twelve saucers, and six bowls or cups[2]—suggests that little in terms of household goods had survived the wardship and that their possessions had been dispersed.

Sadly the surviving records from the time of Thomas de Multon IV tell us little more about the material culture of the Frampton household. For the next generation, however, that of John de Multon I, we are more fortunate in that we have household accounts for 1343–4 and for 1347–8. We are doubly fortunate in that the first of these contains, in addition to the usual diet account, a further account on the dorse of the roll entitled 'Necessary and Foreign Expenses'. Its vantage point is that of the lord, who was itinerant, and it records purchases made for him and moneys disbursed by him and his officials as he travelled around Lincolnshire. Its great advantage to the historian is that it is a dynamic record,

---

[1] See the 'Editorial' to the *Journal of Material Culture* 1 (1996), edited by David Miller and Christopher Tilley, 5–14, esp. 5–6.

[2] *Ciphis.* Various utensils had to be brought in for the kitchen, as well as items for the garden and elsewhere.

affording some insight into the range of items purchased during the course of the year as well as an indication of the quality of material life.

The presence of the lady, Anne, is more apparent here than on the diet accounts. We hear of payment to Roger de Farnham for shoes for the lord and lady near the beginning of the financial year, and a further sum for shoes for them at the end; the cost of the shoes being the same in each case, i.e. 1s for two pairs. Cloth was bought for her for a cloak and for its lining, at 5s and 4s 8d respectively, as well as cloth for Joni, her *damisel*; another 9s. These were relatively expensive items compared with the 23 ells of linen cloth that were bought for the lady at a cost of 3s 6d, and which were most probably for household use. She was also bought silk and pins. The kerchiefs that were bought—including *kerchevez flemez* for 6s 6d and *kercheviez boilez* for 7s 3d—were no doubt primarily for her use. A chest (*ciste*) was bought for her, costing 4s 6d, while 4d was paid for a *harpe* that she gave, perhaps as a present, to William Hardi. This suggestion that music was enjoyed in the house is deepened when we hear of Gige le Harpour being paid 2s.[3] Money was given to the lady for meat for her greyhounds (*levereres*) and on another occasion meat was bought directly for the dogs. The roll allows a sense of the Lady Anne's presence to be gradually built up. Our image of her accords well with the one frequently presented by monumental effigies and brasses, with their fine clothes, including the expensive cloaks and headdresses, and the pet dogs at their feet. This is of course rather one dimensional and reveals nothing of her particular personality. On the other hand, there is every reason to believe that ladies' lives, like their images, were largely conventional.[4]

The lord's own expenses were much greater. Cloth was bought for his use. Much attention seems to have been paid to his appearance. He bought three pairs of gloves, a pair of boots, two pairs of shoes, and two coats. Small sums were spent on a bodkin or small dagger, on a knife of unspecified type, on *layners* (laces or thongs), which we will see later were for use in falconry, and on a purse for him. The goldsmith at Boston was paid various sums for the lord's belt or girdle, to wit 2s 6d, 10s, and lastly 5s of the 14s 6d still owing. This was clearly a major item. There are few indications of the quality of the clothing bought. However, the *cote Wade* he bought at Windsor sounds like a fashionable item. Moreover, ermine was bought on several occasions, which on its own indicates a certain quality of material life. Money was paid over to goldsmiths 'for the lord's work', and various sums were paid to his armourer at Lynn. Girths and circingles were bought for his horses, while two pairs of spurs cost 2s 8d. A minor but vital item of expenditure was the money spent on the lord's seals, that is to say the seal matrices: 2d was spent on mending the lord's seal, at Lincoln, and later three *gurzes* were bought for the lord's seal costing 3d, while another 3d was spent on transporting three seals of the lord from Lincoln Dyke to Frampton. A

[3] However, 4d seems rather cheap for a harp.
[4] See Coss, *The Lady in Medieval England*, 76–83.

lord's seal, often displaying his coat of arms as well as his name and rank, was an important item in terms of his status and identity. That he kept several of these is itself an interesting insight. They may not have been identical, and it was known for a lord to seal with more than one device.[5] A small *premer* was recorded as bought for the lord. This sounds like a primer or prayer book but it seems extremely cheap at 7d. There was some expenditure on his infants: ½d for gloves, and 1s 2d for shoes for them. There was also expenditure on the chapel, including 4s spent on mending its books.

There were also routine purchases for the household: for parchment, for example, on two occasions, for soap and brimstone, for soap specifically said to be for the lady, for a curtain for the lord's use, for canvas for the tables in the hall, for a basin and a laver, i.e. for washing prior to dining, for bowls and other pewter vessels, for pots and pans, and for knives for the kitchen.[6] Two baskets were bought for putting fish into the water around the manor, presumably the moat. Nine cups or bowls were bought on one occasion and four more on another with what was perhaps a drinking horn.[7] John de Multon had only recently come of age and it may well be that some of this expenditure reflected the fact that he and his wife were, in turn, building up the contents of their home rather than making ongoing replacements. As we shall see in the next chapter, many of a previous lord and lady's possessions may have been dispersed in their wills.

These snippets of detail, combined with what we will discover of their diet, suggest a comfortable standard of living in mid-fourteenth-century terms.[8] However, the fact that the 'necessary and foreign expenses' is a dynamic account, allowing glimpses into daily life as it is lived, is in another sense a drawback in that it gives us little sense of the totality of household possessions. For these we have to turn to another source: inventories. These, too, are rare documents, and once again the majority of surviving examples belong to royalty and the higher nobility, where the standard of living is more lavish. However, there are inventories that one can very profitably use, and I will be examining three of these. The diet accounts will be explored alongside them to reveal the content of gentry food and drink.

There is however, one further, indispensable, source for the material culture of the early- to mid-fourteenth-century gentry which we must bring into play. In terms of visualizing the interior of a gentry household and some of the activities that went on there we have an excellent means of entrée in the Luttrell Psalter,

---

[5] For the Multon seal, see Figure 13.1.

[6] Expenditure was recorded on vegetables and tools for the garden and, occasionally, on estate items.

[7] *In iiii ciphis cum i curnekill id ob.*

[8] Improvements to the manor house at Frampton were still being undertaken. Sums of 10s, 13s 4d and 3s were paid out to a master and other masons for the making of a chimney. John and Anne, like his parents before them, were also paying for the services of a carpenter. Timber was transported from Ingleby to Frampton and from Lincoln to Boston.

commissioned by Sir Geoffrey Luttrell of Irnham in Lincolnshire, most probably between *c*.1340 and his death in 1345. It is a famous and much-used source. Until recently, however, the scenes in the Psalter have been reproduced as simply a mirror of medieval social life. Modern study by art historians, in contrast, has tended to see them rather in terms of representations. Michael Camille in particular taught us to position ourselves with Sir Geoffrey Luttrell, that is outside of the manuscript, looking in upon himself and his world; seeing him, in other words, as he wanted the world to see him.[9] We now understand that the scenes in the Psalter are ideologically loaded and that they project an image of the Luttrell household that was intended to convey its status. This realization makes the domestic scenes all the more valuable in the present context, affording us an insight into the mentality not only of the Luttrells but also, by extension, of gentry families in general.

What the Luttrell Psalter depicts is the household at work, elaborately preparing the food, conveying it to the hall and then waiting, efficiently, upon table (Figure 3.1) Sir Geoffrey is shown at the centre of the table, flanked by his spouse, family and guests. The table, like the service, creates an impression of great opulence. The rich textiles behind the table consist of a blue and silver heraldic field, emphasizing the Luttrell arms, fringed by gold brocade. The table itself has a wealth of utensils. Particularly noticeable—as it was intended to be—is the silver plate, most especially the large dish in the centre. As Camille pointed out, these are shown from above rather than from the side to accentuate them. Moreover, the family is being served by the highest officials in the household. Their lowly demeanour at table contrasts with their proud upright bearing in the previous scene, indicating their status within the household itself. The scenes showing the preparation of the meal indicate not only the quality of the food being produced with its accent on roasts, including chicken and suckling pig, but also the size of the household. The lord can afford to have a whole series of servants, each devoted to a specific task. The entire picture is one of aristocratic display. There are other significant features here too. Noticeable is the sheer decorum of the scene. The diners are eating decorously, with no reaching across the table. Geoffrey and his daughter-in-law are shown holding their cups from below. However, the focus of the scene is on Geoffrey as ruler of his house. He is the paterfamilias. What we are seeing, in short, is his household as he would have us see it.

What the Luttrell Psalter indicates to us at the outset of our inquiry into the domestic world of the gentry is an intense desire to be seen to be living up to the standards of one's peers. The need among established families to conform to social expectations in maintaining contemporary standards of behaviour and

---

[9] M. Camille, *Mirror in Parchment: The Luttrell Psalter and the Making of Medieval England* (London, 1998). The most recent study is Michelle P. Brown, *The Luttrell Psalter: A Facsimile* (British Library, London, 2006). This is introduced by a full commentary, including an account of modern interpretations of the psalter.

Figure 3.1. Dining in a gentry household (from the Luttrell Psalter). Add. MS 42131, fos. 206v, 207r, 208r and 208v. © The British Library Board. All Rights Reserved 2010.

consumption is shown to be *as* characteristic of the gentry as the well-known, and often satirized, aspiration among newcomers to achieve recognition and acceptance. Both of these facets must be born in mind as we examine the material culture of the gentry. What, then, can we discover about the range of their possessions?

As it happens an inventory exists from an established family that is very close in time to the household accounts of Sir John de Multon and not too distant from the Luttrell Psalter. This is a list of the possessions of the family of de la Beche of Aldworth in Berkshire. The de la Beches rose through service in the royal household, becoming more significant, and undoubtedly richer, during the early part of the reign of Edward III. Inventories tended to be taken in exceptional circumstances and this must always be borne in mind. In this case the inventory derives ultimately from the forfeiture of Margery, widow of Nicholas de la Beche. In 1347 Margery was staying at the manor of Beams near Reading when a gang, headed by John Dalton, broke in and abducted her. She was most probably complicit in this as she soon married the perpetrator. However, this was no run-of-the-mill abduction. There were abnormal circumstances. For one thing, her uncle, Michael de Poynings, was killed in the incident. For another, the king's children were present, including his son, Lionel, who was officially keeper of England in his father's absence at Calais. The king was outraged and, to avoid the couple prospering from the plan, her lands and moveable goods were confiscated.[10] In the following year the crown placed the property in the hands of Michael Poynings, Margery's nephew.[11] In 1351, following Margery's death, Michael passed them on to Edmund de la Beche, as her closest relative. At this point an inventory of her goods was recorded on the Chancery Rolls.[12]

The inventory begins with the sumptuous furnishings of the chapel and ends with a list of books. Both of these will be given detailed consideration later on in this work.[13] Between these two, however, lies a detailed list of goods belonging to the chamber or chambers, to the hall, to the pantry and buttery, and to the kitchen. Let us leave aside the chambers for the moment and look at how the inventory underpins the famous Luttrell scenes.

The divisions in the inventory are not absolute and some items seem to have strayed across departments. Nonetheless, the details show that the de la Beche kitchen was extremely well stocked with utensils, sufficient to support a luxurious table. There was a great brass pot called 'brounrobyn' together with five other pots, large and small, a cauldron, and four chafers. Whereas a cauldron was normally used for boiling, chafers (round pans with handles) were often used for frying. There were five posnets, that is small cooking pots, as well as three other large pots or *oules* and two brass mortars with iron pestles. There were pails, griddles, andirons (or fire irons) and various other iron implements, one of which was called 'weg', together with twelve *broches de fer*. These last were probably spits used in roasting. Then there were baskets, cases or boxes for wax,

[10] For the details of the case see: *CPR 1345–8*, 310–11, 318–20, 344–5; *CPR 1348–50*, 460; *CFR 1347–56*, 28.
[11] *CPR 1348–50*, 192, 460; *CFR 1347–56*, 36
[12] It is published in *CPR 1350–54*, 137–41.   [13] See below 148–9.

barehides (i.e. undressed skins) for kitchen carts and *costres* (perhaps costrels?) for sauce. Earthenware cooking pots are probably unrepresented here. Many would surely have existed in gentry kitchens. They were not especially valuable, however, and were no doubt treated as disposable. Metal utensils, on the other hand, were more prized. They may not seem especially valuable to us, but, as a recent commentator has said, 'whatever their form and size, metal cooking pans always represented one of the household's major investments'.[14]

Turning to the hall, in addition to more routine items, as it were,[15] we find some highly prized and probably valuable possessions. There were two rich hangings: a red dosel with black stripes and another of Paris work with images. Dosels were found most spectacularly behind the dais as shown in the Luttrell Psalter. For the table there was a drinking horn and a number of mazers, i.e. wooden drinking vessels, usually made of maple. There was also a pair of knives with black handles together with three knives for trenchers (*trenchours*), that is thick slices of bread used as cutting boards for the individuals at table. There were six pitchers made of wood (*fust*) and eight leather pitchers for the buttery. The great mazer and a silver mazer (most probably with a silver rim) both bore the family arms, while two others had the arms of de la Beche and of the related family of Poynings, viz. *barry (6) or and vert, a bend gules*. The dining scene in the Luttrell Psalter once again comes immediately to mind.

If the de la Beche inventory is anything to go by, then, the Luttrell self-image was not so far divorced from reality. However, we should be cautious. The de la Beche family had been doing extremely well in the 1330s and 1340s, with two members high in royal service, who had clearly been enriching themselves. Moreover, it is not entirely clear that the inventory represents only the goods that had been at the manor of Beams. The family possessed other estates and the quantity of items in the inventory may include items from more than one residence. The de la Beche inventory should not be allowed to stand alone in conveying an image of the domestic life of an established gentry family, any more than should the Luttrell Psalter.

One useful comparison that can be made is with the inventory of the possessions of a knight, Sir Edmund Appleby, made a generation later, in November 1374, presumably at his manor of Appleby Magna in Leicestershire.[16] Edmund was a solidly based county knight whose family had been established at Appleby since the twelfth century and who held additional property in several villages within

---

[14] Brears, *Cooking and Dining*, 221.

[15] There were iron forks, round basins, four pairs of andirons, four tables with their accoutrements (*ove la meynee*) and two pieces of canvas, presumably for covering them. The hall was lavishly supplied with linen, including twenty-two tablecloths 'of divers work', and large quantities of towels, some of which were for bread and for spices. There were forty *savenapes* (surnapes?) used in hand washing.

[16] For what follows see G. G. Astill, 'An Early Inventory of a Leicestershire Knight', *Midland History*, 2 (1974), 274–83.

a four-mile radius of Appleby, in Leicestershire, Derbyshire, and Staffordshire. Edmund had been militarily active. He was in Gascony in 1322 and 1324–5 and had participated in the victorious Poitiers campaign against the French in 1356. He belonged to the affinity of the house of Lancaster, not too surprisingly as this area was a centre of its power. At home he functioned as a commissioner of array in the three counties mentioned and as a justice of the peace and tax assessor and collector in his home county of Leicestershire. He was, therefore, a man of some local significance. Given its date the inventory may have been occasioned either by his death and the succession of his son, another Sir Edmund, or for debt, since we know that Edmund had a history of indebtedness. However, there is no reason to suppose this had greatly diminished his household possessions or that his inventory fails to reflect the standard of living of a fourteenth-century knight.[17] This inventory, unlike the de la Beche, includes valuations. The total value was just over £200 of which a little more than half consisted of grain, animals, and agricultural implements, at Appleby and at Seal. It suggests, then, that the home of a fourteenth-century knight might contain possessions to the value of around £100.

Sir Edmund's pantry and buttery contained goods to the value of £17 12s 4d. There was quite a lot of silver. There were two silver bowls with diaper or diamond pattern in gold together with crowns and roses, three silver bowls with covers, two large and one small, one silver ewer, and two other pieces of silver, yet again reflecting the Luttrell dining scene. And there were fifteen silver spoons. There were also four mazers. The Luttrell dining scene may have been ideologically charged, as Camille and others have suggested, but it was clearly not unrealistic.

As we would expect, Sir Edmund had cloths of various sorts, napkins, and towels. He also had twelve barrels, four latten candlesticks, two tubs, four bottles, and six leather pots. All of this was of course to supply the hall. Hence the hall had little under its own name. The items listed there came to only £8 3s 4d, and of this 'a complete embroidery', almost certainly a tapestry hanging from one of the walls (very likely behind the dais) accounted for £6 13s 4d. There were three tables and forms, two basins and one laver, and one *chimone* and iron fork. Basins and lavers (or ewers) were used in the hall for the 'ceremony' of washing hands before dining. This tended to happen, it would seem, at the lower end of the hall or in the cross passage where the diners would be served by an attendant with towels. The Multons had purchased a basin and laver, with other items for their hall in 1343–4. Apart from the tapestry, it will have been noted, the Appleby hall does not appear to have been overly furnished. In this respect it may represent the norm.

---

[17] Ibid. 277. See also Dyer, *Standards of Living*, 76, who points out that the inventory of the fifteenth-century knight, Sir Thomas Ursewick of Essex 'suggests that Appleby's money problems had not caused any great distortion in the types of chattels that were listed'.

Sir Edmund's kitchen housed serving dishes as well as utensils, and here those anterior scenes from the Luttrell Psalter come to mind. Among the items listed was a '*bronderet*' with two hooks.[18] This was a brandreth, an iron stand shaped liked a trivet for supporting a pot directly over a fire. There was also a grater and two knives for the '*dressyngbord*'. The dressing board was where the meal would be prepared. It is shown in the Luttrell Psalter with a dressing knife, which has a convex blade ideal for cutting a suckling pig. This compares with two other kitchen knives, the long chopping knife and the leaching or slicing knife with a straight blade like a modern-day carving knife.[19] The larder was well stocked, to the value of £7 18s 2d.[20] There was a table, a salting trough, and a bin for storing salt. There was also a bakehouse with equipment worth £3 2s 4d.

Altogether, Sir Edmund Appleby may be taking us closer to the standard of the more established gentry of fourteenth-century England, while the de la Beche inventory indicates that a higher level of possessions was possible. Both the de la Beche and Appleby inventories indicate that the gentry hall was relatively sparsely furnished, especially (as we shall see later) in comparison with their private chambers. We have reached the point, however, when we can most valuably turn to the consumption of food and drink. We will then move to examining the private chambers.

The Luttrell Psalter has already suggested to us that dining was a prime area of display and that the food itself, with its high protein content, was a major focus. We are better off when it comes to analysing aristocratic diet, in comparison with other areas of consumption, in that we have surviving household accounts, albeit very few for the gentry. We are exceptionally fortunate in that two of these belonged to John de Multon of Frampton and his wife, Anne, and date from 1343–4 and from 1347–8 respectively.[21] Although household accounts were diverse in form, at the heart of the accounting system lay, invariably, the diet accounts. These were normally drawn up on a daily basis, that is *per dietas*, from which the modern word diet is derived.[22] Consequently, what these accounts tell us most about is food and drink.

From the very start we encounter a heavy protein diet. The Multon household account roll which runs from Michaelmas 1347 to the beginning of Lent 1348 records regular purchases of beef, pork, and mutton, as well as eggs, at the beginning of the week. Veal appears from time to time, as do piglets. Fowl are mentioned fairly regularly, and young pigeons were bought once. The laconic accounts refer not only to purchases but also to items 'from stock'. Ham[23] is

---

[18] There were five dozen pewter vessels and two large serving dishes, also of pewter, together with four brass plates, six brass bowls and a posnet. In addition there were two brass mortars and pestles, three iron spits, a cob and griddle and a frying pan.

[19] I have taken these details from Brears, *Cooking and Dining*, 204.

[20] There were thirty pigs and three oxen.   [21] Multon 160 and 85/2.

[22] Sometimes, however, they were done week by week: Woolgar, *Household Accounts*, i. 7.

[23] The word is *perna*. It may refer to bacon, i.e. *perna baconis*.

found. Among the more unusual entries are haggis (*hagiz*) and brisket (*brusket*). In the Multon diet an equal place to that of meat was occupied by fish. There are regular purchases of herrings, and of dried and salted as well as fresh fish. Cod, plaice, and sprats occur quite often. Oysters occur, as do whelks. Mullet is also found. Salmon occurs on several occasions and conger once. Of freshwater fish, pike and roach are found between September and Christmas. We also find lamprons, that is river lampreys. Of birds less regularly found we encounter plovers, curlews, and pipits. Butter is bought as well as mustard, ginger, galingale, and galantine (a spiced sauce often associated with ginger). Verjuice or vertsauce (*salsamentum*) was also purchased. This was fermented sour juice from grapes. Pepper and saffron were each bought twice during the period of the account. Seven bushels of London salt were bought on 23 October. There is no regular mention of bread or ale, nor of the home baking or brewing which must have taken place very frequently in the Multons' bakehouse and brewhouse. Ale was bought on one occasion, however, 'for lack of malt'. Wine was bought fairly regularly but in small quantities and should not obscure the fact that the staple diet was ale, bread, flesh, and fish of various kinds.

Heavy expenditure was incurred in the run up to Christmas. On 14 December two thousand herrings were bought as well as sixty stockfish and twelve mullets. The same week also saw purchases of ginger and galingale as well as mustard, oysters and sprats, butter and wine. A quantity of *semel* (fine white flour) was also bought. During Christmas week itself the household purchased half a carcass of veal, codling, lamprons, eels, sturgeon, sprats and salt fish, as well as beef, butter and eggs, a quantity of fowl, two piglets and a plover, saffron, galantine and vinegar or sour wine (*vinum acrum*), almonds and rice. More was spent, however, on the Sunday immediately before Lent when 6s 9d was spent on wine for Lord Furnivall and others at the jousts (hastiludes). In addition to the 9s ½d spent on beef, veal and poultry, there was a ham bought for 2s 4d as well as freshly killed pork and four curlews. Saffron, pepper, figs and raisins, almonds and sugar were bought, as well as 10lb of candles. Candles were the commonest non-food purchase. The total weekly expenditure was very variable, from as low as 1s 6d to as high as £1 6s, although it was rarely below 2–3s and not too often above 8 or 9s. Much no doubt depended upon the physical presence of the lord and lady and upon the occasion and, of course, the number of guests.

The food accounted for in the 1343–4 diet account is, not surprisingly, very similar to that contained in the 1347–8 roll. It does, however, widen the range of items. We find the usual sea fish plus sturgeon (twice), porpoise,[24] eels, whelks, oysters and mussels as well as lamprons, salmon, pikerels (small pike), roach, and perch. Among birds in addition to the usual fowl we find larks, a mallard and

---

[24] This occurs in a schedule attached to the account containing the expenses of Stephen the Cook. Most of his purchases were of fish.

teal, and over the Christmas period plovers, *stintes* (birds of the sandpiper family), ducks, bitterns, and a heron. After Christmas half a wild boar was consumed. An occasional insight is provided by the *blaunk seym pur fruturs*, that is fritters or pancakes. We also find 'divers colours for cooking', purchased at a cost of 4s. Among spices we find once again saffron, almonds and sugar, together with rice, while 3s was spent on ginger sauce, mustard, and galantine between Michaelmas and Epiphany. Pears were once bought for the lady and at Christmas there was sugar plate (*sucre de plate*), icing sugar used for the making of confectionary. Candles were regularly bought, and special varieties at Christmas, namely *torches et tortis et autre chaundel*. At the end of the account there is a list of items with which the larder had been stocked, in some cases before Martinmas, the traditional time of culling: meat (beef, mutton, and pork), some of which is said to have been slaughtered, Paris candles, herrings and salt fish, together with cloves, mace, cinnamon flour, cubebs, *suker de platz* for Christmas, fennel, bales of fruit, olive oil, and a gallon of plain 'oil'.

The picture of gentry diet revealed by the Multon household accounts is largely confirmed by those provided by the accounts of Hamo Le Strange of Hunstanton, a family of similar station to the Multons. The earliest Le Strange account roll belongs to 1328–9, with others surviving, with gaps, from 1341 to 1352.[25] They show the same emphasis upon meat and fish. A variety of spices was bought, and salt in some quantity. Baking and brewing were done on a regular basis, although bread was also bought, as was malt for brewing. Ale was clearly the staple drink. Wine figures very rarely. Of non-food items the most regular item recorded is, again, candles. A greater variety of meat seems to have been bought over the Christmas period, including pork, rabbits, capons, hens, and geese. The hens tended to come from rents in kind, while rabbits were often gifts. The most exotic fare, however, was the Christmas day swan, provided by John de Camoys, Hamo's father-in-law. Poultry was bought on a regular basis; pigeons occasionally. Pigeons were also received as gifts. Some butter, milk, and cheese were bought, as well as eggs and, on one occasion, cream. In 1347–8 milk was purchased on various occasions for 'Hamo son of Hamo Le Strange', who was clearly a small child.

The considerable work that has been done by experts on medieval diet in recent years allows us to put the evidence from Frampton in a broader context.[26]

[25] The Le Strange household accounts are in Norfolk Record Office, as LEST/NH 1–12. The earliest roll runs from October 1328 to October 1329. It was partially published by G. H. Holly as 'The Earliest Roll of Household Accounts in the Muniment Room at Hunstanton for the Second year of Edward II [1328]', *Norfolk Archaeology*, 21 (1920–2), 77–96. NH 7, covering the period September 1347 to August 1348, is discussed by H. Le Strange, 'A Roll of Household Accounts of Sir Hamon Le Strange of Hunstanton, Norfolk, 1347–8', *Archaeologia*, 69 (1920), 111–20, where the portion for Christmas 1347 is translated.

[26] Most recently, C. M. Woolgar, D. Serjeantson and T. Waldron (eds), *Food in Medieval England: Diet and Nutrition* (Oxford, 2006), representing the findings of the Diet Group. I have drawn liberally on Dyer, *Standards of Living*, ch. 3 'The Aristocracy as Consumers'. For comparison

The gentry diet, as we have seen, consisted heavily of bread, ale, meat, and fish. As C. C. Dyer points out:

Meat-eating was regarded as both pleasurable and a contribution to health and strength. We can conclude that the average member of a household was supplied with a diet of high calorific content and with plenty of animal protein. Modern nutritional fashion would disapprove of its high fat and low fibre content, and the apparently small intake of vitamins A and C, resulting from the often low levels of consumption of dairy produce and fresh fruit and vegetables.[27]

Dairy produce, fresh fruit, and vegetables did figure in the diet, but they were regarded as of less importance. Vegetables were important of course in the making of pottage. That aside, they seem to have been used essentially as flavourings. Garden produce was considered to be of low status and associated with poverty or penance. For this reason, more vegetables were purchased during Lent. Fruit was used to prepare delicacies, at Christmas for example. Manors often contained their own dairies, even though the consumption of dairy products was limited in high-class households. Milk was given to the young and figured in some medicines. It has also been noticed that milk, cheese and to some extent butter, figured more in households headed by women.[28] These items were also given, as we shall see, to harvesters, boon workers, and other labourers.[29] It was bread, however, that was the basis of the diet. Wheat bread was preferred with maslin (a mixture of wheat and rye) for servants or in places where wheat was less abundant.[30] Households did most of their own baking and brewing, for which barley malt was preferred. Cereals were very largely consumed as bread and ale. Although animals were slaughtered for stock in the autumn and salted, there was nonetheless a supply of fresh meat across the year.

There was, as we have seen, a great variety of fish consumed, not surprisingly given that it was eaten two or three times per week, that is to say on Fridays and Saturdays, and perhaps on Wednesdays too, as well as throughout Lent. The intake of meat and fish seems, therefore, to have been evenly balanced across the year. Even households on the east coast of England still needed to preserve fish.[31] Also fresh fish could be lightly salted, 'powdered', to preserve it for a

---

between secular and ecclesiastical households see Barbara Harvey, 'The Aristocratic Consumer in England in the Long Thirteenth Century', in M. Prestwich, R. Britnell and R. Frame (eds), *Thirteenth Century England VI* (Woodbridge, 1997), 17–37.

[27] Dyer, *Standards of Living*, 64–5.

[28] See C. M. Woolgar, 'Meat and Dairy Products in Late Medieval England', in *Food in Medieval England*, esp. 99–100.

[29] See below 87.

[30] Maslin seems to have been used for trenchers, the thick slices of bread on which other foods were served at table: Dyer, *Standards of Living*, 57.

[31] Christopher Woolgar tells us that there were three forms of preservation available: 'drying (in an English climate, in combination with some salting), pickling in brine and smoking': Woolgar, 'Diet and Consumption in Gentry and Noble Households: A Case Study from Around the Wash', in Rowena E. Archer and Simon Walker (eds), *Rulers and Ruled in Late Medieval England: Essays*

short time. Stockfish, that is dried fish (commonly wind-dried), was a regular sight in the manorial kitchens and larders, as were barrels of herrings, either salted or smoked. Nonetheless, there were regular supplies of a large variety of fresh fish. During Lent one is struck not only by the sheer quantity of marine fish eaten but also by the number of species. And there was also freshwater fish. Like the more exotic varieties of sea fish, these were seen as luxury items and the preserve of the social elite. Hence their consumption on feast days, their value as presents, and their appearance in recipe books.[32] Hence, too, the significance in status terms of the fishpond, like the dovecote, as a manorial appurtenance.

There were of course differences as well as similarities between the consumption of different households.[33] As it happens both of the most valuable sets of accounts surviving for early gentry are from the eastern seaboard. One would expect the quantity and range of fish eaten to have been higher here than in most other parts of the country. The Multons of Frampton often ate fish on Tuesdays, which was perhaps unusual, and even on Mondays, and consumed greater quantities in January and February.[34] Even along the east coast of England, however, household regimes might differ. The Le Strange accounts make occasional reference to fasting, for example during the weeks commencing 25 May 1348 and 23 June 1348.[35] Abstinence on such occasions reflected personal preference, essentially levels of piety, as much as the local circumstances of supply. As Dyer very aptly says, 'abstinence was almost as much an aristocratic indulgence as feasting'.[36] There were other preferences too. Freshwater fish are observable at Frampton, but virtually absent at Hunstanton. In fact, it seems that in the households of both the gentry and the nobility the eating of fresh fish varied more according to individual taste than did meat consumption.[37] In both cases there was considerable consumption of spices. The term is in fact a general one, referring to two types of food. The first is dried fruit—currants, dates, figs, prunes, and raisins—together with almonds and rice. Much of this, much of the time, was out of the reach of all but the wealthiest households. The second type is the strongly flavoured spices—including cinnamon, cloves, ginger, mace, pepper, and sugar. Saffron was the most expensive of all, but—as we have seen—it was consumed by at least some of the wealthier gentry families. It is

presented to Gerald Harriss (London, 1995), 24. For what follows I have drawn heavily on his discussion of the consumption of marine fish. For further detail on fish consumption see also D. Serjeantson and C. M. Woolgar, 'Fish Consumption in Medieval England', in *Food in Medieval England*, 102–130.

[32] See Christopher Dyer, 'The Consumption of Freshwater Fish in Medieval England' in his *Everyday Life in Medieval England* (London, 1994).

[33] For what follows, see especially Christopher Woolgar, 'Diet and Consumption'.

[34] 'Both patterns', says Woolgar, 'would have been very unusual in households located further from the sea': Woolgar, 'Diet and Consumption', 20.

[35] Ibid. 19–20.   [36] Dyer, *Standards of Living*, 66.

[37] Serjeantson and Woolgar, 'Fish Consumption', 129.

one of those strange and enduring myths about the Middle Ages that spices were used to disguise the taste of bland or half-rotten meat. On the contrary, they were valued for flavouring in their own right. They were very much part of normal aristocratic life, and were purchased according to one's purse.

There were differences between households which really do seem to have reflected differences in wealth. In some respects the Le Strange household was less privileged than the Multon. The latter bought more wine, for example, although even then it was far from being a common purchase. The Le Strange accounts show that it tended to be purchased by the lord himself, indicating that it was essentially for his own consumption.[38] The Multons also consumed a greater range of birds. How much we should make of these differences in terms of status is unclear. More fundamental, however, must have been differences between these households and the households of lesser gentry. The surviving membrane of an account of the household of Thomas Bozoun of Woodford near Thrapston, Northamptonshire, running from 1 May 1348 to 28 June 1348, shows that his lifestyle was similar to that of the Le Stranges and the Multons, but more basic. We can locate him socially, at least in broad terms. He was of sub-knightly stock; the sort of man who was coming to be described as an esquire. The inquisition post-mortem of his widow, the lady Alice, shows her holding ninety acres in demesne held as two-thirds of a manor.[39] The household's weekly cash expenditure was a little less than 1s 6½d.[40] Here flour was generally issued for bread-making once a fortnight when the family was at home, always six bushels of wheat and a half quarter of peas. On Saturdays, when the family was home, about a shilling's worth of meat was bought at Higham Ferrers. There were frequent purchases of poultry, eggs, and fish. What is particularly interesting is that when the lord and lady were away the other members of the household were expected to eat from store, without the need of purchases, that is to say, more basically.

At the other end of the spectrum, there were significant differences between the diets of the gentry and of the higher nobility. In the households of the former, as we have seen, wine was rarely drunk. It was much more abundant in the great households. The same is true of venison and of game birds, and in the consumption of a greater range of spices. Christopher Woolgar has made an invaluable study of the diet and consumption of four households from around the Wash. This allows comparison between the Multon and Le Strange households

---

[38] On Christmas day 1347, for example, we hear that the lord had bought two gallons of wine at Heacham, and on the following day Sir John Camoys bought another. For some details from the 1347–8 account see Hamon Le Strange, 'A Roll of Household Accounts'.

[39] *CIPM* xi. 197. As her mother had been at Yelden she must have belonged to the family of Trailly: *VCH Bedfordshire*, iii. 177. The account of the manor in *VCH Northamptonshire*, iii. 256–7 looks distinctly odd as it has Thomas Bozoun as the son of Roger Bozoun and Alice Trailly, the manor coming from her as a joint heiress.

[40] It is printed and discussed by G. H. Fowler, in 'A household expense roll, 1328', *EHR* 55 (1940), 630–4. It is re-dated to 1348 by Woolgar, *Household Accounts*, ii. 695.

on the one hand and those of Joan, duchess of Brittany on the other.[41] The duchess had, as one would expect, a markedly greater level of expenditure. In the half year to 24 March 1378 ordinary expenses of her household departments came to £235 10s 11½d. Her accounts refer to wheaten bread alone, whereas the Hunstanton household has records of regular bakings using both wheat and maslin, suggesting that not only the duchess but also her servants may have eaten better than their gentry counterparts. As we have seen, ale was the staple drink at Hunstanton and at Frampton, with wine purchased only occasionally. In the household of the duchess, by contrast, there were two grades of ale purchased, costing 1½d and 1d a gallon. Wine, however, figured daily in her household, and in some cases there was more than one variety. There were differences, too, in meat consumption. Although all the houses had access to fresh meat, in the gentry households this was less common in winter, that is after the salting which followed Martinmas. The duchess had fresh meat regularly for longer, until December, and more often thereafter. Some meats were delicacies. She had tongue, and veal at feasts and special occasions. Piglets were eaten sparingly in autumn in these households except by the duchess. Consumption of mutton was also seasonal, except for the duchess. She also regularly ate boar. In all of the households a range of birds was often eaten at a single feast. However, exotic birds once again appear more regularly in the household of the duchess.[42] Swans are a case in point. Whereas two occur in the Hunstanton accounts, one on 5 January 1343 and the other at Christmas 1347, the lady's household consumed thirty-one in a half year. Twenty-six of these, like the two Hunstanton birds, were received as presents. Like freshwater fish, the high-status swans and other exotic birds made them ideal as gifts.

In all the households there were some items that figured in restricted quantities and must therefore have been consumed by only a few people. The greater availability of these was an important distinction between the gentry and the higher nobility, as was the longer period of consumption.[43] It is indicative in this respect that Robert Grosseteste instructs the countess of Lincoln in his *Rules* to

Order that your dish be so refilled and heaped up, especially with the light courses (*entremes*), that you may courteously give from your dish to right and left to all at high table and to whom else it pleases you that they have of the same as you had in front of you.[44]

[41] C. Woolgar, 'Diet and Consumption'. The fourth account is that of Abbot Henry de Overton of Peterborough, for 1370–71. Thus both accounts are later than those for Frampton and Hunstanton.

[42] It has been said that 'Birds, even more than fish and other animals, show how those of higher rank in society could exercise choice over the food they ate—and they chose to eat young poultry and wild birds, including species that were both large and striking in appearance': D. Serjeantson, 'Birds: Food and a Mark of Status', in *Food in Medieval England*, 147.

[43] Woolgar, 'Diet and Consumption', 30.

[44] Dorothia Oschinsky (ed.), *Walter of Henley and Other Treatises on Estate Management and Accounting* (Oxford, 1971), 204–5.

As Woolgar has stressed, 'the subtleties of consumption for local display and effect would not have been lost on contemporaries'.[45]

From the accounts then we can learn a great deal of what members of the gentry ate and about how one household might compare with another in accordance with wealth and status. We are less informed about the actual dishes that were eaten, although the accounts include occasional insights. Literary discussions of feasts can be instructive. The earliest detailed menu for an English feast seems to have been that found in the later thirteenth-century *Treatise* of Walter of Bibsworth.[46] He talks first of all of the provision of bread, wine, and ale, all of the choicest. The first course consisted of a boar's head and venison. This was followed by a great variety of cranes, peacocks and swans, kids, pigs, and hens. Then came rabbits in gravy, covered in sugar, *Viaunde de Cypre* and *Mawmenny*, with red and white wine in great quantity. These were followed by a whole series of roasted birds, after which came fried meat,[47] crisps or *crespes* (that is pancakes) and fritters, with a mix of sugar and rosewater. After the table was taken away, there was sweet spice powder with large almonds, maces, cubebs, and plenty of other spicery and wafers. This tells us something of the order in which food was served, with the substantial dishes coming first followed by desserts, which were evidently not confined to sweet dishes. But this is of course a feast rather than daily fare.[48]

In attempting to get closer to what was consumed in the manor house we are fortunate in the survival of some fourteenth-century recipe books, although these, too, have a tendency to concentrate on the exotic. Moreover, they are often laconic, and they lack precise measures. Nevertheless, they do give the flavour, as it were, of thirteenth- and fourteenth-century cuisine. Two groups of recipes were translated from Anglo-Norman[49] into a Middle English collection during the first quarter of the fourteenth century. It was complied under the direction of, and partly it would seem in the hand of, Friar William Herebert of Hereford. It includes the *Viaunde de Cypre* and *Mawmenny*, mentioned by Walter of Bibsworth. Mawmenny was a poultry dish, in a spiced sauce of wine and almond milk. The recipe says that the braun (i.e. the flesh) of a capon should be pounded to powder (*ipolled al to poudre*) and then boiled with the wine. Ground and dried almonds should then be added together with powder of cloves and fried almonds. *Sucre fort* should be added to *abaten the strenythe of*

[45] Woolgar, 'Diet and Consumption', 30–1.
[46] For what follows, see C. B. Hieatt and S. Butler, *Curye on Inglysh: English Culinary Manuscripts of the Fourteenth Century*, EETS (1985), esp. 2–8, 28, 45, 187, 191–2, 200–1, 221–2.
[47] Braun.
[48] For feasts, see W. E. Mead, *The English Medieval Feast* (London, 1931; repr. 1967) and P. Hammond, *Food and Feast in Medieval England* (Stroud, 1993). For cooking, see T. Scully, *The Art of Cooking in the Middle Ages* (Woodbridge, 1995) and Brears, *Cooking and Dining*, which also contains recipes.
[49] They survive in Anglo-Norman manuscripts dating from the early fourteenth century. They probably contain thirteenth-century material: Hieatt and Butler, *Curye on Inglys*, 7.

the specerie. The colour, it says, *schal beon inde* (indigo). *Viaunde de Cypre* was a sweet dish containing sugar (i.e. *cypre*). The Middle English recipe gives the sauce only, but it seems to have been used with fish. This is confirmed by a late-fourteenth-century recipe for *Viaunde de Cypre of Samounre*. This, too, was an almond dish, the basic ingredients being almond milk with rice flour. The early fourteenth-century recipe adds ginger, 'so that hit smacche wel of gynger'. Not surprisingly, its colour was yellow. This recipe also adds 'gyngebred' with 'fasticade'. The gingerbread was apparently not the modern cake-like variety but was made from breadcrumbs boiled in honey with spices. Fasticade (from Arabic *fustaq*) was pistacchio nuts, probably chopped. These last ingredients are indicative of the type of household which these recipe collections envisaged, i.e. royalty and the like. It seems unlikely that cooks at Frampton and Hunstanton had a great deal of recourse to such books. The cuisine here must have been dependant upon the training, skill, expertise, and discretion of the individual practitioner. However, the recipes do give the general flavour of aristocratic meals and a standard against which a kitchen might be judged, or to which it might aspire.

Generally speaking, then, gentry families could not have matched the higher nobility when it came to the consumption of meat and drink. But they could, and did, display the quality and variety of their food. They could also display its plentiful supply, and adopt a spirit of generosity, a quality which was generally linked to gentility both inside romance and without. When Geoffrey Chaucer wished to delineate the characteristics of his aspirant late-fourteenth-century proto-gentleman, the Franklin, he emphasized his hospitality and the quality, variety and aristocratic nature of his food, including meat, freshwater fish, and spices. In short, 'It snewed in his hous of mete and drynke.'[50]

Bishop Robert Grosseteste in his mid-thirteenth-century *Rules*[51] laid great stress on the need for communal dining in hall, and not away from one's household, either alone or with guests. The Luttrell Psalter illustrates how a gentry family should dine, at least when they were doing it properly. If the poet William Langland is to be believed, dining outside of the hall had become commoner by the 1370s.[52] The chronology of this shift is unclear. However, it is noticeable from the inventories that the fourteenth-century hall seems to have been on the whole sparsely furnished compared to, at least, the principal chamber, suggesting that, dining aside, the chambers were the principal foci of family life. As we shall see later, the chamber was certainly where most indoor entertainment took place.[53]

[50] Prologue to the *Canterbury Tales*, l. 345, *The Works of Geoffrey Chaucer*, ed. F. N. Robinson (London, 1957).
[51] See below 65.
[52] *The Vision of Piers Plowman: An Edition of the 'B' Text*, ed. A.V.C. Schmidt (London, 1978), passus x, ll. 96–102.
[53] See below 244–5.

The chamber was also the place where precious possessions were concentrated. The de la Beche inventory contains a long list of bedding. Pride of place is taken with what was clearly the master bed. It had a mattress covered with vermillion sendal (a thin, rich, shiny silk), a pair of curtains of sendal *tulee* (that is tulle, a kind of fine silk net or muslin) with three riddels or curtains 'of the same suit', six cushions of sendal *tulee,* and six tapets or hangings of vermillion 'for the same bed'. There were six cushions of green samite, another rich, silk fabric, a coverture lined with pure miniver (a grey or whitish squirrel fur), the cloth itself being of a red medley (that is, woven of different colours or shades), and so on. A total of forty-seven items are enumerated. What is striking, apart from the sheer quantity, is the colourfulness of it all and the occasionally arresting decoration. There were coverlets and tapets decorated with butterflies, for example, and others covered with swords and oak leaves. There was also a wide variation in quality, ranging from samite to buckram, a (sometimes fine) linen fabric. However, not all of it was new by any means. There was an old doublet covered with green sendal, for example, and a very old quilt covered with sendal *tulee.* Aged items were retained, presumably for as long as they were serviceable. At this point in the list we find six pairs of coffers in which much of the above was probably stored. The coffers are said to be 'for trousseau' which no doubt has a wider meaning than the one that has come down to us.

The list continues with a white *viale* for the chamber and garderobe. The word is obscure, but it may stand for veil and therefore indicate some thin wall covering.[54] There are also two *sales*, which seem more certainly to be wall-hangings,[55] with two bankers (bench covers), again 'of a suit', one of which was said to be better quality than the other and to be powdered with roses and popinjays. It was bordered with the de la Beche arms. There were also one doser (that is, a dosel, a rich hanging or tapestry) with two testers or canopies of worsted (a woollen fabric), powdered with images of knights and ladies. These items conclude this section of the inventory and would seem to be the furnishings of the principal chamber. These were items that were permanently in use, and therefore on display. Here, as in the chapel and at table, the de la Beche arms—*vairy, argent and gules*—were much in evidence as an ongoing statement of identity. The lord and lady's chamber is revealed as one of the principal foci of gentle life.

The existence of older items, however, suggests that this opulence was not acquired overnight but built up over a period of time, a factor which we must bear in mind should we be tempted to allow the possessions of the de la Beches to stand uncritically as the norm among gentry households. On the other hand, it is equally well worth recording that gentry chambers were sometimes the

[54] This seems more likely than vial for phial, i.e. a bottle.
[55] See *Middle English Dictionary* (MED) S-SL, p. 45. Alternatively, it could perhaps be referring to some form of seating.

scene of even more spectacular display. The chamber at Longthorpe Tower near Peterbrough, for example, is covered with elaborate wall paintings depicting a mixture of religious and secular themes, including the Three Living and the Three Dead, the Wheel of Senses, and King David with other musicians, as well as heraldry.[56] The tower was added *c.*1330 to an existing manor house, the builder being very probably Robert de Thorpe, steward of Peterborough Abbey. The plastered and whitewashed walls of many contemporary chambers in gentry houses must have lent themselves to such schemes and there is no reason at all to think that in its day Longthorpe Tower can have been in any way unique. As has been said though, the Thorpe family must have felt that they were living inside an illuminated manuscript.[57] This scenario helps to place the Luttrell Psalter, too, into a wider contemporary context.

Sir Edmund Appleby's inventory begins with the contents of the chamber. Here there were goods to the value of £35 12s 8d. Pride of place was given once again to what appears to have been the master bed, described as being embroidered[58] with three figured cloths, tapets, a half canopy and three curtains, the whole thing having a cord and hook and being worth 8 marks (£5 6s 8d). There were no less than six other beds, the one described as a plain red one with three curtains being the second best.[59] There were also coverlets of various kinds, colours and values, together with mattresses, blankets and cushions (five red and four blue). There were two chests, one white and one red, two leather baskets, two basins and one laver or washbasin. Altogether the chamber seems to have been well provided with furnishings, if not especially richly when compared to that of the de la Beches. It also housed the lord's armour, with a total value of £16 6s 8d.

Once again, Sir Edmund Appleby may be taking us closer to the standard of the more established gentry of fourteenth-century England, while the de la Beche inventory indicates that a higher level of possessions was possible. A final example also suggests that in reality the quality of possessions was quite variable. This takes us a little way back in time, to 1298, when an inventory was made of the wardrobe of Osbert de Spaldington.[60] His inventory is especially valuable in that it contains a list of his personal clothing. Osbert was a younger brother of Robert de Spaldington, a tenant-in-chief who held lands at Northallerton

---

[56] See J. Alexander and P. Binski, *Age of Chivalry: Art in Plantagenet England 1200–1400* (London, 1987), 129 and no. 137, where it is depicted.

[57] Anthony Emery, *Discovering Medieval Houses*, 87.

[58] Or, perhaps, embellished.

[59] The beds were usually defined by their colour. Two were described as being of one kind and worked with devices, presumably meaning they were embroidered. Three of the beds had curtains and/or tapets, and two of them had cords.

[60] What follows is taken from a splendid study by F. Lachaud, with the inventory attached: 'An Aristocratic Wardrobe of the Late Thirteenth Century: the Confiscation of the Goods of Osbert de Spaldington in 1298', *BIHR* 67 (1994), 91–100. Her footnotes contain extremely interesting detail and reflections on the likely value and quality of the items.

in Yorkshire and Santon and Clixby in Lincolnshire. Osbert himself became a knight and was very active on judicial commissions in the 1290s. Active also in the king's service in Wales and Scotland, he was appointed sheriff and keeper of Berwick upon Tweed in May 1296. He appears as a knight of the royal household during 1296–7. However, he fell from favour, seemingly because of some abuse of his office at Berwick. In January 1298 his lands were taken into the king's hands and in June his goods were found at the abbey of Rievaulx and listed.[61] He may well have been trying to avoid their confiscation. In the summer of 1298 he succeeded his elder brother when he was said to be over fifty years of age. It was not until 1303, however, that he was fully restored. What we are seeing then is the property of a successful younger son towards the end of his active life. It probably includes the greater part of what he owned, although perhaps not everything. There is no mention of his armour, for example. However, it certainly seems to include his most valuable goods, and ranges across wardrobe, chamber, and hall. Unfortunately no values are given.

It begins with cloths, namely three cloths of gold and one of *say*, a woollen cloth. The former were of silk woven with gilded thread. They were often patterned and tended to be expensive. These items are followed by his bedclothes. He had a coverlet of linen with a border of sendal, *gris*, that is squirrel fur, with a lining of *paunace,* a woollen cloth of a blue-green colour resembling a peacock, and a canopy of *fil* (probably a type of linen). There was also a green *carde*, a strong cloth used as part of the bed. There was plenty of linen, including table linen. There was a *banquer* or banker and a tapet. Osbert was well set up in terms of tableware. He had four silver goblets (*hanaps*), one of which had a foot, eighteen bowls, seventeen saucers, two salts, a candlestick and a silver cruet.[62] The non-silver items were undoubtedly of pewter. Finally, there was an anlace (a knife) with an ivory hilt, and a trencher or platter.[63]

From what has gone before none of this occasions any great surprise. It is in its lists of clothing, as we have said, that Osbert's inventory is most interesting. He had several robes, each involving a number of garments. The first mentioned was of *ray*, that is a woollen cloth with stripes which was very popular in his day. It consisted of a 'cote', two surcoats or supertunics, a cloak and three *chaperons* or hoods. One of the hoods was lined with miniver, the other with budge or *bouge*.[64] The surcoats were lined with *strandling* and the cloak with

---

[61] What lands he held at this point is unclear. They certainly included property in Micklefield and Sproxton and perhaps already the manor of Willitoft which he certainly held later. He also held the manor of Skiplam in Yorkshire of the abbot of Rievaulx, which helps to explain why his goods were deposited there.

[62] This, at least, is the meaning of *picher* given by the editor.

[63] *Trenchur.* Not in fact a type of knife, as the editor suggests.

[64] A kind of fur made of lambskin with the wool outwards.

bis, both being types of squirrel fur. The second robe was of *pers*, a woollen
material of deep blue, and comprised a tunic, surcoats lined with *strandling*, a
tabard (a sleeveless upper garment) lined with budge and two hoods, one lined
with miniver and the other with sendal. The third robe was of white camelin,
a woollen cloth of high quality. There were two hoods and a *tabard sengle*, that
is without lining, and a closed surcoat, i.e. not open at the front as many were.
There was also a hood of medley, lined with miniver. In addition to these three
robes, there were also some isolated items, namely a surcoat *party de escarlet*,
that is one divided longitudinally with only one side dyed scarlet, two more
tabards, one of cloth of *pers* and the other green, a tunic of striped cloth and
a *corset*, which seems to have been a kind of upper garment richly lined with
fur. There were also three furs for lining hoods, a corset of squirrel fur, and half
a lamb's fur. There were three pairs of new hose, three old hose, two pairs of
sleeves of *pers*, two old sleeves and two *tunicles*, presumably short tunics. There
was also a pair of hose with gilded spurs attached. There were also accessories,
namely four *fermals*, that is brooches used for fastening garments, seventeen
rings, two *flores dor* (perhaps studs in the form of a flower), eight *burses* or
pouches made of say, and five belts. One of these was his sword belt, his *saint de
hernise*.

The quality of Osbert's dress reflects the expectation in the later thirteenth
century that knights and their ladies would want to dress according to their
station. This was recognized in the instructions given to the collectors of
parliamentary subsidies in the time of Edward I. In 1290, for example, the
armour, horses, jewels, vases of gold, silver and bronze, and clothes of knights,
gentiz homes and their wives were exempted from tax.[65] There are also suggestions
in Osbert's inventory that he was abreast of contemporary fashion, in his use
of striped cloth, for example, and most especially in his super-tunic of *mi-parti*.
This was where a garment was half of one colour and half of another. It seems
likely that there was an increasingly strong sense of fashion in dress during this
period in which the gentry were major participants. The Luttrell Psalter indicates,
in the famous dining scene and elsewhere, that this family was à la mode in
its sense of dress, Sir Geoffrey's piety notwithstanding. In the famous dining
scene, for example, Geoffrey's son, Andrew, and his daughter-in-law, Beatrice,
are shown with the long sleeves that were the height of contemporary fashion
(Figure 3.2). They evidently subscribed to the striking new fashions of their
day that have been so eloquently described by Stella Mary Newton.[66] The early

[65] F. Lachaud, 'Dress and Social Status in England before the Sumptuary Laws', in Coss and
Keen, *Heraldry, Pageantry and Social Display in Medieval England*, 113.
[66] Stella Mary Newton, *Fashion in the Age of the Black Prince: A Study of the Years 1340–1365*
(Woodbridge, 1980), 3–5. For more general recent studies see Margaret Scott, *Medieval Dress
and Fashion* (London, n.d.); and F. Piponnier and P. Mane, *Dress in the Middle Ages*, trans.
C. Beamish (New Haven and London, 1997); first published as *Se Vêtir au Moyen Age*
(Paris, 1995).

1340s marked the end of the rectangular look, as sleeves were no longer cut together with the upper part of the garment. They were now separate pieces rounded to fit armholes cut out of the main piece. Both torso and sleeves became tighter fitting. Sleeves themselves had already become shorter and wider at the elbow, forming the shape of a bell. When the arms were bent they hung down. Now they were further lengthened and narrowed so that they hung as a long strip, no longer functioning as a sleeve. These were the famous 'tippets'.[67] The upper garment, moreover, went down to the navel where it met the skirt. In the case of men this terminated around the knee. In the case of women it touched the ground and might lie in folds. Men's skirts were often slit to the waist. Hairdressing for both men and women became more compact. As the waistline was lowered further the overall effect was to elongate the body so that people looked taller. The pull of fashion at this time was not lost on contemporary moralists. The literary manuscript Harley 2253, which belongs to the very same period as the Luttrell Psalter, contains a poem *On the Follies of Fashion* which particularly targets ladies.[68] A rising fashion-consciousness amongst the gentry was very probably one of the underlying causes of the growing desire to control what people might wear in the fourteenth century, which led to the major but abortive sumptuary law of 1363 which attempted to restrict dress and adornment according to social status.[69] It would be too much to argue that the world of fashion was born at this time. However, it does seem to have extended its reach and to have deepened in intensity. An acute awareness of fashion, in dress as in other spheres, was to remain an enduring feature of the gentry.

In short, Osbert de Spaldington owned some items of quality, e.g. cloths of gold, gilt accessories, and silver tableware, not to mention his impressive dress. In quality, if not quantity, he appears somewhat richer than Sir Edmund de Appleby. Of course, he was well placed as a member of the royal household to accrue a reasonable amount of wealth. The possessions of these people pale into insignificance, however, when compared to those of members of the higher nobility.[70] To take a famous example from the late fourteenth century, Thomas duke of Gloucester had possessions valued at £1,910, including a bed of cloth of gold with a canopy of blue satin which alone was worth £182 3s.[71] Richard Lyons, the great London financier, possessed goods and chattels in the capital

[67] For an extended study of this fashion see Robin Netherton, 'The Tippet: Accessory after the Fact?', in R. Netherton and G. R. Owen-Crocker (eds), *Medieval Clothing and Textiles* 1 (Woodbridge, 2005), 115–32.

[68] For Harley 2253, see below Chapter 12.

[69] On sumptuary laws see now Alan Hunt, *Governance of the Consuming Passions: A History of Sumptuary Law* (London, 1996).

[70] Lachaud, 'An Aristocratic Wardrobe', 99–100.

[71] A. Goodman, *The Loyal Conspiracy: The Lords Appellant under Richard II* (London, 1971), 91–4.

Figure 3.2. Fashion in the early 1340s (from the Luttrell Psalter). Add. MS 42131, fos. 186v and 215r. © The British Library Board. All Rights Reserved 2010.

that were valued in 1377 at over £1,925.[72] As far as the material culture of the gentry is concerned, what motivated them primarily was their membership of an aristocratic elite. We sense this when we are talking of residences, furnishings, dress or food and drink. The desire to assert membership, rather than to differentiate themselves from those below or socially aspirant, would appear to be the main inspiration behind their display of possessions and their consumption. Indeed, in maintaining aristocratic standards—standards that were derived, ultimately, from the highest reaches of society—they also played a major part, paradoxically, in determining the contours of wider downward dissemination. We glimpse this in the fragmentary household account of Thomas Bozoun. We find it in literature, in the portrait of Chaucer's Franklin for example, and we see it reflected in the inventories of prosperous townsmen.[73] This is not to suggest

[72] A. R. Myers, 'The Wealth of Richard Lyons', in T. A. Sandquist and M. R. Powicke (eds), *Essays in Medieval History Presented to Bertie Wilkinson* (Toronto, 1969), 303.
[73] P. J. P. Goldberg, 'The Fashioning of Bourgeois Domesticity in Later Medieval England: a Material Culture Perspective', in Kowaleski and Goldberg, *Medieval Domesticity*, 124–44. See also Norman J. G. Pounds, *Hearth and Home: a History of Material Culture* (Bloomington, 1989).

that display was the only criterion. Walls, for example, would have been covered for warmth as well as for decoration. Above all, however, what their surviving inventories show is that materially speaking the gentry enjoyed a reasonably high standard of living in fourteenth-century terms; at least they did so at the level of the Multons of Frampton.

4

Household, Locality, and Social Interaction

In the last chapter we discussed the material culture of the gentry household and the accent placed on display. We now need to try to understand the household dynamically, as a living entity. The seigniorial household, or *familia*, comprised, as is well known, not only the immediate family in the modern sense of the term and sometimes additional kin, but also a panoply of officials and servants together with visitors who came and went on errands, business and social calls of various kinds. The essential purpose of the household was the constant reproduction of the aristocratic lifestyle required by the lord, or by the lord and lady. It follows that much of the life experienced by members of the gentry within the household was a relatively open affair. They became accustomed to living in close proximity, and in some respects in company, with people who were their social inferiors. This was, and was long to be, of the essence of gentry life.

On this basis it is often suggested that medieval lords and ladies lived their lives in public rather than private. Although this view is not entirely without foundation, to put the mater in such terms is to create a false dichotomy and to overlook some of the nuances of medieval life. It is true that the hall could be the site of public business and that the household could accommodate numerous short-term members, but while the external world intruded it did so in a controlled manner. For the gentry the household must still have been a home, a refuge from the outside world and a place of some sentimental attachment. Moreover, life in the gentry household did not preclude a degree of privacy, as the increasing importance of individual chambers, where both physical comfort and intimate interaction were concentrated, and the use of curtains and screens, indicates. Much has been written in recent times on the rise of domesticity in Western culture, most writers seeing it as essentially a 'bourgeois' and a post-medieval phenomenon. A recent study has argued, however, with some validity, that domesticity as a mode of living and as a set of values can be observed in the major towns of fourteenth-century England.[1] Some of the arguments advanced, around hospitality and orderliness for example, and around both private chambers and the home as a place of occupation as well as of retreat,

---

[1] Felicity Riddy, ' "Burgeis" Domesticity in Late-Medieval England', in M. Kowaleski and P. J. P. Goldberg (eds), *Medieval Domesticity: Home, Housing and Household in Medieval England* (Cambridge, 2008), 14–36.

apply equally well to the gentry household. In fact, the latter could be viewed in this context as an antecedent. In short, the gentry household, although it had many dimensions, was a domestic setting.

The present chapter aims to reach a balanced view of the gentry household as a home, as a social organism or institution and as a feature of the social landscape. It will ask a series of important questions, most of them deceptively simple in the asking. Who lived there? Who were the servants and what did they actually do? What were the social relationships involved? How self-contained was the gentry household and how did it relate to the wider world? Who visited the gentry at home? Or, to put the matter another way, for whose benefit was all the display intended? Who saw and appreciated it?

First, then, who lived there? At the heart of the gentry household lay of course the nuclear family together with any other close kin for whom the lord, or in the case of a widow, the lady, was responsible. Thus the Multon household in 1343–4 contained Sir John and Lady Anne, their children, and Sir John's two brothers, William and Thomas. The latter, however, were not regularly in residence, as they were at school in Lincoln, returning to Frampton for Christmas. Even then they were not necessarily at home. Thomas spent part at least of the festive season not with the family but with the neighbouring lord, Roger de Cobeldyke, where money was sent to him on the Monday before Christmas and again at Epiphany. The lord himself, moreover, was only intermittently present. For much of his time he was itinerant. Not only were members of the family apart for significant periods of time but the Multon household as a whole would have been split, with some of its members journeying with the lord.[2]

The outline of John de Multon's itineration during the autumn and winter of 1343–4 can be reconstructed. Around Michaelmas 1343 he was touring his more northerly estates, between Gainsborough and Lincoln. We hear first of the expenses of one John de Basingham at the Multon manor of Heapham, no doubt in preparation for the lord's coming. At Michaelmas wine was bought at Ingleby and Sir John made an offering at Stow: the day after he was at Lincoln where another offering is recorded, and where he made purchases. The following day, Wednesday 1 October, wine was bought for him together with bread for his horses at Kirkby, perhaps in preparation for his journey there. In the week beginning 12 October bread for the horses was accounted for as they brought victuals from Lincoln to Ingleby. Purchases were made for him at Ingleby on 15 and 17 October. Here he was engaging in one of the most famous of aristocratic sports. We find his servant, John de Twycross, and Nicholas his brother receiving 2s 6d in expenses for going to Ingelby with a falconer and two grooms. The *layners* or thongs bought for the lord, the next item on the account, are undoubtedly for the sport. A little later in the account we find 2s given to *le fauconer* himself for his expenses. By 21 October John was again at Lincoln

---

[2] See below 61–2.

where he probably visited his brothers, since he paid out money for their keep. He then moved back to Kirkby, and wine was purchased at Swineshead nearby. On 25 and 26 October, however, he was back at Ingleby. He may then have moved to his most northern properties as another servant, Alain le fitz Robert, was sent to Somercotes. The lord's whereabouts in November are unclear. Some of his servants were on the move: Alain le fitz Robert to Hemingby, Robert del Park to Lincoln, and John de Basingham to Ingleby. During the week beginning 23 November Sir John was at the house (*mesoun*) of John Reignald, where wine was bought for him in small quantities, but we are not told where this was located. He may well have returned then to Frampton. We hear that he had been to a tournament (*hazard*) but there is no indication as to where. Some purchases were made at Boston, and we know that Sir John 'and his company' dined there. We are now approaching Christmas, and the family was probably together at Frampton, although as we have seen the lord's brother, Thomas, seems to have stayed with Roger de Cobeldyke. He and William had journeyed from Lincoln to Frampton Dyke. In mid January an offering was made at Frampton on the day of the jousts at Windsor. It seems likely that both lord and lady were present there. Their presence at the jousts may well be linked with Robert del Park going to Windsor and with the purchase of a 'cote Wade' for the lord there. On Thursday 18 February the lord left Frampton for Ingleby. On the same day grooms and horses travelled to Boston, and the lord himself paid for a dinner with John de Lodlow there. Although Sir John was clearly fond of Ingleby, he probably spent less time away from Frampton in the winter months than he had in the autumn. The lady was not entirely sedentary either. We know a little of her journeys from the expenses given to servants. 'Little Kitte' journeyed with her on one occasion. On another the parson of Frampton's groom was with her at Scrivelsby.

The Multon household was perhaps close to the norm in terms of these activities. The account roll of the minor Northamptonshire lord, Thomas Bozoun, for May–June 1348 tells us that in the third week nothing was accounted for because the lord was away at Northampton for the jousts.[3] On Monday and Tuesday of the following week he was there again, on this occasion for the visit of the forest justices on their circuit. He spent a week in London, for unspecified reasons, between the eve of the feast of the Ascension and Whitsun Eve. He and Lady Alice later spent three days with her mother at Yelden, Bedfordshire. Later still he spent a couple of nights at Windsor while she was away for one night at Thorpe Waterville.

The Multons were close to the norm, too, in terms of the composition of their household. Naturally there were households that were headed by a widow, or even a widower. However, there were other possibilities. The Le Strange roll for 1347–8 is headed 'Expenses of the house of Sir John Camoys and Hamo

---

[3] For the account roll, see above 43.

Le Strange in residence at Hunstanton, with the lady de Camoys, her damsel (*domicella*) and maid (*ancilla*) and with Hamo Le Strange and his wife, with her damsel and maid, and with the free servants (*cum liberis famulis*) living with the aforesaid John and Hamo, that is to say, Richard the Chaplain, the butler, the cook, with the groom (*garcifer*), two boys, and one lad (*garcio*) of the aforesaid Hamo'. John Camoys was Hamo's father-in-law, and in this situation was what was sometimes known as a sojourner.[4] In this situation a guest or guests, with at least their personal servants, stayed on a medium or long-term basis. It was fraught with problems, as Jane Stonor would remind her husband, Thomas, in the fifteenth century. 'It would be better to break up the household than to take sojourners',[5] she advised him. To work, it must have required a close personal friendship. In the Le Strange/Camoys case the two men had served together on the Crécy campaign and at the siege of Calais and had formed a close bond. They had presumably returned from France with the king in the autumn of 1347. Perhaps John was staying with his daughter and son-in law until his own household could be re-formed.[6] The fact that Sir John is mentioned first is no doubt in deference to his seniority. However, this was clearly Hamo's household. He would have needed the same basic staff with or without his in-laws. One further member of the family is not mentioned at the head of the account. This was his baby son, Hamo son of Hamo Le Strange, for whom milk was purchased on various occasions. The purchases were made, in fact, by the lady's maid whose name is revealed in the accounts as Alice.

Each adult member of a gentry family is likely to have had one or more servants who performed duties of a personal nature, including help with dressing. A lady would have a damsel and a maid. In Sir John de Multon's household we hear of Joni, the lady's damsel and of the previously mentioned little Kitte, who was doubtless her maid. We also hear of Margarete who, on one occasion at least, was the lady's companion. Some lowly figures also appear on the male side. We hear of Symme, the lord's groom, and of other, unnamed, grooms.

More significant in terms of status within the household were the free servants or free household, that is to say the relatively high-status officials who were living in. In the Le Strange household, as we have seen, these were the chaplain, who alone is named, the butler, and the cook. Leaving aside the damsel and maid servant of the lady Camoys, we are left with a total of only nine servants. This appears to be a rather skeletal staff, especially when we learn that the contemporary household of the relatively lowly lord, Thomas Bozoun of Northamptonshire,

---

[4] See Woolgar, *The Great Household*, 25, for sojourners.

[5] Christine Carpenter (ed.), *Kingsford's Stonor Letters and Papers 1290–1483* (Cambridge, 1996), no. 106: 'raythere breke up housallde than take sugiornantes'.

[6] Le Strange, 'A Roll of Household Accounts', 112 who suggests that it resulted from the partition of the Foliot estates with Gressenhall and Elsing having been allotted to the other heiress, Margaret's sister Margery and her husband Sir Hugh de Hastings. However, it seems unlikely that John did not have property of his own.

seems to have contained seven or eight people.[7] Surely gentry households were normally larger than this? The Luttrell evidence may shed more light on the issue.

The domestic scenes in the Luttrell Psalter suggest that the family employed a considerable kitchen staff. The cook himself is portrayed as a rather formidable looking character (Figure 3.1). In addition to the kitchen staff, there are men waiting on table. Two of these seem to be the highest officials in the household. A bearded man carries a purse suggesting that he is the steward or dispenser, the man responsible for provisioning the household. The word *spence* was an older term for what had come to be called pantry. The figure in the centre of the scene is perhaps the butler or cup-bearer. His towel seems to indicate his high-status position. He was, of course, in charge of the buttery. These, then, are aspects of the social display we were discussing earlier. Sir Geoffrey Luttrell is showing that he and his guests are served by his highest-ranking officers and that the Luttrells can afford a whole series of servants, each devoted to a specific task.

Judging from the bequests in his will, dated 3 April 1345, Sir Geoffrey Luttrell did indeed employ a staff larger than that indicated for Hamo Le Strange.[8] Geoffrey made a large number of bequests, many of them to members of his household. Robert de Wilford, his chaplain, received a legacy of £1 and his confessor, Brother William de Fotheringay, 5 marks for clothing. The appearance of a confessor in his will is very much in keeping with what we know of Sir Geoffrey's exceptional piety, and is unlikely to have been the norm among the gentry. It is also unlikely that his confessor was resident in his household. The codicil to his will includes a second chaplain, Sir John de Lafford, who also received a legacy of £1. The will certainly reflects Geoffrey's great attention to his kitchen. Two cooks are mentioned. William the Cook (*le Ku*) of Irnham received £2 and a robe, while John of Bridgford received 10 marks and a robe, that is a suit of clothes. Whether they functioned at one and the same time is unclear. In his codicil Geoffrey left John all the brass and wooden vessels belonging to his kitchen, suggesting that he at least was in residence to the end. Two further kitchen servants, William Howet and Robert Baron, received legacies. Both of them were described as 'of my kitchen' (*de coquina mea*).[9] There were also bequests to three children of the kitchen staff.[10]

We are on surer ground with some of the other staff, who clearly have single responsibilities. There was John de Colne, described as his pantryman and butler, William the Porter, and William de Chaworth his chamberlain. The last named received a legacy of £2, the others 10 marks and a robe, the same as John the

---

[7] Dyer, *Standards of Living*, 51. This included, apparently, both family and servants.

[8] The will is Episcopal Register VII (Thomas Bek), Lincolnshire Archives Office, fo. 212. It is published in Eric G. Millar, *The Luttrell Psalter* (London, 1930), 52–4 (text), 54–6 (translation).

[9] They received legacies of £1 and 6s 8d respectively.

[10] There were bequests to: Geoffrey son William Howet, my godson; Geoffrey son of William the Cook of Irnham; and to Robert son of John the Cook.

Cook. This then appears to have been the standard bequest to staff of a certain rank. John de Colne and William the Porter, moreover, also received additional bequests in Geoffrey's codicil. William was to have the furnishings of the hall.[11] John was to have all the utensils and vessels belonging to the pantry and buttery. In other words, they received the items pertaining to their respective offices. Once again we see the household equipment and furnishings being dispersed on the death of their holder. Geoffrey also had a chambermaid, Alice de Wadenowe, who was rewarded with 5 marks. Whether she was in the household at the time of Joan de Meaux, once the lady's maid, is unknowable. Geoffrey's wife, Agnes Sutton, had predeceased him. Joan, however, was remembered in his will, receiving £2. Moreover, it was she who received Geoffrey's bed and all the furnishings of his chamber in accordance with the codicil. Among the other legatees were Thomas de Chaworth of Osberton, described as his esquire, who received a handsome 50 marks, and John of Boothby, his clerk, who received 5 marks. It may well be that both men spent a good deal of time with him.

Altogether at least a dozen of these people must have been resident at any one time under Sir Geoffrey's roof.[12] There may also have been more menial characters that we are not able to take account of. The outline of his *familia* is clear enough. His chaplain(s) and his chamberlain must have taken key roles in the organization of his household. Indeed they might well have functioned as dispenser and receiver respectively. In one respect, at least, his household organization might not have been quite so grand as the Luttrell Psalter suggests. Despite the claims made implicitly by the psalter, John de Colne occupied the offices of pantryman and butler simultaneously, combining two roles that would certainly have been separate in greater households. It is not clear whether Thomas de Chaworth, his esquire, occupied any particular office. If he did, that of steward would seem the most likely.

In passing it should be noted that the will suggests some respect on the part of Sir Geoffrey Luttrell for his staff. Bequests were made not only to them but also to members of their families; these include, in addition to those already mentioned, Eloise, wife of John de Colne, and Lambert, son of Thomas de Chaworth. The latter's groom was also remembered. Notwithstanding the sense of opulence that the Luttrell Psalter attempted to project, however, knightly households are revealed as relatively simple in structure, with less formal division than in the greater households.[13]

[11] *totum apparatum aule mee viz. Dosser & Baunker*. For these terms, see above 47.
[12] Graham Platts, *Land and People in Medieval Lincolnshire* (Lincoln, 1985), 44, notes that Geoffrey had at least twelve employees at his manor of Irnham. This has caused some confusion: Camille, *Mirror in Parchment*, 82–3, appears to confuse household and estate workers. In fact Platts included in this figure a parker, a brewer and a reeve, all of whom received legacies. The several men called *serviens* in the will were also probably estate employees, i.e. serjeants rather than servants. Nonetheless, the number of *household* staff mentioned in the will is at least twelve.
[13] On the organization of the household in general, see also Mertes, *The English Noble Household 1250–1600*, ch. 1.

More understanding of the personnel and actual workings of the household can be gained from the household ordinance of the lord and lady of Eresby, Lincolnshire.[14] The date of this document is uncertain but it appears to emanate from the time of Robert de Willoughby and his wife, Margaret, that is to say during the first two decades of the fourteenth century.[15] The Willoughbys were minor barons, Robert being the first of the family to receive a personal summons to parliament. Given this provenance it is likely to correspond only with the very highest end of the gentry spectrum in terms of the number of household officers. It has a particular value, however, in that it not only lists the household offices themselves but also indicates their respective duties.

The ordinance begins with Sir John de Sturminster, the steward or seneschal. He is aided, it is said, by Henry de Chelreye who functions in his absence. If both were absent their place was taken by Alan de Medfeld. William de Otterhampton is the wardrober. Sir Richard Olyver is clerk of the offices and deputy (*lieu tenant*) of the wardrober when he is away. He is in effect the household clerk. Sir Hugh de Byford is the chaplain and the lord's almoner. He helps in writing letters and other items when the need arises. There is also a chief buyer[16] and John de Horsle, the marshal.

The ordinance pays considerable attention, as one might expect, to accounting by these officials. The household expenses are summarized each evening before

---

[14] The document is TNA C47 3/33. About a third of it was published in Conway Davies, *Baronial Opposition to Edward II* (Cambridge, 1918), 569. There are brief discussions in T. F. Tout, *Chapters in the Administrative History of Medieval England* ii (Manchester, 1920; repr. with minor additions and corrections 1937), 182–3; N. Denholm-Young, *Seignorial Administration in England* (Oxford, 1937; repr. 1963), 7–8; and Woolgar, *The Great Household*, 17–18, who puts it in the general context of the baronial household.

[15] It is written on a single piece of parchment entitled *Lordenance del hostiel mon seigneur et ma dame le v iour de Janeuoir a Eresby lan xij*. Assuming that this refers to the regnal year, Conway Davies, Tout, and Denholm-Young all dated it to 5 January 1284, i.e. 12 Edward I. Tout pointed out that this date was before the tenure of Eresby by the Willoughbys and, against Conway Davies, argued that it must therefore emanate from their predecessors, the Beks. Woolgar dates it to *c*.1319 or *c*.1339 (i.e. 12 Edward II or 12 Edward III), presumably partly on palaeographical grounds. A curiosity of the ordinance is that the lord's main officials seem to have come from the west country. Otterhampton and Chelvey are in Somerset, Sturminster in Dorset. Neither the Becks nor the Willoughbys appear to have had west country interests. However, Robert's wife, Margaret, was the daughter of Isabel de Mohun of Dunster. In all probability the west countrymen are derived from that association. Nonetheless, it is remarkable, and perhaps a tribute to the professionalism of such men, that they came from far afield. Similarly, the members of the Twycross family who served the Multons must have originated in Leicestershire, to judge from their name. However, it seems probable that some direct seigniorial contact motivated these men to move. This seems to point to the time of Robert de Willoughby for the ordinance, rather than that of his son, John. However, Robert died in 1317, which seems to rule out a date of 12 Edward II. Robert's own eleventh year as lord would make it *c*.1311. He had been married to Margaret since at least 1303. The ordinance refers explicitly to the household of lord and lady. However, it could be that it was preserved, if not constructed, during the minority of his son, for the latter's instruction. His mother lived until 1333. John himself died in 1349. For the evidence, see *Complete Peerage*, xii. part 2, 657–9. The lands of Robert de Willoughby are given in *CIPM* vi. no. 60 and of John in *CIPM* ix. no. 201.

[16] Presuming this is what is meant by *chef atatur* (for *acheteur*?).

the steward (or one of his named deputies) and the wardrober, if he is present. However, the 'ingrossing' (that is, drawing up a fair copy) of the account waits until Sir John (the steward) and Henry (his deputy) are present. The wardrober, it is stated, acts as the chief auditor of the account. In his absence the chaplain keeps a counter roll of the expenses of the household. The chaplain summarizes the expenses of the household when the lord is away from it and he accounts for this to the wardrober before the steward of the household (*seneschal del hostiel*). Sir Richard Olyver accounts for, and is present at, the livery of oats (the oats, that is, given out as fodder for the horses). Moreover, all the expenses of the household and wardrobe were to be overseen and examined four times per year by the high steward (*le haut seneschal*) and the stewards of the household or others 'as it pleases the lord to assign and ordain'.

There are two cooks and larderers (*cues et lardiners*), with two *garceons*. There is also a *stiverer* (presumably a man who makes stews), called John le Stiucier; he is, it says, the sauce-cook (*saucier*). There are two pantlers and two butlers (*panetiers et butillers*), also with two *garceons*. There are two ushers and chandlers. There is a poultryman, William le Poletur, a porter or gatekeeper (*portier*), two farriers with their *garceon*, a baker and a brewer, and a laundress with a *garcette*. Philip the Baker, it says, has his own *garceon* 'either his brother or another'.

Altogether, including the menials, a household of around thirty persons is envisaged,[17] although they were perhaps rarely all under the same roof at any one time. Some of the most important figures were frequent absentees. The named stewards seem to have been present only rarely. Another frequent absentee was, of course, the lord himself, while the wardrober probably tended to be away with him. The lord also took one of the cooks, one of the pantlers, one of the farriers, and sometimes a girl to do the laundry.

The frequent to-ing and fro-ing had cost implications. The wardrober is specifically stated to have two horses, the implication being that when he is present these, and no more, are a charge on the household. The wages of a knight when he goes on the lord's business is 2s 6d per day. For a clerk or an esquire with two horses it is 1s 6d, or if they have one horse only it is 1s. Each horse, it is added, 'draws' $\frac{1}{2}$d per day. The provender for a horse travelling overnight is calculated as $\frac{1}{2}$ bushel (of oats). As we have seen, the clerk of the offices oversees and accounts for the provision of horses that are being stabled by the marshal. These, then, were closely regulated matters.

The ordinance, however, is a curious mix of formal arrangements and current reality, with many of the servants, even quite lowly ones, being named. Of the farriers' garcons, for example, 'Colle will follow the great horses and Gillot will follow the lord'. Nevertheless, we cannot assume that all of the personnel detailed

[17] Not counting any knights or esquires and omitting the brothers (*freres*) with their *garceon*. These, in the absence of the chaplain, will have a clerk and will look after the members of the household. The *garceon* will serve the brothers and help them in the chapel. The Willoughby chapel is clearly an elaborate affair.

in the ordinance were actually in place in the Willoughby household. Armed by what we have seen with the Luttrells we must be alive to the possibility that the ordinance may reflect to some degree how the Willoughbys saw themselves, or would have liked to have been seen. However, their social position suggests that in size and complexion their household lay between those of the great lords on the one hand and the upper ranks of the gentry on the other. We see the same emphasis upon the kitchen and the hall as is implied in the Luttrell Psalter. At the same time we see more servants, high and low, than the Luttrells could muster. We also see the absence from the household of high officials, and the skeletal nature of the Le Strange household seems to be partly explained. Some of the duties of household officials have been revealed to us, as well as the heavy emphasis upon accounting.

With this in mind let us return to John de Multon and his household accounts for 1343–4. We cannot calculate the precise size of the household, but we can be sure that it was closer to the fifteen-strong household of the Luttrells than to the thirty-strong household of the Willoughbys of Eresby. We can certainly put names to some of the Multon officials. We hear of Nicholas the Chaplain, of Stephen the Cook and, on one occasion, of Robert the Chamberlain. A schedule attached to the foot of the household account roll contains the expenses of Stephen the Cook. Most of these are unremarkable.[18] However, he also made various payments on behalf of the lord. He occurs again on the roll for 1347–8.

More light is shown on the role of the Multon chaplain in the manorial accounts of 1324–6. The ale and victuals provided for the then chaplain, Sir Henry, and the reeve in the autumn suggests that they were jointly responsible for feeding the customary tenants at harvest time. A similar role was performed by the Le Strange chaplain, Richard, at Hunstanton. We see him dealing with estate workers. In a separate account of the autumn expenses of 1328 we find that Richard had accounted for four men and four women, four ploughmen and one groom, a shepherd, a cowherd, and a porter maintained at the lord's table up to 29 August. Overseeing their provision was clearly one of Richard's responsibilities. There are no further surviving rolls until 1341. In the 1340s, however, we find Richard the Chaplain making, or at least authorizing, intermittent purchases of food for the household. In the household of the Northamptonshire and Warwickshire knight, Sir Thomas Murdack, we find that his chaplain was also his dispenser.[19] This may also have been the case at Hunstanton. In the Multon household of the mid-1320s we find Henry the Chaplain being jointly responsible for supervising the giving of oats to the horses of John Pecche, a relative of the Multon family, on a visit to Frampton. This is reminiscent of the role of Sir Richard Olyver,

---

[18] The largest expenditure was for fish. On the reverse of the schedule is a list of cocks and hens received as rent. These were no doubt handed over to Stephen.

[19] See below 66.

'the clerk of the offices' in the Eresby Household Ordinance. In many gentry households, less well-endowed with personnel, the chaplain would be expected to undertake a variety of tasks that required recording, in addition to priestly and pastoral duties and the writing of the lord's letters as envisaged in the Eresby Ordinance. In the household of the Cobeldyke family, neighbours of the Multons at Wyberton, we find that in 1327–8 Sir Roger the Chaplain also acted as the lord's receiver (*receptor*). Moreover, the same man actually wrote the manorial account. He seems, therefore, to have combined three roles in one: chaplain, clerk, and receiver. At Frampton, by contrast, the Multon manorial accounts of 1324–6 were written by Robert the Clerk. The fact that he received two bushels of maslin 'of the lady's gift' suggests that he was a member of the household. The general rule seems to be that the less elevated/wealthy the household, the more it lacked specialization. In lesser households there was also perhaps less rigid division as to who was responsible for what. While the terminology itself is derived from great households, and ultimately from royal ones, where there were more offices with precise responsibilities, in the gentry household there appears to have been some combining of offices, some fluctuation in designations, and perhaps some degree of latitude in terms of precisely who did what. It was this that the Luttrell Psalter was trying to gloss over, if not actually deny.

Whatever else a gentry household needed, however, they had to have someone to receive their money for them and someone to oversee the spending of it. Thus the Cobeldykes had, in addition to their receiver, Roger the Chaplain, a dispenser (*expenditor*) named Sir Roger de Stikeford. This basic arrangement appears to have been replicated at Frampton. The Multon accounts, however, are not rich in designations. The most prominent figure in Sir John de Multon's household was Nicholas de Twycross. The editor of the household accounts calls him Sir John's receiver, and there is no doubt that among his duties was the receiving of rents from collectors. Whatever the correct nomenclature may have been, however, he was undoubtedly Sir John's principal household officer. He had his own staff. He had a groom called John de Twycross, who was presumably a relative, and another called William.[20] Nicholas was surely related to the John de Twycross who had served Sir John's father, Sir Thomas de Multon. This John had received an allowance of £3 16s 1½d in March 1326, suggesting that he had a considerable area of responsibility. We hear of oats being fed to his horses the previous year, suggesting that he was to some degree itinerant. It was he who shared responsibility with Henry the Chaplain for supervising the giving of oats to the horses of John Pecche. He may well, then, have been Thomas de Multon's household steward or dispenser. That he was a highly trusted figure is beyond question. In 1326, as John son of Herbert of Twycross, he was one of two men who was formally granted the manor of Frampton so that they could

---

[20] On one occasion we hear of John de Twycross and his brother Nicholas, who may or may not be the same Nicholas de Twycross.

re-convey it to Sir Thomas and his wife. Furthermore, in 1332 John de Twycross served as attorney, together with Thomas Pecche, for giving seisin of the manor of Heapham to Thomas's eldest son, Sir John.[21] These were commissions of an extremely high order.[22]

Another household figure in the years 1324–6 was Thomas de Gower. He handed money to the lord, received money from a collector and himself received an allowance. There is no designation to aid us, but it seems likely that his role mirrored that of Roger the Chamberlain in 1343–4. John de Twycross and Thomas de Gower in 1324–6, Nicholas de Twycross and Roger the Chamberlain later, were responsible for the household economy. A gentry household needed a minimum of a household steward or dispenser and a wardrober or chamberlain. There was often an additional estates steward who might also function as a receiver. A variety of arrangements, some of them probably ad hoc, persisted below this level. There was normally a chaplain, a cook, and a butler. The receiver or steward was unlikely to be a permanent resident of the household. The chamberlain or wardrober may have itinerated with the lord.

The Multon household can be fleshed out a little further by returning again to the manorial accounts of 1324–6. Richard the Cook figures here, who, like Stephen the Cook after him, had the responsibility of receiving cocks and hens from the unfree tenants. John de Twycross, the chaplain Sir Henry, and Robert the Clerk we have already met. Robert was the man who wrote both of the account rolls. Reginald le Porter, who received a bushel of peas and beans for feeding sows in 1325/6, presumably within the *curia*, may well have been, as his name suggests, the gatekeeper. The Willoughbys and the Luttrells had such a figure. Robert le Baker who received maslin from the lord may also have been a regular member of the household. Some higher officials also make an appearance in the manorial account rolls. Richard de Scopeholm and Geoffrey de Wynceby appear to have been the lord's estate stewards. They were two of the three men who extended, that is surveyed, the manor in 1326. In 1324/5 we hear of oats for their horses and in 1325/6 of their expenses. They came to hold the courts. Geoffrey came more often than Richard, who appeared in fact only at the Michaelmas great court and at the court held at Candlemas 1325. This may suggest that Richard was the more significant figure with wider responsibility across the Multon estates than Geoffrey, although the details are hidden from us.

The existence of several members of the Twycross family, and across two generations, suggests that service to the gentry may have persisted in particular families. The appearance of Walter Gowerre in the manor court rolls in 1331 as *custos* of the manor, probably meaning in this instance some form of bailiff, suggests that the Gowers, too, had a history of service to the Multons.[23] Longevity of individual service may also have been common, if Richard the Chaplain and

---

[21] Multon, 87a, 37.   [22] See below 206.   [23] See below 125n.

John the Cook who served the Le Strange family were at all typical. Clearly, these factors have implications for how we should understand the relationship between the gentry and their servants. What can we say about such relationships in general?

The Luttrell Psalter lays great emphasis upon the role of the lord as paterfamilias and upon the general decorum of the dining scene. Allowing for differences in scale, this accords well with what was said in Bishop Robert Grosseteste's *Rules*, first written for the countess of Lincoln, perhaps around 1240–2, but in wider circulation during the second half of the thirteenth century and after.[24] His instructions on how to govern a household place heavy emphasis upon obedience. Clause 14 says that all servants, whatever their rank, should carry out their orders 'fully, quickly, and willingly and without grumbling or contradiction', while clause 18 warns against having household members who create strife or discord. All members of the household should pull together and obey those who are set above them.

Courtesy towards guests was vitally important. Clause 20 instructs the lady to order emphatically (*fermement*) that all her guests, both secular and religious, are received promptly, courteously and with good cheer (*a belle chere*) by porters, ushers and marshals. Special attention is given to decorum at meal times. Clause 22 reads:

Let your free household and guests (*vostre fraunche maysnee e les hostes*) be seated at tables on either side together, as far as possible, not here four there three and when the free household (*la fraunche maynee*) are seated all the grooms (*garcuns*) shall enter, be seated, and rise together. Strictly forbid that there is loud noise during meal-time and you yourself be seated at all times in the middle of the high table. That your presence as lord or lady is made manifest to all and that you may see plainly on either side all the service and all the faults.[25]

Most of the instructions are given in general terms, but it is clear that dinner in hall is already overlaid with ceremony. The Luttrell Psalter suggests that the gentry took these matters seriously, at the very least in the world of their imagination. How well order was actually kept must have depended both on senior members of the household and upon the calibre of the lord himself, or upon the lord and lady combined. The Eresby Ordinance makes it clear that the lord himself is ultimately in control, so that when he is absent he makes such arrangements, through his marshal and esquires, as he sees fit. At the same time it suggests that one of the duties of the chaplain is to look after the household, perhaps in a behavioural as well as purely spiritual sense. In the case of Sir Geoffrey Luttrell, it is very likely that he regarded this as ultimately his

---

[24] Oschinsky (ed.), *Walter of Henley*, 196–9. Works on courtesy and etiquette were produced, in Latin, in the twelfth century. Vernacular texts appear in the thirteenth century. See J. Nicholls, *The Matter of Courtesy: Medieval Courtesy Books and the Gawain-Poet* (Woodbridge, 1985), esp. 145–76.
[25] Ibid. 398–407.

own responsibility. It is indicative that he was himself godparent to two of his cooks' children.

However, order and obedience was only one dimension to relationships within the household. Normative texts, in laying emphasis upon such matters, suggest a distance, perhaps even a coldness, in the relations between masters and servants. In practice, however, members of the gentry must have formed closer relationships with key persons in their household. To make an obvious point, despite the clear differences in social rank, both lord and lady must often have enjoyed intimate relationships with those who looked after their bodies. For the lord, in particular, there was also the effect of life on the road. A lord like John de Multon, journeying around Lincolnshire and elsewhere, is likely to have formed some sort of bond with those who travelled with him. Daily contact and long service are bound to have produced intimacy, whatever the social distance involved. The lord's chamberlain or wardrober, for example, must often have been someone to whom he was close. His receiver may well have been another. As we have seen these men could be placed in positions of particular trust. Even mundane matters, the carrying of messages for example and frequent journeys on the lord's behalf, also involved a degree of reliability.

Of course trust could sometimes break down. It did so quite spectacularly in the case of the midland knight, Sir Thomas Murdack, who was murdered by his household in April 1316. The first to be indicted of his killing were Juliana his wife, Alice le Chaumberere and Adam le Someter. Alice's name suggests that she was the lady's chambermaid, while Adam was probably a groom, a *sumpterer, sumpter* being a word for a pack horse. Three other women were mentioned in connection with the crime, one of whom, Matilda Hastang, may well have been the lady's damsel. The name is that of a major gentry family in Warwickshire and elsewhere and reminds us that a member of one gentry family could be brought up in the household of another. However, when the details of the crime began to emerge it became clear that the weapons were wielded by the male members of Thomas Murdack's own household. These were William son of Richard de Bodekisham, his dispenser, Robert the Chaplain, who was also described as the victim's steward, and Roger the Chamberlain. Furthermore, the crime was said to have been abetted by William Shene, the cook, and by Adam the Palfreyman, who is probably identical with Adam the Sumpterer (palfrey being another type of horse). Altogether seventeen people were indicted, although only one, his widow, paid the penalty.[26]

Such occurrences, however, must have been rare. The fact that servants and household officers often figured in wills is indicative of regard, if tinged perhaps with a sense of duty and social expectation. If servants could be remembered in

---

[26] She was executed, the murder by a wife of her husband being classified as 'petty treason'. For the details of the case see Coss, *The Lady in Medieval England*, 131–8, where the Murdack household is revealed as similar in size to that of the Luttrells.

wills they could also receive presents from time to time. These might include items of clothing, although it is difficult to separate largesse on the one hand from the duty to provide on the other. Both considerations, moreover, involved an element of social display. John de Multon for example spent 3s 10d on a cloth for a coat for Nicholas the Chaplain, which seems to have been by prior agreement, 5s on six tippets or hoods for the grooms and a further 3s 3d on the two bought for the *gens de meister* (household officials). But these were incidental. The main cost in clothing, outside of dressing the immediate family, must have been for the household livery. Here we should note the 6d spent for bread and farriery for six horses of the lord when he was at Boston to buy his livery. This was an important matter. Most of what we know about the clothing of servants comes once again, as one might expect, from the great households, where livery was given once or twice a year and varied according to rank.[27] Either the cloth itself or ready-made clothing was given, sometimes cash, and sometimes a combination of the two. Whether it was regularly worn is perhaps another matter, but there can be no doubt that it was an item of display and that it was used on major occasions and for effect. There is every reason, therefore, to expect the gentry to have employed the same system.

For the Multons of Frampton there is further direct evidence that they did. On 7 April 1327 John de Multon's father, Sir Thomas de Multon of Frampton and his wife, Elizabeth, entered into an agreement with William son of John Godesone of Boston whereby, in return for the messuage in Boston called *Bayard*, they undertook to provide him with his maintenance throughout his life in their household at the table of the servants *de officio*, with one robe of the servants' suit, or 10s to enable him to acquire such, and half a mark for his shoes.[28] The term *de officio* would seem to mean that William would sit with the higher ranking servants, the *libera familia*, and not with the grooms. A robe in this context probably meant a complete outfit, with undergarments, and not just the tunic. This was a serious matter. The agreement contains a clause allowing William to distrain, not only on this messuage but on the two other messuages which his father John Godesone had conveyed to Thomas, in case of default. What was established here was a corrody, a set of privileges attached to a long-term sojourner or lodger. It was by this time quite a common occurrence in monasteries. In fact it was in the late thirteenth and early fourteenth centuries that the system reached its peak.[29] Commonly, the corrodian would hand over a piece of real property in perpetuity in return for their maintenance for life. Corrodies do not appear to have been common in the secular world; or, at least, if they were they are not much evidenced.

[27] On these matters, see, for example, Woolgar, *The Great Household*, 31–4, 172–5.
[28] Multon 122.
[29] For a full discussion of monastic corrodies see Barbara Harvey, *Living and Dying in England 1100–1540: The Monastic Experience* (Oxford, 1993), ch. vi.

The picture of dinner in the hall at Frampton is completed by an agreement of July 1326 between Alan de Cobeldyke and Sir Thomas de Multon of Frampton. This allowed Alan to pay 10d per annum for certain lands in Kirton instead of the old rent which had consisted of 5d at the feast of St Botulf (17 June) together with four cocks and four hens at the feast of St Stephen (26 December). In return for the latter Alan had received a meal for four men from the said Sir Thomas on the day of its payment; presumably this now lapsed.[30] We can thus envisage the meal in hall with a high table consisting of family and guests and the servants sitting below, the officers first and the grooms and others at the bottom. Perhaps we should envisage a figure U, with two tables at right angles to the top one, as suggested in the *Rules* of Robert Grosseteste.[31]

The lord's 'table' was swollen from time to time by occasional employees working in the *curia*. Hugh the Carpenter, who was kept busy during the rebuilding at Frampton during the years 1324–6, was sometimes said to be paid 'in wages at table'.[32] This does not necessarily mean, however, that he was eating in hall. He could well have been taking meals elsewhere within the *curia*. He was by no means the only casual worker to be found in the *curia*.[33] We find similar figures in 1343–4 such as John Oliver, carpenter of Frampton, who was paid for work at the manor house from time to time and who is probably identical with the John le Carpentur who also figures. Employees like these constituted one of the regular links between the Multon household and the local society and economy.

Altogether the curia was the scene of much to-ing and fro-ing. As we have seen, major officials such as Nicholas Twycross came and went. Lesser figures were sent on errands. The Lady Anne had her own commissions. Little Kitte was given 1s 4d on one occasion for her expenses travelling from Frampton Dyke into *Arderne* (presumably the forest of Arden) with a man and a horse. She was very likely going to the related Pecche family at Hampton in Arden. Amabel de Cobeldyke was given 5s for 'the lady's business', which is unfortunately unspecified. There was probably a steady stream of people coming on estate business from the other Multon properties. Others came bringing presents from their masters. This no doubt explains the 8d paid out on Monday, 8 December 1343 for a dinner for the men of Lady Ros by order of the lord, together with 4d for bread and hay for their horses. In January 1344 Sir John returned the compliment. In passing we learn something of how hazardous winter travel could be. The account records 5d paid to five porters for helping the lord's wagon which was in peril on its way to the Lady Ros with a present. We know what the present consisted

---

[30] Multon no 11a.   [31] Oschinsky, (ed.), *Walter of Henley*, 402–3.

[32] He was generally paid wages at piece rates. For larger projects, however, he was sometimes paid under contract, or as the account says 'by covenant'.

[33] The same accounts reveal payments to Andrew the Smith for various ironwork and Richard le Ploghman who was paid a substantial sum for roofing the barn. There were also a few regular employees, such as the gardeners, who were in the broadest sense part of the Multon household.

of: one carcass of beef costing 12s, 2 calves costing 6s, and two pigs and two swans whose cost is unrecorded because they were from store (*de estor*). One is reminded forcibly of the scene in the Luttrell Psalter where a wagon is stuck and is having to be pushed, a procedure involving great physical exertion. Further activity took place at the *curia* once per month when the Multon manor court was held, almost certainly in the hall.

How often tradesmen came to the *curia* is unclear. We know that the Multons made local purchases of various kinds. We also know the names of some of the men they did business with at Boston, men like Thomas Marchaunt, John Driffeld, from whom they purchased ermine, and Little Watte 'le Mercer'. The Le Strange accounts also show that the household used regular suppliers, of meat, fish, candles, and spices. One of those who regularly supplied fish was Thomas de Sandfort. Interestingly, in the late 1340s he appears as a purchaser for the household, perhaps a chief buyer, mirroring the official noted in the Eresby Ordinance.[34] Unfortunately these accounts do not tell us who was responsible for the transport of the goods, nor indeed where the transactions were conducted. Multon servants probably went to market from time to time. The account of the Le Strange household at Hunstanton tells us that Richard the Chaplain was sent to Lynn market in January 1348 and returned with 'flour de Rys', ginger, galingale, oil, and sugar.

It would be quite wrong, then, to give the impression that the gentry household was a self-contained world. The expenses that occurred during Sir John's itinerary also give some indication of the range of his social contacts. They included the Lady Ros, Lord Daubeny, Sir Saer de Rochford, and Sir Geoffrey de Cotes with whom he dined, probably at Boston. Nearer to home we find contact with the prior of Frampton and the neighbouring lord, Roger de Cobeldyke. The two manorial account rolls of Sir Thomas de Multon widen our knowledge of local intercourse. The Cobeldykes of Wyberton appear again, as does Sir John de Kirton, another Frampton lord. We are told of the giving and receiving of presents. The abbot of Revesby sent a cart with victuals to Frampton, for example, in 1325–6. We also hear of visitors. The related Sir John Pecche came in the autumn of 1324. The Cobeldyke account of 1327–8 is also instructive in respect of visitors. The foreign expenses section of this account records 6s tax paid on the moveable goods at Cobeldyke towards the subsidy of 1/20th that was granted by parliament in 1327 but collected in two instalments in 1328. Most interestingly, the reeve also accounted in the same section for 2s spent on breakfast (*gentaculum*) for the taxers and the curial clerk. A further 13s 3d, moreover, was paid from Wyberton towards the same tax and an additional sum

---

[34] One at least of the Le Strange suppliers was a significant figure in his own community. John de Brunham, who is probably identical with John the Spicer or Grocer, was a property owner in the town and became its mayor: *The Making of King's Lynn*, ed. D. M. Owen, British Academy Records of Social and Economic History, new ser. 9 (London, 1984), nos. 138, 185–7, 203–4, 324, 388.

(probably 2s 11d)[35] on breakfast for them. These were of course sweeteners, the giving of which was not an uncommon practice.[36] The Cobeldykes seem to have been generous with their breakfasts. Sir John de Willoughby and his *familia* stayed one night with them and were duly breakfasted. The cost came to 6s 10½d. Six horses also had to be fed. On another occasion 6d was spent on food and drink for two men of the prior of Spalding who brought bream to Wyberton and who stayed the night and had breakfast. Where they consumed this is not clear as the money was given for the lord to reimburse the prior. All of this was nothing, however, compared to the two quarters seven bushels of provender that were expended on looking after the thirty-six horses of Master Henry de Cliff and the clerks of the Chancery. Whatever its value to the lord he could not have welcomed too many such visits.

The Multon records, however, are limited in what they tell us about the visitors who came to the manor because the household accounts do not include expenditure on horse provender. A much fuller picture of the social dimension to visiting is provided by the Le Strange accounts. During 1328–9 Hamo le Strange was visited by Sir John Coleville twice, each visit lasting for two days, by Sir Roger de Swanton on four occasions, by Adam de Brancaster, by Sir John Curzon, William Howard and William de Sedgeford together, by John de Cayley, William de Sedgeford and John de Blunville together, by Sir John Curzon again, by John de Blunville on four further occasions for one or two days, by Sir John Caley again, by Lord Lovel and, on a separate occasion, by Lady Lovel. These names are sometimes given in the margin of the account roll but in most cases their presence is indicated under expenses in terms of the fodder provided for the horses.[37] It is not known whether the men were accompanied by wives, or what servants they brought with them. However, Sir Roger de Swanton always came with two horses, as did Lady Lovel, whereas Sir John Coleville came with three, as indeed did Lord Lovel. The list of horses provided for shows that there were other comings and goings, from officials and others on business, as opposed to guests.[38]

Who were these guests? Some were undoubtedly very local[39] (Figure 4.1). The Lovels held a manor at Hunstanton itself. They were related to the Lovels of

---

[35] The reading is uncertain.

[36] The manorial accounts of the manor of Cuxham, held by Merton College, regularly show both the cost of entertaining the assessors and payments to ensure leniency or favourable consideration: P. D. A. Harvey, *A Medieval Oxfordshire Village: Cuxham 1240–1400* (Oxford, 1965), 105.

[37] The rolls are not consistent. The earliest, for 1328–9, gives the expenditure on horse provender at the beginning of the week, and has some notice of guests in the marginalia. Other accounts do not list horse provender. NH 7 has notes of who is staying among the marginalia together with indications of absences by the lord and lady. The horses catered for are given at the end of the week, as they are in NH 8.

[38] In addition to the steward we find a Robert Oruch, a Geoffrey le Foun, and a Richard Brad (perhaps accompanying the steward). A person's status is not always clear in the text. Peter le Foun who stayed for a week on one occasion and for two days on another may well have been an estate official.

[39] For the details which follow, see *Feudal Aids*, 6 vols (London, 1899–1920), iii, *passim*.

Titchwell, along the north coast but within the same hundred of Smethden. It is difficult to know which Lovel family the Le Stranges were on especially good terms with, but it is more probable that it was their close neighbours. From within the same hundred came members of two sub-knightly landowners: Adam de Brancaster, who held ½ knight's fee at Brancaster; and William Sedgeford who held ½ fee at Sedgeford and Thornham of the bishop of Norwich. A third figure of similar stature was William Howard, who held at Winch just south of King's Lynn and had additional property at Terrington to the west of that city.[40] The knights, on the other hand, tended to come from a little further afield, but many of them can be shown to have held land in north Norfolk. Sir John Curzon came from Barningham, south-east of Holt. Sir John Cayley's chief residence was at Oby but the family also had property nearby at Wolferton, between King's Lynn and Hunstanton. The Colevilles were primarily a Lincolnshire family but they also held Norfolk property at Walsoken, Walton and Walpole, near Wisbech. The Swantons held Foulsham and Themelthorpe, on the road from Fakenham to Norwich. Sir Roger de Swanton, however, might well be the cleric of that name who was parson of Little Dunham.[41] John de Blunville probably came from the family of that name holding at Deopham, south-west of Norwich and with interests in and around Wramplingham. Of course, John, like others, may well have had further property closer to Hunstanton. He is probably the royal escheator of that name whose office covered Norfolk, Suffolk, Essex, Cambridgeshire and Huntingdonshire.[42] The knights were men of significance. Sir John Cayley (or Cailly) was to be sheriff of Norfolk and Suffolk a few years later (in 1332–3), while Sir John Curzon was MP for Norfolk in 1318 and again in 1319; he was commissioner of array in the years 1324–6. Hamo le Strange was already well-connected in north Norfolk.

The Le Strange family were still receiving a steady stream of guests twenty years later. In 1348–9 Sir Thomas de Felton came with four horses, while John de Camoys and Ralph de Camoys came on one occasion with eight. It is not clear how often John de Camoys was actually present in the household, but the list of provender shows him there on other occasions, with two or three horses.[43] The largest gathering was in 1348 when eight men are recorded staying with eleven horses. Five of the men, including Sir Thomas de Felton, were knights. The 1347–8 roll also indicates in the margin the presence of guests, such as Sir Thomas de Felton, Sir Hamo de Felton, Sir Ed[mund] de Hetherset,

---

[40] In 1330 William was pardoned for granting rent in Middleton and Wormegay to the prioress and nuns of Blackborough, Norfolk, without licence: *CPR 1330*, 552.

[41] *CPR 1330–34*, 172.

[42] *CPR 1327–34, passim*. John also functioned from time to time on peace commissions and commissions of oyer and terminer, and as taxer, in Hertfordshire.

[43] On one occasion we hear of his three horses and an additional three, it seems, that pulled his wagon. Another visitor in this year was Roger de Swatching who came with three horses and stayed two nights.

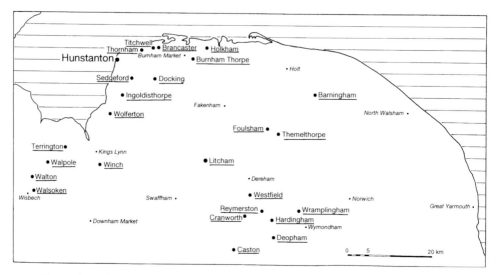

Figure 4.1. Places of origin of Hunstanton visitors.

Sir John de Camoys, Sir William de Ingoldisthorpe, Roger de Swatching, the parson of Ingoldisthorpe, and William de Burgh, with their horses sometimes explicitly provided for. The stables also housed the horses of estate officials, like Thomas the steward of Gressenhall and Elias the reeve of Gressenhall, who were very probably the men of John de Camoys, and Thomas the hayward of Heacham.[44] The horse of Richard the serjeant of John de Docking was provided for, and that of the parson of Stanfield, who seems to have stayed over as he is noted in the margin.[45] The Le Strange stables saw a good deal of activity. So, too, did the household. No doubt it was often hectic. Sometimes we hear of extra food being brought in because of guests as, for instance, in the autumn of 1342 when R[obert] de Somerton, Thomas de Snitterton and his wife, William Maret and John Barun were dining.

The most prominent among the visitors in these later years were the Feltons with a manor at Litcham, between Swaffham and Dereham and other property further away at Burgh and Oxnead, north of Norwich. Sir Edmund Hetherset held ¼ knight's fee at Westfield, south of Dereham. William de Burgh held the manor of Caston, a little further south still. John of Docking must have come from Docking close by, while Roger de Swatching may well have come from Swatchings in Hardingham, not far from Deopham, and from the family who

---

[44] Marginal notes suggest that the Gressenhall steward was called Thomas de Oxenburgh and the Hexham Hayward (*messor*) was Thomas Gouste (on another occasion called Thomas Gouer).

[45] John the chaplain, whose horse figures, seems to have come with William de Burgh. The status of John de Banastre who came with Elias the reeve, and who stayed over, is unclear, although he sounds more like a guest than an official.

held at Reymerston and Cranworth nearby. Thomas de Snitterton held several properties but the closest was at Hunstanton itself where he held ¼ knight's fee of the bishop. William Maret may well be William Marit of Hindringham who is recorded in 1344 with an interest in Holkham and (Burnham) Thorpe. A John Barun also occurs at Holkham.[46] Although some of these visitors seem to have been relatively minor figures, others came from families that provided MPs, JPs, commissioners of array and taxers in the early to mid-fourteenth century: those of Camoys, Felton, Hetherset, Ingoldisthorpe, Snitterton, and Somerton.

What we see, then, is the Le Strange family on intimate terms with some prominent knightly families, some with interests quite near and others at some distance, and with some sub-knightly families whose interests tended to be local. This is perhaps what one would expect. Both in 1328–9 and again in the late 1340s a group of knights were particularly frequent visitors, although there does not appear to have been much continuity across generations. It seems that each generation forged its own relationships, but that these were based largely on the broad locality within which their principal manor was situated. No doubt what we are witnessing in these accounts is a general round of visiting, in the manner of the coaching society of later centuries. We do know from the accounts of one occasion when Lady Le Strange returned the visit to the Feltons. These are only glimpses into their social life, of course, and a very great deal remains hidden from us. One would dearly like to know, for example, what brought the eight men, five of them knights, together at Hunstanton in 1348. Was this business, pleasure, or perhaps both? What is abundantly clear in all of this is that much of the social world inhabited by the gentry, as revealed by household and manorial accounts, was intensely local. It was not an entirely self-contained world, to be sure, but it was nevertheless severely circumscribed, not least of course by the time it took to travel. It is not surprising that we hear much about stables and stabling, as horses provided the only means of contact with the outside world. As we have seen, close account was taken of the livery of oats. The Eresby wardrober was restricted to two horses. Thomas Murdack and John de Vaux, his host at Stourton Castle where he was murdered, had special servants for their horses, palfreymen, and sumpterers. Every lord had his grooms. Horse knowledge and indeed horse medicine were vital aspects of practical wisdom. Men needed to know their horses. Hamo Le Strange regularly had between one and three horses in addition to stotts or affers, that is work horses. He also had a hackney or carriage horse. In the late 1340s he had three horses, one of which was called '*Romesleye*'. The Multons had two stables, one for 'horses' and one for palfreys. The inventory of Sir Edmund Appleby's stables boasted a horse 'for the lord', namely a grey worth £5, together with another grey, a dun and a bay, of varying

---

[46] *Lordship and Landscape in Norfolk 1250–1350: the Early Records of Holkham*, ed. W. Hassall and J. Beauroy, British Academy Records of Social and Economic History, new ser. 20 (Oxford, 1993), 460.

but lesser values. Altogether they were worth £10. In the stables there were also five carthorses and two iron-framed carts with the necessary accessories.

Part of the answer, then, to the question of who saw and appreciated the elements of social display that were discussed in the previous chapter was the stream of guests who visited the *curia*. Prominent among these were local personages including other gentry, major freeholders or sub-gentry, and clerics. But they could also include government officials. In some cases, visitors could be more elevated. The de la Beche family, for example, were entertaining royal children when Margery de la Beche was abducted. Display must also have impressed locally in that it showed their elevated status in comparison with most people living in the vicinity. As we have seen, and as we shall see again later, the *curia* was visited by a considerable range of local people in a wide variety of capacities. Finally, and this is by no means the least important dimension, display was also an expression of self-identity, a sense of family worth, pride in pedigree, and esteem. This is the central message of the display contained in the Luttrell Psalter.

The gentry household was a social and cultural crossroads. The visitors who came might admire the buildings, the food, the tapestries, the silverware and so on. But they also came with ideas and with news and gossip: from Westminster, for example, and hence from Scotland and from overseas. That is to say they imported the values of the external world. They also would go away with impressions, perhaps even gossip. In these ways pre-existing ideas and values were constantly reinforced. At the same time the social relationships involved in the running of the household (and indeed the running of the estate, as we shall see later) kept the gentry constantly in touch with more mundane concerns. Conversation among the gentle can have ranged, therefore, from who was in and who was out at the centre of power to the price and availability of local artefacts. Household interaction had other cultural implications, too, including linguistic ones. There can be no doubt that families like the Multons spoke in English with their servants and probably in a mixture of the two vernacular languages with those of the highest rank. Moreover, the local world was culturally more complex than one might have supposed, and this is a topic to which we will return later in the study. In the meantime, however, we need to turn our attention to another dimension to local life: gentry estates.

5

The Gentry Estate
The Locus of Production

In the next three chapters we shall turn our attention to the gentry's estates, their attitude towards those estates and towards their tenants. What did they bring to the running of their estates, and in what ways did their experiences of landholding condition their values and assumptions? These are not easy questions to answer for this early period, given the nature of the sources that are available to us, but it is vital that we make an attempt given the high significance of rural production and estate management within gentry history. In order to do so, however, we need to understand something of the structure and of the economy of gentry estates. This is a more straightforward matter given that our sources, even though they are not abundant, lend themselves relatively easily to it.

This chapter will be devoted to a detailed examination of two estates whose records survive in the archive of the Multons of Frampton. One, unsurprisingly, is Frampton itself, the home farm of the Multons. It represents the knightly, more established, end of the gentry spectrum. The other is the estate of the Cobeldykes, centring upon Wyberton, representing the sub-knightly stratum of the gentry whose upward striving did so much to broaden and strengthen the character of the gentry. Their meagre patrimony was boosted by the profits of service of various kinds. The fact that their respective account rolls are both from precisely the same period, the mid- to late-1320s, makes their comparison all the more valuable. We will examine these estates in terms of both their structure and their exploitation. Before doing so let us briefly rehearse what we know about gentry estates in general. We can then be sure that the Multon and Cobeldyke estates were not atypical.

For the composition of gentry estates during the period of its formation, that is from the later thirteenth to the mid-fourteenth century, historians have two major sources to rely upon, namely the Hundred Rolls of 1279–80 and manorial extents, principally those embedded in the *Inquisitions Post Mortem*. The Hundred Rolls are the surviving returns of the Domesday-like survey which

the government of Edward I commissioned in March 1279.[1] One of the great
virtues of the survey is that in its full coverage of the landholdings within each
hundred it allows us access to the structure of estates belonging to the smaller lay
landlords who have rarely left us their own archives.[2] Unfortunately, the surviving
returns are confined to parts of the Midlands and East Anglia. Nonetheless, their
value is unique. The majority of the surviving returns—those published by
the Record Commission in the early nineteenth century—were analysed by
the Russian Academician E. A. Kosminsky in the 1930s, in a thorough study
which has not yet been superseded.[3] Kosminsky classified the manors it revealed
according to type. Those classed as type A are the 'typical' manors with a
demesne, villein land and free holdings. The other types are those lacking one or
more of these components. Kosminsky found considerable variety in manorial
structure, but also found that more than half belonged to the classical type.
However, he also classified them according to size, that is to say large manors
with over 1,000 acres of arable, medium manors with 500–1,000 acres, and
small manors with less than 500 acres. In general terms the larger the manor, the
smaller the percentage of demesne, and the higher the percentage of villein land.
Major ecclesiastical institutions tended to have large manors of the classical type,
worked by customary labour. As regards the great lay lords he found that large
manors predominated, but were by no means universal. Below this social level
he found that the 'line . . . between the "small" and the "medium" manor was
apparently approximately that which determined whether a holding was knightly
or not'.[4]

As regards the gentry, then, we can expect to be dealing with medium or
small manors, at least in terms of Kosminsky's classification. It is important to
note, however, that Kosminsky found no clear boundary between free holdings
and manors, nor between peasants and 'small landowners', in each case the one
moving imperceptibly into the other. The Hundred Rolls reveal, therefore, not
only the estates of knights and other 'established' members of the gentry but also
the complexity of landholding below these levels. Kosminsky gives a particularly
useful example in Robert Danvers of Oxfordshire, who had a series of holdings
much of which comprised freehold land that brought in only small amounts of

[1] The making of the survey and the state of play in the analysis of the surviving returns have been
recently explored by Sandra Raban in *A Second Domesday? The Hundred Rolls of 1279–80* (Oxford,
2004).
[2] Ibid. 6. For its value in studying the fortunes of smaller lay estates during the mid-thirteenth
century see my *Lordship, Knighthood and Locality: A Study in English Society c.1180–c.1280*
(Cambridge, 1991).
[3] Kosminsky's work was published in English in 1956 as *Studies in the Agrarian History of
England in the Thirteenth Century*, edited by R. H. Hilton (Oxford, 1956). Some of his findings
were inevitably coloured by his particular concern with the origins of capitalism.
[4] Ibid. 108.

rent. Using this example Kosminsky was able to suggest that some manors were in fact in process of formation.[5] In this context one thinks especially of those administrators and lawyers who were increasingly prominent in this and succeeding generations, many of whom carved their own place among the gentry, men like Robert de Stoke, of Stoke near Coventry, and Robert de Madingly, of Madingly near Cambridge.[6] The Hundred Rolls show us something of the largely free holding base on which their property accumulation was predicated.[7] The work of other scholars on the structure of landholding tended to support Kosminsky's picture,[8] and more recent scholarship broadly confirmed these findings.

The structure of estates is also revealed by manorial extents. They give details of demesne land by category together with rents and other forms of income. They also give land values and areas. Although extents were often generated by lords themselves, for lay lords—and more especially for the gentry—the historian finds them surviving most often within the *Inquisitions Post Mortem*. An inquisition post mortem was an inquiry conducted by a royal official known as an escheator on the death of a tenant-in-chief of the crown. The crown needed to know the configuration and value of estates so that royal rights over them could be protected. The most lucrative of these was the wardship of an estate, should the heir prove to be under age. Hence the inquisitions often contain detailed extents. Beginning in the mid-thirteenth century, they become increasingly numerous precisely for the period under study here.[9] The great value of the inquisitions is that they deal with a cross-section of lay landowners and that they are countrywide.[10]

---

[5] Ibid. 262–7.

[6] For Robert de Stoke, see my *Lordship, Knighthood and Locality*, 312–15; and for Robert de Madingly, see E. Miller and John Hatcher, *Medieval England: Rural Society and Economic Change 1086–1348* (London, 1978), 172, citing E. Miller, *The Abbey and Bishopric of Ely* (Cambridge, 1951), 267–8.

[7] Kosminsky was also aware, of course, of the existence of regional variations in the structure of estates, the greater proportion of free tenants in the eastern counties, for example, and the tendency in areas further west for large manors, more villein land, and comparatively insignificant freehold land.

[8] See, esp., Barbara Dodwell, 'The Free Tenantry of the Hundred Rolls', *EcHR* 14 (1944), 163–71, and R. H. Hilton, 'The Social Structure of Rural Warwickshire', *Dugdale Society Occasional Papers*, 9 (1950), repr. in his *The English Peasantry in the Later Middle Ages* (Oxford, 1975).

[9] Kosminsky regarded them as an unreliable source, especially when compared with accounts, as there were incentives to undervalue: ibid. 58–67. See also R. F. Hunnisett, 'The Reliability of Inquisitions as Historical Evidence', in D. A. Bullough and R. L. Storey (eds), *The Study of Medieval Records* (Oxford, 1971), 206–35. Equally, of course, as Kosminsky well knew, the Hundred Rolls are by no means without blemish. See also Raban, *A Second Domesday?*, 127–30. Recently, however, the inquisitions have been rehabilitated by Bruce Campbell: *English Seigniorial Agriculture 1250–1450* (Cambridge, 2000), 37–40. They are at their 'most precise and informative', he points out, between 1323 and 1342. See also Campbell and Bartley, *England on the Eve of the Black Death*, ch. 3.

[10] A national IPM database has now been produced: ibid. 47–8.

A comprehensive study of the *Inquisitions Post Mortem* recording the property of over 1,800 tenants-in-chief between 1300 and 1349 has recently been undertaken.[11] Seventy per cent of the property recorded was in the hands of the higher nobility, while 20 per cent was in the hands of knights and the remaining 10 per cent belonged to non- or sub-knightly estates. Although the evidence is inevitably skewed towards the higher reaches of secular landholding, the *Inquisitions* do in fact document a wide range of lay estates. The knights, the hard core of the emergent gentry, held one-fifth of the recorded property. A few of them, such as Robert de Willoughby (d.1317) enjoyed revenue in excess of £250.[12] However, three-quarters of all knightly estates were valued at below £50 and more than half at less than £25. Of the 700 non-knightly estates, nearly ninety per cent were worth less than £25. Their mean value was a mere £12. As far as the composition of their revenue was concerned, 90 per cent of seigniorial revenue came from agricultural production and from rents.[13] They were, therefore, as Campbell and Bartley say, 'in a very real sense landlords'.[14]

When we come down to the *structure* of the individual manor, their findings also tend to mirror those of Kosminsky. Thus the demesne was of relatively greater significance on small manors, rents and services—both free and unfree—on middle-sized manors (those worth £20–£60), and customary rents and services on the largest manors of all. Profits from courts and mills, markets and fairs, advowsons and knights' fees also tended to be highest on large estates, giving them a more balanced portfolio of resources.[15]

Small manors were by far the most numerous type. Although the demesne was of proportionally greater importance on the small manor, in absolute terms it was often not very extensive. Demesnes of 50–150 acres were the most numerous on secular seigniorial estates as a whole, with the average 'upwards of 150 acres'.[16] As to land use on the demesne, on average 55 per cent of its value was from arable land, 35 per cent from pasturage and 10 per cent from woodland and various other uses. There were, of course, wide variations.

---

[11] Campbell and Bartley, *England on the Eve of the Black Death*, esp. ch. 6.

[12] There appear to have been only twelve knights in this bracket.

[13] On average lay lords gained 42 per cent of their income from their demesnes, 48 per cent from rents and services, 2 per cent from the profits of seigniorial justice, 5 per cent from sources such as mills, forges, markets, fairs, and boroughs and 3 per cent from items such as advowsons and profits from knights' fees.

[14] Ibid. 77. As to the size of estates, these authors calculate that a 'good middling-sized estate' would have had around 2,000 acres of land and a small estate probably less than 500. A large number of minor lay lords held only a single demesne containing less than 200 acres of land in total. This classification, although it differs from Kosminsky's in that it introduces a category of 'good middling-sized estate', nevertheless tallies with his findings, most especially when it comes to small manors.

[15] Ibid. 80.

[16] Ibid. 90. This is a minimum figure. It is not always clear whether the fallow land, or how much of it, was recorded. Demesnes of less than this are more numerous than any other.

With these points in mind let us turn to the first, and better sourced, of our two south Lincolnshire gentry estates, that of the Multons at Frampton,[17] where 80½ acres plus 1 rood of demesne arable land are listed in fifteen locations. All of the acres were said to be of the same value (3s 5d) and measured by the same rod of 20 feet. This would make them approximately one-and-a-quarter times the size of statute acres. The value of the land in each location is written between the lines (interlined) and the total comes to £13 15s 10¾d.

Then comes 60 acres of fallow in *le Newelond*, valued at 1s 6d per acre, that is (as correctly interlined) £4 10s. This would suggest a two-field rotation. However, the demesne appears to have been held in severalty, as seems to have been common in this region, and not intermingled with the land of the customary tenants. The names of the locations suggest enclosure: crofts, tofts, and holms.[18] That the fallow was new land suggests that the field system had been reorganized in the not too distant past. Moreover, the references to Old Newland, Lady Newland, and Newmarsh among the locations of cultivated land indicate that reclamation had taken place in stages. The fields of the Multon manor at Frampton were very probably the product of around a century of evolution.

In addition to the arable there are six pieces of pasture and herbage, amounting to 7½ acres and 4 roods, valued at £1 6s 10d, plus the sheepcote with pasture on the sea marsh worth £2, and two other items,[19] the total amounting to £3 8s 5d. In various locations in Frampton and Kirton 74½ acres and 6 roods of meadowland are listed, at valuations of 3s 4d, 4s and 6s per acre. The total of the stated values (again interlined) comes to £14 13s 5½d.

So far we have omitted the items given at the beginning of the extent. No manor house is recorded as such. Instead we are told that the manor close 'has not been extended because it does not suffice for the repair of the houses of the manor', that is to say there is no value beyond the cost of maintenance. However, outside the close there was a messuage called the Lady Hall which was worth 10s per annum. This was presumably the value at which it was, or could be, rented. The garden of the close was itself worth 4s in herbage and 5s in 'fruits'. The total value thus far is £37 6s 9¼d.

---

[17] Multon Adds 11. The extent is on a single membrane of parchment. The hand is small. The sums are often omitted in the text and interlined in the same hand. Where sums are in the text they are often underlined. On the dorse is the actual statement of the jurors. This manor was extended for Sir Thomas de Multon on 17 April 1326 before three officials and by the oaths of both free tenants and bondmen of the manor. The officials were Sir Thomas de Tynton, Richard de Scopeholm, and Geoffrey de Wynceby.

[18] Only one 'field' is mentioned, *le Westfield*, where there was one demesne acre, said to be in two places. Perhaps here the demesne is mixed with tenant land and was the product of joint endeavour. It need not have been extensive. 'Field' in this region tends to refer to a furlong of strips, all of which lie in a single direction.

[19] 1s 3d from *Honypyt*, and 1 selion at *Brynholm* worth 4d.

Table 5.1.   The Extent of Frampton Manor, 17 April 1326

From the demesne	£	s	d
Arable land (80 ½ acres, 1 rood)	13	15	10¾
Fallow land (60 acres)	4	10	–
Pasture and herbage	3	8	5
Meadow	14	13	5½
Lady Hall		10	–
Garden of close		9	–
Subtotal:	37	6	9¼
From the tenants:			
Rent of assize (free tenants)	3	12	10½
Rent of customary tenants	1	14	8
Customary tenants of Wyberton		10	10¾
Rent from 4 cottages in Frampton		16	8
Newly-accrued rent		10	8
Tallage	5	–	–
Rent in kind (pepper, salt, hens and cocks)		7	¾
Windmill	1	6	8
Customary works	7	–	6
Court	2	10	–
Subtotal:	23	10	0
Total:	60	16	9¼

Having given the composition of the demesne lands, the extent now turns to the rents. The rent of assize from the free tenants, customary rents from tenants at Frampton and Wyberton, rents from cottages at Frampton, and 'newly-accrued rent',[20] yielded in total £7 5s 9¼d. However, income was also coming from the tenants in other ways. There was tallage, an annual tax which the unfree tenants paid to the lord.[21] There were rents in kind.[22] There was the yield from the windmill. There was the income from the three-weekly court and the customary works of the unfree tenants.[23] In short, the amount taken from the tenants in addition to the stated money rent comes to a further £16 4s 2¾d, or rather £9 3s 8¾d plus works. The total value of the estate as recorded in the extent is £60 16s 9¼d, or £53 16 3¼d plus works. A little under two-thirds of this was accounted for by the demesne, the remaining being provided in one way or another by the tenants.

What can we tell of the nature of this estate from the extent? First of all, the manor was a small one in terms of overall acreage. The demesne is not especially large: some 140 customary acres, perhaps 175 statutory acres, of arable together

[20] For the significance of this see below 122.
[21] £3 came from Frampton, 13s 4d from Kirton, and £1 6s 8d from Wyberton.
[22] 4s 3d from cocks and hens plus 1 lb pepper worth 1s, and salt from various men at Bicker worth 2s 9¾d.
[23] The text says 31½ works, but 32 is interlined. £7 0s 6d is an estimate, the extent says, 'as they have not been valued for certain'.

with a sizeable amount of valuable pasture and meadow. Although we are not given the acreage of tenant land, we know from a later source that the size of the unfree tenements was small. On the other hand, there would seem to be a large number of tenants, many of them unfree and owing customary works as well as money rents and some renders in kind. The manor extends principally over three settlements, i.e. Frampton, Kirton, and Wyberton, from all of which the lord is taking tallage. The court is active and so is the lord's mill. There is also a free tenantry. A sizeable share of the income seems to have come from meadowland and the valuable summer pasture in the marshland by the sea. There was also a sheepcote. Despite its small size, in terms both of value and range of resources, it has the characteristics of a medium-sized manor according to Kosminsky's typology, that is to say it is 'typical' of a knight's manor.

In structural terms the Multon manor appears to have been fairly typical of the area. There were two other manors in Frampton for which we have extents within *Inquisitions Post Mortem*. The Huntingfield estate was extended on the death of William de Huntingfield in 1314.[24] It was valued at £43 16s 10d.[25] The land values are well below those we find on the Multon manor in 1326. Otherwise the estates were similar. The Frampton manor of the Earl of Richmond was extended in 1280.[26] No total value is given but it was in excess of £44.[27] The rent roll was comparable, except that the Multon manor took a good deal more from explicitly free tenants. The value of customary works was also higher on the Multon manor. Whether we are talking of arable, meadow or pasture, land values are once again higher on the Multon than on the Richmond manor.[28] In most respects, the Multon, Richmond, and Huntingfield manors were similarly structured. They bear the characteristics of the medium sized manor in pre-Black Death England, a type of manor that was common among the established gentry and well-known among established lords in general.

There are two respects, however, in which the Multon manor differed from its neighbours. One, as we have seen, is the higher land values. Land values are comparatively high in this area in any case. On the Multon manor they seem to be among the very highest in the land.[29] It is difficult to know whether these were due to more fertile soil, a more aggressive attitude toward leasing or greater commercial penetration. The most striking difference between the Multon estate

[24] TNA C134/34/4; *CIPM* v. no. 471. It had also been extended in 1303: C133/108/1; *CIPM* iv. no. 1303. For land use on various manors in Kirton Wapentake, as revealed by the extents, see Hallam, *Settlement and Society*, 183 ff. and table 3.
[25] Or £43 12s 6d net after the payment of 4s 4d in rent resolute for sheriff's aid.
[26] TNA C133/26/6; *CIPM* ii. no. 381. This document is badly smudged in its latter part, leaving numerous obscurities.
[27] £44 2s 7½d is the total of the items for which values are given. In addition there are further works of customary tenants and the renders in kind of 4 quarters 3 bushels (of unspecified grain) worth 1s 3d (per bovate?).
[28] Only with the outlying meadow at Boston does the Richmond manor reach Multon values.
[29] See Campbell, *English Seigniorial Agriculture*, 347–55, and esp. table 7.09.

on the one hand, however, and the Richmond and Huntingfield manors on the other is the size of villein holdings. This requires some comment.

The extent of the earl of Richmond's manor in 1280 includes 9 bovates of customary land containing 316 acres. These bovates comprised, therefore, 35 acres.[30] On the Huntingfield manor in 1303 there were 7 bovates. The figure of 300 written above would seem to indicate the acreage. This would make the bovate on this manor a huge 43 acres. H. E. Hallam noted that the bovate in Lincolnshire was often 20 acres, but noted the particularly large bovate on the Richmond manor. He pointed out that where soils were heavy, on the estates of the prior of Spalding for example, villein holdings tended to be larger.[31] Elsewhere he points out that in the saltlands the bovate could be as much as 40–100 acres 'because it had grown as new settlement in the fen and marsh took place'.[32] The real surprise at Frampton, therefore, is when we realize that on the Multon estate the bovate was exceptionally small. As we shall see, around 1340 the labour services from customary holdings here were 'arrented', that is given a monetary value that would allow them to be sold to the villeins. This is when we learn that the standard holding was a mere 4 acres. There were at that date fourteen standard holdings and eleven which are multiples of four. There appear, therefore, to have been twenty-eight four-acre holdings at some time in the past.[33]

How do we explain this difference within a single settlement? The Multon *curia*, as we know, was at Sandholme on the eastern side of the settlement at Frampton, almost against the sea bank. The Multon tenants were also most probably physically divorced from the main settlement and fields of Frampton. Perhaps the Multon bovate reflects later settlement than the others, when population pressure was high and there was considerable land hunger? This may have been in the second quarter of the thirteenth century when we first encounter the Multons. The services due from the four-acre units were not especially light. It may also be the case that the soil on the seaward side of the settlement was particularly rich. Even so, one suspects that the tenants must have had additional means of livelihood.

Although one can deduce a good deal from them in terms of the range of enterprises and of the variety of resources enjoyed by the gentry, the extents, like the Hundred Rolls, provide only a static picture and concentrate on landholding. In order to understand something of the *running* of estates we need to turn to other sources.

---

[30] The bovate must have been variable as there were another 10½ bovates pertaining to the same manor at *Fraunchundred* which contained 133 acres of arable, meadow and pasture. Here there were 12.66 acres to the bovate. For the history of the standard holding and its increased territorial definition, often around the early thirteenth century, see P. D. A. Harvey's 'Introduction' to *The Peasant Land Market in Medieval England* (Oxford, 1984), 7–19.

[31] Hallam, *Settlement and Society*, 5.   [32] Hallam, *Agrarian History*, 594.

[33] See below 125.

In his recent magisterial study of English seigniorial agriculture, Bruce Campbell states that no 'single source provides fuller, more systematic and more precise information on the practice, performance and profits of husbandry' than the annual accounts rendered by the reeves and bailiffs of individual manors at the end of each farming year.[34] Like the extents, the manorial accounts are a thirteenth-century phenomenon. After 1250[35] they became increasingly common and increasingly standardized in form and content. During the last quarter of the thirteenth century they spread to most classes of estate in central, southern and eastern England. By the 1280s a Norfolk lord like Henry le Cat, the holder of a sub-manor at Hevingham, was keeping his own accounts.[36] Nevertheless the surviving accounts are very strongly biased toward ecclesiastical estates and towards large manors in general, with very little evidence for how minor landlords were running their estates.

We are fortunate, therefore, that for the Multon manor of Frampton there are two surviving account rolls, for 1324–5 and 1325–6. As the former is severely damaged in its first membrane, it is better to start with the more complete picture afforded by that of 1325–6. The reeve who accounted was Robert son of Alexander, an unfree tenant of the manor. The account is in standard form, that is to say, an account of all cash receipts and expenses, with a stock or 'grange' account on the dorse. The latter gives receipts and losses of all produce and provides our starting point. The reeve accounted for the following:

- 31 quarters, 1 bushel of wheat
- 102 quarters, 6½ bushels of mixtil
- 46 quarters, 5 bushels of peas and beans
- 29 quarters, 2 bushels, 3 pecks of oats.

Mixtil, normally rendered in English as maslin, was generally a mixture of wheat and rye. In eastern England, however, it might be a mixture of wheat and 'bere', that is winter barley. Given that the Multons sowed bere at Frampton it might well be the case here too. Either way, mixtil or maslin was commonly used to make bread. The account roll tells us in fact not only what was produced but also what was done with it. Let us begin with the wheat. It is important to note, at the outset, that that not all of the wheat accounted for was home grown: 4 quarters, 7 bushels came—in two instalments—from the reeve at the Multon manor of Miningsby, some way to the north of Boston. A further

---

[34] Campbell, *English Seigniorial Agriculture*, 27. See his footnotes 3 and 4 for the most important studies of manorial accounts. I have drawn especially on P. D. A. Harvey, *Manorial Records of Cuxham, Oxfordshire, circa 1200–1359* (London, 1976), particularly 12–71. Still useful as an introduction to the subject is J. Z. Titow, *English Rural Society 1200–1350* (London, 1969).

[35] Most of those that survive from before 1250 are ecclesiastical, although there are accounts from the honours of Clare and Gloucester.

[36] Campbell, *English Seigniorial Agriculture,* 28. See also B. M. S. Campbell, 'The Complexity of Manorial Structure in Medieval Norfolk: a Case Study', *Norfolk Archaeology*, 39 (1986), 239–42.

quarter came as a gift from John de Kirton, a neighbouring landowner. Such gifts and loans, as we shall see, appear to have been a common phenomenon within the gentry world. Only 25 quarters, 2 bushels, therefore, were produced at Frampton. Of the total, no less than 20 quarters are stated to have been consumed in the household, together with 1½ bushels given to Richard the Cook as his pastry allowance, and 3 quarters that were put in with the mixtil for allowances to the household staff. A further 3 quarters, 2 bushels went to Alan Robert in repayment of his loan of the previous year, and one quarter went to the Dominican and Franciscan friars of Boston 'by equal portion' as a gift from the lord. A total of 2 quarters 3½ bushels were sown. Only 2 bushels remained in store when the account was drawn up. Wheat, then, was not produced as a commercial enterprise but for household consumption. Even then, the manor was not necessarily self-supporting in this respect, with additional grain coming from another Multon manor.

What of the mixtil? Again, not quite all was produced on the demesne. Seven quarters were received from Alan Thormond, the manor's rent collector, and presumably therefore came from rents in kind, and 13½ quarters came from perquisites of the lord's mill, no doubt as 'multure', that is the charge upon the peasants who were compelled to grind their corn there. In this case 9 quarters, 6½ bushels were sown. Most of the mixtil was consumed by the household or given out to estate workers. Two bushels went to the household for bread on 25 January. One quarter five bushels were given to Robert the Reeve as 'allowance' from Michaelmas to Thursday 13 February when the lord arrived at Frampton. The implication is that he and the other officials ate bread made from mixtil, not wheat bread, as a matter of course, at least when the lord was not in residence. Robert the Reeve was allowed a further 4½ bushels for the period from the lord's departure on 23 July until 8 September, when the account ends. The same amount was allowed Henry the Chaplain for the period from Michaelmas to 13 February, although deletions in the text at the audit make the sum uncertain. This, too, was for household consumption. Robert the Clerk received 2 bushels and Alan Hubert 2 bushels 'by the lady's gift',[37] while 1 quarter 4 bushels was sent by the lord's gift to Robert le Baker, no doubt in recognition of services rendered. Nearly a third of the total—30 quarters—were used for malt and a further 6 were given to Ivette Godeson for (making) 5 quarters of malt. A further 7 quarters 6 bushels was consumed in the household.

The manor's regular employees needed to be fed: 16 quarters, 5 bushels were given to the regular ploughmen and a gardener for their extensive services during the year. Additionally ½ quarter was given in baked bread for 34 ploughmen using 17 ploughs at the winter sowing and 20 carters carrying turves from the marsh, while 3 bushels were used for bread for the customary tenants carting

---

[37] Alan Hubert does not seem to appear again in the Multon records. However, the Cobeldyke account for Wyberton of 1328 records the payment of 10d to Alan Huberd for measuring land.

roofing materials for the houses at Swineshead and thereabouts and for the 50 customary tenants weeding the lord's corn for a day. Five quarters two bushels were baked for the customary tenants in the autumn, presumably for the harvest boon. In addition, 1 quarter was given to the ditchers working around the manor close, 1 quarter to the diggers of turf and half a quarter to builders employed in the close, in each case it says 'for goodwill and by covenant' (*ad bonitatem per convencionem*). In addition the reeve of Miningsby was given 5 quarters, most probably for sowing, and 1 quarter was given to the Carmelite and Augustinian friars 'by equal portion' by the lord's gift. They would seem to have been less favoured, therefore, than their Franciscan and Dominican brethren who received wheat. Finally, 10 quarters 6 bushels are noted as having been sold, with 2 quarters, 2 bushels remaining at the end of the year, although some bargaining with the reeve followed at the audit. Only ten per cent of the mixtil reached the market.

Of the other grains, 1 quarter 2 bushels of 'bere' were bought, and sown, while 1 quarter, 6 bushels of barley (i.e. spring barley) had been produced but were mixed with oats in the account, presumably because of its poor quality. This leaves the oats. Again, not all of the oats were produced on the manor. One quarter came as a gift from Sir John de Kirton, a neighbouring landowner, and 8 quarters, 2 bushels had been bought. Only 5 quarters, 1 bushel were sown. Some was used in the form of pottage for the *famuli* while 2 quarters, 2 bushels were made into flour 'for the lord's maintenance'. Most, as one would expect, was used as provender for the lord's horses and those of visitors. In sum, 27 quarters 1 bushel were used, and 2 quarters, 1 bushel, 3 pecks were sold on account, i.e. charged to the reeve.[38]

Finally, we come to the legumes. Of the 46 quarters 5 bushels of peas and beans, 10 quarters 6 bushels were sown. In this case not far short of a quarter of the produce was used as seed. Much of the rest was used for feeding animals. Five quarters, six bushels went to the reeve of Miningsby, 1 quarter, 2 bushels were loaned to Sir Henry (presumably the Henry the Chaplain) 'by the lady's precept', 7$\frac{1}{2}$ bushels were mixed with the oats for bread and 2$\frac{1}{2}$ quarters were sold on account, i.e. once again they were charged to the reeve.

This was not, then, a greatly market-orientated manor. Under sales of corn (in the cash receipts section of the account) the reeve accounted for only £4 3s. One or two items may have been held back until the end of season prices, but they do not add up to a great deal.[39] What of livestock husbandry? In the account of stock we find the normal range of horses, oxen, cows, geese, and

---

[38] That is to say that the reeve was penalized, either because he should have done better or because he had done better but was concealing some of the profit. I owe this point to Barbara Harvey.

[39] 1s 1d came from the sale of $\frac{1}{2}$ quarter of peas and beans sold on 24 June. £1 14s came from 1 quarter, 5 bushels of mixtil, 8 quarters, 7$\frac{1}{2}$ bushels of peas and beans, 1 bushel of peas and oats, and 6 bushels of malt.

capons. The account tells us—in minute detail—the origin of the stock and what happened to it. Once again then, very little was sold on the market. The animals at Frampton seem to have been overwhelmingly for consumption or for traction to keep the arable operation going. The manor is shown, however, to have been working in concert with that of Miningsby, which may have been more livestock orientated. In addition to the geese, salt, and cocks and hens, the reeve of Miningsby received the sows and their piglets, while the cow had been received from, and was later returned to, him. Forty-six of the cocks and hens had been received from him as pullets. All of the oxen were handed over to Reginald Bishop, as were the two affers (working horses). He appears to be some form of stockman. He is mentioned elsewhere as an unfree tenant of the manor, and may well be identical with Reginald the Reeve who features in a similar capacity on one occasion.

The receipt section of the account shows that the cash income of Thomas de Multon's manor of Frampton came overwhelmingly from other sources. The account of the rent collector, Alan Thormond, which follows the livestock account on the dorse of the roll, shows that £6 13s 9d was gathered from free and bond tenants at Frampton and parts near.[40] A further £13 14s 1d came from land and houses at farm, £5 came from tallage of the bondmen and a £13 13s 9d from the profits of the lord's court. The other major source of income on the manor was the herbage, the payment for the use of pasture. It came to £9 15s ½d. It included a variety of sources including herbage from the sea wall and from the tide, from the stubble, from the fallow, from the 'Fenland', and from 'Newland'.[41]

We are now in a position to calculate the cash income of Frampton manor in 1325–6, drawing on the reeve's account of receipts and the collector's account. The total comes to £53 18s 2¼d. Less than £5 of this was from sales (Table 5.2).

The picture would not be complete, however, without looking at the expenses listed in the reeve's account. There are: expenses relating to the improvement of the manor; expenses relating to production, including equipment and threshing; purchases; wages and payments to officials; and the expenses of the lord. Let us take them in reverse order.

The expenses of the lord refer to money handed over on his visits to the manor. Other sums were handed either to the lady or to the lord's servants. These were running expenses. Monies were clearly being handed over to lord, lady, and officials as required during the course of the year, underlining the ongoing interaction between household and estate which must have characterized gentry life.

---

[40] i.e. Kirton, Wyberton, Skirbeck, Bicker, and Fleet.
[41] It also included summer herbage for the agistment of (i.e. renting of pasture for) animals, herbage in Multon *Heeng* and fallow in Papworth. The item of account known as foreign receipts includes various sums from sales amounting to 13s 3d in total.

Table 5.2. Cash income from Frampton Manor[42]

Herbage	£9	15s	$\frac{1}{2}$d
Corn sold	£4	3s	
In stock		5s	3$\frac{3}{4}$d
Foreign receipts		3s	3d
Rent	£6	13s	9d
Farms	£13	14s	1d
Tallage	£5		
Perquisites of court	£13	13s	9d
Total	**£53**	**18s**	**2$\frac{1}{4}$d**

Notes: No cash income is noted from the lord's mill, suggesting perhaps that the income was entirely in the form of multure. The income from the court seems very high this year, and way above the £2 10s noted in the extent.

In terms of sums paid to officials themselves, we may note first that Richard de Scopeholm and Geoffrey de Wynceby were paid 2s in expenses for the Michaelmas court. Robert the Clerk was paid 6s 8d for writing the roll for the preceding year. His writing of the current roll is also noted but no sum follows. No doubt he was due for payment at the beginning of the next accounting year. Wages were given to John Slegh and Peter Baret, the ploughmen, to John le Gardener, to Robert le Oxhird and to William de Cockewell, whose occupation is unspecified.

We come now to the production costs themselves. First of all, the cost of ploughing. Maintaining the necessary equipment was costly.[43] The total sum came to 14s 2d, not counting the 2s 6d per annum by which a smith had been retained. The ploughing itself was less costly than the provision of equipment. The winter ploughing depended upon the services provided by the tenants. Food was provided for them in the form of bread, a goose, and a hen from store, and by the purchase of ale, mutton, and cheese for breakfast. This was not cheap. The bought items alone cost 5s 5d. Carting, too, had its running costs, with a total of 7s 11d expended. The shoeing of affers was separately costed at 1s 6d, while the cost of threshing and winnowing came to £1 7s 9$\frac{3}{4}$d.

Back in the fields, weeding was done by the customary tenants, who were provided with a daily meal of bread, cheese, and butter. Mowing was done by twenty-one mowers with twenty-four customary tenants doing the hay making. The latter were given, from store, sufficient bread, cheese, and butter or herring, at two meals a day, while the mowers were treated daily to meat and to cheese at noon.

Finally, we come to the corn harvest. The customary tenants were provided with meals consisting of bread, cheese, and butter or herring for reaping, carrying

[42] Excluding all arrears and money received for improving the manor. The foreign receipts include a large sum of money received from the lady for repairs and improvements to the manor. These were receipts as far as the reeve's account is concerned.

[43] The details indicate that both horses and oxen were employed in ploughing. The Multon manor seems to have been using mixed plough teams. On demesne plough teams see John Langdon, *Horses, Oxen and Technological Innovation* (Cambridge, 1986), esp. ch. 3.

corn, serving the stacker and carrying turves from the marsh: 140 herrings had to be bought, together with 6½ stones of butter and 6½ stones of cheese. The cost was 13s 5¾d. Moreover, 10 stones of cheese were received from Miningsby for this purpose. The meat for the mowers cost 3d. The wages for the stacker of beans through four days was 8d and the wages for two men stacking the turves within the manor for one day was 3d 'of the lord's food' (*ad cibum domini*). Finally, the wages of the man stacking the corn in the barn for five days and stacking the beans for two days was 1s 2d plus 2d 'of the lord's food'. This presumably means that they ate in the *curia*, although probably not in the hall.

The agricultural services performed by the tenants may seem considerable at first sight, but in fact they were relatively light, consisting of seasonal works rather than week work. In addition, various workers had to be paid; sometimes, as in the case of the smith, this was by contract. Wages, as we have seen, were given to the regular farm workers, the *famuli*, who worked on the demesne. These workers are best known from studies of large estates but were clearly of some significance here.[44]

The recorded production costs on the arable side, not counting the supply of customary food and ale, comes to £3 14s. If we add wages and the expenses that are given this increases to £4 15s 8d. This is, of course, a false figure, in that it takes no account of other dimensions to the operation, including livestock husbandry and the salaries of higher officials. Moreover, it focuses on the operation of the manor, whereas in practice the running of estates and household were strongly intertwined. However, the figure does at least indicates that basic running costs were high, even if the year 1325–6 may not have been quite the norm.

But if the cost of maintaining equipment seems to have been high this particular year, it was nothing in comparison with the amount spent on buildings. As we have seen earlier, there appears to have been something of an overhaul of the manor house and of the close. The total cost of building, restoring, and furnishing came to £17 7s 6¼d. There was also the cost of canvas for the sails of the windmill, which came to 11s 4½d. The bulk of this expenditure was unusual in that the manor was being repaired after the effects of the minority of the lord and the consequent wardship. The repairs began, as we have seen, during the previous year when the most basic and urgent items had been dealt with. The foundations were laid for the further developments that took place the following year.

To complete the picture we need to look briefly at the account roll for 1324–5. It is not surprising, after what has been said, to find that virtually no grain had been sold during the year 1324–5. Under the category of corn sold we find only 4 bushels of mixtil that came from the payment of multure at the lord's mill. A later entry refers to a further 2 quarters, 9 bushels sold for 10s 3¾d. 120 eggs were

[44] The classic study is M. M. Postan, *The Famulus: The Estate Labourer in the XIIth and XIIIth Centuries*, EcHR Supplements 2 (1954). See also M. Morgan, *English Lands of the Abbey of Bec* (Oxford, 1946).

sold as well as profits of the garden, i.e. 1s 9d from *chibols* (small onions) in the summer, 3s 4d from apples and pears and 1s 8d from plums and juice. These are perhaps items that would not normally be marketed, as though the manor was looking for something to sell. Not much had been spent on threshing during the year. One man worked by agreement for one day in autumn for 2d at the lord's table, and another for one day at piece work. Additionally, two men worked for a day threshing at piece-work and at the same time threshed 4½ quarters, 1 peck of oats for provender for the horses of Sir John Pecche.

On the other hand grain had to be bought, some of it at least for sowing. Five quarters of wheat and 'bere' were bought from Alan de Cobeldyke, a neighbouring landowner, by indenture, for which he was owed £1 5s. A further quarter of wheat and bere was bought for 4s from him explicitly for sowing. It seems fairly certain that Walter of Henley's advice to sow with another man's seed was being adhered to. This, it was believed, would increase the yield.[45] There were other purchases, too: three-quarters of a quarter of beans from Alan de Cobeldyke, 6 quarters of oats, a further 5 bushels of oats, 1 bushel of barley for sowing, and 1 bushel of vetch also for sowing. Thirty-two geese were also bought, twenty of them in the autumn 'for stock'. The total purchases of grain and stock were said to be £5 4s 9½d.

The grain and stock accounts amplify the story and give us the details of the crops sown. They consisted of 8 quarters of mixtil;[46] 3 quarters, 2 bushels of wheat (loaned from Alan Robert); 1½ bushels of barley; 12 quarters of peas and beans; 1½ bushels of vetch; and 5½ quarters of oats. By putting these figures together with the home production recorded in the grange account for 1325/6—that is, 25 quarters 2 bushels of wheat; 79 quarters 2½ bushels of mixtil; 20 quarters 3 pecks of oats; and 46 quarters 5 bushels of legumes—we can gain some idea of the yield (see Table 5.3).

These figures are almost certainly net of tithe, which would have been taken directly from the field.[47] The yield ratios envisaged by the author of the late-thirteenth-century treatise, *Husbandry*, were 5 for wheat, 6 for mixtil, 7 for rye,

Table 5.3.   Multon Yields, 1325

	Wheat	Mixtil	Oats	Legumes
Yield ratio	7.76	9.91	3.65	3.89
Yield per acre	20.2	33.39	24.73	12.23
	(10 acres)	(19 acres)	(6 ½ acres)	(30 ½ acres)

[45] Oschinsky (ed.), *Walter of Henley*, 325. In the following year, Frampton and Miningsby may have been exchanging seed for a similar reason.

[46] The greater part of the 25 quarters, 2 bushels of mixtil accounted for went on liveries to employees and on food at boon services.

[47] cf. Harvey, *Cuxham*, 52; however, there is no mention of tithe in the account rolls.

and 4 for oats. (He gives no figure for legumes.)[48] Against this, the Multon yield from oats is in line with what one would expect, the yield from wheat high and that from mixtil especially so. This requires further exploration. To obtain the yield, three items have been deducted from the total of mixtil in store, i.e. the grain that came in via the rent collector, the perquisites of the mill, and the 3 quarters of wheat that were added to it. The result is 79 quarters 2½ bushels. Even so, the yield seems very high and it could be that the amount of mixtil in store has been inflated in some way. It is possible that there is an element of old stock, although this seems unlikely give the context and the scale of the enterprise. The small quantity of grain threshed in 1324–5 hardly suggests this. The other figures seem more credible. The crop yields from the well-documented manor of Wisbech Barton over the period 1313–1429 show an average yield ratio of 2.9 for legumes, 3.9 for oats, 4.5 for wheat, and 5.7 for mixtil, with maxima of 6.2, 6.4, 9.7, and 8.8. The corresponding yields per acre are on average 9.4 for legumes, 17.3 for oats, 10.2 for wheat and 16.4 for mixtil with maxima of 24.7, 30.2, 20.2, and 25.3.[49] Compared with these figures the Frampton yield in terms of oats and legumes seems to be reasonable but not especially impressive, the wheat yield again high and the yield of mixtil, as we have said, extraordinarily so. On the other hand, it might be relevant that the Wisbech figure for bere alone is higher than for mixtil. There was no fixed ratio of wheat to bere or rye in mixtil. It could be that the mixture at Frampton contained a lower proportion of wheat. Nevertheless, these yields are very high for medieval England.

But they are not impossible. Bruce Campbell, looking at sixty-two demesnes in eastern Norfolk, an area where there were many high-yielding demesnes, found that before 1350 the maximum recorded yield ratios were 10.3 for wheat and 10.5 for mixtil.[50] However, yield per acre is now seen as a better measure of productivity given that variations in seeding rates could produce different yields even where yields per seed were actually the same.[51] The maximum recorded

---

[48] Oschinsky (ed.), *Walter of Henley*, 401. Bruce Campbell has recently argued that these expectations were unrealistic except, under favourable conditions, for wheat: *English Seigniorial Agriculture*, 321.

[49] D. Stone, *Decision-Making in Medieval Agriculture* (Oxford, 2005), 38. The Husbandry says that wheat ought to yield to the fifth grain, oats to the fourth: Oschinsky (ed.), *Walter of Henley*, 418–19.

[50] Bruce M. S. Campbell, 'Arable Productivity in Medieval England: Some Evidence from Norfolk', *Journal of Economic History* 43, no.2 (1983), 79–404; repr. in Bruce M. S. Campbell, *The Medieval Antecedents of English Agricultural Progress* (Aldershot, 2007). See his table 1. To put these yields in perspective, however, we should note also his calculation that the highest yielding demesnes averaged only 6.8 for wheat and 6.1 for mixtil.

[51] Ibid. 385, citing P. F. Brandon, 'Cereal Yields on the Sussex Estates of Battle Abbey During the Later Middle Ages', *EcHR* 2nd ser. 25 (1972), 403–20 (at 406–15). Even yields per acre do not give 'a true measure of productivity', Campbell adds, because the frequency with which the land was cropped was an equally important factor: ibid. 390. Campbell has developed a more sophisticated measure known as WACY (Weighted Aggregate Crop Yields). This takes a variety of factors into

from eastern Norfolk in the same period was 34 for wheat, 33.2 for mixtil, 33.5 for oats, and 26 for legumes.[52] The Multon yields are not quite as high as they look in comparative terms, given that Frampton acres were one-and-a-quarter times statute acres. The seeding rate for wheat was on the low side, but higher for the other crops.[53] Nevertheless, the Multon yields were very respectable. Clearly, if the circumstances were right, gentry estates could lie at the higher end of productivity. Economic historians have recently been emphasizing the variety of factors that helped determine yields.[54] Here, however, it seems undeniable that soil fertility was a crucial factor. We must remember that Frampton was located in the reclaimed silt Fenland, one of the most fertile areas of England, where one would expect yields to be comparatively high. In the particular case of the Multon manor the yields seem to reflect the very high valuation placed on the land.

Although the yields were high, there is every reason to believe that the Multon estate of 1324–5 was not running at full capacity. Only 66 acres were sown that year. The extent of 1326 talks of 80 acres 3 roods under cultivation with 60 acres lying fallow. If this represents a two-year system of rotation, then the figures would correspond. However, the sown area in 1325–6 seems to have been no more than in the previous year.[55] There was some slight variation in the quantity of each crop sown and the acreage under each, but it is not very significant. The small quantity of barley that was sown in the earlier year did not do well and was replaced by bere. Perhaps there was some experimentation going on. The seed sown per acre was more or less the same, except that oats were sown less densely.[56] To some small degree, the regime was feeling its way. In terms of stock the picture is similar. The reeve accounted for four affers received from the lord, one foal of issue, fourteen oxen received from the lord, twenty capons received by indenture, and large numbers of cocks and hens, viz. forty-four received by indenture and seventy-one as Christmas rents. It looks as though the manor was being stocked.

account, but is dependent upon the existence of more robust evidence: see *Seigniorial Agriculture*, ch.7 'Arable productivity'. For estates with limited sources like that of the Multons, yield ratio and yield per acre are the best data on productivity that can be produced.

[52] Campbell, 'Arable Productivity', 385 and table 3. The highest yielding demesnes averaged 25.1 for wheat, 21.4 for maslin, 24.6 for oats, and 26 for legumes.

[53] The Multon account for 1324–5 records the wheat was sown at a rate of '2½ bushels per acre plus one bushel more'. Mixtil was sown at '3½ bushels per acre plus one bushel', oats at a rate of '6 bushels plus one peck' and legumes at '3 bushels 1 peck per acre plus 3 pecks more'. Campbell's figures range from 2–4 for wheat and maslin, 3.3–7.8 for oats and 1.9–4 for legumes: ibid. table 3.

[54] These include labour input, techniques of husbandry and the quality of management as well as the weather and the prevalence of pests and diseases. For a recent discussion of productivity see C. C. Thornton, 'The Level of Arable Productivity on the Bishopric of Winchester's Manor of Taunton, 1283–1348', in Richard Britnell (ed.), *The Winchester Pipe Rolls and Medieval English Society* (Woodbridge, 2003), 109–37.

[55] 61.25 acres are enumerated, plus 2 further selions under wheat and a few acres under bere.

[56] At 5 bushels 1 peck (plus 4 pecks overall) compared with 6 bushels, 1 peck the following year. It is interesting to note, however, that sowing rates were not static.

There were the usual production costs.[57] The customary ploughing and harrowing services seem to have been in place. In fact, curiously, customary services appear to be more extensive than those accounted for in 1325–6. Nevertheless the lord needed to find extra help. Ale was given to the four men of Alan de Cobeldyke who went at two ploughs for a day to help with the ploughing. The other customary services also seem to have been in place, that is to say weeding, mowing, reaping, and carrying. All of this came at a cost in terms of food provided. Wages were paid to a gardener, to Robert Randolf the ploughman and John le Deye (the dairyman). Although the first membrane of the account is badly damaged, it is clear that the rents were being collected with reasonable efficiency.[58]

What we see, then, is a lord pulling his estates together after a wardship. Although the rents and labour services had continued to be paid, the demesne economy seems to have been somewhat run down and the buildings were certainly in disrepair. Perhaps the most startling lack was sheep, especially given the frequent mention of the sheepcote. It may be that sheep were being concentrated elsewhere, perhaps at Miningsby. It seems likely, however, that the demesne flock was a victim of the long wardship. That this is the most probable explanation is suggested by the arrentation of customary services that was conducted around 1340, where it appears that the standard villein holding owed the services of washing and rearing sheep.[59] The surviving accounts for two neighbouring manors, the Huntingfield manor at Frampton[60] and the Cobeldyke manor at Wyberton,[61] reveal demesne flocks in 1331–2 and 1328 respectively.

On the other hand one must be careful not to exaggerate the extent to which the basic economy was run down. The manor clearly was functioning[62] and a process of recovery was well underway. This explains the making of the extent in 1326, i.e. to provide the new lord with a full picture of his estate. It explains the survival of various other items of documentation from this period, including the manorial accounts and a memorandum regarding the behaviour of the lord's unfree tenants on the land market. Everything points in the same direction: the manor was being revitalized and lordship was being asserted.

---

[57] Ploughing equipment was costed at 13s 11½d. The costs incurred at the ploughing was almost as much, totalling 13s 8½d (*recte* 13s 2d).

[58] £3 17s 4½d came from free tenants and £5 from the bond tenants. £14 10s 4d came from farms and £5 7s 5d from the perquisites of the court. A few further items brought in sums of 1s 3d and 5s 4d, making a total of £29 1s 8½d.

[59] See below 129. It is also implied, however, that sheep were not always being reared on the manor.

[60] The account of the Huntingfield reeve, Geoffrey de Stalworth, survives in the Magdalen archives as Multon Add 5.

[61] Multon Add 24. The opening of the account is missing but 2 Edward III is written on the dorse.

[62] The amount that needed to be spent on repairs to equipment does not seem to have been excessive when compared to that on the Huntingfield and Cobeldyke manors.

In some respects, however, the Multon account rolls give an incomplete picture. Ideally, one should be able to understand the Frampton manor within the entire portfolio of Multon estates. Unfortunately, the lack of sources means that this is not possible. Nonetheless there are indications in the accounts that the Frampton manor was functioning as part of a larger enterprise. From the appearances of the reeve of Miningsby we can see that intermanorial transfers were taking place. It is likely that some specialized activities were occurring on some of the Multon manors. Frampton was producing largely for consumption rather than for sale, and in 1324–6 at least it was putting little produce on the market. It is may well be that other manors were more commercially orientated.

Let us turn now to the second of our south Lincolnshire estates, that of the Cobeldykes of Wyberton. In both structure and exploitation it provides an interesting contrast. The Cobeldykes were a family with a very different history from that of the Multons, although by the time of their account role they were of more comparable status. In order to understand the nature of the Wyberton estate we need to remind ourselves that the type of manor held by the likes of Multon, Huntingfield, and Richmond was not the only variety in the area. There were also some very small manors. An inquisition into the lands held by rebels in the wapentake of Kirton after the battle of Evesham in 1265 includes one such, held by Walter Malreward in Wyberton and Frampton.[63] Walter had the following:

- 60 acres of arable, valued at 8d per acre, worth £2;
- 9 acres of meadow, valued at 1s 6d per acre, worth 13s 6d;
- rent of free men amounting to 12s 6½d.

The recorded total is £4 0s 0½d.[64]

The source is relatively early—sixty years before the Multon extent—and, given its provenance, in the aftermath of war, perhaps a suspect one. Nonetheless it is indicative of the existence of very small manors to set alongside the three larger ones that centred on Frampton. Other small manors were held by Sir Richard de Casterton in Wigtoft, and no less a person that Sir Roger de Huntingfield in Bicker and Wibtoft, valued at £2 12s 4½d and £5 6s 8d respectively. The most striking features of these properties are the high proportion of demesne land and the lack of unfree tenants, features which, as we have seen, Kosminsky found characteristic of small manors.

The Malreward case is particularly interesting to us in the present context because it is the heart of the Cobeldyke estate for which the account roll survives for the year 1327–8. Something of the history of this estate can be put together, and it is most instructive. In 1242–3 Richard 'Maureward' was said to hold a

---

[63] TNA C145 28/1; *CIM* i. no. 791.
[64] The sums do not tally. The sum should be £3 6s 0½d.

knight's fee at Wyberton[65] and Robert de Cobeldyke one-eighth of a knight's fee in Frampton and Kirton. The former was the small manor that belonged to Walter Malreward in 1265. By 1303 it had passed to Roger de Cobeldyke, presumably through marriage or purchase. This was shortly after the violent death of William 'Maureward' the previous year.[66] Roger, the descendant of Robert de Cobeldyke of 1242–3, had therefore united the two small estates. He was a man on the rise, and doing well for himself. He was undoubtedly a lawyer-administrator. By 1298 he had become the steward to the earl of Lincoln for his Lincolnshire lands.[67] In 1305 he acted as one of two attorneys for the earl, who was going overseas on the king's business. In 1303 he was a justice of oyer and terminer and in 1306 he was placed on a commission of walls and ditches in Lincolnshire.[68] He died in 1325. His inquisition post mortem puts the account roll in context.[69] At Cobeldyke itself, which is within Frampton, he held an amalgam of properties: a messuage and 10 acres from Thomas de Multon by knight's service, rendering 14s yearly, together with a further 10 acres in Frampton from William de Cobeldyke by knight's service for 3s 4d yearly, and 14 acres of arable, 20 acres of meadow and 18s rent of the earl of Richmond in socage (that is, non-military free tenure) for 5s 4d yearly. At Wyberton he held what was clearly the Malreward estate of Roger de Huntingfield, by the service of one-quarter of a knight's fee, 5s 6d for sheriff's aid and 2s to the Earl of Richmond. He also held a house in Boston of the earl which was worth 13s 4d per annum, that is 'in fair time when it could be let'. He held additional properties elsewhere in Lincolnshire, all of them small and all held by different lords. His heir was his son, Alexander de Cobeldyke, said to be aged 34 and more. It was Alexander who was lord at the time of the manorial account.

By this time, however, Alexander had inherited further property from Alan de Cobeldyke. The account roll itself speaks of 5s from the farm of a house once Alan de Cobeldyke's in Coningsby and of 8s from his land there leased to Robert Osgot, who is now dead. In the future, the roll says, the house and land will be leased for 13s 6d. There is also a sheepcote which, the account says, is not in use this year but will be leased next year, 1d rent of assize from John Drab, and 3s 4d from two doles of meadow 'sold this year'. Under Kirton we have a memorandum in the margin against which there is a hand with a long forefinger pointing to the statement that the serjeant (*serviens*) received last year, and this year, £2 16s from Alan the Marshal for *Toteeland*:

but because it is not decided between the lord and his parceners of the inheritance of Alan de Cobeldyke how much the lord will have as his share, the serjeant is not charged as yet, but will hold the money until it is decided.

[65] It was later said to constitute one-quarter of a knight's fee.
[66] *CPR* 1301–7, 37, 336; *Feudal Aids*, iii. 164.
[67] *A Lincolnshire Assize Roll for 1298* ed. Walter Sinclair Thomson, Lincolnshire Record Society cvi (1944), 215.
[68] *CPR* 1301–7, 189, 380, 478.   [69] *CIPM* vi. no. 600.

Cobeldykes seem to have been ubiquitous in this area in the early fourteenth century, and the relationships between them are difficult to decipher. Alan de Cobeldyke occurs in Frampton deeds from 1297 to 1326. He was apparently associated with the Multons. In 1305 he was among fifteen men who were placed under royal protection going to Ireland with Thomas de Multon.[70] From 1322 to 1327 he was holding the castles of Bolingbroke and Lincoln as royal constable, being among those minor figures to whom the king had committed the castles forfeited after the rebellion against him in the former year.[71] How precisely he was related to Roger and Alexander de Cobeldyke is uncertain, although everything suggests that he represented a junior line and was making his way in the world by an alternative means from those being employed by Roger, that is by military service. The Cobeldykes were a family that had clearly been clawing its way up.

Whatever the relationship among the Cobeldykes may have been, Roger's son, Alexander, was among Alan's heirs. The account roll also shows that Alexander held additional property, most especially a manor at Freiston, also in Holland but north of the River Witham.[72] He had a house, garden, and some land with a barn at Cobeldyke, and a substantial manor at Wyberton which was subject to periodic visits. However, his household seems to have had its main base at Freiston. Coupledyke Hall, a seventeenth-century L-shaped house, still survives half a mile south of that village. There was, however, a Cobeldyke Hall on the south side of Frampton, and here the Cobeldykes were relatively close neighbours of the Multons. What is certain is that they were of more lowly social origins. By the time we come to the 1327–8 account roll the Cobeldykes had secured themselves a place within the gentry. Nevertheless, as lords of any status they were newcomers on the scene.

The nature of the Wyberton-centred estate, however, reflects this history, and it reveals some important characteristics of Kosminsky's small manors. According to his analysis 'small manors, like land in free tenure, brought further entanglement into the cobweb of feudal connections, as its separate parts belonged to various fees'.[73] The Cobeldyke account roll of 1328 reveals this most clearly in its list of outgoing rents, indicative of how the estate was brought together in a piecemeal fashion. In addition to 5s 6d paid for sheriff's aid and frankpledge, money was being paid out to neighbouring lords. Thirteen outgoings were listed, ranging from 1d to £1 4s 8d. The recipients included Sir Thomas de Multon, the Earl of Richmond, the lord of Huntingfield, the lord of Scrivelsby and the prioress of Stixwould. Furthermore, money was being paid out for land that was once Alan de Cobeldyke's, viz. 8s for the tenement in Coningsby, and 4d for *Ploghbetilland*

[70] *CPR* 1301–7, 337.
[71] *CFR* 1319–1327, 119; John Rickard, *The Castle Community: The Personnel of English and Welsh Castles, 1272–1422* (Woodbridge, 2002), 38, 289, 292.
[72] *CIPM*, vii. no. 597; *Feudal Aids*, iii. 231, 234, 241.
[73] Kosminsky, *Studies in Agrarian History*, 274.

in Kirton. The total of these outgoings was £3 6s 2½d, a not insignificant reduction in the profitability of the estate.

Let us look more closely at the Cobeldyke income from Wyberton and places that accounted with it as recorded on the account roll of 1328. The recorded total is £69 13s 8½d. The largest income was from grain, and the greater part of this came from mixtil (£11 10s 7½d) and from legumes (£8 6s 4½d). However, wheat, barley, dredge (a mixture of barley and oats), and oats also figured. Almost all of the grain accounted for was produced on the manor, except in the case of wheat where more than a third of the 39 quarters 6 bushels came from outside. The grange account informs us of its destiny. Of the wheat, 21 quarters 1 bushel was sold, that is almost as much as was produced on the manor, and 3 quarters were used as seed. Seven quarters were sent to Freiston. Of the 192 quarters 1 bushel of mixtil accounted for, 78 quarters were sold, 22 sown and 22 turned into malt. Of the small quantity of bere produced 2 quarters 5 bushels were sown and the remaining 15 quarters 5 bushels used, 13 of them for malt. Of the 62½ quarters of oats accounted for, only 4 quarters were sold and 3 quarters 2 bushels were sown. Some went on horse provender and on potage. However, nearly half of it was sent on to Freiston. One hundred and ninety-four quarters of peas and beans were accounted for, of which 5 quarters had been bought and the rest produced on the manor. Of these 50 quarters 6 bushels were sold, and 19 quarters 6 bushels were sown. Almost all of the rest was consumed on the manor in various ways, for example 51 quarters 3½ bushels of malt were produced. Of this, 36½ quarters were sent to Freiston. Once again, we are reminded that manors were not self-contained worlds and that a gentry estate really ought to be seen as a whole, if only we had the sources to do it. Freiston begins to appear as a consumption centre. Wyberton on the other hand was more of a production centre, over and above, that is, the cost of sustaining itself.

The manor was reasonably well endowed on the livestock side, despite ongoing losses from murrain. Total income accounted for on this side came to £19 7s 3d. The greater part of this came from the sale of wool. Pigs and piglets, chickens and geese, cheese and butter were largely produced for consumption. Much was sent on to Freiston. Geese were reared especially on the Cobeldyke holding at Tuddebach. Broadly speaking, the purpose of livestock rearing was the same as that on the estate of Peterborough Abbey: oxen for traction, sheep for wool, horses for transport and some ploughing, and pigs for meat.[74] The principal commodity was wool (Figure 5.1): £12 10s was earned from two sacks sold. A further 2s 6d came from the sale of 'locks' (i.e. collected remnants after shearing). The stock account naturally reinforces this picture, and gives us a sense of the scale of the enterprise. 171 wethers were accounted for, 157 ewes, 140 hoggs and 190 lambs. Wethers, it should be noted, produced

---

[74] Kathleen Biddick, *The Other Economy: Pastoral Husbandry on a Medieval Estate* (California and London, 1989), 125.

Figure 5.1. A Sheepcote (from the Luttrell Psalter). Add. MS 42131, fo. 163vs. © The British Library Board. All Rights Reserved 2010.

the heaviest and largest fleeces. Sixteen of them were sold during the period of the account. Nothing at all was wasted. Necessarily so, given the heavy losses through murrain.[75] Organizationally speaking what stands out here is the degree of intermanorial transfer, with the shearing done at Wyberton. No doubt the Cobeldyke enterprise lacked the resources that would enable further specialization.[76] Once again, however, the main picture is of Freiston as a consumption centre and Wyberton as a locus of production.

The second highest earner for the Cobeldykes was from their pastoral resources. Basically pasture was sold to the peasant sector in return for cash. Altogether the animal husbandry of others brought in £8 12s 11d. One gets the strong impression of a highly managed enterprise, where all available resources are put to use.[77] The official's expenses are equally illuminating. The outgoing 'rent' aside, there is no doubt that the major costs in terms of running the manor were in labour. Under wages we have the cost of employing the permanent farm workers. This amounted to £2 5s 6d and was paid out to ten employees, including two ploughman, an oxherd, a shepherd, a carter, a dairyman, and a keeper of stabled animals.

The costs of weeding, mowing, and haymaking are not broken down but they were also of course labour costs. The autumn costs consisted of £7 6s 2d in wages

---

[75] Eighteen woollen pelts from dead sheep were sold and 4 lamb's pelts were paid in tithe. Thirty-five lambs' pelts were sent to Freiston to be made into fur. Eight shorn pelts and 7 low-grade lambs' pelts remained in stock. Six carcasses were used in autumn expenses and 2 poor-quality ones were salted and remain in stock.

[76] On the Peterborough Abbey estate, by contrast, some manors specialized in rearing wethers, others in ewes. See Biddick, *The Other Economy*, chapter 5, for the Peterborough sheep flocks.

[77] The management had an acute sense, for example, of the quality of grains. At some point after the harvest 1½ quarters of barley was put in with the mixtil as was half a quarter of wheat, while 1 quarter 7 bushels of oats was put with the harvested dredge.

for reaping, gathering and binding, together with 10s for three ploughmen, 7s 5d in flesh, fish and herring bought for the serjeant, the harvest overseer (*messor*), the dairyman (le Dye) and the ploughmen, 9d for a stacker (*tassor*) to cover the beans and 5d for a woman employed for five days on miscellaneous tasks. Repairs to the sea ditches and muck-spreading involved further expenditure, as did milking the ewes.[78] The costly and time-consuming threshing was done by three men working at task taking 1½d for a full day and 1d for a half day. They threshed the whole range of arable produce—wheat, mixtil, bere, barley, oats, peas, and beans—with profit, that is the difference between heaped and razed measures being allocated to them. They also did the winnowing.

Other classes of running costs, for example ploughing, carting, housing repairs, repairs to the mill and the miscellaneous category called 'necessary items' also involved labour costs. There were carpenters, smiths, makers of harnesses, and coopers, not to mention men carrying beans into the barn. We hear of Walter the Carpenter who made a door and who worked on the great gates, and of Joceus the roofer. The cost of keeping sheep involved paying for their washing prior to shearing—465 sheep were washed this year. Wages were paid to a man making 'hebbes' and 'cribbes'. There was the cost of bringing cow's milk to the lambs, of candles during lambing, of unguents, and so on.

Wages, however, were not the entirety of the labour costs. The grange account includes the livery of 56 quarters, 4½ bushels of mixtil to the *familia*. It is noticeable that almost as much mixtil was consumed by the *familia* as was sold. Even the 56 quarters was not the entirety. A further 2 quarters 5 bushels went on autumn expenses, half a quarter to the reapers 'by agreement', and half a quarter to the mowers also 'by agreement'. The mixtil was costly to produce. It is salutary that of the total of 192 quarters 1 bushel which were accounted for only 78 quarters, 2 bushels were sold. In addition to gifts and other minor items, 22 quarters were used as seed and 22 quarters were turned into malt. There is no mention of malt being sold so that it must have been consumed in the household. There were other liveries too. The serjeant was provided with a superior diet, receiving 4 quarters 4 bushels of wheat, at a rate of 1 quarter per ten days. He obviously did quite well. Among his perks was 6s 8d for shoes. Otherwise smallish quantities of the various grains (and animals) went in autumn expenses while 2½ quarters of oats and 2 bushels of peas and beans went into potage for the *familia*. A lamb was given to the shepherd 'by custom'. Some produce was paid out in rent. There were also gifts of produce, however, by the lord himself, or on behalf of the lord.

All in all, the Wyberton manor appears to be enterprising but costly to run. Wages and liveries in kind were high, the more so perhaps as the Cobeldykes, unlike the Multons, did not have much in the way of services of unfree tenants

---

[78] Sums amounting to £1 3s 10½d are recorded for these items, not including the digging of a new ditch at *Couppeland*. Milking was done by women.

to draw on. On the other hand, although its demesne was no larger, it was a more market-orientated manor than that of the Multons. Does this simply reflect the relationship between Wyberton and Freiston on the one hand and, say, Miningsby and Multon on the other, as integral parts of larger enterprises? Or is there a difference in commercial attitude and acumen between established gentry on the one hand and aspirant gentry on the other? It is to the relationship between the gentry and estate management that we must now turn.

6

Commercialization and Estate Management

The Multon and Cobeldyke manors employed a large number of people in many capacities, all of them increasing, at least potentially, the range of local contacts the gentry enjoyed. We may wonder how well Alexander de Cobeldyke knew his ploughmen and Roger le Deye, who, judging by his name, was his dairyman. How well did he know John Douay, his gardener at Cobeldyke, or Roger Aynald, the keeper of his stabled animals? What terms, if any, was he on with his hayward, William White or his serjeant, whose name is, unfortunately, unknown to us?

How much contact he had with such people must have depended very largely on how he managed his estate. Before we turn to this question, however, we must ask another. How commercially orientated were gentry estates? Here the starting point is, once again, the pioneering work of Kosminsky. He argued, famously, that the smaller manor tended to be more price-sensitive and its proprietor more entrepreneurial than was the case with larger estates.[1] His analysis was coloured by his preoccupations, since he was looking to the gentry, or at least the minor gentry, as the harbingers of capitalism. For him the smaller estates were more market orientated and their holders likely to invest on a larger scale than the greater landlords.

In what is undoubtedly the most significant study of the manorial accounts of gentry estates in this period, first published in 1980, Richard Britnell put Kosminsky's arguments to the test.[2] He looked at four sets of accounts from four small estates in north-east Essex, all held by minor lay landowners.[3] All of the manors conformed to the structural characteristics suggested by Kosminsky, in being small manors, with relatively little in the way of customary labour and a high proportion of land in demesne. The only partial exception was Langenhoe, where Lionel de Bradenham was the principal landlord and where he held courts. He also had higher than usual rents of assize and more in the way of pasture,

---

[1] Kosminsky, *Studies in Agrarian History*, 273–8.

[2] R. H. Britnell, 'Minor Lords in England and Medieval Agrarian Capitalism', *Past and Present* 89 (1980), repr. in T. H. Aston (ed.), *Landlords, Peasants and Politics in Medieval England* (Cambridge, 1987).

[3] These rare survivals 'yield information of much the same quality as that to be extracted from those of larger estates, except that they are too few to provide anything but "still pictures" ': ibid. 3.

Langenhoe being a marshland manor. These manors, as Britnell pointed out, were ideal for testing Kosminsky's hypotheses.

Britnell's findings were as follows:

First of all he found that the dependence on demesne agriculture as a source of cash was 'unmistakable'. Moreover, it was clear that the sale of livestock was also an important component, even on a predominantly arable manor. Of the manors he examined, only Langenhoe was a home manor, supplying the household. Even here, however, a large surplus of cereals was put on the market. None of the other manors examined sent grain to the lord's household. This was itself an important finding for it showed that small estates could have 'distinct home manors' and 'cash manors' just as large ones did.[4] This, as we have seen, was clearly the case with the Multons of Frampton and the Cobeldykes of Wyberton.

Secondly, he found that investment was indeed relatively high on these small estates. His evidence matched his deductive reasoning that with little customary labour the cost of repairs and maintenance was likely to be higher. At the same time, however, he found that much of the expense was in dealing with dilapidation and replacement of stock rather than in improvements. This does not in itself indicate greater commercial acumen or orientation. Furthermore, all landowners, of whatever hue, had expenses of one sort or another to find and are likely to have been concerned to have tightly managed estates and to sell their grain surpluses at a profitable price. He therefore concluded that 'Kosminsky's a priori argument linking investment ratios to different qualities of entrepreneurship is accordingly a weak one'.[5]

Thirdly, Britnell's estates provide evidence that small estates played the market, holding back grain until prices had risen well above the harvest price. However, he adds a strong argument that smaller landlords are likely to have been forced to sell grain early because their money income depended upon it. The money was needed for wages, purchases, and the lord's own needs. In short, contrary to Kosminsky's reasoning, it would seem that in practice smaller landowners were less likely to obtain the best prices for their produce.

Finally he points out that those improvements in farming methods that did occur affected large landowners at least as much as small ones, that traditional methods of production and low capital investment were endemic. In short:

Neither the importance of trade for small landlords nor their greater dependence on wage labour can be shown to have made them more capitalist than large ones in any sense likely to be useful for the interpretation of long-term social change.[6]

How well do our South Lincolnshire manors fit with Britnell's findings? Here, Langenhoe provides a particularly useful case for comparison.[7] For this manor there are no fewer than five early account rolls, between 1324–5 and 1347–8. Its

---

[4] Ibid. 14.   [5] Ibid. 14.   [6] Ibid. 21.

[7] See especially Britnell's earlier study of this manor: 'Production for the Market on a Small Fourteenth-Century Estate', *EcHR* (1966).

lord, Lionel de Bradenham, was a very minor light amongst the English landlords
of the day and this was his only manor. Nonetheless he had a serjeant running
his manor for him, grew wheat as a cash crop and kept livestock in the adjoining
village of Abberton during the 1340s. Across the five accounts 30 per cent of his
produce was sold on the market.[8] Lionel de Bradenham was able to increase his
income from rents (by substituting leasehold rents for customary money rents)
and to increase the manor's production of grain to the limits of the available
arable land.[9]

Lionel's situation was obviously different from that of the Multons. With only
one manor he needed it to provide both produce for his household and cash
for his own income. The Multons could afford to arrange things differently. As
we have seen, the Multon manor of Frampton did not market a great deal of
its produce, at least in 1325–6. It was clearly a home farm, geared largely for
consumption. Moreover, the Multons were drawing a substantial cash income
from Frampton in other ways. The relatively small size of the Multon demesne
may also be a factor. It is noticeable, however, that the single surviving accounts
for the nearby Huntingfield and Cobeldyke manors show that they marketed
more produce. The Huntingfield manor had a somewhat larger demesne.[10] It
earned a total of £28 2s 8d from the sale of arable produce in 1320–1, most of
it according to the account 'at divers prices'. This might of course indicate that
the market was being played, although it is by no means certain. In addition,
sales of stock, leather, skins, wool, hay, dairy products, and fruits of the garden
brought the total value of the sales to £45 2s 3d. Although, as we have seen, the
higher reaches of the gentry were itinerant around their estates in the fourteenth
century, it is unlikely that the Huntingfields spent a great dealing of time at
Frampton. In contrast to that of the Multons, this manor was not a 'home
farm'.

The Cobeldyke manor of Wyberton, although it had a demesne no larger than
the Multons, was certainly more geared to the market. The situation here was
closer to that of the Bradenhams of Langenhoe. In 1328 a total of £25 7s 3d was
earned from the sale of arable produce. When we add in the profits from animal
husbandry (£8 12s 11d), the £2 14s that was earned from the sale of turves and
tiles, and the small sum (2s 6d) earned by the dairy, the total comes to £36
16s 8d. As we have already seen, nothing was wasted, and one gets the strong
impression of a highly managed enterprise, where all available resources are put
to use. An example of this is the use made of turf. Four thousand thraves of turf
were accounted for in the marsh and a further thousand that had been dug. Of
these 2,000 had been used in making tiles and 1,400 sold, leaving 1,600 in stock.
Under the heading of 'tiles at the tilery' (*tegule apud tegularium*) we learn that

[8] Actually 29.9 per cent as against 22.8 per cent used to feed the household, 21.4 per cent used
for seed, and 18.9 per cent as wages.
[9] Moreover, pasture farming brought the lord more cash than the sale of grain did.
[10] It was said to have 155 acres of arable in demesne in 1314.

44,000 tiles had been produced; of these 3,000 had been sold leaving 41,000 in stock. In addition to the £2 4s from the sale of turf, some of it sold where it was dug, 10s came in from the 3,000 tiles sold to Martin the Baker, presumably for his ovens. Naturally, the manufacture of tiles was not without its cost. The turf, used here as fuel, involved transport costs—£1 6s 8d for carrying 2,000 thraves from the place where they were dug up to Witham and from there up to *Slop(er)scote,* at 1s 4d per 1000. Then there was the cost of digging, turning, and drying. The actual manufacture of the tiles, including the maintenance of the kilns, involved heavier costs, amounting to a total of £2 10s 11½d for 44,000 tiles.[11] The tilery hardly seems cost effective on the figures given, until we take into account the heavy stock that was being held over. The reason for this is far from clear. It is possible that the intention was to use them in refurbishment of the Cobeldyke manors. However, the majority may have been intended for the market the following year.

It may well be that the Cobeldykes, with greater outgoings in rent and labour costs, may have been looking out for further resources to exploit. It could be argued that their relatively lowly origins made them more enterprising in this respect. It is also clear, however, that having made it into gentry ranks they were behaving in traditional ways in terms of largesse. We hear of gifts of produce, either by the lord himself or on his behalf. The Franciscans of Boston were the recipients of both wheat and mixtil, while other gifts of grain went to individual laymen. Oats were used, of course, for provender for the horses of guests. Two bushels were given to William de Stiken(ey) of Newcastle by the lord. Intriguingly oats were also provided for the horses of those coming in from Kesteven and elsewhere for the fairs. An affer was given to William Doget by the lord, who was also liberal with cheeses, three weighing one-and-a-half stone going to the nuns of Stamford and one weighing half a stone going to William de la Bruere. One cannot helping wondering what those who managed the estate thought privately about this, and indeed about the 'lord's expenses' in general.

The degree to which manors were marketing their produce depended, then, upon a variety of factors, internal as well as external, including location. Perhaps only a minority were able to hold back their produce to claim the highest prices. Commercialization cannot be measured by sales alone, however. Estates of all sizes were heavily involved in the steady commercialization of English society that had proceeded throughout the thirteenth century and beyond.[12] The direct management of demesnes dictated and encouraged it. A myriad purchases were made for the estate and the household. The expanding land market, which

[11] Clay was available locally but sand had to be transported in. For the manufacturing process see John Cherry, 'Pottery and Tile', in J. Blair and N. Ramsay (eds), *English Medieval Industries* (London, 1991), 190–3.
[12] See, especially, R. H. Britnell, *The Commercialisation of English Society 1000–1500* (Cambridge, 1993).

increasingly involved peasants, townsmen, and many others, encouraged lords to expand their use of contractual rents and leases of various kinds. And then there is the purchase of labour. The seasonal services of the customary tenants are often given high profile both in the accounts and by historians. These services were important and were guarded by the lords, even if they necessitated expenditure on food and needed to be enforced. However, we should not lose sight of the fact that even on a manor like that of the Multons, where villein services persisted, most of the labour was undertaken by paid employees. Threshing and winnowing, for example, had to be paid for. They were costly items, because of the time involved. Stacking was paid for on a daily basis. Those employed for this included the *tector* (roofer) who covered the beans and who was aided by customary tenants. This, no doubt, involved some skill and ability to direct others. Carpenters, smiths, roofers, and others could be paid by a written agreement for some major work, at task (with or without such an agreement), or by the day.

There are clearly some grounds for thinking that gentry lords were often more burdened with labour costs than was the case with, say, large ecclesiastical estates, and that they could be—perhaps had to be—more acute in seeking out additional forms of income. There are also good reasons for thinking that it was at the level of the Cobledykes rather than the Multons or Huntingfields, at the lower and aspirant end of the gentry, that imagination in finding new ways of enhancing income was more likely to be found. At the same time, however, we find them buying into largesse and hospitality, traditional values amongst the most established landowners. Although there undoubtedly were differences between estates, including differences between small and large manors and between lay and ecclesiastical estates, the effect of these can be exaggerated. Some recent work on ecclesiastical estates indicates just how acute their managers could be in playing the market. Although the manorial accounts were not profit and loss accounts, as J. Titow pointed out some time ago, it is relatively easy to calculate profits from the information they provide. Indeed, there is evidence that some lords were doing just that.[13] In 1986 David Postles reviewed this issue, looking at memoranda derived from the estates of a few 'lesser or medium sized' ecclesiastical lordships.[14] The main components of the calculation (the *proficuum manerii*) were the liveries of cash to the household and the value of grain and stock delivered to the household or to other manors within the lord's estates. A further, more sophisticated calculation was to include the grain left in the granary and the natural increase of livestock during the accounting year, and to deduct the arrears, but this seems rarely to have been done. There were other

[13] Titow, *English Rural Society*, 26 citing Denholm-Young, *Seigniorial Administration*, ch. 4; and E. Stone, 'Profit and Loss Accountancy at Norwich Cathedral Priory', *TRHS* 5th ser., 12 (1962), 25–48. See also Harvey, *A Medieval Oxfordshire Village*.

[14] The estates of Merton College, God's House, Southampton, the Bishopric of Lichfield, Southwick Priory and Bolton Priory: D. Postles, 'The Perception of Profit Before the Leasing of Demesnes', *AgHR* 34 (1986), 12–28.

possibilities, such as checking the current account with the extent, as advocated by Walter of Henley, for example,[15] or with accounts from earlier years. This may explain why we have both an extent and manorial accounts surviving for the Multon estate from 1324–6. However, it is the basic calculation which seems to have been the most widespread. As Postles points out, this recognizes the value of the supply to the household as much as the proceeds from the sale of produce, which must have been an important consideration for many of the holders of small- to medium-sized estates. It emerges from his study that there was an increasing interest in making these calculations from the 1280s and that zenith of its use may have been limited to the 1290s and first two decades of the fourteenth century. It also emerges that the calculation was done for estates of all types, from where there were high levels of sales to where the main function was to supply the household, from the 'classical' manor to the estate where a high proportion of the lord's income came from rents.[16]

More recently, David Stone has re-examined the level of decision-making on the later medieval manors, in a study based, in the first instance, upon the bishop of Ely's manor of Wisbech Barton.[17] This takes us, once again, to the Wash, this time its southern coast. Wisbech Barton produced a sizeable cash surplus for the bishop whilst at the same time helping to supply his household. The range of crops sown, not surprisingly given the location, was similar to Frampton's. A major difference was in terms of livestock. At Wisbech there was a heavy emphasis on sheep breeding, with steady transfer of immature animals to the bishop's manor of Beaudesert which concentrated on the production of wool.

For the 1330s and 1340s the Wisbech accounts allow us to see the monthly distribution of sales of winter-sown crops. What Stone found was that the cheapest grains were sold first: bere between January and March, mixtil between March and May, and wheat between May and July. In other words, the most valuable tended to be held back until the 'hungry gap' preceding the next harvest, when prices were at their highest. However, some wheat could be sold very early on, to test the market. This would influence the amount sown in November and December.[18] This was only one aspect of marketing strategy. The relative prices of the grains affected the amount of each that was sown. For example, when the price of wheat fell during the 1320s and early 1330s there was a shift away from wheat towards mixtil and bere, due to an increase in their price relative to it. Moreover, as mixtil usually produced better yields than wheat, and bere better still, the financial return on these grains could be as good as, if not better than, the return on wheat.[19] Nonetheless, the market was not the only influence. The more stable yields from crop mixtures like mixtil were also a factor, while there

---

[15] Oschinsky (ed.), *Walter of Henley*, clause 21.

[16] Some also recorded investment in buildings, marling, ditching and other improvements. 'In this respect', Postles suggests, 'the memoranda reflect that lords were conscious of the value of investment in their estates, even if the general level . . . was low' ('Perception of profit', 13).

[17] Stone, *Decision-Making*.   [18] Ibid. 49–50.   [19] Ibid. 52–3.

were also environmental fluctuations to be respected. In particularly wet years the reeves attempted to maximize income from spring crops, particularly oats.

Widening out from Wisbech Barton to include other, ecclesiastical, estates, Stone comes to some general conclusions about the standard of demesne farm management: 'The behaviour of medieval farm managers by this reckoning could be sophisticated, rational, and much more 'modern' than historians have previously given them credit for.'[20]

One wonders, then, whether the distinctions between small and large manors has tended to be exaggerated, at least as regards the level of commercialization. In most cases commercial concerns coexisted with traditional ones to a greater or lesser extent. There were certainly many traditional elements in the way gentry lords treated their estates. We have seen for example, the importance of gifts, and indeed of counter gifts. We have seen neighbourliness. It was a social and cultural world in which there were a variety of non-commercial obligations, and where *largesse* or open generosity was highly prized.

If there was a distinction to be made between large and small landowners did it lie more in the area of management? Were the gentry more 'hands on', as it were, especially where the lord was resident? Evidence for this, though never abundant, is relatively less sparse for the fifteenth century.[21] However, the economic climate was by then very different. As far as the pre-1370 period is concerned, one might well wonder whether on gentry estates the reeves really had quite the freedom of action that David Stone envisages. Perhaps when we speak of farm management we should think more in terms of collective decision-making by a small group. How far, for example, were forward decisions made during or immediately after audit? And was the lord himself directly involved? Although we may never get very far in answering these questions, we can at least penetrate the process of audit.

Manorial accounts were 'a record of obligations and their discharge'[22] rather than a balance sheet and were drawn up for the benefit of the landlords—who were often absentees, or at least semi-absentees—whose first concern had to have been whether their officials were acting honestly and efficiently. The accounting official, reeve or bailiff, presented a record of all the items of revenue received, or which should have been received, and of the items that had been bought, received or produced on the manor. This was totalled. He then accounted for the expenditure and for all outgoing items or losses, including consumption on the manor. The balance left was paid over or, in the case of livestock, carried over to the next year. Items were included that were not truly income and

[20] 'Perception of profit', 194–5. Stone points out that the calculations of profit became increasingly common, and there was a tightening up of administration on many estates during the last years of the thirteenth century, reflecting a growing concern with profitability. The explanation for this he sees in the falling prices and rising taxation: ibid. 198–200.
[21] See, for example, the remarks of David Stone: *Decision-Making*, 224–30.
[22] Titow, *English Rural Society*, 25.

others (uncollectable rents, for example) would be written off at the end under 'Allowances'. How did the Multon reeve fare? Robert son of Alexander will have turned up at the Michaelmas accounting in 1326 with considerable evidence of his operation over the year, including many tallies justifying his expenditure. The system worked like this. The tallies were used as receipts, for money or goods. The sums were shown on the tally by means of notches of different widths, depths and intervals according to usage. The tally was split down the middle, allowing both parties to have a record. In addition to the notches that were cut by a knife, the transaction was also explained in ink upon them. They were not, therefore, as was once thought, a substitute for literacy.[23] In fact the system was a quite sophisticated one.

The reeve's account for Frampton in 1326 began with a statement of the arrears from the previous accounting year, that is 17s 10d and an allowance of 19s by tally. When the totals were added up it was found that £30 15s was due and that the reeve owed the lord £4 15s 4¾d. In the margin is added a memorandum that he did not respond, that is account, for several items. However, this was not the whole story. The roll, written, it tells us at one point, by Robert the Clerk, contains many deletions and interlinings. These corrections are made by Robert the Clerk himself, not, or at least not for the most part, because he was working carelessly from a draft and having to make corrections. Occasionally the deletions were because an item was being accounted elsewhere. Interlineations were sometimes for clarification. However, many were substitutions for deleted items. These substitutions tended to be sums that were less than those given in the account. It seems highly likely that they followed from the discussion, or indeed haggling, which took place and this may well have been a downright disagreeable process. For instance, in the expenses in repairing the buildings, 'a carpenter working for four days' was amended to three days and the wages correspondingly reduced from 8d to 6d. The cost of roofing was reduced at one point from 2s 3d to 8d and at another point from 10d to 8d. The 2d claimed for the wages of a roofer's mate was deleted. Under 'minor necessities', a man helping the household in various duties, including daubing, over four days, at a cost of 4d, was deleted—that is, disallowed—as were various purchases amounting to 1s 9d. And so it goes on. The value of the bere sown was reduced from 5s to 4s 2d. One of the sums handed over to the lady, 12s 4d, was disallowed despite the tally which it shared with a previous item. Under the stock account, thirty-five geese remaining was written above thirty-two deleted. An interesting item occurs in the grange account where two quarters, two bushels of mixtil were handed over to Sir Henry the Chaplain for board, presumably for the household, during the periods when the lord was absent. This was from Michaelmas to 13 February,

---

[23] As Michael Clanchy has pointed out, tallies 'were not a primitive survival from the preliterate past, but a sophisticated and practical record of numbers. They were more convenient to keep, less complex to make, and harder to forge': *From Memory to Written Record: England 1066–1307* (London, 1979), 124. Tally sticks are pictured as figure 8.1, with further commentary.

on which day the lord arrived, and from 16 July to 8 September, when he was again away, a total of twenty-seven weeks according to the account. This was at the rate of one quarter per twelve weeks. All of this is deleted in the account and above is written '4$\frac{1}{2}$ bushels [presumably per twelve weeks] is allowed by the lord'. The difference was quite considerable. *En passant* we may note that this tells us when the lord was present at Frampton and when he was not, and that in his absence the household ate bread made from mixtil. In the present context what is suggested is that the accounting took place in two stages, one in which the account was drawn up, probably with just the clerk and the official present, with the tallies and other information, and one where the sums were checked and where necessary amendments were made. The totals below each section of the account must have been added at this stage, a space having been left. Then, or afterwards, someone went through the account and underlined some figures that were thought significant. The impression given is one of thoroughness, especially in terms of checking the honesty of the accounting official.

How did the reeve, or his predecessor[24] fare in the previous year? On this roll there is less in the way of emendation, but the same underlining of some of the sums occurred. The total of all expenses came to £49 16s 9$\frac{1}{2}$d, and the reeve was found to owe £4 4s 2d. However, by the lord's grace he was allowed the 3s 4d from the amercements of Alan Cullul with which he had been charged. He was also pardoned 6s from the farm of Emma Stot from the house in Boston which, by misfortune, had burned down and the farm due from Hugh de Castleford. The latter must have been quite a bit for the total of this came to £3 3s 4d. This still left him in debt. He was then pardoned 3s rent from *Gotelynholm* by the lord, leaving him 17s 10d net in debt. This was indeed the sum in arrears with which the account for 1325–6 opens.

This later roll also contains the account of Alan Thormond, the collector. His responsibility went beyond the collecting of free and bond rents, and farms, to encompass also the collection of tallage and the perquisites of the manor court. The total came to £39 1s 7d. He had to account for his dispersals to the lord and, most particularly, to the lady—no doubt because she was the greater presence during the course of the year—and to the various other officials. He accounted for £33 10s 1$\frac{3}{4}$d. He was found to owe £5 11s 5$\frac{1}{4}$d, of which he had given £1 11s 8d to the lady by tally. He was pardoned a further £2 'by the lord's mandate' from the amercement of Robert son of Alexander, the reeve, and 13s 4d was found to have been received by Thomas de Gower, another official. Two other amercements, which presumably remained uncollected, were waived. Attempts at a new summary were deleted followed by the information that 4s 2d had (since?) been handed over to Robert son of Aleyn and 6s 7d had been pardoned by the lord's precept. He was allowed in total £4 19s 6d. In the end, he owed 11s 11$\frac{1}{4}$d.

---

[24] The name is lost through damage.

Whether the lord himself was present at the audit is unclear. If not he was certainly represented by someone who guarded his interests and had his ear. What is certain from the 'corrections' is that he was involved in some way, either formally or informally, in the proceedings. The process seemed to consist of harshness in the first instance followed by pardons, especially it seems of sums that could not be collected. It could work out, however, that the accounting officer ended up in credit, as did Alan Cullul, the collector, who in 1331 was found to have expended £33 11s 9¾d when his accounts registered that he in fact owed £32 10s 7¾d. The account concludes that the lord owed him £1 1s 2d.

The evidence from the reeves' accounts sits well with the normative texts on estate management produced in the thirteenth century and in wide circulation by the early fourteenth.[25] Walter of Henley warns against pecolation. A reeve or other servant, he tells us, should love and fear his master. When it comes to making a profit he should think of it as though it were his own. When it comes to an expense he should think of it as another man's. However, he says, few actually behave like this. On the contrary, they extort and cover up their unfaithfulness.[26]

The *Seneschaucy* is more specific.[27] For example:

No bushel, half bushel, or cantle should be handed over to the reeve from the threshers over and above the foresaid measure. The heaped measures and the bushels, half bushels, and cantles and any odd amounts which enter the garner without tally or number bring the lord little profit.

No sales of corn and stock should be conducted by bailiff or reeve without warrant by writ . . .

No reeve ought to make an allowance nor permit anybody to have one unless he is entitled to it.

No reeve, on any manor, ought to keep open house and receive visitors at the lord's expense without special warrant by writ . . .

The role of the auditors and the importance of the audit is made clear. Auditors should be loyal, prudent, and experienced. They should know everything relating to accounts. Accounts should be audited at each manor. The auditors should hear the account, becoming aware both of profit and loss and of the quality of each official:

Whenever they have made a profit or caused loss during the year this will be seen through the audit *in a day or two* [my italics]; and it will be easy to recognize good sense and improvements or folly, if such has been committed.

[25] For the texts and commentary, see Oschinsky (ed.), *Walter of Henley*. This work should be used in conjunction with P. D. A. Harvey, 'Agricultural Treatises and Manorial Accounting in Medieval England', *AgHR* (1972), 170–82.

[26] Oschinsky (ed.), *Walter of Henley*, cl. 111–12.

[27] For what follows, see *Seneschaucy* in Oschinsky, (ed.), *Walter of Henley*, cl. 9, 39, 41, 43, 46, 70–6.

The audit, then, could be drawn out and was likely to be a heavy-handed affair. The author of the *Seneschaucy* seems to be assuming that the lord himself is not involved in the routine procedures. How he made his presence felt is difficult to penetrate. However, we must bear in mind that this text was written for estate managers and that it is the great estate that it has constantly in mind. Even so, the *Seneschaucy* makes it perfectly clear that the ultimate responsibility is the lord's own. He should take advice only from experienced quarters and appoint only the right sort of men. He should ensure that the audit is carried out. Moreover he should carry out ad hoc enquiries through his household officials when he arrives at a manor.

Walter of Henley's Husbandry was written after the *Seneschaucy* and by contrast was written for the more modest landowners themselves rather than for their officials.[28] It assumes that the lord, rather than the steward, is supervising his property himself. Even so, it envisages him working through appointed officials. *Walter of Henley* can only take us so far. The question that remains is just how far were knights and other lesser manorial lords involved in the running of the estates, beyond overseeing appointments, making demands for produce and cash, and ensuring that mechanisms were there to see that their estates ran reasonably efficiently and reasonably honestly?

Even on small manors like those studied by Britnell, much of the responsibility both for production and for commercial transactions must have devolved, as he says, upon manorial officers.[29] His study shows that they generally had a serjeant (*serviens*) or occasionally a reeve. On the small Fitz Ralph manor of Pontes the terms were interchangeable. Lionel de Bradenham had one serjeant at Langenhoe and another on his outlying holding at Abberton. The serjeant's duties must have varied according to the manor. At Kelvedon Hall the serjeant had a considerable number of subordinates, including a hayward (*messor*). In cases like this he must have devoted himself to supervision and commercial transactions. On the manor of Pontes, on the other hand, the serjeant also acted as cowman, as shepherd, and at harvest-time as reap-reeve. On small estates, as Britnell suggests, a low level of specialization may well have been common, mirroring what we have seen in the case of gentry households.

At Frampton and at Wyberton we know the names of officials, and sometimes the name given to the office they held. At Wyberton, as previously noted, we hear of Sir Roger the Chaplain, the lord's receiver, and of Sir Roger de Stikeford the lord's dispenser, from whom the accounting official in 1327–8 had received the sum of £1 6s 8d.[30] However, there is mention of a serjeant, and the *curia* contained a serjeant's chamber (*camera servient'*). There is also, as we have seen,

[28] On these issues, see Harvey, 'Agricultural Treatises', 175–6.
[29] Britnell, 'Minor Lords', 7.
[30] Curiously, a note on the outside of the roll and another on the dorse refer to him as the reeve of Wyberton.

a *messor*, a hayward or overseer. Some lords were no doubt more 'hands-on' than others by nature, and one might expect minor landlords to have been more personally concerned with the details of manorial administration than the lords of large estates. It may be indicative that the Cobeldyke manor had a sheep-shearing feast and that the lord was personally involved. In 1328, 6s 1d was spent on ale bought for the lord and others with him at the shearing (*pro domino et aliis secum ad tons[ionem]*): 4s 1d was spent on meat over two days and 5d on pike and other fish for the lord, 'because it was Tuesday', 6d was spent on a gallon of wine and 5d on wheat bread. In addition one pig and five piglets were supplied from stock together with two cheeses weighing one stone and a half stone of butter. The expenses are couched in such a way, however, as to suggest that the lord and his fellows feasted separately from the rest. Perhaps, like Lionel de Bradenham, he was 'able to exercise a close control over the running of the manor'.[31]

It may well be that lords like Thomas de Multon, with multiple estates, preferred to behave like greater lords through a panoply of officials. If they were wise, however, they must have found some way of keeping their finger on the pulse. It has to be admitted that it is extremely hard to enter into gentry perceptions. There is, however, one other avenue open to us, that is the ownership of the books on estate management. The *Rules* of Robert Grosseteste, the first known treatise on estate management, was followed by the *Seneschaucy*, *Walter of Henley's Husbandry*, which was probably written around the 1260s, and the treatise entitled simply *Husbandry* which belongs to the end of the thirteenth century.[32] Although such treatises were written primarily for estate administrators, there are nevertheless indications that secular landowners were among the owners of copies and that they were part of the intended audience when copies of texts were produced. Numerous copies of the *Seneschaucy*, dated from around 1300, were included in legal textbooks. Two copies are especially interesting in this respect.

One was in fact a conflation of the *Seneschaucy* and *Walter of Henley* and is found in a fair copy of a legal compilation known as *Fleta*, written around 1290 by an inmate of Flete prison.[33] What is particularly noteworthy about this text is that it appears to have been adapted to apply to a smaller estate than the one envisaged in the original *Seneschaucy*. It envisages a single steward for household and estate, with a good deal of the estate work devolved onto the shoulders of the bailiff. Moreover, the lord is thought of as an active presence.

The other copy of particular interest is in a large legal textbook of the early fourteenth century which includes a collection of texts concerning estate management. It contains an introduction to the *Seneschaucy* which, together with additional pieces of advice within the text, was probably provided by the compiler

---

[31] Britnell, 'Minor Lords', 7.

[32] I am following P. D. A. Harvey's revision of Oschinsky's dates, in 'Agricultural treatises'.

[33] For the manuscript see Oschinsky (ed.), *Walter of Henley*, 20, and references given there, and for a fuller discussion, 99–106.

himself.[34] The former addresses secular lords. It tells us that the treatise is one of
instruction for stewards of noble men to the great advantage of lords and to the
great profit of their manors. It goes on to say that a lord who pays attention to
these things will be one of high reputation, a *prudome*, and live his life honestly
without wronging others. It is not without interest that this uses language that
we encounter in chivalric literature, i.e. a man of great worth (*grand preu*), a
prudome.[35]

The author is considered to have been one John de Longueville of Northampton, on the basis of annotations to the copy of the legal treatise known as *Britton*
within the same manuscript. Unfortunately, the identity of this man is uncertain.
The editor of *Britton* identifies him as John de Longueville, burgess and MP for
Northampton in the later years of Edward I's reign, and conflates the evidence
for this man with that for Sir John de Longueville who was MP for the county of
Northampton. This Sir John was a justice of assize, oyer and terminer, and gaol
delivery in the following reign, as well as a collector of parliamentary subsidies,
commissioner of array, and one of the justices who was assigned to investigate
the conduct of sheriffs and other officers of the crown in 1323–4. He tentatively
identified him as Sir John of Orton Longueville in Huntingdonshire, who was
listed as a banneret in the *Parliamentary Roll of Arms* of *c*.1308.[36] Oschinsky
accepted this identification and considered the compiler of this manuscript to
have been John of Longueville, 'an eminent Northampton lawyer who lived
during the late thirteenth and early fourteenth centuries'.[37] However, this John
de Longueville, burgess, who was also a lawyer and a knight, is a myth.[38] The
most likely candidate for the compiler was Sir John de Longueville lord of
Little Billing, a settlement in close proximity to Northampton. It was he, and
not Sir John of Orton Longueville, who held the judicial commissions during
the reign of Edward II.[39] The evidence strongly suggests, then, that the John
de Longueville who owned and annotated the manuscript was a landowner
with a strong interest in the law, and perhaps some legal training. The contents of the manuscript are appropriate to a lawyer/administrator, but also to

[34] This manuscript is discussed by Oschinsky on pages 24–5.   [35] Ibid. 297.
[36] F. M. Nichols (ed.), *Britton*, 2 vols (Oxford, 1865; repr. Holmes Beach, 1983), lxi–ii.
[37] Oschinsky (ed.), *Walter of Henley*, 24.
[38] There is no evidence that the burgess, John de Longueville, was a lawyer. In fact, his attendance
at a convention of merchants in 1303 suggests a rather different career (*VCH Northamptonshire*,
iii. 8). The identification of this John as the compiler of the manuscript rests primarily on the fact
that the manuscript contains a fragment of a custumal of Northampton. However, as we have seen,
the contents of the manuscript, if they point us in the direction of a lawyer, also suggest someone
with a strong interest in a rural estate.
[39] Sir John de Longueville of Huntingdonshire died in 1316 (*VCH Huntingdonshire*, iii. 191).
Sir John of Little Billing, on the other hand, held his land from at least as early as 1301and died
around 1325. An active county knight, he was also associated with the city of Northampton in that
he gave land and rent at Little Billing to the hospital of St John there in 1299. His son George,
moreover, gave a messuage to the Austin Friary there in 1323. It may well be, of course, that all of
these men were related.

an active county knight interested in both his estate and in the operation of the law.

A figure similar to Sir John de Longueville was John de Solers of Dorstone in Herefordshire. He owned a manuscript which contained, in addition to the great legal treatise known as *Bracton*, a copy of *Walter of Henley's Husbandry*.[40] Indeed, it may have been owned previously by his uncle or grandfather, Henry de Solers, who held the manor of Dorstone in 1303 when John was holding Postlip in Winchcombe, Gloucestershire.[41] Henry had been against the crown in 1265, had been sheriff of Herefordshire in 1291–3 and had been called for military action against the Scots in 1297. Around 1312 he conveyed his estates to John de Solers, at which point he may also have given him his books. By this time what had originally been two separate 'books' in the form of loose quires appear to have been put together. John de Solers was a tax collector in Herefordshire and Gloucestershire in 1313 and 1319, and a commissioner for array for Gloucestershire in 1322. The manuscript was used as a notebook by John de Solers, and perhaps by Henry before him, into which were written transcripts of family deeds and related matters. At the bottom of folio 10r was added the accounts of the tax collectors of 1313–14 for Gloucestershire (Nicholas de Kingeston and John de Solers) and of those for Herefordshire for 1320–1 (John de Barewe and John de Solers). John also wrote a line against Piers Gaveston and his accomplices and partisans. One should be wary of assuming that Henry and John were the compilers of these texts as opposed to the owners, and only John's ownership and insertion of extraneous matter is beyond doubt.[42] Even if we take a minimalist position on this, however, the fact that men like John de Solers and John de Longueville owned manuscripts containing, amongst other things, treatises on estate management raises the possibility, indeed the probability, that there existed lay landowners whose interests in their estates went beyond the intermittent supervision of their officials.

There were no doubt landowners whose sense of the viability of their estates hardly went beyond the intuitive, making them dependent upon the expertise and honesty of others. It was felt by at least some contemporaries, however, that careless landowners were themselves blameworthy. In 1300 John de Barham reported to the king on the lands of the late Earl of Hereford in south Wales:

There is a very fine and great lordship in those places, and, if well managed, they would be worth not less than 2,000 marks a year, but there have been bad and disloyal stewards and bailiffs, and the earl was lax.[43]

---

[40] For a discussion of this manuscript, see Oschinsky (ed.), *Walter of Henley*, 25–8. See also the astute comments by Paul Brand, *The Earliest English Law Reports*, vols 1 and 2, Seldon Society (London, 1996), xxviii–xxxiv.

[41] *Feudal Aids*, ii. 295, 380.

[42] Paul Brand considers that the only certain owner was John de Solers and that neither he nor his predecessor compiled the texts (*Earliest English Law Reports*, xxxiii).

[43] See *CIM* i. no. 1870.

Consumption needs were, of course, of vital importance, but landowners in general, or at least their officials, required a degree of commercial sense if manors were to be run successfully. Although the search for agrarian capitalism in this period has tended to muddy the waters and there was no new spirit of enterprise enveloping the smaller landowners, it remains likely that some of the gentry were interested in estate management and even in farming techniques. We know well enough from later centuries that direct interest in such matters was extremely variable amongst members of the gentry but that some developed a fascination, even a passion for it. If, in the early to mid-fourteenth century, the majority were operating at one remove from the running of their estates, this passion may already have existed amongst some of them, at least in embryonic form.

7

Human Resources
The Lord and His Tenants

The household was the principal locus of gentry consumption, the manor that of production. They were of course closely linked, with the one largely dependent upon the other. In the previous chapters we have glimpsed some of the constant interaction that took place between the two. So far, however, we have said very little about the gentry's relationships with their tenants. It is to this subject that we must now turn. In the famous *bas de page* scenes of the Luttrell Psalter the labour in the fields is anterior to the depiction of the household; justly so, for the household could not exist without it. The manner in which the agrarian scenes are presented in the psalter gives rise to two observations.

The first is that, as Michael Camille pointed out, they de-emphasize the land in favour of the depiction of the peasants and their activities.[1] We can be sure that this was felt to be of great significance not only by Sir Geoffrey but also by his contemporaries. Lordship of men had traditionally been considered to be as important, if not more important, than lordship over land. When, in the fifteenth century, the Pastons wanted to prove that they were gentle and of 'worshipful blood', the first thing they stressed was that they had possessed a court and 'many and sundry bondmen' since time immemorial.[2] Even though serfdom was in sure and rapid decline in the fifteenth century, tenants, and in particular unfree tenants, still had considerable significance in terms of the meaning of lordship. The significance must have been so much greater in the early fourteenth century.

The second observation is that the psalter paints a picture of deep social harmony at Irnham under the benign lordship of Sir Geoffrey Luttrell. It also indicates that lordship was considered as natural and, indeed, divinely sanctioned. The peaceful harvest is made possible through the blessing of the Lord and under the earthly good lordship of Sir Geoffrey Luttrell. The content of the psalms that figure at this point, the Luttrell arms in the margin and the harvest scenes all

[1] Camille, *Mirror in Parchment*, 180–1.
[2] I discuss this in more detail in *The Knight in Medieval England 1000–1400* (Stroud, 1993), ch. 1.

point to a close interconnection between divine lordship, on the one hand, and the power and protection provided by the secular lord on the other. What we have, as Camille neatly puts it, is 'a vivid portrayal of the customary labours on a fourteenth-century manor, that sought to cement social hierarchies and idealize feudal obligations'.[3]

Once again, the Luttrell Psalter is shown to be ideologically charged. Having said that, can we get any closer to the real relationship between the gentry and their tenants? What was the situation like, as it were, on the ground? For our period we lack the gentry correspondence of later ages which yields direct insights into what people actually felt and thought. Nevertheless, it is worth looking first at the experience of their descendants in the succeeding centuries because it does furnish us with some clues.

When, in the sixteenth and seventeenth centuries, members of the gentry sought to benefit from the rising prices and the greatly expanded market opportunities of their day by engrossing land and by introducing technological improvements, they tended to find themselves in contention with paternalistic values that were considered traditional. These values were hammered into them through the family 'advice literature' of the period and reinforced from the pulpit.[4] At the same time, however, proactive estate management was also prized. It has been observed of this period that although 'managerial technique is ultimately a matter of individual aptitude and character' two groups among the gentry were especially prone to exploit their estates to the full, namely 'newcomers' and those who were financially embarrassed.[5] The resulting tension was often considerable, and many landowners seem to have paid little more than lip service to tradition. Others, no doubt, were genuinely affected by it.

It is worth asking, however, how old these paternalistic values actually were. They seem to have been there in the fifteenth century. In 1465 John Paston I wrote to his wife, Margaret, emphasizing that 'ye be a gentilwoman and it is worshep for yow to confort yowr tenantis'.[6] However, the context of this needs to be understood. The Pastons faced rival claimants to some of their estates. Moreover, these were particular circumstances in particular times, when the landlord–tenant relationship was especially fragile. Colin Richmond may well be right, however, in detecting in Margaret some genuine compassion for her tenants, especially those of her ancestral manor of Mautby which she brought to her Paston marriage. The Paston contemporary, John Hopton,

[3] Camille, *Mirror in Parchment*, 209.
[4] See the examples given by Felicity Heal and Clive Holmes, *The Gentry in England and Wales 1500–1700* (London, 1994), 102.
[5] Ibid. 114.
[6] For the Paston evidence see, for example, Davis, *Paston Letters and Papers, I,* nos. 73, 178, 210, and Colin Richmond, 'Landlord and Tenant: the Paston Evidence', in J. Kermode (ed.), *Enterprise and Individuals in Fifteenth-Century England* (Stroud, 1991), 36.

was prone to pardon his tenants' fines on grounds of their poverty.[7] One is left to wonder just how rare, or how common, such compassion had been, and how often it was encountered in our period when the land was teeming with people and would-be tenants, that is before the Black Death of 1348–9.

What had intervened was a series of savage plagues and their momentous consequences. The generation that followed 1348 witnessed considerable tension between lord and tenants. The latter sought to maximize the advantages that their new bargaining power had given them by the drastic and continuing fall in population. Tenants and estate workers were increasingly at a premium. Landlords responded individually in various ways to bolster their regimes, the so-called 'feudal reaction',[8] while national legislation empowered local justices to hold down wages to pre-Black Death levels and put the brakes on peasant mobility, measures deliberately designed to prevent people seeking better conditions. The justices of labourers tended to be members of the gentry, putting them into direct conflict with labourers. Little wonder that the poet, William Langland, counselled landlords, during the 1360s, not to vex their tenants. 'Let mercy be the taxer', he wrote, and warned of the consequences for the vexatious lord in terms of the perils of purgatory. How far Langland's strictures can be seen as relating to the 'normal' world of pre-1348 is a moot point. His warnings were certainly prescient, as the world of labour laws and truculent peasants was soon to experience a major revolt: the Peasants' Revolt of 1381.[9] Meanwhile problems were stacking up that would spell the doom of the old agrarian regime. Falling prices from the mid-1370s and increasing wages put landlords in the famous price scissors which led to the gradual abandonment of direct demesne farming in favour of leasing, while serfdom, in the wake of peasant revolt and the foregoing economic changes, was to wither away. These changes are outside of the time frame of the current book. Nonetheless, evidence from succeeding periods provides some clues as to how we might read evidence from the pre-plague period. Against the version of reality depicted in the Luttrell Psalter, we have sporadic evidence of peasants being chastised for their failure to show the necessary deference.[10] We also have the evidence of disputes between lords and

---

[7] Colin Richmond, *John Hopton: A Fifteenth Century Suffolk Gentleman* (Cambridge, 1981), 47.

[8] See, for example, R. H. Britnell, 'Feudal Reaction After the Black Death in the Palatinate of Durham', *Past and Present* 128 (1990), 28–47. See also John Hatcher, 'England in the Aftermath of the Black Death', *Past and Present* 144 (1994), 3–35.

[9] For the origins of the revolt, see, especially, R. H. Hilton, *Bondmen Made Free: Medieval Peasant Movements and the English Rising of 1381* (London, 1973); and Christopher Dyer, 'The Social and Economic Background to the Rural Revolt of 1381', in R. H. Hilton and T. H. Aston (eds), *The English Rising of 1381* (Cambridge, 1984), 9–42, repr. in Christopher Dyer, *Everyday Life in Medieval England* (London, 2000), 191–219.

[10] See the references in Coss, 'An Age of Deference', in Rosemary Horrox and W. Mark Ormrod (eds), *A Social History of England, 1200–1500* (Cambridge, 2006), 38–9. The examples come from ecclesiastical estates, but they are nonetheless indicative.

tenants across the thirteenth and fourteenth centuries.[11] At the same time the
divine sanction and the peaceful relations depicted in the psalter are not so far
removed from the God-fearing paternalism espoused in early modern England
and this may have some bearing on how we interpret the pre-plague reality.

How then should the historian trying to understand the relations between
gentry and peasants in our period proceed? One avenue of approach is through
the normative legal literature of the age, which presumably must have had some
impact not only upon landlord–peasant relations but also upon the gentry's actual
perceptions of their tenants. Under the common law of villeinage, customary
tenants were consigned to the jurisdiction of their lords, and denied access to
public courts, virtually assimilating them with the descendants of slaves. The
terms villein (*villanus*, inhabitant of a township or vill) and bondman, neif or serf
(*nativus*) became essentially interchangeable. The legal texts list the numerous
disabilities which the unfree suffered as a consequence of their condition. The
greatest expression of this subordination is that a lord could sell his serfs singly,
as well as part and parcel of an estate. Either way, they were sold with their
goods, chattels, and offspring. Nothing can convey the social gulf between lord
and serf more clearly than this. As the legal historian F. W. Maitland pointed
out, the same Latin word (*sequela*) was used in the documents for the offspring
of both cattle and unfree tenants.[12] One might also invoke courtly literature,
which differentiates between noble men and women, who were generally capable
of refined behaviour, and peasants, of whatever status, who were not. Hence
our terms villain and villainy (from *villein*) and churlish and boorish (from old
English *ceorl* and *gebur*). All of this must have had some impact upon the world
of the gentle and the would-be gentle, with their social aspirations and their
exclusive manners.

In reality all of this was tempered by practical considerations. We know,
for example, that many of the disabilities outlined in the normative texts
were tempered by need, by custom, and by peasant resistance. There was, for
example, a great deal more certainty in peasant lives than the normative texts
allow. Their labour services were generally fixed by custom. Even the annual
payment of tallage, theoretically at the will of the lord, was in reality a fixed
render. Moreover, lords can hardly have regarded their serfs as some sort of
separate or sub-species when in practice they were indistinguishable from free
tenants. Furthermore, tenure and status did not necessarily coincide. In the
land-hungry thirteenth century it became increasingly common for free men
to take on unfree tenures. Equally, out in the countryside, the precepts of
courtly literature can hardly have been taken entirely at face value. Wider

[11] The *locus classicus* here is R. H. Hilton, 'Peasant Movements in England Before 1381', *EcHR*
2nd ser. Ii (1940), 117–36. Hilton's findings have been much amplified since, by himself and by
other scholars.
[12] F. Pollock and F. W. Maitland, *The History of English Law*, 2 vols (Cambridge, 1895; repr.
1968), I. 380–1.

evidence suggests a much more complex situation and hence more nuanced perceptions.

At the same time the inherent antagonism in landlord–tenant relationships should not be too readily cast aside. It was closely integrated into the manorial economy, with labour partly provided by the services of the peasants. Lords were extracting income from their peasants in a whole variety of ways. Consequently, the relationship was in large measure one of coercion. This can be shown analytically. There was no necessary reason, from their point of view, why peasants should yield a proportion of their surplus to the lords. The antagonism can also be seen in the sporadic resistance that we witness in court records. This resistance has a direct bearing on the observation by some recent historians that lords failed to extract as much from their peasants as might have been expected, given the apparatus of coercion. Significant in this respect is the comment by C. C. Dyer that lords in the thirteenth and fourteenth centuries 'often appear to have treated their tenants gingerly'. The same historian, however, is insistent that lordship cannot be regarded as benevolent.[13]

Faute de mieux we have no choice but to approach the issue of gentry–tenant relations through the institution of the manor court, the primary instrument of local social control, even though in doing so we may risk putting too much emphasis upon the coercive components of the relationship. Manors were extremely variable, and many factors influenced the level of seigniorial control over the tenants. In order to understand a gentry family's situation apropos their tenants we have to place their manors in their local context. With this observation in mind, let us return to the Multons of Frampton. They had a considerable number of both free and unfree tenants in and around the three settlements of Frampton, Kirton, and Wyberton. As we have seen all three of these were populous and prosperous communities and all three had multiple lords.

Once again, we are fortunate in the survival of documents. A series of Frampton manor court rolls survives for the years 1330–2. The court was held at three-weekly intervals. It was quite lucrative to the lord, although the income was extremely variable, ranging from £1 6s 3d from the court held in July 1331 to only 3d from the court held in the previous May. The total from sixteen courts held during the complete year 1330–1 comes to £4 11s 9d, beginning with the great court held on 8 October 1330 and ending with the court of 10 September 1331.[14] The income was also variable from year to year. For 1325–6 the collector, Alan Thormond, had accounted for £13 10s 8d from ten courts. The sum is considerably higher than in 1330–1, although the number of courts is fewer. Without court rolls for the 1320s it is impossible to know why the sums

---

[13] Christopher Dyer, 'The Ineffectiveness of Lordship in England, 1200–1400' in Christopher Dyer, Peter Coss, and Chris Wickham (eds), *Rodney Hilton's Middle Ages: An Exploration of Historical Themes* (Oxford, 2007) 69–86, at 79 and 85.

[14] The Collector's Account for 1330–1 contains £3 9s 10d from perquisites of the court, plus 7s 5d from the relief of Lawrence Illory, making £3 17s 3d. (Multon Adds 9.)

from 1325–6 were so high. The most likely explanation is that the court was exacting money that had not been gathered during the last years of the lord's minority. Around £5 per annum was perhaps the normal annual yield from Sir Thomas de Multon's court.[15] The court, although it dealt with tenants at Frampton, Kirton, Wyberton, and elsewhere, was invariably held at Frampton, almost certainly in the hall of the manor. It was clearly quite a flourishing court, unsurprisingly given the high number of tenants.[16] From where precisely did this income come?

The short answer is largely from 'fines' and 'amercements', that is to say in modern terminology fees or licences on the one hand and imposed fines on the other. The courts were used to enforce the lord's rights vis-à-vis his tenants. They were also used for cases between tenants, both free and unfree, so that we find cases for debt, trespass, damage, and defamation.[17] The Multons' court had a further dimension to its power, in that the lord had view of frankpledge. This was a matter of delegated public authority, which allowed the lord to ensure that peasants properly belonged to the mutual security system centred on the (normally) ten-man tithings. The payments involved, which normally accrued to the sheriff, now went to the lord. It also meant that the court dealt with minor offences against the public order which were not matters for the ordinary manor court, e.g. minor acts of violence that led to the shedding of blood, the policing of the hue and cry, and obstructions to public utilities such as highways and ditches. Such matters were dealt with by the same manor court wearing, as it were, a different hat, at Michaelmas and sometimes at Easter too. Some lords had received royal grants of the view of frankpledge, many others had usurped it during the thirteenth century. Often associated with it was the assize of bread and ale, which allowed lords to regulate the price, the quality and, indeed, the measures used by bakers and brewers, and to punish those who did not comply. In reality, they were using this to charge retailers a licence fee to operate. Strictly speaking this was a separate franchise and could function without view of frankpledge.[18]

Two of the recorded Multon courts were frankpledge courts, namely those held on 8 October 1330 and 3 October 1331. We find in the rolls items that we

[15] In 1324–5, the first year of Sir Thomas de Multon's tenure, the court had yielded £5 7s 5d.
[16] A recent study of the yield from seigniorial courts from the *Inquisitions Post Mortem* of the first half of the fourteenth century shows that three-quarters of all courts were worth less than £1 per annum and that the mean was 16s. Only one in twenty yielded £5 or more per year: Campbell and Bartley, *England on the Eve of the Black Death*, 269–75.
[17] See Mark Bailey (ed.), *The English Manor c. 1200–c. 1500* (Manchester, 2002), 168–170; chapter 4 of this work gives a good general introduction to the subject, together with an excellent bibliography.
[18] Another franchise was free warren which gave the lord the exclusive right to hunt minor animals on his land and to punish poachers, who were almost always their tenants. See, for example, the court rolls of Walsham le Willows: Ray Lock (ed.), *The Court Rolls of Walsham le Willows 1303–50* (Woodbridge, 1998). The Multons, however, did not have free warren, at least not at Frampton.

would expect to find at this level of court, including amercements arising out of the hue and cry and for the shedding of blood. There were also amercements for infringing the assize of ale, although the assize of bread does not figure. These were lucrative additions and enhanced the value of the court both in terms of income and of social control. Curiously, there is no mention of view of frankpledge itself in the surviving court rolls, despite the headings specifically calling it a franchise court. Perhaps the annual payments due under this heading were taken outside of the court by the collector, whom we know organized the annual payment of the tallage due to the lord from his unfree tenants. It is important to note that the recorded annual income from the court is minus these matters.

In addition to being able to calculate the income from the Frampton court, we can also use the rolls to understand something of the relationship between lord and peasant.

We will concentrate for the moment on the unfree tenants. The serfs or *nativi*, who were personally unfree, were obliged to attend the court by reason of their tenure. Indeed, they would be amerced if they failed to do so. Just as they were obliged to attend the lord's court, so they were equally obliged to do labour services on the lord's demesne. As we have seen, the reeves' accounts afford us a glimpse of what this meant in practice.[19] The labour services amounted to seasonal work only, including harvest boon services, but not week work throughout the year. They did ploughing, harrowing, weeding, mowing, carrying of both hay and corn, and of course reaping. In addition, eight of the customary tenants were obliged to help to cover the stacks of beans and forty-six tenants carried turves from the marsh. How onerous these were within the overall peasant economy is arguable,[20] but there is good reason to think that they were not always performed with the best will. One of the seasonal services at Frampton was certainly resisted. At the court held on 29 October 1330, more than a dozen tenants were amerced for their failure to perform the service of carting the lord's beans as they were obliged to do.[21] At the court held on 10 December 1330, five more tenants were amerced for the same offence. As the issue did not surface the following autumn it would seem that either these peasants had knuckled under or that the lord had backed down. It may be that the lord had been trying to extend the service of carrying of corn to apply to beans.[22] There is no mention of the carrying of beans in the account rolls.

Another bone of contention that had featured in the court rolls was the obligatory use of the lord's mill for grinding the tenants' corn. On 8 July 1331,

[19] See above, Chapter 5.
[20] For the strongest argument that villein tenants were often better off than their free counterparts see John Hatcher, 'English serfdom and villeinage: towards a reassessment', *Past and Present* 90 (1981).
[21] The amercements were 3d, 6d, or 9d according to whether a half day, the standard day, or one-and-a-half days' work was due.
[22] I owe this suggestion to Barbara Harvey.

four tenants were fined for having withdrawn suit from the mill, i.e. they had refused to take their corn to be ground there and pay the multure fee, the fraction of grain (one-sixteenth or whatever was the custom) charged at the mill, the remainder being received back as flour. Another tenant was similarly fined at the following court. Meanwhile, however, Reginald Buckle, who was similarly charged, claimed that neither he nor his predecessors had ever milled there. The case was put in respite until the lord could be consulted. Most of those who owed suit of mill across the country were undoubtedly unfree. However, it has been suggested recently that suit was a matter of custom rather than tenure, and that other tenants were drawn in. One owed suit if one's ancestors had done so in the past.[23] The case of Reginald Buckle suggests that this might have been what was at issue here.[24] The mill was a useful addition to seigniorial income, and from the lord's perspective his right to suit was well worth preserving.[25]

Much of the manor court's business was directly concerned with the peasant tenements. The extent of 1326, after giving the value of free and then customary rents, contains a statement to the effect that 10s 8d of rent had newly accrued from thirty-one acres of land 'which various bondmen (*nativi*) of the manor acquired in fee from various free tenants'. These acquisitions may have been ratified in court by license of the lord. On the other hand, they may reflect the development of an unregulated land market during the wardship of the estate. By the early fourteenth century a peasant land market had long been in existence and had long involved both free and unfree land.[26] By and large, landlords seem to have been concerned not so much to prevent their unfree tenants from exchanging, leasing, or even buying and selling land but rather to control and profit by it. Vigilance varied, but it clearly applied to gentry as much as to other lords. An undated, and indeed untitled, document in the Multon collection, but which undoubtedly dates from around 1324–6, sheds further light on the situation at the beginning of Sir Thomas's tenure.[27] It contains four memoranda of matters to be inquired into concerning the conveyancing of land by *nativi*. This involved the leasing or selling of parcels of land to free men. These parcels

---

[23] See John Langdon, *Mills in the Medieval Economy* (Oxford, 2004), 275–8.

[24] There is nothing to suggest that Reginald was an unfree tenant.

[25] As we have seen, the Multon mill was a windmill. The evidence of the *Inquisitions Post Mortem* indicates that the average windmill brought in a net income of just under £1, although there was a tendency to under-valuation: Campbell and Bartley, *England on the Eve of the Black Death*, 280. The extent of 1326 values the Multon mill at £1 6s 8d.

[26] The most important studies are M. M. Postan's introduction to *Cartae Nativorum*, ed. C. N. L. Brooke and M. M. Postan, Northamptonshire Record Society no. 20 (1960), ch. 2, 'The Charters of the Villeins', and P. D. A. Harvey (ed.), *The Peasant Land Market in Medieval England* (Oxford, 1984), especially the editor's introduction and conclusion. See also P. R. Hyams, *King, Lords and Peasants in Medieval England* (Oxford, 1980), ch. 5. For a recent, and broader, discussion of peasants and land, see Phillip R. Schofield, *Peasant and Community in Medieval England 1200–1500* (Basingstoke, 2003), part I.

[27] Multon Hall 128/11.

could then go through several hands and the services due from them would be lost.[28] It appears that during the time of Thomas de Multon of Frampton's long wardship a land market had developed, as a result of which unfree land held by Multon tenants who were also personally unfree had been passing into the hands of free men. It was vital to the interests of the lords that they should reassert control. Presumably, as with the newly accrued rent noted in the extent, these 'discussions' resulted in an increase in income for Thomas de Multon. But it was equally important for him to exercise control over the activities of his bond tenants. Otherwise the integrity of the tenements, and most particularly the services due from them, could have been compromised. The Multon court rolls show the continual need for vigilance in keeping track of tenancies. This must have been a particular problem in an area such as this, with so many small tenancies, so many free tenants, a thriving land market and the intermingling of lordships. Free men entering the manor was a particular problem. When it was found at the great courts of October 1330 and October 1331 that unfree tenants had conveyed land to free men without licence, they were fined and the land taken into the lord's hands. This is not to say that there was an absolute ban on this sort of transaction, but only that it should be regulated. There was no problem when the transaction was done legitimately.

All demises, in fact, needed to be licensed and thereby recorded. There are many cases of licensed demise, most of them involving small pieces of land. Even direct exchanges of land needed to be licensed.[29] The lord, of course, profited from regulating these transactions, generally known as 'surrender and admission'. What passed between the tenants in terms of money was not the court's concern, as long as the lord received his fine. What was especially important was that the lord's own rents should be safeguarded. The question was who, in contemporary parlance, was to perform the services? Consequently this tended to be stipulated when the transaction was licensed.

As far as the unfree tenants were concerned, it was a restrictive regime. And it was one from which it was difficult to escape. It was presented, for example, at the great court of October 1330 that three *nativi* of the lord had withdrawn themselves from the lord's fee, i.e. left the manor, and they were therefore in mercy (supposing of course that they could be found). And then there was the licence for marrying one's daughter. Known as merchet, this was one of the common law's tests of villeinage. It was regulated by custom. At Frampton it appears to have been due only if a daughter married a free man or married outside of the fee.

The unfree tenants could be called upon to hold office. At the great court held in October 1330 'the homage' presented Alan Thormond or Geoffrey Elryk to

---

[28] Two of the tenants concerned were said to be *nativi* of Sir Thomas de Multon and Sir Thomas de Kirton jointly.

[29] Nicholas son of Robert Pinder exchanged land with his son, Thomas, but they still had to pay a fine of 1s.

the office of reeve at the lord's will and Walter[30] son of William or Robert son of Robert Gardener or John son of Robert Gardener to the office of collector. Presumably the lord chose from the names on offer. In the latter case we know the upshot, for on 26 March 1331 Robert Gardener accepted the office and took his oath to perform faithfully and efficiently. However, de did not function for long. At the great court on 3 October 1331 Alan ad Pontem junior was made collector and took his oath.[31] The unfree tenants could be called upon to perform other, more ad hoc, duties too. On 7 May 1331 six of them were sworn to make a survey of the land of the lord's *nativi* in Wyberton (that is, literally, to measure it) and report back to the next court. One of them was Alan ad Pontem. Another was Reginald Bishop whom we have met in an earlier chapter as the lord's stockman.

There are a few cases which take us a little further in terms of the relations between lord and tenant and the effect on the tenants' lives. On 5 December 1331 it was presented that Thomas Henery, *nativus* of the lord, had died. His tenements were taken into the lord's hands, pending an inquiry into the services he owed. The four sons who were his heirs came into court and paid a fine. The two who were of age also swore fealty. The other two were minors and therefore did not. They and their tenements were handed to their mother, who was to look after them and render account when the time came, presumably to the court. In another case it was a male relative who rendered account. The custom seems to have been, therefore, that an under-age heir and his property was looked after by a male or female relative.

This entry relating to the late Thomas Henery shows a joint inheritance system at work which had increased the number of tenants rather than the number of formal holdings. It also shows that the unfree tenants swore fealty and that they did so in court. As the lord was demonstrably not present in court it was not sworn directly to him, but presumably to the official holding the court. At the manor of Cuxham, where the warden of Merton College presided, we have a full statement of the conditions of tenure of the free and unfree tenants recorded in the year 1329. Under the heading *fidelitates nativorum* we are told that they *make fealty* and acknowledge that they hold specified property of the lord in bondage for specified rent and services and three-weekly suit of court.[32] The clauses are, of course, essentially formulaic and they are repeated in the court rolls as individuals take on their tenure. The same *formule* occur on the Multon court rolls.

---

[30] The roll says William, but it probably an error for Walter son of William who appears elsewhere.
[31] The collector's responsibilities were wide and included not only collecting rents but also tallage and the fines from the lord's court. Oddly, the collector who finally accounted for the lord's rents for 1330–1 was Alan Cullul: Multon Adds 9. Either Robert Gardener had been superseded or he held a subordinate office.
[32] P. D. A. Harvey, *Manorial Records of Cuxham*, 657.

We learn more about the Multon serfs from a document that was drawn up barely a generation later, *c*.1340. This is an 'arrentation' of the services due from the *nativi* that was undertaken in the time when Sir Henry Hillary was guardian (*custos*) of the young John de Multon.[33] As guardian Sir Henry appears to have been holding some, if not all, of the Multon property during John's minority, from *c*.1337 to 1343.[34] The 'arrentation' gave a money value for each labour service or 'work', allowing them to be sold back to the tenants for cash or, indeed, commuted into rent on a longer term basis. Reluctance on the part of the unfree tenants to perform the services may well have been a factor in this decision. Given also the customary outlay on meals, it may also have been considered more economical for the lords to hire the necessary labour. Hired labour was still relatively plentiful on the eve of the Black Death and was in any case already employed on the Multon manor for other tasks, such as threshing. This document, entitled 'good evidence for the works of the *nativi*', can be used by the historian as in effect a 'custumal', informing us of the range of services owed by the unfree tenants before their 'arrentation'.

Twenty tenancies in all are named. There were 14 standard units of four acres each, and a total of eleven multiples, making 25 four-acre units in all. Moreover, the fourteen-acre tenement held by the heirs of Gilbert the Cook may well have comprised a further multiple tenancy of twelve acres together with two additional acres, perhaps of assart. This would mean that there had once been (notionally if not actually) a total of 28 standard units, plus three additional acres, two now held by the heirs of Gilbert the Cook and one held as a separate tenancy by Reginald Loveless. If we leave out of account for the moment not only the Cook and Loveless but also the Thormond and Dereboght tenancies, which were held on favourable terms, the following services were due. From each of the 24 four-acre units we have one person working from the beginning of weeding to the end of harvest, and we have twenty-four man days of ploughing and twenty-four man days of harrowing twice yearly, plus twenty-four men carrying three cartloads of hay each and carrying corn for one-and-a-half days. In addition, when it is required, men would be called upon to wash and sheer sheep.

The remainder of the services, strictly speaking, related to the household rather than the estates, i.e. twenty-four men carried two cartloads of turf each (from the marshes as an account roll points out), which were presumably required largely for domestic fuel, and, most interestingly, twenty-four men dealt with the roofing and with carrying timber and roofing materials for the *curia*. For each item of service the number of repasts that the tenant is entitled to is carefully stipulated. Three tenancies, however, were held on favourable terms. The heirs of Henry

---

[33] Multon 165/30. This is a booklet comprising 16 leaves of paper, and unbound. It was written in the early fifteenth century but consists in large part of rentals of mid-fourteenth-century date. Sir Henry was not, however, *custos* of the manor in the sense that Walter Gower had been in 1331. Henry was a knight and *custos* here means guardian.

[34] See below 198-9.

Dereboght perform only half the service. One strongly suspects that Henry or his forebears had performed the entire service. Alan Thormond was required for harrowing, mowing, reaping, and the carrying of turves, taking the number involved in these activities up to twenty-five. However, he was exempted from ploughing or any of the other labour services. Again this was almost certainly a recent concession. The Cook tenancy was required to do the carting of hay and turves. In addition, however, it supplied three women with sickles for a day in the autumn, boosting as it were the harvest boon services. Also outside of the norm were the services owed by Reginald Loveless for his one-acre tenement. He was required to find a woman to work in the fields from the beginning of weeding until the end of harvest, in what appears to have been a relatively heavy burden, although he paid no money rent. The acre held by Reginald was most probably a relatively recent tenancy, as were the extra acres held by the heirs of Gilbert the Cook.

The following observations can be made. The first, with the court rolls in mind, is that there is no mention in the 'custumal' of the carrying of beans that had caused such contention in 1330. This would seem to reinforce the suggestion that the lord had attempted to impose an extra burden beyond custom, ultimately unsuccessfully. It underlines the fact that manorial customs were not static in practice but represented a certain amount of negotiation between the peasant community and the lord. It is surely indicative that the number of peasants fined for not carting in 1330 amounted to no less than seventeen (plus the heirs of Thomas Randolf), representing the great majority of the unfree tenements. These tenants constituted only part of the village of Frampton. Nonetheless, they appear to have a constituted a 'community', at least in the sense that they could resist their lord collectively. A second observation is the connected one that the customary obligation on the part of the lord to provide food and ale was vital to the continuance of the entire operation. Any attempt to introduce 'dry' or 'hungry' boons would undoubtedly have led to heavy resistance and the breakdown of the system.[35]

A third observation concerns the role of women. In his famous study of the Luttrell Psalter, Michael Camille highlighted the fact that the artist's depiction of the harvest shows three reapers with sickles, all of whom are women.[36] One of them is patently suffering from backache. This depiction is strikingly unusual. In his essay on harvest work Michael Roberts examined ninety-four visual representations of reaping and found that only one other (from twelfth-century Germany) from before 1400 showed women reapers. With this and the evidence from manorial accounts he concluded that reaping as such was 'man's labour'.[37]

---

[35] For dry and hungry boons, see H. S. Bennett, *Life on the English Manor* (Cambridge, 1937; repr. 1969), 19, 111.

[36] *Mirror in Parchment*, 194–7.

[37] Michael Roberts, 'Sickles and Scythes: Women's Work and Men's Work at Harvest Time', *History Workshop* VII (1979). There are eight examples from after 1400.

Figure 7.1. Reaping and Stacking (from the Luttrell Psalter). Add. MS 42131, fos. 172v and 173r. © The British Library Board. All Rights Reserved 2010.

In Camille's view, therefore, the Luttrell Psalter is by no means a representation of reality: 'here we have an example of where an image in the psalter depicts what probably did *not* go on in fourteenth-century fields'[38] (Figure 7.1).

And yet, the evidence from the Multon 'custumal' must give us pause. Emanating from the same county and at not too great a distance from the Luttrells at Irnham, the Frampton evidence suggests a quite heavy involvement of women at harvest time. This was not because of the demands of harvest requiring all hands, but because by custom *one person*, male or female, was required from each tenement. The basic holding, we are told, 'will find one man or one women in the hay and corn from the beginning of weeding until the end of autumn'. This statement seems to be amplified by details of the service owed by Reginald Loveless for his one-acre tenement. He has to find 'one woman from the beginning of weeding up to the end of autumn for weeding, reaping

---

[38] *Mirror in Parchment*, 196.

and making hay stacks in the meadow when hay is carried'. She will also 'reap and weed around the ditch of the lord's meadows'. It is quite possible that the majority of those reaping the lord's corn at Frampton were, in fact, women. Perhaps the male tenants considered a woman's contribution more expendable in terms of work on their own tenements. This scenario is reinforced by the services due from the abnormal holding of the heirs of Gilbert the Cook from which was due the service of three women with sickles[39] for one day in autumn, and from the service due from Reginald Loveless who found a woman for the entire harvest period for weeding, reaping, and connected duties. Nor does this evidence stand entirely alone. The author of the *Husbandry*, written at the end of the thirteenth century, advises engaging reapers as a team, 'that is to say five men or women, whichever you wish, and whom are termed "men"'.[40] He is talking here of wage labour, but it is nonetheless indicative. None of this, of course, deprives the Luttrell Psalter of its ideological force. It does, however, make the depiction of the harvest closer to at least a south Lincolnshire reality.[41] The Frampton 'custumal' is close to the Luttrell Psalter's depiction of the agricultural services in other respects too. If weeding and reaping is done by women, the other services—enumerated in the one and depicted in the other—are done by men, perhaps because these tasks were considered to be even more strenuous. Could the fact that the tenants were more likely to send women have encouraged commutation?[42] In an age when labour was abundant it might have been thought preferable to commute the services and hire more robust men.[43] However we read this evidence, it does suggest that the employment of women as reapers was not solely a post-Black-Death phenomenon as a reaction to the shortage of labour.[44]

[39] I am presuming that *cum falc'* refers to sickles. The work of M. Roberts (above) suggests that it would have been most unusual for women to mow with scythes. They were never shown with scythes in the illustrations: 'Sickles and Scythes', 5. However, the word *falx* could mean either. Alternatively, *cum falc'* could conceivably stand for *cum falcatoribus*, which would suggest women undertaking ancillary work (raking, gathering, and binding) alongside the mowers.

[40] Interestingly, he seems to envisage no difference in productivity, for twenty-five 'men' can reap and bind ten acres a day, working full time: Oschinsky (ed.), *Walter of Henley*, 444–5.

[41] It may also help to explain 'the rent called Womanswerk' on the Abbey of Crowland's manor at Langtoft: F. M. Page, *The Estates of Crowland Abbey* (Cambridge, 1934), 95. This seems to refer to commuted service.

[42] On peasant tenements Barbara Hanawalt assumes that the reaping will normally be done by the man: *The Ties That Bound: Peasant Families in Medieval England* (Oxford, 1986), 126–7.

[43] This is, of course, a controversial subject. For a discussion of the value attached to women's work, but concentrating on the period after the Black Death, see Sandy Bardsley, 'Women's Work Reconsidered: Gender and Wage Differentiation in Late Medieval England', *Past and Present* 165 (1999), 3–29; and the ensuing debate between John Hatcher and Sandy Bardsley in *Past and Present* 173 (2001), 191–202.

[44] Nevertheless, the post-Black-Death conditions are likely to have increased the value of women's work. It could be argued that the fifteenth-century copy of the arrentation of *c*.1340 has been 'contaminated' by subsequent social changes. However, the other aspects of the custumal are consistent with what we know from the manorial accounts of 1324–6 and the names of the tenants are entirely consistent with the 1340s.

Finally, it should be noted that the services that were 'arrented' here were the arable services only, together with the carting of turves. Why the washing and shearing of sheep is not included is unclear. The 'custumal' tells us that if the work was not required no payment could be made in lieu. The same was true of carrying services, including those involved in repairing the houses of the *curia*. In this case, it may have been felt that it was prudent to retain these services, given that the need was occasional rather than regular. It was the agrarian services that were costing the lord and which, most probably, caused most in the way of truculence from the peasants with the consequent need for rigorous supervision. The fact that carrying and pastoral works could not be 'sold' to the peasants when they were not required suggests that as regards the arable enterprise 'the sale of works' did indeed feature at Frampton, although, if the extant account rolls are anything to go by, it did not go back as far as 1324–6.

The 'arrentation' of *c*.1340 does not stand alone, however, as a means of understanding the situation of the Multon tenantry. The collector's account of 1330–1 gives the rent of bond tenants at Frampton as £1 6½d, a sum close to the £1 2s 3½d 'besides works' recorded in the custumal.[45] The acreage is similar too. In 1330–1 the rent is from 104 acres of bond land of old demesne in Frampton, while the later calculation is 117 acres. Clearly, acreage and rent had increased slightly in the meantime. The greater part of the Multon unfree tenants in the area appear to have been Frampton tenants, with relatively few living in Kirton and Wyberton. These bond tenements, however, were not necessarily the entirety of the land that the *nativi* held, as the extent of 1326 indicates. Indeed there is a list of additional holdings contemporary with the arrentation. This is one of a series of documents emanating from the beginning of Sir John de Multon's tenure, mirroring the survival of documentation that followed upon his father's majority. As we have seen, there is a household account from 1343–4 as well as a diet account from 1347–8. Furthermore, the fifteenth-century booklet which contains the arrentation of *c*.1340 contains a group of additional rentals that were clearly drawn up around the same time. The first item in the booklet is a rental of all the tenants, without reference to individual status or tenure, who paid at the several terms of the year. This rental is also said to belong to the time of Sir Henry Hillary. Most of the *nativi* of the arrentation figure here too.[46] More interesting is the item which follows the arrentation. It lists the free land which the ancestors of the lord's *nativi* had acquired 'of military fee', echoing the newly accrued rent in fee mentioned in Thomas de Multon's extent. Many of the *nativi* of the arrentation also figure here, suggesting that it, too, is close in date. Some of these men were paying rent for the additional parcels of land to

[45] Multon 9.
[46] Henry Dereboght, Reginald Loveless and the heirs of Stephen Miller are missing. Robert Randolf has lost his brother Alan, while Alan Thormond has gained a brother called Roger. Robert son of Elias appears to have been replaced by Alan son of Robert, presumably his son. This suggests that the rental might be slightly later than the arrentation.

several people in addition to their own lord. For example, Reginald Parker (*alias* Reginald Benet) and Athelard his nephew pay rent to the lord and to no less than eleven other people. These items suggest that the Multon *nativi* tended to be better endowed with land than the arrentation alone would suggest. They could hold considerably more land than their standard bovate and were well able, it would seem, to pay good money for the opportunities it brought.

There was, of course, nothing new about this in the 1340s. The collector's account of 1330–1 records unfree tenants paying substantial rents 'at the will of the lord' and others jointly paying 12s rent from the free land they had purchased. Unfree status, then, was no necessary barrier to holding free land. Altogether these men probably had substantial holdings. The national taxation records tell the same story. Geoffrey Elryk, for example, a Multon serf at Wyberton, paid the very substantial sum of 4s 2d to the lay subsidy of 1332. Allan Cullul, who accounted as collector for 1330–1, paid the more modest but still substantial sum of 2s 6d. When we are talking about the lord's relationship with his unfree tenants, therefore, we must bear in mind that we are not necessarily talking about insubstantial men. There is every reason to suppose that the reeves and collectors were chosen from among the more substantial of those who were Multon tenants.

This brings us to confront more squarely the issue of the lord's attitude towards his unfree tenants. The question of direct contact between the lord and the unfree tenants, such as the reeve and the collector who ran his estate, is problematic. However, it is hard to believe that they never met face-to-face or that when they did they could not communicate with a degree of mutual understanding, if not exactly 'civility'. It was not unknown, moreover, for a *nativus* to be employed on 'household' duties. One clear example is Robert del Park. We first encounter Robert in the court rolls. In 1330 he was one of those amerced for failing to do carrying service. In the arrentation we find him holding a regular four-acre tenement with its rents and labour services. At the same time, however, the household account of 1343–4 shows Robert going on journeys for the lord—to Lincoln on two occasions and once to Windsor—and being paid expenses. What, then, of those *nativi* who had come to hold their standard bovates on 'favourable terms'? Alan Thormond, the collector in 1325–6, held his tenement by money rent and very light labour services. Is there a connection between his low rent and his service to the lord? Similarly, is it conceivable that Gilbert the Cook's heirs held on favourable terms as a result of service in the household? And what do we make of a deceased *nativus* called Walter of the Kitchen? Is it possible that gentry families like the Multons drew some of their more menial household servants directly from their estates? The least we can say is that the relationship between a lord and his dependant tenants was likely to have been a more complex one than the normative legal texts might lead one to suppose. It was perhaps more complex, too, than the manor court rolls might suggest, given that these portray life as largely determined by the consequences of tenure.

Let us turn now to the free tenants. As one would expect they are largely revealed to us through their recorded rents: in the 1326 extent, the collector's account within the 1325–6 manorial account roll, the free-standing account of the collector for 1330–1, the rental of free tenants at Frampton and Kirton of 1343 (the only Multon rental to survive as an original document) and the further rentals belonging to the 1340s which survive in the early-fifteenth-century booklet. The collector for 1330–1, Alan Cullul, accounted for £9 8s 8¼d rent plus £13 10s 4d from farms. Several items indicate an increase in the exploitation of assets since 1325–6. There was 9s coming from the farm of *Pecchehall* plus 2s 3d increment,[47] 13s 5d comes from the farm of four houses at the Lane End which the account says used to render 9s. It looks as though more houses had been built at Lane End as only one was recorded in 1325–6. Some additional items are also new.[48] We see a similar level of exploitation of assets, later, in the time of Sir John. A surviving rental records the rents and holdings of free tenants of Sir John de Multon in Frampton and Kirton.[49] The farms are omitted, but can be supplied to some degree from the rentals in the fifteenth-century book.[50] Enough material survives to indicate that the Multon lordship remained an active one in terms of the exploitation of its resources.

Many of the free rents coming from Frampton and its neighbouring settlements were individually quite modest. There were, however, some substantial figures among the tenants. Hugh de Castleford, for example, paid £1 12s per annum for land in Skirbeck in 1325–6, and was recorded in 1343 as having paid £2 8s for 16 acres there. Thomas de Welby of Kirton had paid two large farms of £4 13s 8d and £2 8s in 1325–6. He contributed 4s 9d to the lay subsidy of 1327 and 5s 2d in 1332. The relationship between the Multons and many of their free tenants must have been purely contractual, especially those who were holding individual items for a period of years at farm. In some cases, however, there must have been some social contact. Thomas de Welby, for example, witnessed a number of Multon deeds during the 1320s and 1330s, where he occurs with other local men of similar station: William de Cobeldyke, Athelard de Welby, John del Meres and Alan son of Alan.[51] William de Cobeldyke contributed 4s 3d to the lay subsidy at Frampton in 1332, Alan son of Alan 10s at Kirton in 1327, John del Meres 4s ¼d at Kirton in 1327 and 6s in 1332. The last mentioned, however, held a mere two acres of the Multons at Kirton in 1343, paying 1s 1d per annum. This is a clear warning against assuming that

---

[47] A note adds that it will render 12s the following year.
[48] For example, the 17s 1½d coming from three acres, three roods and fifteen perches of land in *le Newemersh* put at farm to Simon son of Alan and the 4s 6d for ½ acre in *le Stewemersh* put at farm to Thomas son of William.
[49] Multon Add 7.
[50] The quality of the transcription deteriorates and there appear to be omissions from the rentals on which the writer is working. The names of tenants suggest that these rentals are a little later than that of 1343 but not by very much.
[51] Multon nos 1a, 11a, 26c, 29a.

a small parcel of land in a rental was necessarily held by someone of little consequence locally.

We should not assume, either, that the lord necessarily had more dealings with tenants solely because they were free. Free tenants held their land on considerably better conditions, although their money rents could be noticeably higher than those paid by villeins. As is well known, they were not invariably better off. Many free tenants were cottars, that is cottagers, often holding very small parcels of land. As this was insufficient land on which to support a family, they needed to supplement their income by wage labour and/or by a variety of other occupations. England enjoyed an expanding and commercializing economy in which there were opportunities, as well as rural poverty. Nowhere was this more the case than in the Fens. At the same time we should not make the mistake of assuming that all free tenants were peasants. They included minor ecclesiastics, officials of various kinds, townsmen as well as substantial local craftsmen, and even the lords of neighbouring manors. M. Barg has compiled figures indicating that in the three counties of Oxfordshire, Huntingdonshire, and Buckinghamshire, in particular, more than half of the freehold land recorded in the Hundred Rolls was held by people who were not peasants but were drawing rents from those who were actually cultivating the land.[52] It is important to be alive to this. Some of the Multon tenants at Frampton and its environs were certainly in Barg's categories of non-peasant, although the majority do in fact appear to have been cultivators. On the other hand, as we have seen, some unfree tenants were also substantial farmers, in the modern sense of the term. This can be shown in outline, but not in detail, for some of the Multon tenants. Robert son of Alexander the reeve, for example, who was later amerced for failure to perform service and for not using the lord's mill, held in addition to his servile holding, land in Kirton for which he paid a farm of £1 5s per annum in 1325–6 and *Pecchegrene* and *Loyrigges* for which he paid another 6s 8d. The Thormonds seem to have functioned at a similar level. Such men then were as wealthy as some fairly substantial free tenants and they took additional land outside of customary tenure.

What can the court rolls tell us about the relationship between the lord and his free tenants? And how did this differ from the institutional relationship with the *nativi*? At Cuxham a free tenant would make fealty and would be given a day at the next court to demonstrate what he held of the lord and by what services. Afterwards he would come and acknowledge what he held of the lord for homage and fealty and by specified services, in this case of course money rent not labour. It is stated that the lord will have custody and marriage (of the heir) when this accrues, and that the free tenant also owes three-weekly suit of court. Finally he would be given a day for making homage to the lord within forty days 'wheresoever the lord may be found'. As the lord, the warden of Merton College,

[52] M. A. Barg, 'The Social Structure of Manorial Freeholders: an Analysis of the Hundred Rolls of 1279', *AgHR* 39 (1991), 108–15.

presides over this court, the clear implication is that this is performed outside of the court. A major difference between the unfree and free tenant in terms of status—aside from labour services, merchet and the other disabilities—is that the free tenant performs homage and does so out of court.

Although we have no direct statement of custom, the same *formule* are applied with regard to free tenants at Frampton. At the great court of 8 October 1330, for example, Laurence Hillary, heir of Thomas, who was of full age, came into court and swore fealty for his tenement and was given a day at the next court for demonstrating what he held and by what services. And homage, it says, is respited until the next court. On 29 October it was ordered to levy a relief of 7s 6d from him. It might be assumed from the respite that homage was made in court. In fact, we have a case which makes it clear that this was not so. On 11 February 1331 another free tenant came into court and swore fealty for the tenements he 'claimed to hold' of the lord by hereditary succession. He was told that he should go to the lord to pay homage. At this moment in their lives at least the free tenants seemed to come face-to-face with their lord.

Even for free tenants their tenure could involve irksome restrictions. The Multons had the right to the marriage of some, at least, of their under-age free tenants; that is to say they had feudal wardship.[53] Marriage and wardship were valuable 'feudal incidents' and it was obviously important for a lord, or at least his agents, to keep track of them. This is no doubt why the mid-fourteenth-century rentals of Multon tenants differentiate between tenures. Some tenancies are said to be held by military tenure, while others are held in socage—that is non-military free tenure—and therefore by implication not subject to wardship and marriage.[54] In such cases these matters were not within a lord's jurisdiction. The collector's account for 1330–1 is also explicit in differentiating between tenures. In his account tenements are held by free tenants, by bond rent, in socage, at farm, and at the will of the lord. Those who were free tenants without qualification seem to have been subject to wardship and marriage.

No doubt some free tenants valued an association with a particular lord. The Welbys, as we shall see, had a military relationship with the Multons of Frampton.[55] There are certainly others who would have wanted to break it. On 12 July 1330 it was ordered to distrain eleven men for homage and fealty. This was repeated at the next court.[56] A particular bone of contention was suit of

[53] The question of the marriage of a free tenant occurs, for example, at the great court held on 8 October 1330 with regard to Jocens son of Geoffrey Augrim, 'who is under age and whose marriage belongs to the lord by reason of the tenements which he holds of the lord's fee and of which his father died seised', and who was given into the custody of Peter son of Robert and John Basilneve, who pledged to produce him unmarried.

[54] Those holding by military tenure had presumably been liable to pay a contribution to scutage (shield money) when the king called out the host.

[55] See below 200–1, 286.

[56] One of them at least continued to resist. At the great court held on 3 October 1331 it was presented that Sir John de Kirton ought to come and does not; therefore he is in mercy. It was

court. In this world of kaleidoscopic lordship and free tenures, the exercise of
power and authority could be difficult matters. Suit of court was a more general
bone of contention, as we shall see below.

Free tenants figure centrally in the standard interpretation of the development
of manorial court rolls in England.[57] The explanation for the proliferation
of these, it is argued, lies with the development of the common law courts.
Landlords were able to ensure that their villein tenants did not gain access to
the royal courts, so that they could keep control of them, their tenements and
their labour.[58] Free tenants, however, were more of a problem for landlords as,
unlike villeins, their access to royal courts could not be denied. Lords reacted by
making their own manorial courts more attractive to freeholders by introducing
some of the new procedures developed in the royal courts, such as the recording
of proceedings.[59]

The most significant procedural development was the use of juries of various
kinds. These had been used for some time to produce manorial surveys and
extents. Now they began to displace inquests conducted by the entire court and
were introduced for personal plaints as well as disputes over land. An important
study of the introduction of these new procedures by John Beckerman argues
that the first quarter of the fourteenth century, roughly speaking, was 'the
heyday of jury trial in English manor courts'.[60] Another procedure that was
transferred from royal to manorial courts was the jury of presentment. Initially
this was confined to crime and to public matters as many landlords took over
the business of the sheriff's tourn in their 'views of frankpledge'. From the early
fourteenth century, however, it was extended to deal with seigneurial rights and
offences against manorial custom. It is possible that the slow introduction of this
procedure was due to peasant resistance, given that it generally strengthened the
landlord's position. This was so because persons who were presented by a jury as
guilty of infractions tended to be summarily convicted.

There were, however, considerable benefits for tenants in the introduction of
additional legal instruments into the manorial courts. For one thing, they now
recorded economic transactions of numerous kinds and added to the security of

further presented that he has withdrawn service from the lord, namely homage and fealty and
4d per annum for two selions of land in Kirton. It is ordered that he be distrained. For a man
of his stature—himself the lord of a manor—this recognition of subordination, aside from the
practicalities, must have been especially irksome.

[57] For what follows see Zvi Razi and Richard Smith, 'The Origins of the English Manorial Court
Rolls as a Written Record: a Puzzle', in Z. Razi and R. Smith (eds), *Medieval Society and the Manor
Court* (Oxford, 1996).
[58] For an indispensable exploration of this, see Paul R. Hyams, *King, Lords and Peasants in
Medieval England*.
[59] Although some manor court rolls were already being produced during the first half of the
thirteenth century, at least for large ecclesiastical estates, they began to proliferate in the 1260s and
1270s: Razi and Smith, 'The Origins of the English Manorial Court Rolls', 40.
[60] John S. Beckerman, 'Procedural Innovation and Institutional Change in Medieval English
Manorial Courts', *Law and History Review* 10 (1992), 214.

tenure. Not all the influences were one way, that is to say from royal to seigniorial courts. The procedure of 'surrender and admittance', whereby a tenant gave the property back to the lord who passed it to a new tenant, paved the way for the Statute of *Quia Emptores* of 1290 which established substitution rather than subinfeudation with regard to property held in fee simple. This in turn seems to have increased the incidence of 'surrender and admittance' in the manorial courts. By this procedure the new tenant became responsible for the rents and services and paid the lord an entry fine, in addition to whatever had passed between the old and the new tenant, which was outside of the business of the court. In the late thirteenth and early fourteenth centuries it became the standard means by which customary land passed from one tenant to another. The various procedures can be seen in operation at Frampton. Surrender and admittance has already been observed. Inquests by trial juries occur with some frequency. Presentment also occurs, though only it seems at the frankpledge courts.[61] The Multons were not spectacularly successful, however, in retaining the attendance of their free tenants.

A few of the free tenants had suit recorded in the 1343 rental as a condition of their tenure. Certainly more free tenants owed suit at Frampton than is indicated in the rental since they appear in the list of essoins (excuses) recorded at or near the opening of the court, either as essoiners or as their substitutes. It seems highly likely that most of the free tenants owed suit at Michaelmas. Getting them to attend, however, was a difficult matter.[62] The attendance of Sir John de Kirton seems to have been a dead letter, while the Cobeldykes were also problematic. But did free tenants owe suit to the manorial court itself? In some cases, at least, it seems that they did, as they are found there too among the essoins.[63] Of course others may well have attended regularly without mention in the rolls. However, the number one encounters among the known free tenants is not large. Their attendance was probably intermittent. Despite the difficulties they encountered with the many Cobeldykes and others, the Multons nevertheless strove to maintain the attendance of free tenants where they could.[64]

[61] On 8 October 1330 we hear that it was presented 'by the homage' that many persons who ought to have come to the court had not. The whole homage was amerced 2s for failure to present this default. A further ten matters were presented, mainly concerning the hue and cry and breaking of the assize of ale, although two seigniorial matters were also presented. It is not clear whether the homage spoke in practice through a jury, although it may well be that they did. In October 1331 we hear of eleven presentments regarding the breaking of the assize of ale, the hue and cry, shedding blood and theft.

[62] At the Michaelmas court of 1330 the homage presented a list of seventeen persons who ought to come but had not, that is to say, in fact, that they had neither come nor essoined, while there is a further list of free tenants who were ordered to be distrained for homage and fealty. Given that they were resisting Multon lordship they were hardly likely to appear in court. There were also suitors who paid an annual sum to be free of attendance, that is to say their suit was commuted.

[63] One of the free tenants had suit at the Michaelmas court only recorded in the rental.

[64] The history of the Hillary tenancy suggests this. Between the court rolls and the rental of 1343, Laurence Hillary seems to have died. Hugh de Dowesby acquired a portion of his land. Suit

It is important to ascertain, however, whether the free tenants of Frampton and Kirton, and elsewhere in the area, *were* bringing cases to the court. From this perspective cases were of two kinds, i.e. those brought by free men against unfree Multon tenants and those brought against one another. In these latter cases it was more a matter of choice as to whether one chose the manor court or a public court. The first variety certainly occurs. There were numerous cases brought by free men against unfree tenants for debt.[65] By contrast, however, clear cases where free tenants were suing one another are conspicuously absent. Cases of unfree versus unfree, on the other hand, abound. Overwhelmingly, those who brought pleas of debt, transgression, and the like were unfree tenants. Everything indicates that the *nativi* were the mainstays of the Frampton seigniorial court. The evidence suggests that the Multon court at Frampton was not especially popular with the free tenants of the area, and that the Multons were fighting a continual battle to keep their suit. It may be that free tenants had a stronger presence in other local courts, at the commercially vibrant Kirton, for example, with its local market, or at the Hungerfield or Richmond courts. One should not extrapolate from the evidence of one court at one point in time, but the Multon evidence suggests that the need to retain the presence of free tenants was not the sole catalyst for change. The pressure for more effective courts was probably more widespread within the tenantry. Moreover, in this as in other matters, lay landlords tended to borrow ideas and procedures from one another.

What role did the lord play in the court? Things were done in his name, but Sir Thomas de Multon neither attended nor presided, whether the court be the manorial or the frankpledge court. This is not to say that no secular lord ever presided in his own court. However, at the level of the Multons there is every reason to think that this would have been very unusual. On 8 July 1331 an issue regarding tenure was respited until the lord could be consulted. He was there, then, in the background, operating at one remove from the court through his officials, much as he did in matters concerning the estate.

The question as to what contact a gentry lord actually had with his peasants is therefore a complex one. In the case of his unfree tenants as a body, the answer is probably not a lot, although, as we have argued, he may have had some contact with some of them as individuals, if they held manorial office or had dealings with the household. As we have seen, however, they swore their fealty by means of induction, as it were, at the court and in the absence of the lord. The allowance of ale and victuals to Sir Henry the Chaplain and the reeve which we find in the account roll for 1324–5, at the end of the provision for

---

of court was included in his tenure. Moreover, it was written above the entry that the land had been 'sold' by the lord *with suit of court*; it obviously mattered.

[65] For the significance of inter-peasant debt, see P. Schofield, 'Dearth, Debt and the Local Land Market in a Late Thirteenth-Century Village', *AgHR* 45 (1997); and 'Access to Credit in the Early Fourteenth-Century English Countryside', in P. R. Schofield and N. J. Mayhew (eds), *Credit and Debt in Medieval England* (Oxford, 2002).

the customary tenants during boon services, strongly suggest that it was they and not the lord who presided over these proceedings. On the other hand, we do have the evidence that Roger de Cobeldyke was present at the sheep-shearing festival.

Free tenants on the other hand were expected to perform homage to the lord. There is no guarantee that this was not done via a major official, as the lord's proxy, although it is not what the records say. Even if they paid homage directly their subsequent contact with the lord may well have been quite minimal. Most of the free tenants of the Multons at Frampton, Kirton, and Wyberton held only small parcels of land from them, although we cannot assume that this necessarily reflected their overall economic status. On the other hand, Roger de Cobeldyke was a lord in his own right and there were others among the Multon tenants who had some status. The witness lists to charters suggest some real contact between tenant and lord. Hugh de Castleford paid his rent personally into the lord's coffers, as did Emma Stotte for her house in Boston. This may have been partly a matter of convenience, but it was also perhaps a mark of their status that they paid directly and not through the lord's collector. It cannot be doubted that local society was strongly hierarchical and that this affected the lord's perception of individual tenants and helped determine the level of social contact, if any, with them.

There are some interesting suggestions of social interaction between the tenantry and the household. The accounts of 1343–4 show Amabel de Cobeldyke being given the sum of 5s for the lady's business. Where she fits into the Cobeldyke clan is unclear. However, the rental of 1343 shows her as a free tenant of the Multons, both in Frampton and in Kirton. She seems to have had a collecting role, for she handed directly to the receiver the sum of 13s 4d at Michaelmas 1343 together with £2 16s 8d from *Neuvand* (presumably for Newland) for the entire year and 6s for winter pasture. She was a substantial figure in her own right. She is presumably identical with the Amabel widow of William de Cobeldyke who paid £1 0s 4d to the 1332 lay subsidy at Frampton. Amabel seems, therefore, to straddle household and estate. Nor was she the only one to do so. The household chaplain had done so since the endowment of the chantry at Frampton around 1260.[66] Nicholas the Chaplain appears prominently in the household accounts. His duties were clearly multifarious and went well beyond saying mass. He, too, is found travelling, this time on the lord's business. As we have seen, a predecessor, Henry, was involved in organizing the harvest boon services in 1324–5. The reeve's account reveals Henry taking cloth and lining to Ingleby. Robert the Chamberlain received a sum of 6s 8d at Frampton in 1343–4, indicating that he probably functioned there. He is very likely the same Robert Chamberlain who witnessed a deed with other local free tenants in 1337, suggesting that he was considered to be one of them.[67] He paid 2s

---

[66] For the endowment and the early chaplains, see below 144.   [67] Multon no. 21.

11d to the 1332 subsidy at Frampton.[68] The household also had dealings of an economic nature with their tenants, one being Ivette Godeson, who was clearly a maltstress,[69] just as it had economic contacts with many other men and women who were not Multon tenants.

We lack the sources to penetrate the gentry's personal perceptions of their tenants. If there were sometimes elements of paternalism in the relationship we rarely perceive it in our sources, although we do have evidence of social contacts which certainly do not preclude it. On the other hand, that there was some latent antagonism in the relationship is certain. Our overriding impression, admittedly from a limited range of sources, is that the gentry saw their tenants primarily as assets to be exploited. However, these assets were human and their exploitation must have involved some negotiation. This was naturally the case when it came to leases, farms, and other contracts. It was also true when it came to conflict resolution. Conflict arose from the lord's demands and from peasant resistance, institutionalized at the manor court. The evidence from gentry sources does not reveal secular landlords regarding even unfree tenants as a subspecies with bestial characteristics. What the gentry records point to is neither this nor indeed the idealized world of the Luttrell Psalter, but a more hard-headed, matter of fact view of the world.

If the attitude of lords towards their tenants was based in large measure upon economic calculation, the legal 'underpinning' of the landlord–tenant relationship, most especially where the latter was personally or tenurially unfree, retained considerable coercive potential should this need to be invoked. And, as we can see from the experience of landlords in succeeding centuries, the basic medieval set up could take landlord–peasant relations in different directions according to the 'quality' of lordship and the presiding social and economic conditions.

In the meantime we can certainly find examples of particularly avaricious gentry landlords. Work on the Hundred Rolls of 1279–80 has shown that the highest rents tended to be taken by some of the lesser lords, men like Wydo de Waterville whose rents from Orton Waterville in Huntingdonshire averaged an enormous £1 per virgate. Sandra Raban's study of Normancross hundred in that county has led her to conclude that if 'rapacious lords' existed, 'they were more likely to have been knights [than the ecclesiastical landlords of earlier historiography], many of whom had relatively modest resources and were therefore driven to take action'.[70] As in later centuries levels of exploitation varied and attitudes probably did so too. There is some evidence from our period that when landlords were in financial difficulties they might well try to increase the burdens on their tenants. Jean Birrell's study of the court rolls of Alrewas shows Sir Philip de Somerville

---

[68] There is nothing to suggest, however, that he held directly of the Multons.

[69] See above 84. The collector's account of 1330–1 shows that she was a tenant of the Multons in Boston, which was where the Godesons seem to have originated.

[70] Raban, *A Second Domesday?*, 137.

doing precisely that during the 1330s and coming into conflict with his tenants as a result.[71] An especially exploitative attitude on the part of newcomers can certainly be seen in the thirteenth and fourteenth centuries just as in a later age. Good examples come from those thirteenth-century *curiales* who have been the subject of study, men like Geoffrey de Langley who, at Stivichall near Coventry, for example, used his muscle to increase his rents and to change the terms on which his tenants held.[72] In these respects the evidence tallies with that from the sixteenth and seventeenth centuries. Much must have turned on the structure of estates and on whether there or not there was a strong peasant community able to resist a landlord's attempts to revise the level of exactions in his favour.

The history of the relationship between the Multons and their tenants is lacking in spectacular or sensational episodes. Indeed, it comes across as mundane, even humdrum. Unfortunately, the Multon archive fails us just at the point that peasant–landlord relations became especially strained, in the decades after the Black Death. All the evidence suggests, however, that in the Multons of Frampton, at least as far as the early to mid-fourteenth century is concerned, we have a good example of a middle of the road gentry family who were not especially rapacious towards their tenants but were nonetheless very conscious of their rights and made the most of the opportunities they had to take what they could from their tenants.

[71] Jean Birrell, 'Confrontation and Negotiation in a Medieval Village', in *Survival and Discord in Medieval Society: Essays in Honour of Christopher Dyer*, ed. Richard Goddard, John Langdon, and Miriam Müller (Turnhout: Brepols, 2009).

[72] P. R. Coss, 'Sir Geoffrey de Langley and the Crisis of the Knightly Class in Thirteenth-Century England', *Past and Present* 68 (1975), 3–37; repr. in T. H. Aston (ed.), *Landlords, Peasants and Politics in Medieval England* (Cambridge, 1987).

8

The Church as Cultural Space

It goes without saying that religious belief and practice are central to the understanding of any, or at least almost any, culture. As far as the gentry is concerned religious sensibility and religious observance immediately raise issues around internal and external worlds and around the possibility of a fundamental dichotomy between private and public spheres. However unwittingly, the historian cannot help but have one eye on the Reformation and the debates it engenders. In this chapter, I intend to approach the religion of the gentry in its formative period, initially though the uniquely revealing phenomenon of the private chapel. Here we can examine belief and worship in their most intimate setting: in the *curia* itself. Although the *curia* conditioned a great deal within gentry life, it was never a self-contained world, as we are used to emphasizing by now. Hence, sooner or later any study of the religious dimension to gentry culture takes us into the external world and, more specifically, into the broader institutions of the church. It is here that a particularly significant development took place in our period, a development that would govern the role of the gentry within the church for many centuries. I refer to the shift in patronage and support from the religious orders to the parish church.

As we shall see, many gentry passed though an intermediate phase of support for the friars before centring their activities upon a parish church or churches. A crucial change in behaviour was the transfer of burials, and their attendant sepulchral monuments, from the monasteries to local churches. The sheer variety in the types of monument encountered from the later thirteenth century is arresting and, as many scholars have appreciated, offers a spectacular means of entrée into contemporary modes of thought.[1] This shift of location did not take place in a cultural vacuum, however, and has to be understood in terms of the striking expansion of visual representation within churches during the twelfth and thirteenth centuries. The monuments themselves, moreover, have several layers of significance. Whilst their central purpose was as an aid to salvation, they added qualitatively and quantitatively to the visibility of lordship and family prestige. The development of the parochial mausoleum in particular must have impacted powerfully on local communities in terms of awareness of the power

---

[1] See the ground-breaking survey by Nigel Saul: *English Church Monuments in the Middle Ages: History and Representation* (Oxford, 2009).

of aristocratic lineage. Issues of identity, status, social display, and social stability were inexorably intertwined here with more explicitly religious concerns. For these reasons, then, gentry commemoration within the parish church demands our particular attention.

There is, however, one further dimension to the relationship between the gentry and the church whose resonance remained strong until recent times. This is the matter of church livings. In this period we begin to see clearly, for the first time, the social impact of the gentry's involvement in the presentation of local rectors. Although the role of religious institutions was to remain strong in this area for several centuries, bishops' registers allow us to observe, at this early date, the appointment by local lords of clients and relatives, including younger sons, to livings under their control. This and the broader gentry role in the patronage of the local church was to play a major part in entrenching their social position thereafter.

These, then, are the matters which this chapter will cover. Let us begin, once again, with the *curia*. The natural starting point is with the needs of the household. The Luttrell Psalter affirms pictorially the traditional view that the head of the household, the paterfamilias, was responsible for its general tone and there is every reason to suppose that under this regime its members were expected to conduct their outward lives in accordance with the Christian faith.[2] Sir Geoffrey Luttrell even acted as godfather to the children of some of his servants.[3] Whether this was a common phenomenon is unclear. However, it can hardly be doubted that in this respect, as in others, the lord and the lady determined the moral complexion both for the immediate family and for the household as a whole. The household chaplain was a significant figure, one who played an important part in gentry life. His duties, as we have seen, could be quite wide. By the later thirteenth and early fourteenth centuries the private chapel had become a traditional feature of the manor house. It was, of course, essential for prayer. It was more valuable to the gentry family, however, if the chaplain had the power to say mass; if, that is, the household chapel was the site of a chantry and its incumbent of course a priest (as seems normally to have been the case).

Once again, the Multon archive allows us to take this family as an example. A fourteenth-century copy of an original, but undated, licence survives in the Multon collection by which the rector of Frampton, Philip de Eya, gave permission 'as far as was in his power' for Sir Thomas de Frampton to have divine service celebrated daily in the chapel 'which he has in his *curia*' at Frampton.[4]

---

[2] See Mertes, *English Noble Household*, ch. 5: 'The Household as Religious Community'.

[3] See above, 58; and Camille, *Mirror in Parchment*, 83.

[4] Multon 94a. The catalogue is useful here but there are omissions and some inaccuracies. Philip de Eya was dead in 1277 when Thomas de Huntingfield was presented to Frampton church: F. N. Davis (ed.), *Rotuli Ricardi Gravesend Episcopi Lincolniensis, 1258–1279*, Lincoln Record Society (1925), 75.

This was granted, formally at least, on the grounds that Thomas was unable to visit his parish church on a daily basis and to be present at divine service there, despite his 'pious desire' to do so, because of its distance from his house (*domum*) and the inconvenience of the roads. This was probably a common excuse for such requests, although it is perfectly true that the manor house at Sandholme was some way from the parish church.[5] A chaplain was to be maintained, at Thomas's own expense, to celebrate daily in the chapel, upon condition that the chaplain would never administer the sacraments to any parishioner nor do anything to defraud or injure the parish church and that Thomas would swear to pay over all offerings justly due to the parish church. Thomas and his heirs were to visit the church to hear divine service on at least the four feasts of Christmas, Easter, Whit Sunday and the Assumption of the Blessed Virgin Mary each year, 'providing they were present' (at their manor house). Thomas was at liberty to acquire confirmation from the bishop of Lincoln and from the cathedral chapter. In return for this permission, Thomas granted to the rector and his successors an acre of land in Frampton,[6] and 1s annual rent to be paid at the feast of St Botulf.

The original of this seems to have been a chirograph sealed by both parties. It was, in fact, a composition serving to regularize the situation. It may have followed some actual local contention. However, such compositions had become normal practice. The Huntingfield Cartulary, to take another example from the same locality, contains just such a composition between Roger son of William de Huntingfield and the rector of Toft over Roger's chapel and chantry in his *curia* there. The abbot of Crowland, the prior of Freiston and the bishop of Lincoln were all parties to the arrangement.[7] This was necessary because they all had rights, that is to say they had income, to safeguard.

As an account of the founding of the Multon chantry, however, the composition is slightly misleading. The inspiration behind it was undoubtedly Thomas's mother, Margery, who actually endowed it. The date is uncertain but seems likely to have been somewhere around the middle of the thirteenth century.[8] Margery's husband, Sir Alan de Multon, had died in 1240. She moved swiftly

---

[5] Distance and the state of the roads, especially in winter, seem to have been the most common reasons proffered. See, for example, Rosalind M. T. Hill (ed.), *The Rolls and Register of Bishop Oliver Sutton 1280–99*, 7 vols, Lincoln Record Society (1948–75), vol. iv (1958), 37, 57, 67, 125. Sir Hugh de Bibbesworth and his wife added that she was unable to attend during pregnancy, and Walter de Molesworth that his mother was old and frail and his wife very fat: ibid. 46, 156. For a discussion of such chapels and chantries and the conditions under which they were licensed see Hill, *Rolls and Register*, vol. ii. (1950) xiv–xvii.

[6] i.e. the acre lying next to the barn 'which he had newly built'.

[7] Huntingfield Cartulary, LRO, fos. 15v–16r.

[8] Multon 4. This document was witnessed by a group of local worthies: Sir James de Bussey, Sir William de Kirton, John de Hoyland, William de Frampton, Stephen his brother, Alan de Cobeldyke, Denis de Cobeldyke, and John de Gisors. It carries a curious seal—*sigillum Margarete de Cer* . . . In a separate deed (Multon 135) the grant is confirmed by her son Thomas. It recites Margery's deed at length and carries his mother's same seal, viz. *sigill' Margarete de Ceritun*, suggesting perhaps that Thomas did not yet possess a seal of his own.

to acquire wardship of his estates and of their three children, Thomas and his two sisters, in 1241.[9] How long the wardship lasted is unclear. Margery was still active in 1272. Thomas was certainly married by 1269 when he and his wife Beatrice are recorded.[10] As the records relating to the chantry make no reference to her, its foundation is undoubtedly before their marriage. On the other hand, Thomas was already a knight by the time that the chantry was endowed. The evidence seems to suggest, therefore, a date around 1250–60, perhaps closer to the earlier date. The property with which she endowed it was her own, acquired during her widowhood and most probably for this specific purpose. The chantry was located in the presumably pre-existing chapel of St James within Thomas's *curia* at Frampton.[11] Her indented deed provides an income for the maintenance of the chaplain, Robert de Miningsby, and his successors. She was inspired to do this, she says, 'for the sake of divine love and out of pious devotion' for the souls of herself, of her late husband, of Sir Thomas de Multon of Frampton (her son and heir), and of their parents, brothers, sisters, relatives, friends, ancestors, and successors. It was done, she says, with the consent and goodwill of the said Sir Thomas, as her son and heir. The fact that the chapel was said to be in his *curia* rather than his house (*domus*) suggests perhaps that the chapel was a free-standing structure and not integral to the manor house.

The chaplain, Robert de Miningsby, and his successors were to celebrate both mass and the office for the dead on every day of the year, at matins and at vespers, 'fully and assiduously'. There were, however, to be various exceptions to this routine. These were: at Christmas and the four days following, at the Circumcision of the Lord, at Epiphany, at the Purification of the Virgin Mary, at Easter and the three days following, at the feast of the Holy Trinity, at both feasts of the Holy Cross (that is the Invention and the Exaltation), at the mass of the blessed Virgin Mary (i.e. on her various feast days), at Michaelmas, at both feasts of St John the Baptist, on all the feasts of the Apostles and the Evangelists, at the mass of All Saints and on a number of specified saints' days, as well as on Saturdays and Sundays. On all of these occasions he was to use the offices specifically for those days together with the mass of the Blessed Virgin Mary with a second special collect for the souls of family members and of all the faithful departed. The chaplain, moreover, undertook to maintain a sufficient altar light in the chapel and to find a suitable clerk to minister there, 'without defect', at his own cost. In addition he undertook to maintain the cultivated land, houses, rents, and buildings attached to the living in at least as good a state as he found them. In case of infringement of any of the above the chaplain would be removed unless the situation were to be remedied within a period of forty days to allow

[9] Multon 80. She occurs as a widow on 1 January 1241: Multon 105.
[10] Multon 22, 97a.
[11] . . . *ad sustentacionem cantarie capelle sancti Jacobi site infra curiam dicti domini Thome apud Frampton.*

for admonition and for a final decision to be made by Margery or her heirs. In such case another suitable chaplain would be instituted.

The endowment consisted of land in Frampton and property in Boston. Its location was precisely described. In addition to a toft in the village, there was the land which Margery had acquired from Geoffrey le Baye, son of Hubert, in the same village, namely in Popildyke. In Boston the chantry was endowed with the lands and their buildings which she had acquired from Roger the Chaplain, son of William son of Gilbert of Boston, outside the Bardyke and near the hall and houses of the Earl of Richmond.[12] The chaplain was to pay 6d annual rent to Alan de Cobeldyke for the land in Popildyke. In short, the chaplain would become at one and the same time a member of the household, a tenant of the Multons and a member of the village of Frampton and its community, although he was unlikely to have cultivated the land himself.

The conditions were intended to be taken very seriously. One of the chaplain's successors was not up to the job and the penalty clause was in fact invoked. This was in 1298 when a new chaplain, Robert de Burwell, was presented by Sir Thomas de Multon II. An inquiry held by the official of the archdeacon of Lincoln had shown that the previous incumbent, Robert de Wenham, had been mad for five years. He had been summoned to defend himself against the charge of having infringed the conditions of the chantry but had failed to appear. The new incumbent was charged with taking care of him until other provision could be found.[13]

Although, as we have seen, there is nothing out of the ordinary in the Multon composition itself, it is unusual in the liturgical detail it contains. What, then, does it tell us about gentry religion and about Margery's religious propensities in particular? How much room was there for the expression of individual piety and how far can we detect it? That Margery comes across from the composition as a traditionally, and perhaps intensely, pious woman goes almost without saying. Little else is known of her outside of property deeds, but she did give £2 annual rent to the nuns of the church of St Michael next to Stamford.[14] To understand something of her needs we can turn to another source: books of hours.

Ladies like Margery de Multon were prominent among the owners of these from the earliest days of their production. In fact the very first book of hours was produced by the Oxford illuminator, William de Brailes, around the year 1240 for an otherwise unknown Lady Susanna,[15] a lady roughly contemporary with

[12] As contained, we are told, in the writings between her and William son of Gode and Peter Parlebeyn. The background deeds relating to Margery's acquisitions are extant: Multon, 32, 36, 100, 114, 123, 125. She paid £41 for the Boston property.
[13] Hill (ed.), *Rolls and Register of Bishop Oliver Sutton*, V, 222–3. Robert de Wenham had been presented by Thomas son of Lambert de Multon in 1287, following the death of the previous chaplain John Kepas: ibid. 103.
[14] Multon 140/19.
[15] For what follows, see Claire Donovan, *The de Brailes Hours* (British Library, 1991).

Figure 8.1. Lady Susanna (from *The de Brailes Hours*). Add. MS 49999, fo. 95r. © The British Library Board. All Rights Reserved 2010.

Margery de Multon. Susanna's portrait occurs at least four times in historiated initials to prayers and again in the psalms where it is used to portray the biblical Susanna, presumably indicating the lady's name (Figure 8.1). At the end of the process of production of his book, William added a leaf celebrating St Laurence. This is a clear indication of special devotion to a particular saint, and is mirrored by a sequence of scenes in the Gradual Psalms which tell the story of a burgess who lived in the parish of St Laurence. To the west of the city of Oxford lies the church of St Laurence, North Hinksey, which may well locate Susanna geographically, if not socially.[16] It is precisely in the choice of saints to whom one might wish to turn for favours and for intercession that the personal element entered contemporary religion. Some choices no doubt reflected the shrines that the pious subject had visited and other, more particular, circumstances.

---

[16] Most of the land in this area was held by or from the abbey of Abingdon. The abbey had numerous military tenants, and Lady Susanna may well have belonged to the family of one of these: *VCH Berkshire*, iv. 407. Donovan, however, sees her belonging to a burgess family rather than an aristocratic one: ibid. 24, 129.

While the increase in the ownership of books by the laity reflected the development of literacy, it also reflected a different attitude to books. Fashion was moving away from the grand ceremonial books of the twelfth century to a more compact form of illuminated book designed for personal reading and for study. A new type of book had been created to meet the requirements of a new market. These developments also reflect the Church's courting of the laity, as the resolutions of the Fourth Lateran Council of 1215 show. Lay people were being encouraged to take responsibility for their own salvation through prayer, penance, and charitable works. As Claire Donovan says, the book of hours 'with its small format, large script and many images, and with its concentration on the Virgin, was the perfect devotional manual for a lay woman'.[17]

Understood in terms of devotional need, the success of the book of hours is hardly surprising. Over the next thirty years, with the addition of the Calendar and the Office of the Dead from the psalter, it gradually became a familiar devotional volume and was ultimately to outstrip the psalter's popularity among the laity. Eight other manuscripts of English books of hours survive for the thirteenth century, from 1250 onwards, and another twelve from between 1300 and 1330. Increasing numbers survive from then on.[18] In addition to the de Brailes book, five other thirteenth-century books of hours depict their first owners. All are lay and all 'give the most prominent place' among the donor-portraits to women. A sixth was made for a woman, although she is not depicted.[19] It would be wrong to suggest that books of hours were used solely by women. Nevertheless, they provide a strong insight into the pious needs of ladies like Margery de Multon. We cannot say for certain that Margery de Multon actually possessed a bible or a psalter—although there must be a very high probability that she did—let alone a book of hours. It may well be the case, however, that in nominating the saints who would be directly called upon in the Frampton chantry she was exercising a degree of personal choice similar to that which seems to have been exercised by Lady Susanna when commissioning her book of hours. Some of those she chose were perhaps almost obligatory for the pious lady. St Margaret of Antioch, for example, was the patron saint of childbirth. St Katharine was another popular martyr, while St Mary Magdalen was 'a great source of hope to penitent sinful women'.[20] Others probably indicate a regional preference, i.e.

---

[17] Ibid. 23.

[18] This is, of course, survival rate and not rate of production. Donovan's figures do not include books where the Hours are combined with Psalters. If these are included the numbers go up to thirty for the thirteenth century and 104 for the fourteenth: Eamon Duffy, *Marking the Hours: English People and their Prayers 1240–1570* (New Haven and London, 2006), 10, 180.

[19] Donovan, *The de Brailes Hours*, 155. On this subject see also Kathryn A. Smith, *Art, Identity and Devotion in Fourteenth-Century England: Three Women and their Books of Hours* (London, 2003).

[20] C. Scott-Stokes, *Women's Books of Hours in Medieval England* (Woodbridge, 2006), 14.

for the saints of eastern England: St Edmund, for example, and St Hugh of Lincoln.[21]

In the founding the chantry in St James chapel, Frampton, Margery de Multon was not doing anything particularly unusual. On the contrary, by the time of its creation the proliferation of such institutions was well under way.[22] To understand fully, however, why they were popular amongst landowning families we need to recall some important aspects of Christian practice and belief. A chantry, unlike a chapel, was not a place but an institution. It was essentially an endowment of masses, 'chanted' for the souls of a person or persons, and could be either perpetual or for a given period of time.[23] The entire phenomenon is predicated upon the idea of intercession, by the Lord and his saints, and upon the concept of pardon for venial as opposed to mortal sin. It is also predicated upon the evolution of purgatory within Western thought.[24] This has its ultimate roots in St Paul and its origins in St Augustine. A matter of popular belief, it was systematized by the schoolmen of northern France in the twelfth century and raised to the level of dogma at the second Council of Lyons in 1274. Although purgatory was regarded by theologians as more of a state than a place, it came to be imagined as a location between Heaven and Hell. This was where the majority of Christians, it was believed, would find themselves as they went through the process of purgation from sin. This process could be speeded up, not by the dead themselves but by the living, through suffrages, that is prayers, masses and alms. Fear of the sufferings of the soul in purgatory was a stimulus, therefore, both to good works, especially charitable bequests, and to the endowment of special altars where intercessionary prayers could be said and masses celebrated. Wealth used in this way was, in Eamon Duffy's famous phrase, a form of 'post mortem fire-insurance'.[25]

It is beyond doubt that such chapels were a matter of status as well as convenience. Every residence of a great lord is likely to have had one. In size they could range from small 'closets' within the main dwelling to separate buildings, sometimes of considerable size. From the mid-fourteenth-century onwards they

---

[21] The full list is: St Laurence, St Edward, St Thomas the Martyr (the Translation of), St Nicholas, St Edmund, St Martin, St Hugh the Confessor, St Mary Magdalen, St Katharine, and St Margaret the Virgin (presumably Margaret of Antioch).

[22] Sir Geoffrey de Langley had one in his manor house at Pinley near Coventry as early as 1222 when he received a grant from Ralph de Manewaring, parson of the chapel of St Michael's, Coventry, to the effect that during Ralph's life Geoffrey could have a chantry 'in his free chapel' there, as long as St Michael's sustained no injury thereby and provided that the chaplain who celebrated there made canonical obedience to him: *The Langley Cartulary*, ed. P. R. Coss, Dugdale Society Main Ser. 32 (Oxford, 1980), nos. 384–5, 524. By Margery's time such chantries must have existed in considerable numbers.

[23] The classic study is K. L. Wood-Leigh, *Perpetual Chantries in Britain* (Cambridge, 1965). See also Joel T. Rosenthal, *The Purchase of Paradise* (London, 1972).

[24] There is a good treatment of purgatory, including its roots and its historiography, in Paul Binski, *Medieval Death: Ritual and Representation* (London, 1966), 21–8, 181–99.

[25] E. Duffy, *The Stripping of the Altars* (New Haven and London, 1992), 302.

Figure 8.2. The Stonor chapel.

were increasingly built in stone. They could be entirely free-standing or partially attached to the main house.[26] A good example of a once free-standing chapel is at Stonor in Oxfordshire, where a detached chapel was built to the south-east of the manor house and enlarged or rebuilt in 1349 (Figure 8.2).[27] Another is at Lytes Cary in Somerset where the still detached but contiguous chapel was built, it seems, for Peter le Lyte around 1343.[28] An equally good example of an entirely integral chapel is in the fortified manor house completed in brick by Petronilla and William de Nerford in Suffolk in the late thirteenth century. The chapel contains a carved figure on the roof boss said to represent St Petronilla whose cult was popular in, and largely confined to, East Anglia.[29] This is a reminder that chapels could contain devotional images. The chapel, moreover, retains a pair of brackets on either side of the east window which were undoubtedly for religious sculptures.[30]

It is not surprising to find that the lavish household furnishings of the de la Beche family extended to their chapel. Their inventory shows it to have been well-stocked with priestly vestments and fabrics for the altar. Seven sets of vestments are itemized. Five surplices are also noted, as well as an *accon* (presumably a 'haketon' or tunic) embroidered with a leopard's head in gold. A few items are said to be old or worn, but for the most part they are of fine quality and carefully described. One set of vestments, for example, is described as of cloth of gold, lined with green sendal and powdered with stags, hounds,

---

[26] Mertes, *English Noble Household*, 140–1; Wood, *The English Medieval House*, 227–40.
[27] J. Sherwood and N. Pevsner, *The Buildings of England: Oxfordshire* (London, 1974), 792.
[28] N. Pevsner, *The Buildings of England: South and West Somerset* (London, 1958), 228.
[29] Coss, *The Lady in Medieval England*, 63–4.
[30] R. Marks, *Image and Devotion in late Medieval England* (Stroud, 2004), figure 40 and pp. 55–6, where the author adds: 'Almost certainly the large numbers of exquisite ivory images of the Virgin and Child which survive from between c. 1250 to c. 1350 began life as prized objects of personal devotion in a domestic context.'

and peacocks. It comes as no surprise to find that the de la Beche arms figure here too. One set, of murrey velvet, is embroidered with the family arms, while another of camaca cloth of gold is both powdered with griffons and embroidered with the de la Beche arms as well as being lined with green sendal. The same is true of the corporals and frontals for the altar. A large frontal of purple velvet and another of murrey velvet both carry the de la Beche arms. The arms of related families also figure. A set of jewels for an amice has the arms of Bacoun, for example, while an old frontal is powdered with divers arms but pre-eminently with those of Bacoun and Poynings (the family of Margery de la Beche). Various other fabrics are itemized. There was also a lantern, a bell, a box (*boist*) a chalice, a superaltar (a portable altar, that is), and an ivory image of Our Lady. As one would expect, there were also books: a missal with a black cover, a gradual, an antiphoner, a psalter, an old *porthors* (perhaps a *portiforium* or *portas*, that is a portable breviary), another *porthors* with a red cover, a primer, and a *troper* (or *tropier*).[31] It comes as a surprise to find that none of these, nor indeed the chalice, is said to carry the de la Beche arms.

Of course, we should not assume that all gentry chapels were so opulent or so well-equipped. The inventory of Edmund de Appleby suggests that his chapel was sparsely furnished in comparison.[32] On the other hand there is no reason to suppose that the de la Beche family were exceptional. Piety and display, once again, went hand in hand. These twin features of contemporary society were by no means confined to the gentry. Indeed, both in the construction of household chapels and in their furnishing, the gentry and their forebears were aping the higher nobility. There was nothing at all new in this. Emulation is the stuff of gentility, and the history of monasticism had already revealed its force. The nobility, together of course with royalty, had been the founders of monastic houses.[33] In many cases these became the family houses of the founder's descendants and the churches themselves became family *mausolea*.[34] The progenitor of the Berkeleys, for example, founded St Augustine's at Bristol in 1141. Apart from the founder's son, all holders of the Berkeley barony were buried there until 1361. Similarly, throughout the twelfth century most, if not all, of the

---

[31] The meaning of the last is unclear. Could it conceivably be a book of hours?

[32] See above 36–7.

[33] For a discussion of their motives, see, for example, Emma Mason, 'Timeo barones et dona ferentes', in D. Baker (ed.), *Religious Motivation: Biographical and Sociological Problems for the Church Historian*, Studies in Church History 15 (1978), 61–75; and Emma Cownie, *Religious Patronage in Anglo-Norman England, 1066–1135* (Woodbridge, 1998), ch. 9. For a good regional study, see Janet Burton, *The Monastic Order in Yorkshire, 1069–1215* (Cambridge, 1999). From the point of view of the services rendered by the monasteries, see Benjamin Thompson, 'From Alms to Spiritual Services: The Function and Status of Monastic Property in Medieval England', in Judith Loades (ed.), *Monastic Studies II* (Gwynnedd, 1991), 227–62.

[34] For what follows see the splendid essay by Brian Golding, 'Burials and Benefactions: An Aspect of Monastic Patronage in Thirteenth-Century England', in W. M. Ormrod (ed.), *England in the Thirteenth Century* (Harlaxton, 1984), 64–75.

Clares were buried at their foundation at Clare itself in Suffolk.[35] More minor nobles were generally less able to found monasteries, of course, although quite a few did so.[36] When they did there is no doubt that it was a matter of considerable family pride. The Huntingfields of Frampton, for example, were founders and patrons of the Cluniac priory of Mendham in Suffolk.[37] The fourteenth-century *Huntingfield Cartulary*, although it is otherwise concerned only with their Lincolnshire properties at Frampton, Toft and Boston, lists the founders and patrons of the priory.[38] This was clearly a matter of immense significance to them.

There were regional variations. In Gloucestershire the only case of a knightly family founding a monastery appears to have been the priory of Leonard Stanley, founded by Roger de Berkeley *c*.1131.[39] In Lincolnshire the situation seems to have been rather different. As Dorothy Owen informed us, the seventy years after 1130 witnessed 'a rapid, almost feverish' series of monastic foundations in the county.[40] Some of these were houses of Austin and Premonstratensian canons; others were Cistercian or belonged to the English order centred on Sempringham. Cells of alien priories were also established. Many of the new houses were set up on unreclaimed land or in heavy woodland, with economic as well as spiritual benefits to the founders. The founders need not have been especially wealthy. Some were not tenants-in-chief but mesne tenants, like Eudo de Grainsby, for example, who founded Greenfield Priory, although there was no necessary correlation between tenure and wealth.[41] More often, however, such men followed their overlords in supporting the latter's foundations or choices. A late twelfth-century list of the charters of the Lincolnshire abbey of Revesby, for example, includes many confirmations by barons of grants by knights who were their under tenants.[42]

---

[35] From the early thirteenth-century, however, having acquired the earldom of Gloucester they transferred their mausoleum from Clare to Tewkesbury. Similarly, the Bohuns, having acquired the earldom of Hereford in 1200 through descent from Miles of Gloucester, the founder of Llanthony by Gloucester, chose this house as their burial place. After they acquired the earldom of Essex they switched to Waldon in Essex (a house founded and patronized by previous earls) although not immediately.

[36] See, for example, Burton, *Monastic Order in Yorkshire*, ch. 7.

[37] For the history of the priory see *VCH Suffolk*, ii. 87.

[38] *Fundatores prioratus de Mendham*: William de Huntingfield founder of the priory; Sibyl his wife; Roger I, second patron; Alice de Senliz his wife; William II, second, third patron; Isabel de Fenyll his wife; Roger II, fourth patron; Joan de Bobing(ton) his wife; William III, fifth patron; Emma le Grey his wife; Roger III, sixth patron; Jocasta d'Engayne his wife; William IV, seventh patron; Joan de Hastings (Astyng) his wife; Roger IV, eighth patron; Emma de Northwick his wife; William V, ninth patron; Elizabeth de Willoughby his wife. For the *Huntingfield Cartulary* see below 187–9. For their genealogy see *Complete Peerage*, vi. 664–73.

[39] N. Saul, 'The Religious Sympathies of the Gentry in Gloucestershire, 1200–1500', *Transactions of the Bristol and Gloucestershire Archaeological Society* (1980), 105.

[40] For this and what follows, see Dorothy Owen, *Church and Society in Medieval Lincolnshire* (Lincoln, 1971), 48–9.

[41] Eudo was a tenant of the honour of Richmond and of the fees of Arsic and Scotney.

[42] There is a large literature on the subject. See, for example, J. C. Ward, 'Fashions in Monastic Endowment: the Foundations of the Clare Family, 1066–1314', *Journal of Ecclesiastical History*, xxxii (1981), 427–51.

In these ways, then, lesser nobles had participated in the monastic fervour. In some cases over-enthusiastic endowment could cause embarrassment to later generations, as rent charges that were established way back in time were sometimes resisted. This was the case, for example, with the Multons of Frampton. In 1339 the sheriff of Lincoln received a writ ordering him to recover £20 due to the prior of Watton representing ten years' arrears on a rent charge of £2 granted by Thomas de Multon back in the thirteenth century and about which there had been law suits in 1297 and 1324–5. The rent charge was noted as reducing the income from Frampton manor in 1368.[43] In many cases, too, there was regret over the granting of advowsons—the right to appoint the rector of a parish—to monasteries so that more often than not the livings became appropriated by them with the duties being undertaken by vicars. A major feature of twelfth- and early-thirteenth-century piety, the granting of advowsons seriously declined during the second quarter of the thirteenth century and even went into reverse as some families sought to retrieve them (unsuccessfully, more often than not) through the courts.[44] Where advowsons did survive in lay hands, they were regarded as a valuable appurtenance to a manor.

These problems, however, lay in the future. Meanwhile, especially in terms of salvation, burial in a monastic church was a prize worth having, the more so if the house in question, and indeed its order, had a reputation for spirituality. Not surprisingly, lesser nobles were often buried in monastic churches, and this continued into the thirteenth century. In Gloucestershire, to take one example, we find that two thirteenth-century members of the St Amand family, lords of South Cerney, were buried in Cirencester Abbey, to which they were benefactors.[45] By this time, however, there was a plethora of institutions worthy of support, and the old monastic orders had lost their primacy. John Smyth, the historian of the Berkeleys, listed the benefactions made by Robert II, who died in 1220. He made substantial grants to St Augustine's, Bristol, where obits were established for himself and his two wives, but he also made grants to Christchurch Priory (where he was received into confraternity), to the Cistercian abbey of Kingswood, to the houses of Stanley and Bradenstoke, to the Knights Hospitaller and to the hospital of St Katherine's outside Bristol which he himself had founded. Moreover, he was a benefactor to the parish church at Berkeley and had founded chantries in his private chapels at Portbury and Bedminster.[46] The Berkeleys were an important noble family, of regional significance. Their actions are doubtless indicative of a widespread trend across the nobility, high and low. The fact

---

[43] Multon no. 137. Watton was a Gilbertine House in Yorkshire: *VCH Yorkshire*, iii. 245.

[44] For further details and for the literature on the subject, see my *Lordship, Knighthood and Locality*, 268–9, and *The Origins of the English Gentry* (Cambridge, 2003), 103, and references given there.

[45] Saul, 'Religious Sympathies of the Gentry', 103; *The Cartulary of Cirencester Abbey*, vol. 2, ed. C. D. Ross (London, 1964), nos. 642–4.

[46] For this and what follows, see Golding, 'Burials and Benefactions', 71–2.

that the benefaction was being spread more and more thinly gave considerable annoyance to the older orders, and this comes through clearly in the works of monastic chroniclers and annalists. This annoyance was particularly focused on the friars, not least because spiritual leadership passed increasingly to them and with it considerable popularity among the laity. What gave special offence was burial elsewhere than in an older, monastic church. According to Matthew Paris, for example, 'the friars hung around the deathbeds of magnates and the wealthy so that they made secret wills commending themselves to the friars alone'.[47] What the monks feared, of course, was the drying up of benefaction which was often strongly bound up with the descendants of their founders and of early benefactors.[48]

Where the higher nobility led, the gentry tended to follow. They, too, patronized the friars. The Gloucestershire knight, Sir Anselm Gurney, who died in 1286, for example, made bequests to the friaries at Bristol—the Franciscans, the Carmelites and the Friars of the Sack—as well as to numerous small hospitals in Bristol and to six churches of parishes where he held land.[49] In order to acquire a fuller picture let us look in detail at the will of the knight Walter de Gloucester, drawn up on 22 August 1311.[50] Walter was a wealthy knight with considerable property. In Gloucestershire he had manors at Uley, Alweston, Brockworth, and Elmbridge. He also held the manor of Tadlington in Worcestershire and property in Surrey, at Southwark and at Chertsey. In Lincolnshire, apart from property in Lincoln itself and its suburb, he held at Haydor, Culverthorpe and Swarby, and at South Witham.[51] His heir was his son Walter, aged 17. His executors were Sir John de Foxley, knight, Hawise his wife, Sir Robert le Venour, rector of Medbourne, Leicestershire, Master Henry de Gloucester, rector of Heydon Boys, London diocese, and Laurence de Cirencester,[52] rector of Tillington, Chichester diocese. John de Foxley was a fellow Gloucesterhire knight. The clerics reflect the widespread nature of his interests.

Walter de Gloucester's will is a fairly conventional one, although it contains a striking number of bequests, some to individuals and some to institutions. The latter are particularly interesting. Money was given to the fabric of five churches, each representing an area of interest. St Mary, Badgeworth in Worcester diocese received £2 and St Giles, Uley in the same £1. The church at Haydor in Lincoln diocese received another £1 while St Nicholas in Newport in the suburbs

---

[47] Golding cites the specific example of a monastic annalist who complained that when William IV, earl of Warwick, was taken ill at Elmley he 'in the absence of all his friends made his will on the advice of Brother John of Olney, who changed his mind so that he chose not to be buried with his ancestors in the [monastic] cathedral church of Worcester, but among the Friars Minor'.

[48] Ibid. 73.

[49] Saul, 'Religious Sympathies of the Gentry', 100, citing J. W. Willis Bund (ed.) *Register of Godfrey Giffard*, 2 vols, Worcestershire Historical Society (1898–1902) ii. 295–6.

[50] His will is contained in *The Register of Walter Reynolds, Bishop of Worcester, 1308–13*, ed. R. A. Wilson, Dugdale Society (1928), 25–27.

[51] *CIPM* v. no. 350.   [52] ? *Cicestre*.

of Lincoln received a mark and St Margaret, Southwark, ¹/₂ mark. The parish chaplain serving the latter received another ¹/₂ mark and the clerk 2s. Equally interesting is the number of bequests to friaries. No less than ten friaries received sums of either £1, 1 mark or ¹/₂ mark. All four orders of Dominicans, Franciscans, Augustinians and Carmelites were represented, in London, Gloucester and Lincoln. The Dominicans of London, in whose church he wished to be buried, also got his purple vestment, with tunic, dalmatic and other things belonging to it, and his chalice. Several of the bequests to individuals were also to friars, namely to Friar Luke, executor of the king, £2, to Friar Edmond Damnory £2, and to Friar Thomas de Westwong 1 mark.

The same tendency to spread bequests is found even more in the wide-ranging will of Sir Geoffrey Luttrell. He made no less than thirty-two institutional bequests. Fourteen were to the upkeep of chapels and to the fabric of churches. Four were to monasteries and six were to friaries. Four others were for the upkeep of images in London, Canterbury and York. Finally, corn was to be supplied to the mendicant poor of four parishes, namely Irnham, Hooton Pagnell, Bridgeford and Saltby. The total came to £29 6s, and 100 quarters of corn. To this extraordinarily long list the codicil to his will adds further specific bequests to the churches: a pair of silver basins to the great altar of the holy mother church of the blessed Mary at Lincoln, jewels to the shrine of St Hugh and the tomb of St Robert, both at Lincoln, further jewels to the shrine of St Thomas at Canterbury, to the high altar at St Paul's, to the image of the blessed Mary at Walsingham, and so on. Sir Geoffrey was unusual in his bequests and in the strength of his piety, no doubt, but many wills display the same features.

As far as the gentry was concerned there was a general correlation between major benefaction on the one hand and place of burial on the other. Nigel Saul has shown very clearly for Gloucestershire that the evidence of wills and tomb monuments matches that from monastic cartularies.[53] By the early fourteenth century, however, monastic benefaction was tending to peter out. This did not mean that relations between gentry and religious houses were necessarily poor. Some maintained links with local monasteries, especially where there was an historical association. John de Multon, for example, was on good terms with the abbot of Revesby. They may have had family members in religious orders, sometimes in high positions, as they did within the secular clergy. Sir Geoffrey Luttrell was closely related by marriage to Bishop Oliver Sutton.[54] His will contained a legacy of 10 marks to his son, Robert, who was a Knight Hospitaller. Gentry children could be sent to school at religious houses, including nunneries as well as monasteries. And, of course, nunneries were depositories for

[53] N. Saul, 'The Religious Sympathies', 99–112.
[54] Sir Giles de Badlesmere gave his best horse to his kinsman (*consanguineus*), Henry Burghersh, bishop of Lincoln. The will is in the Register of Bishop Burghersh, Lincoln Record Office, Episcopal Register V. It is cited inaccurately in A. Gibbons, *Early Lincoln Wills* (Lincoln, 1888).

daughters, although it is one of those dubious historical generalities that they were 'unwanted' ones. One is not at all surprised to find that Geoffrey Luttrell had two sisters and another relative, Lady Joan de Sutton, who were all nuns at Hampole, and that he had a daughter, Isabel, who was a nun at Sempringham. There is a genuine element of piety here, although whether it was strictly the girls' own piety is another matter.

Notwithstanding the fact the monastic orders were included in some gentry wills, there is no doubting the serious decline in benefaction towards them and that the greatest beneficiaries, at least in the first instance, were the friars. Although it is clear that friaries became popular burial places of the gentry during the second half of the thirteenth century, the incidence is very difficult to quantify. There survives, however, an invaluable list of names of those who were buried in the Franciscan church at Coventry. It gives not only some indication of the number of gentry who chose burial in a friary within a particular locality but also goes a long way towards explaining its popularity.[55] It survives in British Library Harley 6033, a curious manuscript which contains only ten items and many blank leaves. The items include lists of burials at the four London friaries—White Friars, Black Friars, Augustinians, and Grey Friars—as well as those at Grey Friars, Coventry. The final item is a list of 'funerals as have been served by any of the Officers of Arms since Sept I 1596 to July 1599'. On one of the blank leaves at the beginning is the name Robert Treswell Blewmantle. Robert was made Bluemantle Pursuivant in 1589 and Somerset Herald in 1597. He was presumably the owner, and very probably the compiler, of at least some of the contents, including the Coventry list. This, however, is undoubtedly a copy of a pre-existing list, possibly made before all of the monuments in the church were destroyed.[56] There are some errors due to copying: the name Capworth for Lapworth, for example. The antiquary's list of burials is embellished with details. Some of these, as we shall see, will have come from the lost sepulchral monuments; others must have been supplied by the antiquary himself. Not all of these are accurate. Nonetheless the list is rare and invaluable.

The first section is entitled 'Names of the founders of the Friars Minor', indicating from the third name onwards that they were buried there. This has confused at least one commentator into believing that they were all buried in the church. The list begins with Ranulf (III) *illustris* earl of Chester, lord of Cheylesmore, who died in 1232, and his wife[57] Clemence. Ranulf was buried,

---

[55] The list of names has been printed in 1888 by Benjamin Poole in his *Antiquities of Coventry* and more recently by Iain Soden, *Coventry: the Hidden History* (2005). Soden suggests that it is a copy of an original dating from c. 1450–75.

[56] Little remains of the church today. The buildings were largely destroyed at the Reformation, leaving only the fourteenth-century tower and spire. This was incorporated into Christ Church, built in 1830–2. This church in turn perished in the 1940 Blitz, all that is except the tower and spire which survived once again.

[57] The word used here is *consors*, as it is with the Montalt and Hastings wives who follow.

'with great pomp' the *Complete Peerage* says at St Werburg's, Chester, and his heart at Dieulacres Priory.[58] The successor to the childless Ranulf III as Coventry's secular lord was Hugh Daubigny, earl of Arundel, the second founder according to the antiquary, and he was certainly not buried in the friary.[59] It is when we come to the third founder or founders that the authentic burials begin. These are of the Montalts, Roger and Cecily. Cecily was one of the sisters and coheirs of Earl Hugh and hence she and her husband acquired the lordship of Coventry as their share of his inheritance. The antiquary tells us that Roger lies in the choir in the middle before the high altar with the Lady Cecily[60] 'in the middle on the left'. In 1249 Roger and Cecily had conveyed their lordship at Coventry to the Benedictine Priory there, apparently in order to finance his participation in a forthcoming crusade, but with major reservations, including the manor house and park at Cheylesmore (the successor to the castle as the caput of the lordship) and the Franciscan friary which Ranulf had founded in its grounds. The association with the friary was therefore a strong one. Roger died in 1260. Cecily survived him, although the date of her death is not recorded.

The antiquary continues with the following names:

* John de Montalt his[61] son
* Robert de Montalt younger son *germanus* (i.e. german, of the full blood) of the aforesaid John
* Sir Roger de Montalt elder son of the aforesaid Sir Robert with Lady Joan his wife, daughter of Sir Roger de Clifford.
* Isabella, wife of Sir Robert de Montalt the younger, daughter of Sir Roger de Clifford.[62]

The implication is clear. These were all buried in the choir. The list ends with an apparently unrelated name, that of Sir Thomas Hastang, described as *miles strenuissimus* (most valiant knight), and his wife[63] who lie on the north side. These, then, are clearly the names of those buried in the body of the choir. There then follows a list of fifteen individuals, described by the antiquary as 'other friends' who are buried on the steps of the chancel.

We will return to these shortly. In the meantime let us note that what we have here is clearly a later thirteenth-century Montalt mausoleum, located in the choir. John must have predeceased his father, Roger. Robert, who succeeded to his inheritance, including Coventry after his mother's death, died in 1275. His

[58] It is just possible that he was re-interred at Coventry, as Ian Soden has suggested, but it seems unlikely. On the other hand the text does name the earl *with* rather than *and* the Lady Clemence. She lived until 1252. Her place of burial is unknown but it could conceivably have been Coventry. It could therefore be argued that the antiquary was led into the assumption that Ranulf was buried here too.
[59] He died in 1243, 'in the flower of his youth', and was buried with his ancestors at Wymondham Priory. He is widow was buried much later at Marham in Norfolk.
[60] His *consors*, whom the antiquary mistakenly calls sister of Earl Ranulf.   [61] *Sic.*
[62] A genealogy is given below this list of names.   [63] *uxor* here not *consors.*

son, Roger, who made his own grant of land to the Grey Friars for the extension of their precinct in 1289, died in 1296. His wife, here called Joan but elsewhere Juliana, seems to have predeceased him. She was indeed daughter of Roger de Clifford. Robert his brother succeeded.[64] He died in 1329 and was buried in Shouldham Priory, Norfolk; his widow was buried in Stradsett church, also in Norfolk. The Montalt mausoleum at Grey Friars, Coventry, was active, in the sense of receiving new burials and hence no doubt monuments, until the end of the century. It did not receive the last Montalts, however; perhaps because there was no-one to ensure this.[65]

The Montalts were great lords and where they led others were likely to follow. Theirs was not the only mausoleum, however, at Grey Friars, Coventry. Off the chancel on the north side and towards its west end lay the Hastings chapel. Here were buried Sir Henry de Hastings, lord of Allesley near Coventry, and his wife, Lady Joan, daughter of Sir William de Cantelupe. He died in 1269, she in 1271. They were presumably the founders of this chapel. Their son, Sir John and his wife, Isabella, daughter of Sir William de Valence, earl of Pembroke, were also buried in the chapel, she dying in 1305 and he in 1313.[66] John, meanwhile, had acquired the lordship of Abergavenny from his mother, Joan. Nonetheless, he was buried in his father's chapel in Coventry. In the late thirteenth century the Hastings were not the elevated lords that they later became. Henry himself was lord principally of Allesley near Coventry, which his family had held of the earls of Chester and then of the Montalts.

Our antiquary lists those buried in the Hastings chapel. He begins with Sir Henry de Hastings and his wife,[67] the Lady Joan, daughter of Sir William de Cantelupe. He adds that she was the sister of the bishop of Hereford; the bishop in question was, of course, Thomas de Cantelupe who was later to be canonized. He then notes Sir John de Hastings and his wife, Lady Isabella. Two other burials were Lady Joan de Huntingfield, their daughter, and Lora (otherwise called Lorna) de Latimer, daughter of Henry de Hastings himself. We have here two examples of married ladies returning in death to their family mausoleum; no doubt this was because they willed it so. Also buried in the chapel was Robert de Shottesbrook, described in the text as 'most valiant esquire and sometime-standard bearer of the same Sir Henry and afterwards his steward'.

---

[64] He is recorded as having married Emma widow of Sir Richard FitzJohn who died around August 1297. If the antiquary is correct and he had married another daughter of Roger de Clifford, she must have been an earlier wife and we have one of those examples of a double marriage, brothers marrying sisters. It seems quite possible that Roger de Clifford should have had a daughter called Isabella, given that his was his mother's name. Sir Robert de Montalt's first wife, if this is accurate, probably died in the 1290s.

[65] Curiously, another Montalt, Roger de Montalt the younger, is found buried in the body of the church.

[66] *Complete Peerage*, vi. 345–8.

[67] The word *consors* is used again here, and for Sir John's wife.

The details in the antiquary's list of burials here is derived from an earlier, probably medieval, description of the contents of the chapel. It is written in French and was published in Dugdale's *Antiquities of Warwickshire*.[68] It reinforces the information that we have but adds further valuable details. It tells us, as we expect, that two knights are buried in the chapel. One is Sir Henry de Hastings. His wife clearly lies next to him. She is identified as Joan, in precisely the same terms as in the antiquary's list, and displays the Hastings and Cantelupe arms. The other knight has the arms of Hastings surrounded, it says, by those of Valence, 'his name being John de Hastings'.[69] Next to him lies Dame Isabel de Valence herself, with the Hastings arms. There is no indication of precisely where any of the arms are displayed until we come next to Dame Joan de Huntingfield, daughter to Sir John de Hastings and Isabel de Valence. Joan was the wife of William de Huntingfield IV, son of the Roger de Huntingfield for whom an account roll survives for his Lincolnshire manor of Frampton. She wears a gown powdered with the arms of Hastings and Huntingfield.[70] On her mantle above she displays a different set of arms—*argent, 2 bars gules*[71]—and on her sleeves the arms of Valence. She has a pillow beneath her head showing the arms of Hastings and Huntingfield quartered, that is to say *or, a manche gules* and *or, on a fess gules 3 roundels (torteaux) argent*.

There then follow the details on Henry de Hastings and Joan, and John de Hastings and Isabel. The precise dates of the deaths of the latter couple are given, i.e. 9 March 1312 in the case of John and 3 October 1305 in that of Isabel. All these details, in Latin, are preceded by the statement that they are written on the table (*En le table estoit escrit*), strongly suggesting that they are derived from a tomb chest. Joan de Huntingfield is said to lie to the right of the table. There then follows the notice, in Latin, of Robert de Shottesbrook, Sir Henry's steward, in exactly the same terms as in the antiquary's list. This, too, seems to have been an original inscription on or near the tomb itself. We then find a notice, again in Latin, that John, Edmund and Henry, sons of Sir William de Hastings, son of Sir John de Hastings, lie here, and John Huntingfield, son of William de Huntingfield and Lady Joan his consort, information that is not in the antiquary's list. Oddly, however, there is no mention of Lora de Latimer nor

---

[68] W. Dugdale, *The Antiquities of Warwickshire*, 2 vols, rev. W. Thomas (London, 1730), i. 182–3. There is a translation in *Monasticon* VI—3 (ed. J. Caley, H. Ellis and B. Bandinel, London 1830), 1533. There is an account derived entirely from these in W. G. Fretton, 'Memorials of the Franciscans or Grey Friars Coventry', *Transactions of the Midland Institute, Archaeological Section* (Birmingham, 1882), 34–53.

[69] It is not therefore entirely clear whether he is actually named on the monument: *L'autre chivalier est ove l'armes de Hastings enseint ovesque lez armes de Valence, son nome estoit Johan de Hastings*.

[70] *En une gowne pudre des Armes de Hastings, & or, a fess gules* (i.e. Huntingfield).

[71] It actually reads *argent deux fesses gules*. These arms occur again in the description of the windows as *argent deux barrs de geules ove une label de Valence*. I have not been able to definitively identify them, but clearly there is a Valence association.

of Edmund son of Sir John de Segrave, whom the antiquary tells us also lay in
the chapel.

The Segraves were lords of Caludon, on the other side of Coventry from
Allesley. They were of similar station to the Hastings and were also destined
for great social heights. The two families were related by marriage. Stephen de
Segrave, minister of Ranulf III, earl of Chester, and later royal justiciar, who died
in 1241, had married Ida de Hastings. Edmund was probably one of the sons of
Sir John de Segrave, who died in 1325.[72] He seems to be the only Segrave who
was buried at Grey Friars. For generations they were buried at Chacombe Priory
in Northamptonshire.

There is a further feature of the Hastings chapel which the French account of
the chapel furnishes for us, and that is the description of the stained glass. Indeed,
the account begins with the glass. Some of this, at least, was clearly contemporary
with the monuments and was meant to compliment them. The windows were
adorned with heraldic glass. Four are noted, one in the north, two in the east
and a fourth in an unspecified location. All contained the Hastings arms together
with others, probably in vertical columns. One of the east windows contained
the arms of Hastings, Cantelupe, and Valence.[73] Another window had the arms
of Hastings and Huntingfield at the bottom, presumably impaled, with three
other sets above.

What do these details tell us, then, of the Hastings chapel as a gentry
mausoleum created in the late thirteenth and early fourteenth centuries? The
first observation is that it must have appeared impressive, reflecting the wealth
and local significance of the family. The complementarity of the glass with the
monuments not only added to it aesthetically but also reinforced the sense of
family presence. It held essentially two generations of Hastings lords and ladies
together with a variety of close relatives who were not themselves heads of the
family, some non-inheriting children of the next generation and one member
of a more distantly related but associated family. There was, however, another
person buried here: Henry's standard-bearer, Robert de Shottesbrook. This is
a reminder, should we need it, of the strong military outlook of much of the
nobility of this period and hence the military content of the process of burial and
of many sepulchral monuments. His burial here also indicates, of course, a close
relationship in peace and war, an insight deepened by the fact that this man was
allowed burial in what was the family mausoleum.

Robert was not the only officer to be buried in the church, however. In the
nave we find Roger the chamberlain of Sir Thomas Blund. Thomas, *recte* Blount,
was the second husband of Juliana, widow of the second John de Hastings. He

---

[72] *Complete Peerage*, xi. 609.

[73] The other east window contained the arms of Hastings with those of the Leybourns and the
Despensers, representing the two marriages of John de Hastings II. This suggests a slightly later date
for the glazing of at least this window.

was lord of Tibberton in Gloucestershire and a steward of the royal household. We might also note the burial in the church of Joan de Sackville, once damsel (*domicilla*) of the lady of Segrave and that of John of Tanworth who died at 'Bergavenny', presumably in the service of the Hastings family. We have here some clear indications of the strong relationships that the gentry could have with key members of their households, the probability of which we spoke earlier and to which testamentary bequests seem to allude.

The mention of Abergavenny is a reminder that the Hastings mausoleum did not endure beyond two to three generations. Lord John de Hastings, the second baron, was buried at Abergavenny when he died in 1325. It was time for the Hastings family, soon to be earls of Pembroke, to move on. Meanwhile something of the character of Grey Friars in the late thirteenth and early fourteenth centuries in terms of burial and commemoration has been revealed.

The Hastings were not the only gentry family to find burial at Grey Friars in the late thirteenth century. Another of the most significant families in the area, the Langleys did so too. Geoffrey de Langley, who died in 1274, was one of the most notorious of Henry III's forest justices. A considerable property accumulator in Warwickshire and elsewhere, he had been an object of attack by the baronial opposition to the crown during the 1260s. He was lord of both Pinley and Shortley near Coventry and a property holder in the city itself. The antiquary's list notes the burial of Geoffrey and Matilda his *consors,* and a little later of Walter his son. Walter, by virtue of a profitable marriage arranged by his father, was independently lord of Wyken, another local manor. He died in 1280. Wives did not necessarily follow suit. Alice de Langley, Walter's widow, as we shall see, was buried elsewhere.

The Langleys were buried somewhere in the body of the church at Grey Friars. In addition to those buried in the Hastings chapel and the Montalt mausoleum, including the 'interloper', Thomas Hastang, and the fifteen buried at the foot of the presbytery, another 124 persons are noted as buried in the church, presumably in the nave and aisles. A considerable number of those buried there were gentry, including in fact the first fourteen named.[74] An early burial in the nave was that of John de Pontefract, sometime steward of the prior of Coventry, although he is given here as John Pomfrett, bailiff, and Agnes his wife. This is surprising given the antagonism between the monks and the friars, for which we have specific evidence in 1269. John was dead by 1280; perhaps by then this antagonism had died down.[75] Another early burial in the nave was probably that of Sir Robert de Verdon the elder and Margaret his wife. They held at Bourton on Dunsmore, east of Coventry.[76] Among the earliest may well have been the two heart burials

[74] We have no means of knowing how the list was compiled. Did it begin at the east end or in one or both of the transepts? Or were the names recorded in a single circuit?

[75] *The Early Records of Medieval Coventry*, ed. P. R. Coss, British Academy Records of Social and Economic History, new ser. 11 (Oxford, 1986).

[76] For the Verdons, see *VCH Warwickshire*, vi. 39–40.

recorded near the presbytery, those of Sir Thomas de Bray and Sir Richard de Amundevill. Thomas de Bray held of the Hastings family at Stretton upon Dunsmore. One time sheriff of Bedfordshire and Buckinghamshire, Thomas was a justice of gaol delivery in Warwickshire during the 1280s and a justice of oyer and terminer.[77] The history of heart burials and the papal condemnation of 1299 strongly suggest that the heart in question belonged to this Thomas de Bray rather than his son, another Thomas, who was holding the manor at Stretton in 1313.[78] Richard de Amundeville was undoubtedly the lord of Berkswell to the south of Coventry. His will was dated 20 March 1299. He bequeathed his body to Chacombe Priory in Northamptonshire to lie near his father's grave but his heart to the oratory of the Grey Friars in Coventry.[79]

Dates are not always easy to establish, given the repetition of Christian names within families and our comparative lack of knowledge where the deaths of ladies are concerned. It would seem to be clear though that the number of gentry burials in the friary grew at the beginning of the fourteenth century, reached its apogee during the second quarter and continued into the third. In this second quarter they were increasingly encroaching upon the holiest part of the church, as was often the case at this point in time. We have already noted that Sir Thomas Hastang and his wife were buried in the choir close to the Montalts. They were both living in 1340 and he in 1343. He was the head of an important family, holding at Hopsford, Leamington Hastings, and Budbrooke in Warwickshire.[80] Of the fifteen people said to be buried (heart or body) on the steps of the chancel, twelve were gentry and one, Sir Nicholas Hastang, was rector of Leamington Hastings.[81] The twelve include William Rivel of Clifton, Brownsover, and Fenny Newbold. He was living in 1316 but dead by 1325.[82] Another was Sir John de Odingseles, knight, glossed in the text as once lord of Long Itchington. This was probably the John who was pardoned for his part in the death of Piers Gaveston and who died in 1337.[83] The heart burials we have mentioned. A striking feature is the number of women who figure here. In addition to Alice, mother of William Rivel, there is Lady Joan de Chaunceus, Lady Margaret de Braundeston, lady of Lapworth, Emma lady of Wappenbury, Lady Eleanor West, Lady Beatrice de Bishopton, Lady Margaret de Hartshill, and Agnes, daughter of the lord of Bradeston. Some of these can be located and to some degree dated. Margaret

---

[77] Coss, *Origins of the Gentry*, 153, 156; *VCH Warwickshire*, vi. 242.

[78] For heart burials, see Brian and Moira Gittos, 'Motivation and Choice: The Selection of Medieval Secular Effigies', in Coss and Keen, *Heraldry, Pageantry and Social Display*, 146–7 and references given there.

[79] Dugdale, *Antiquities of Warwickshire* ii. 980. See also Coss, *Origins of the Gentry*, 153.

[80] *VCH Warwickshire*, iii. 66–7, and vi. 255, 266.

[81] East Leamington in the text. The Hastang family had apparently conveyed the church to Nostell Priory and the living had been appropriated in 1232: *VCH Warwickshire*, vi. 154. It seems, therefore, odd to have had a Hastang rector at this date.

[82] *VCH Warwickshire*, vi. 65–6, 175.

[83] Ibid. 126. He is glossed in the text as one time lord of Long Itchington.

de Braundeston occurs in 1282.[84] Her husband died in 1299 but she was still holding in dower, at Grandborough, in 1312. Eleanor West, wife of Sir Thomas West, was a Cantelupe. She was living in 1333. Beatrice was married to John de Bishopton. Both were living in 1337.[85] Margaret de Hartshill was a Stafford. Her husband died in 1368, aged around 73.[86] All of these ladies seem to have been buried where they wished, and away from their husbands.

Among the gentry buried in the nave we find some of the same characteristics. We find, for example, a number of ladies buried singly. Among the first fourteen names are Joan, daughter of Sir William Bagot, Lady Maryon de Birmingham and Lady Alice de Welles, as well as Isabella Otteley and Alice de Draycote. Joan Bagot sounds at first like an unmarried daughter, but in fact she is very probably the Joan whom William Bagot enfeoffed jointly with Roger de Coningsby of the manor of Morton Bagot in 1296, with reversion to Henry Bagot. The other two ladies, Maryon and Alice, are more obviously gentry wives or widows. There is also the above-mentioned Joan de Sackville, damsel of the lady of Segrave. Elsewhere, in fact named immediately after Geoffrey de Langley and his wife Matilda, we find Lady Margery de Pinkeneye. The Pinkeneys were a major Northamptonshire family, Margery being the wife of Sir Henry who succeeded to his estates aged 40 in 1296. She was widowed in 1315.[87] There is also Juliana, 'once lady of Asthill'. Asthill was one of the small manors in the Coventry area and she must be either the wife of William d'Aubigny who is among the fourteen or the widow of Oliver d'Aubigny who was living in 1279. Finally, one should note Sarah wife of Robert de Stoke. He was very probably the lawyer-administrator of that name, who was living in 1322 and who had carved himself a lordship and position of prominence in the area.

That pious ladies were attracted to the Franciscan order in the fourteenth century is certain enough. There were some, however, buried jointly with their husbands. Among the aforementioned fourteen are Sir Robert de Verdon the elder, knight, and lady Margaret his wife as well as John de Clifton and Lucy his wife. Later we find Henry Verney and Alice his wife. They are probably related to Henry de Vernoye, who is mentioned among the first fourteen and described as the founder of two friaries in Ireland. Among the other men were two knights, Sir John de Solneye and Sir Nicholas Pecche, knight. The latter was a relatively late arrival in the church. He was a commissioner of array in 1338 and taxer in 1348. He presented to the church of Honiley in 1354 and died sometime before 1366.[88] The Pecches, as we shall see later, were related to the Multons of Frampton. Among the most curious is the burial of Thomas son of William Boteler of Warrington, baron. The Butlers of Warrington held the manor of Exhall north of Coventry.[89] However, their seat was far away in Lancashire and

84 *VCH Warwickshire*, v. 110; vi. 95.   85 Ibid. iii. 261; iv. 202–3.
86 Ibid. iv. 132.   87 *CCR 1313–18*, 223.
88 *VCH Warwickshire*, iii. 121, 123.   89 Ibid. vi. 88.

they played relatively little part in Warwickshire affairs. It is as though the Butlers were making a token burial at Coventry as an expression of their local lordship, rather in the way that lords made bequests to churches and friaries in the various localities in which they held property. The last of the fourteen is Geoffrey de Whitley, holder of a small local manor.

Finally, one should mention Sir John de Langford, 'knight and constable of Kenilworth' and John de Verdon, knight, another member of the Verdon family of Bourton on Dunsmore. The former occurs as constable of Kenilworth in 1335 and 1341.[90] Sir John de Verdon was living in 1346. He was undoubtedly the son of Sir Robert de Verdon who was MP for Warwickshire 1297, 1307 and 1313, and commissioner of the peace 1307. Robert died shortly after 1327. He may be distinct from the Robert who was active as a justice of gaol delivery and of oyer and terminer in the 1270s and 1280s. Which of these is Robert de Verdon the elder, noted above as buried at Grey Friars, is unclear.

The chronology of burials at the Franciscan friary in Coventry is plain. The first to be buried in the church were Roger de Montalt and his wife Cecily, lords of Coventry, patrons and descendants of the founder. They lay in the most privileged position in the church, that is in the choir before the altar. This development took place some time after 1260. This was followed by the Langleys in the body of the church and by the Hastings family in their own chapel. The chapel was further colonized by descendants and a retainer of the Hastings family in the late thirteenth and early fourteenth centuries. Other burials and commemorations were taking place in the last decades of the thirteenth century and the number seems to have expanded in the second quarter of the fourteenth century. There were other gentry burials in the church. The first fourteen names mentioned in the sixteenth-century text were overwhelmingly gentry. They may well have been clustered towards the east end of the nave or in the transepts, and this would explain why they were listed first. Some gentry families were local, others came from a little further afield, but mostly from within Warwickshire. Burial on the edge of the chancel probably began with the two heart burials, one of which belongs to 1299, and gathered pace in the 1320s and 1330s. In the mid-fourteenth-century we find the Hastangs encroaching in the choir. Some of the burials in the body of the church were earlier than these and tend to be gentry or to have seigniorial associations.

Gentry families tended to follow greater lords, and even within the gentry the wealthier stock tended to lead the way. For some gentry families burial at a friary was an intermediate before turning to colonize parish churches. A good example is the Langleys. At Grey Friars the name of Sir Walter de Langley is followed by John de Langley. This could be his son, who was lord of Pinley near Coventry

[90] He came from Longford in Derbyshire, held the manor Killamarsh there in 1302 and died in 1304: *Feudal Aids*, i. 251; G. J. Brault, *The Rolls of Arms of Edward I*, 2 vols., Society of Antiquaries (London, 1997), ii. 264.

and of Siddington in Gloucestershire. However, it is unlikely, for John was a thoroughly committed Gloucestershire knight. His offices were largely exercised there. St Peter's Siddington became the family mausoleum and members of the family, including John, were commemorated there. The John de Langley at Grey Friars is more likely to have been the Coventry merchant of that name, who was distantly related to the gentry family and who was living in 1324.

Among the gentry, and those who followed them, burial with the friars seems, however, to have been a distinct and relatively short-term phase, although legacies to them did not cease. The singularly most enduring feature of the second half of the thirteenth and early fourteenth centuries in terms of the relationship between the gentry and the church was the growing emphasis placed by the gentry upon the parish church. This was a real sea change. Nigel Saul has shown that of the ninety-seven known burials of knights and esquires and their ladies in Gloucestershire between 1300 and 1500, seventy-seven were in parish churches.[91] Occasionally, one of them broke ranks. According to Leland one of the Pauncefots was buried in the hospital of St Bartholomew, Gloucester. However, his burial appears to have been the only one of note there. The tombs of other members of the family were in their parish churches of Much Cowarne, Crickhowell and Ledbury.

Ladies were not necessarily buried with their husbands, however, and sometimes preferred to lie with their natal family. This may have been particularly the case with heiresses. Alice de Langley, for example, whose husband Walter and father-in-law Geoffrey de Langley lay in the Franciscan friary in Coventry, willed her own body to the church of Wolfhamcote in Warwickshire, one of the three manors of which she was heiress. She and her husband Walter were married in 1243–4. He died in 1280. She, however, lived until 1300. In her will she commends her soul to God, the Blessed Mary and all the saints, and her body to be buried in the church of Wolfhamcote before the altar of the Blessed Peter. She left 30 marks for the exequies around her burial and £5 to the fabric of the church. There is no mention of her husband.

Although for some gentry families burial at a friary was an intermediate phase, the gentry in general in this period 'tightened their grip' over the parish churches.[92] This development was to have a profound effect, not only upon the interior of parish churches but also upon how the lord was perceived in relation to the church and the parish community. It is to the parish that we now turn.

---

[91] Saul, 'Religious Sympathies', 103.   [92] Ibid. 109.

9

The Gentry and the Parish

In order to understand both the motivation behind this tightening grip and its effects we need to look closely at the changes that were affecting the parish church more generally in the thirteenth century. In visual terms the interior of the church was truly revolutionized.[1] Some devotional imagery certainly existed in twelfth-century churches, especially Christ on the cross (rood), occasionally flanked by the Virgin and St John, and the Virgin herself. However, the thirteenth century witnessed a very considerable growth in the number of images of Christ, the saints and the events of Holy Scripture. There can be no doubt that this was connected with the introduction of the elevation of the consecrated Host so that Christ's body could be seen by the congregation.[2] Images of the Virgin spread exponentially. Although the inspiration here was originally monastic, by the late twelfth century some parish churches already had altars dedicated to her. In the thirteenth century Marian images were much used for meditation and private devotion. Stories of the Virgin increased this appeal and her role as intercessor becomes increasingly evident.[3] In addition to the Virgin, and the rood images, there was a proliferation of images of other saints during the thirteenth century. This reflected the importance not only of the patronal saints but also of saints more generally as personal intercessors and helpers and, in return, as the recipients of prayers and offerings through their images. The rood remained the central focus, and was joined by images of the saints grouped around the high altar in the chancel. It was the nave, however, the public space of the church, that was truly transformed, with carved images, murals, and stained glass. The inspection of churches belonging to St Paul's Cathedral in the diocese of London conducted during the year 1249–52 shows that images were occurring in rural churches by the middle of the century. By the end of the century their incidence had greatly increased. Many churches were becoming 'image rich'. There were numerous 'standard' saints such as Peter, Paul, Michael, Nicholas, Christopher, Mary Magdalen, Margaret, and

---

[1] For what follows, see in particular Marks, *Image and Devotion*, esp. chs 2–5.

[2] Ibid. 41–2. In addition to carved statues or reliefs, there were also paintings on walls and sometimes on piers. For wall paintings, see especially the comprehensive study by Roger Rosewell: *Medieval Wall Paintings* (Woodbridge, 2008).

[3] It is no coincidence that there was a shift in the representation of her from a stiff and remote Romanesque figure to a 'more empathetic, smiling image of mother and child': ibid. 55.

Katherine, there were English saints like St Edmund and there was also some
regional diversity.

But it was not only images of saints that transformed the churches. We also
observe a veritable intrusion of secular images into sacred space.[4] This intrusion
began in the late twelfth century and seems to have reached its peak in the middle
of the fourteenth. In the thirteenth century St Thomas Aquinas, observing
that it was praiseworthy to beautify a church, also commended the building of
monuments because they incited men to pray for the souls of the departed.[5] The
clergy were bound to pray for their benefactors and by the late thirteenth century
it was a common theological position that monuments were an aide-memoire to
such prayer.

Sometimes a parish church must have been totally dominated by the image
of the lord and, coincidentally therefore, of lordship. A good example of this is
the church of St Michael's at Moccas in Herefordshire. It is small and simple in
structure. There is a nave, a chancel, and an apse.[6] The church was modernized,
however, in the early fourteenth century. The two decorated windows in the
chancel date from *c.*1300, while those in the nave are mid-fourteenth century.[7]
As was so often the case, reconstruction or additions to a parish church
were accompanied by more emphatic signs of a local family's predominance
(Figures 9.1 and 9.2). The church is dominated by an early fourteenth-century
stone effigy of a cross-legged knight on a tomb chest with shields in quatrefoils.[8]
The tomb is in the middle of the chancel, which does seem to have been its
original position. But this is not all. In the middle of the fourteenth century a
fine set of four glazed windows were installed in the nave. The upper half of two
of these survive on the north side. They have magnificent canopies with two tiny
figures on each side. Above the two are the arms of the Fresne family—*gules, two
bars per fess indented azure and argent*.[9] The arms are again within a quatrefoil.
Within the red and gold glass on three of the leaves there are green birds, while the
top leaf has a helm with a scarf waving, perhaps indicating a crest. On the south
side only two sets of arms survive, but there is little doubt that the same glass
was replicated four times. Pevsner thought it 'curious' that the artist was allowed
to do this. Cost was no doubt a factor in replicating the images, but Pevsner's
observation largely misses the point. The lost figures and the inscriptions below

---

[4] This was famously examined by Andrew Martindale in 'Patrons and Minders: the Intrusion of
the Secular into Sacred Spaces in the Late Middle Ages', *Studies in Church History* 28 (1992).

[5] Ibid. 169; Saul, *English Church Monuments*, 121.

[6] As Nikolaus Pevsner pointed out, 'if it were not for the bellcote and some tall decorated
windows which help to let light into the interior, [this] would be the perfect example of a Norman
village church', *Buildings of England: Herefordshire* (London, 1963), 253. There are three original
windows in the apse, one in the north wall and one high up on the west, and two Norman doorways
with weathered tampana.

[7] There is also a decorated timber south porch.

[8] The effigy, writes Pevsner, has been 'depressingly cleaned-up', *Herefordshire*, 253.

[9] See Brault, *Rolls of Arms of Edward I*, ii. 183–4.

Figure 9.1. The effigy of the Fresne knight at Moccas.

them must have been considered sufficient to make each panel individual, but decoration for its own sake was not the primary purpose. The effect, in this small building, must have been to produce an overwhelming impression that this was the Fresnes' church.[10]

The Fresnes were an ancient family who held a knight's fee of the earls of Hereford.[11] It consisted of one half fee at Moccas and the other at Sutton. In 1291 Hugh de Fresne received a grant of free warren in all his demesne lands in Moccas and Sutton. He was living in 1293 but dead by 1303 when John de Fresne was lord of Moccas and Sutton was in the hands of Margaret de Fresne, presumably as dower. John was returned as lord of Moccas again in 1316. It is not clear when he came into the estate at Sutton except that it was before 1346. Nonetheless he was probably comfortable at Moccas, where he received the grant of a weekly market on Tuesdays and of an annual fair on the eve of the nativity of St John the Baptist (23 June). He was dead by 22 January 1347, when he was described as a knight.[12] The chronology suggests that the most likely candidate as the subject of the effigy is Hugh de Fresne and the most likely 'creator' of

---

[10] Richard Marks, incidentally, cites Moccas as an example of a lord of the manor glazing a church entirely at his expense: *Stained Glass in England during the Middle Ages* (London, 1993), 4.

[11] It was of old enfeoffment, that is before 1135.

[12] The death of his son, Henry, who was just a fraction under age when John died, followed in June 1360. His son was aged only 14.

Figure 9.2. The Fresne glass, Moccas.

the newly Fresne-centred parish church was John de Fresne, lord from before 1303 to 1347. They held a fairly compact estate, with its twin centres not too far apart.[13]

The wealthier the family the more they were able to accommodate this new-found fashion for celebrating their status while securing their salvation, by reconstructing the parish church. A good example is at Spilsby in Lincolnshire where John de Willoughby, son of the Robert and Margaret de Willoughby who were responsible for the Eresby household ordinance, endowed a chantry within the existing church of St James. In fact, John went further than this. On 26 January 1348 he paid £100 for a royal licence to create a college with a master and twelve chaplains, endowing them with the three churches of Eresby, Over Toynton, and Kirkby. Spilsby and Eresby were contiguous settlements,

---

[13] *The Book of Fees, Commonly Called Testa de Nevill, 1198–1293, 3 vols* (London, 1920–31) 813; *Feudal Aids*, ii. 378, 380, 394, 397; *CChR*, ii. 407 and iv. 90; *CIPM*, viii. 679, x. 574; Brault, *Rolls of Arms of Edward I*, ii. 183. There are extents of both manors on the death of Richard son of Richard de Fresne, knight, in 1375: *CIPM* xiv. 130.

and the Willoughbys were lords at both. John's plan was not carried through in his lifetime, however, for he died in June 1349; he was buried at Spilsby. The following year his son, John, first Lord Willoughby, acquired licence to give lands to the chapel that was to be built at Spilsby to celebrate divine service daily in honour of the Holy Trinity 'for the good estate of the grantor and his wife Joan and their children, for their souls when they are dead, and for the soul of the said John, the father'.[14] The chapel was a spacious one. At around the same time a new and equally wide south aisle was constructed. A limestone monument was duly erected to John and Joan (who died in 1354). It was placed in the middle of the new chapel, facing the altar.[15] John's shield carried the arms which the family acquired from the Bek family, that is a *cross moline*.[16] Robert de Willoughby, who had borne the arms *or, fretty azure* at the siege of Carlaverock adopted the Bek arms of *gules, a cross moline argent* after inheriting Eresby from John de Bek.[17]

The monument was described by the seventeenth-century antiquary Gervase Holles:[18]

A very ancient Monument in the middle of the Quire—On which lyes the portrayture of a Chevalier cross-legged, in complete armour, his hands elevated, upon his left arm a shield, in which a Crosse scarcely, his sword hanging in his belt buckled upon his belly, the belt and scabbard garnished in divers places with crosses scarcely; under his feet a lion. On his right hand lyes his wife, her hands elevated, about her head a border of Reves, under her feete a Talbot . . . . At the ends 4 old great and high Pillars set with statues of men and women much defaced and ruyned.

The effigies themselves are of high quality, although in more or less standard form. The sculptures, however, are unusual. The pillows are supported not by the normal angels, but by male figures which Holles identified as reeves (Figures 9.3 and 9.4). These are very much extant. Whilst his specific designation is very doubtful, they look like contemporary laymen and could conceivably be ministerial.[19] The statuettes at the four corners, on the other hand, were in a

[14] *CPR 1348–50*, 8, 537. John paid a further 10 marks. See also *VCH Lincolnshire*, ii. 236. For the family details that follow see *Complete Peerage*, xii part 2, 657–61.

[15] Following the Reformation and the dissolution of the chantries the interior of the church was rearranged. The spacious chapel of the Trinity now became the chancel and the fourteenth-century south aisle became the nave. The old medieval chancel was transformed into the Willoughby (later Bertie chapel), and a screen erected dividing the erstwhile chancel and nave. See John Lord, 'Repairing and cleaning of the said burying places', *Church Monuments* ix (1994), 86–91.

[16] William de Willoughby, father of Robert, had married Alice, first daughter and co-heiress of John Bek.

[17] Earlier still he bore *argent, a chevron sable*. See Brault, *Rolls of Arms of Edward I*, ii. 456.

[18] R. Cole (ed.), '*Lincolnshire Church Notes made by Gervase Holles A.D. 1634 to A.D. 1642*', Lincoln Record Society, vol. 1 (1910), 89.

[19] There are four of them, two on the outer side of the pillows and two at the inner ones, joined. These last appear to have wings. The later effigy of Sir Robert and Elizabeth de Willoughby has similar figures but only at the lady's head. They are without wings. Could Holles have been confusing the two monuments?

Figure 9.3. The effigy of John, Lord Willoughby (d. 1349), and Joan his wife (d. 1354) at Spilsby.

bad way in the seventeenth century and have clearly been heavily restored; how faithfully it is impossible to say. They are two sets of two. Those on the lady's side are of a bearded civilian above and a lady below (Figure 9.3). They must have been an equally striking feature in their original time. The four corner buttresses are lavishly decorated. The pinnacles are clearly not original and it is probable that the buttresses once supported a canopy. The effect must have been truly startling.

Like the knight himself, the tomb chest displayed heraldry. Almost nothing remains of this, although Holles described it. His details are surprisingly unhelpful in supporting the presumed identity of the figures. The arms of the Deincourts, Joan's family, do not appear to have been present. In heraldic terms the modern viewer is far better served by the alabaster tomb held to represent the younger Lord John Willoughby, who died in 1372. This splendid tomb has five coats of arms on each side of the tomb chest, representing no doubt families with whom the Willoughbys were associated. They include the engrailed cross of the Uffords, representing John's marriage to Cecily, sister and co-heir of William de Ufford, earl of Suffolk. One of the other coats probably represents the Huntingfields, a family that we have met on several occasions during the course of this study,

Figure 9.4. The effigy of John and Joan de Willoughby (detail).

since it comprises three roundels on a fess.[20] The relationship between the two families, however, is unclear. Interestingly, the tomb chest appears to carry both coats associated with the Willoughbys. At the lord's feet were the *fretty* arms which John's father had borne at Carlaverock and below his head and helm, the *cross moline* (Figure 9.5). These monuments were joined in due course by an alabaster tomb to the younger John's son, Robert, third Lord Willoughby (d.1396), and his wife Elizabeth.[21] The Willoughby chapel, then, became the Willoughby mausoleum.

In this respect it was but one example among many such constructed in the fourteenth century. Another good example is at Aldworth where eleven effigies of men and women of the family of the prolific Sir Philip de la Beche, known locally as the Aldworth giants, were added to the enlarged parish church in the middle of the fourteenth century. The church itself was turned into an evocative and stylish mausoleum. In 1351, Edmund de la Beche, archdeacon of Berkshire and the last of Philip's sons, acquired a royal licence to found a college at

---

[20] The Huntingfields bore *or, a fess 3 roundels argent*.

[21] This last has been the subject of considerable restoration. There are also brasses to this lord's former wife Margaret Zouche (d. 1391), third wife of Robert, third Lord Zouche, and to William, the fifth Lord Willoughby (d. 1410), and his wife.

Figure 9.5. Effigy of John, Lord Willoughby (d. 1372).

Aldworth for the spiritual benefit of himself and his ancestors. The college and the mausoleum would preserve the memory of the de la Beche family, sometimes lords of Aldworth, for all time.[22]

The various media employed by the gentry in self-commemoration transformed the interior of parish churches during the period under discussion.[23] Of the varieties of sepulchral monument surviving in these churches from the thirteenth century onwards, it is the knightly effigy that is perhaps the best known. As one would expect, royalty and higher nobility figure prominently among the earliest knightly effigies, most often in much grander settings. From the middle of the thirteenth century, however, these effigies become increasingly common in churches throughout southern and middle

[22] The Aldworth effigies were the subject of a meeting of the Church Monument Society at Aldworth on 16 June 2007. B. and M. Gittos are preparing the findings for publication. Meanwhile see the interim statement by Nigel Saul in *English Church Monuments*, 135.

[23] Saul, *English Church Monuments*, ch. 4, brings discussion of the various media together.

England.[24] The prominence of knighthood within the visual representation of lordship is apparent wherever one looks, and the last quarter of the thirteenth century and the first half of the fourteenth saw the veritable colonization of England's churches by the knightly effigy, both in stone and in wood.[25] Although they were increasingly (but not invariably) sophisticated, they were built around a number of standard features. The knight was normally shown either in an attitude of prayer or sword handling. The effigy combined militarism and social rank, within a religious setting. The stone effigy of the lady was a little later on the scene. H. A. Tummers lists only forty-four effigies of ladies belonging to the thirteenth century, less than a handful being dated securely to before 1280. However, by the early fourteenth century they, too, were proliferating fast. What they lack in vigour in comparison with the military effigy, they often make up for in serenity and in fashion-conscious elegance.[26] They also illustrate, by means of heraldry, the female involvement in chivalric culture.[27]

During the early fourteenth century, however, commemoration by means of the new medium of the monumental brass became a distinct fashion among some members of the gentry. Brasses, it has been said, are better understood than any other type of medieval funerary monument.[28] The broad history of brass design has been reconstructed, the main centres of production identified and the sequence of styles analysed. In the late thirteenth century the patrons of figure brasses were largely the bishops and other senior clergy. In the early decades of the fourteenth century they were joined by the gentry and by country clergy and academics. Their emergence from more modest forms of commemoration is relatively easy to comprehend. In the van amongst the gentry were the Camoys, Septvans, and Cobham families, the last two related by marriage. The Cobham family and its monuments have recently been studied in depth by Nigel Saul.[29] There are no fewer than twenty medieval brasses in Cobham church in Kent, the majority of them—mainly those of the Cobham family and their kin—being located in the chancel where they form two rows. The fact that some related

---

[24] The standard work on thirteenth-century effigies is H. A. Tummers, *Early Secular Effigies in England in the Thirteenth Century* (Leiden, 1980). The fourteenth century lacks, as yet, a similarly comprehensive treatment. For a regional survey, however, see Brian and Moira Gittos, 'A Survey of East Riding Sepulchral Monuments before 1500', in C. Wilson (ed.), *Medieval Art and Architecture in the East Riding of Yorkshire* (British Archaeological Association, 1989), 91–108.

[25] As a rough guide, of the 143 knightly effigies assigned by Tummers to the thirteenth century more than half (seventy-seven) are said to belong to the very end of the century, with another nine assigned to the period 1270–90 (*Early Secular Effigies*, 135–43). For the social context see P. Coss, *The Knight in Medieval England*, ch. 4, 'The Triumph of Chivalry in England'.

[26] See Coss, *The Lady in Medieval England*, ch. 4, 'Visual Representation and Affective Relations'.

[27] See Coss, 'Knighthood, Heraldry and Social Exclusion', 47–8.

[28] By Nigel Saul in: 'Bold as Brass', in Coss and Keen (eds), *Heraldry, Pageantry and Social Display in Medieval England*, 169–94. I have drawn on this authoritative work for the remarks that follow.

[29] Nigel Saul, *Death, Art and Memory in Medieval England* (Oxford, 2001).

Cobhams beyond the immediate family came to be buried there has prompted Saul to see Cobham church as 'a mausoleum not just for one branch of the family but for the whole clan'.[30] As to why they chose brasses, Saul points to several factors. The first is the popularity of the medium itself. The second is the pressure on space. This naturally became a more significant factor with time, but it was a particular consideration where a collegiate foundation was concerned; space was required for the 'free flow of processions'. The third factor was an aesthetic one. The sheer visual impact of artistic patronage was surely intended and should not be marginalized in our minds by other factors.

At the same time, however, an over-concentration upon the full-figure effigy and the monumental brass of the fourteenth century can obscure the understanding of the broader evolution of sepulchral monuments and distort our full appreciation of the gentry's visual invasion of the parish church. Notwithstanding the emphasis which is often placed on the three-dimensional stone effigy, the most popular form of memorial in the thirteenth century had, in fact, been the Purbeck marble coffin-shaped slab. These were not, as has sometimes been supposed, for the less advantaged sectors of society. The very fact that someone could afford commemoration indicated in itself both wealth and status. Modern scholars have concentrated heavily on relief effigies and on brasses, partly because they are perceived as having had more visual impact than incised slabs. However, cross slabs and incised slabs did not necessarily lack impact in their own day, as the recent renewed attention to them is beginning to show. There is growing material evidence for the use of polychromic line filling and applied decoration, as well as line colouring. Moreover, the lack of means of identification in the persons being commemorated in the dull monochrome that is seen today also indicates that these monuments must have been more elaborate in their time.[31] As has recently been pointed out, in their day incised slabs would have been 'eye-catching'.[32] The London marblers, who were responsible for incised slabs as well as brasses, also produced mixed-technique slabs, with incised figures and brass inlays.[33] There were also slabs with inlaid relief features. These possible combinations together with the intrinsic merit of incised slabs ensured their survival into and through the centuries of monumental brasses. In addition to the London workshops, which were responsible for about one third of the surviving incised slabs in England and Wales, there were a number of regional centres.[34] The Londoners dominated the market in the south-east of England.

---

[30] Ibid. 81–2.

[31] Sally Badham, '*A New Feire Peynted Stone*: Medieval English Incised Slabs', *Church Monuments*, xix (2004), 20–52.

[32] Ibid. 49.

[33] A common origin for brasses and incised slabs was suggested by the pioneer student of incised slabs, F. A. Greenhill. As far as the London workshops are concerned it has been put beyond doubt by Sally Badham and Malcolm Norris, *Early Incised Slabs and Brasses from the London Marblers*, Society of Antiquaries of London (1999).

[34] For what follows, see Badham and Norris, *Early Incised Slabs and Brasses*, ch. 3.

Of the others, only that of north Wales, it seems, was involved in large-scale regional production. The next in importance, on the basis of surviving evidence, were the Hereford and Lincoln 'schools'.

The Hereford 'school' was responsible for what appear to be the earliest effigial incised slabs commemorating members of the laity surviving in England. One of these is a mid-thirteenth-century military effigy of a member of the Solers family at Sollers Hope, Herefordshire, whom we have met earlier.[35] The effigy has a full-length knight, sideways-turned and shield-bearing, with a flat-topped pot-helm. It is one of four incised slabs that were discovered when foundations were being laid for the vestry in 1887. They presumably lay in the nave of the church. From the early fourteenth century there survive incised effigies of ladies produced by the same 'school'. The incised slab to Maud de Edvin at Edvin Ralph, Herefordshire is unusual in its Latin inscription for not only does it tells us that she is Maud, widow of Sir Thomas de Edvin, but adds that whoever will say a *Pater* and an *Ave* will gain thirty days pardon via the bishop of Worcester and sixty days pardon via the bishop of Hereford for Maud's soul (in purgatory). Thomas, who died in 1329, was lord of Edvin. Maud's slab carried two shields. The arms on the lady's left are lost; those on the right show a *fess and in chief three mullets pierced*. They are presumably those of Edvin. The lady wears a wimple. She has distinctive hands, possibly holding an object. There are two dogs at her feet. The slab dates, then, from around 1330.[36] It helps to put the other early fourteenth-century monuments in the church in context, in that families did not necessarily prefer one medium to another. There is also a double effigy of the early fourteenth century. The man's head rests on the characteristic double pillow of the period. The same arms are found on his shield. A second effigy is of a knight with two wives and appears to be a generation later than the other.[37] In addition there is a diminutive female effigy, probably closer in time to the earlier effigy, although whether this represents an adult or a child is not entirely clear. The church itself is of simple structure, in that there are no aisles. Like Moccas, it is another example of a Norman church that was restructured in the thirteenth and early fourteenth centuries, often reusing Norman materials and features, making it quite long. In the north wall of the chancel are two fourteenth-century tomb recesses, each with a carved head above. There can hardly be any doubt that these housed the effigies, although they are now located under the Tower. They must have literally overpowered the chancel. The same mixture of media is found at nearby Woolhope, although the balance is different.

---

[35] Another is to an unknown knight, once in the church of Avenbury but since moved to Bromyard. This is particularly fine. The dating, however, is insecure and the Bromyard figure, it seems, may have been produced later in the thirteenth century: ibid. 18.

[36] It has features in common with the inscribed effigy of a lady holding a heart at Tong, Shropshire. Incised figures with colour inlays were still being produced in the Hereford area at the end of the fourteenth century.

[37] The knight's shield carried *a fess between 3 fleur de lis*.

This much-altered church shows signs of rebuilding around 1300. Here there survives an early-fourteenth-century effigy in bas-relief of a young man, a civilian, with crossed hands. He is complemented by a series of incised slabs, including one of a lady and another with two crosses and curious foliage. The combination of media in these examples is different from that at Moccas, but the overall effect, even if less startling, must have been similar, i.e. of an overwhelming seigniorial presence.

As we have seen, among the other centres of production was Lincoln.[38] Lincolnshire has over forty surviving effigial slabs from before the Black Death. However, only a minority of these were produced at Lincoln. Most were imported from Tournai.[39] The important point is that effigial slabs were clearly being produced in increasing numbers during the second half of the thirteenth century for seigniorial families. This continued into the fourteenth century, when in fact they extended down the social scale in the same way as monumental brasses were to do.

Our brief survey of commemorative media employed by the gentry would not be complete, however, without a further word on glass. During the late thirteenth and early fourteenth centuries parish churches began to be glazed with a combination of grisaille and heraldic glass. Extant examples include Selling in Kent and Norbury in Derbyshire. From there it was but a step to more ambitious and complex windows in the Decorated Style, often accompanied by 'donor portraits' of the families, as we have seen at Moccas. Heraldry was to transform the means by which donors could be recognized.[40] The joint donor portrait of husband and wife became popular during the fourteenth century, as did the double effigy. In both media the arms of the two families now allied by marriage were a normal feature. In short, many English churches of the fourteenth and fifteenth centuries seem to have featured armorial glass and depictions of donors.[41] The wealth of art that has been lost from then, sometimes recoverable in the notes and drawings of early antiquaries, distorts our modern perception of the interior of medieval churches, as does the lack of colour in the great majority of surviving monuments. By means of heraldry, monuments and glass were also used to broadcast a range of relationships with other gentry families and with higher lords.[42]

Sepulchral monuments intruded into the most holy places within the churches. In the twelfth century burials were either in the churchyard or in the nave. It was bishops who led the way into the chancel. In the 1230s they were being

---

[38] Another was Bristol. See Badham and Norris, *Early Incised Slabs and Brasses from the London Marblers*, 17.

[39] For the incised slabs at Boston, see below 277.

[40] Marks, *Stained Glass in England*, ch. 1: 'Donors and Patrons'.

[41] Coss, *The Knight in Medieval England*, 89.

[42] On this point, see Coss, 'Knighthood, Heraldry and Social Exclusion', where examples are given.

buried in the eastern parts of the cathedrals of Wells, Exeter, and Worcester. Their example was soon followed by royalty and members of the higher nobility. By the 1260s princely mausolea were being created in France in the eastern part of the abbeys of Royaumont and St Denis, and in England at Westminster. A generation or two later we find mausolea of great splendour being created for magnate families like the Despensers in the choir of Tewkesbury Abbey and the Berkeleys at St Augustine's, Bristol. From the beginning of the fourteenth century, however, the gentry were breaking out of their confinement to recesses along the nave aisles or in side chapel or transept to join their superiors and invade the holiest places.[43]

So far we have merely described this intrusion. How do we explain it? In his study of secular intrusion into sacred places, Andrew Martindale suggested that the reasons for change remain elusive given the lack of contemporary comment.[44] This is of course undeniably true in an absolute sense, but it now seems to have been unduly pessimistic. The underlying cause was beyond doubt the spread of the doctrine of purgatory. In consequence there was a growing preference by the socially influential to be buried immediately next to the high altar. The high altar was *ad sanctos*, close to the saints and under their protection. It was widely believed that burial here would speed the soul's passage through purgatory. Once concealed under arched recesses, in the fourteenth century tombs came, as Nigel Saul puts it, 'out into the open'. The ideal medium from this point of view was the floor brass. Compared with tomb chests, floor brasses minimized the physical intrusion into the area of liturgical celebration. Some of the considerations were religious, but others were undoubtedly more secular. The key is what is often called 'family pride'. The local church was seen increasingly as a family chapel. The whole phenomenon is a manifestation of the gentry's obsession with display, at the heart of which lay affirmation that they were members of the elite.

Contemporaries are unlikely to have perceived any fundamental dichotomy between the religious and the secular and neither, arguably, should we. There were nonetheless important seigniorial concerns and we ought not to neglect them. The parish church was of vital and, during the period under study here, of increasing importance to the gentry. Equally important was the relationship between lords of the manor and the priests in whose parishes their manors lay. Apart from the question of local stability and influence, parish rectors were employed, as we shall see, as executors and as trusted agents when it came to the creation of such vital matters as jointures and enfeoffments to use.[45] As noted above, however, many parishes had passed into the hands of religious foundations and, in consequence, had had their livings appropriated, turning the rectors into vicars. Some advowsons—that is, presentations to livings—were in the hands of the crown, providing benefices for royal clerks. Yet others belonged

[43] Saul, *Death, Art and Memory*, 75–6.   [44] Martindale, 'Patrons and Minders', 177.
[45] See below 206–7.

to great lords, allowing them to support household clerks by means of the church. During the thirteenth century advowsons had often been purchased from lesser lords with this in mind. Nonetheless, a large number remained in the hands of the gentry. The prosopography of the parish clergy of this period is still in its infancy, but is already producing interesting results. A study of the beneficed clergy of three deaneries in north-east Lincolnshire between 1290 and 1340, in the time, that is, of Bishops Oliver Sutton (1280–99), John Dalderby (1300–20), and Henry Burghersh (1320–40), shows that of their 104 benefices 52 were rectories, 42 vicarages, and 10 curacies (in appropriated benefices where no vicar had been ordained).[46] Exactly half, then, had been appropriated, while no less than sixty-eight livings were in ecclesiastical hands. This is in keeping with the findings for the diocese of Lincoln as a whole where 65 per cent of all livings were in ecclesiastical hands by 1320. Within the three deaneries the gentry held sixteen benefices, the baronage eight, and the crown four. Work in this area has tended to focus, understandably, upon the question of the calibre of the clergy, against the standard criticisms often levied by contemporaries as well as by historians. In terms of the appointment of foreign clerks, of clerks in minor orders (i.e. not yet priests), of clerics who were insufficiently educated, of absentees and of pluralists, the clergy of these deaneries come out much better than earlier scholars often thought.[47] Of particular interest here is the proportion of incumbents who were local men. The provenance of 197 out of the 361 who were appointed in the period 1290–1340 is known. Of these, 156 (79 per cent) came from within the diocese, 144 (73 per cent) from Lincolnshire itself. Moreover, eighty (40 per cent) originated within the three deaneries. Furthermore, of the forty who are known to have originated outside, thirteen came from the East Riding of Yorkshire and only one from overseas. Presentations by members of the gentry have to be seen in this context, emphasizing once again the intensely local nature of their lordship.

The published register of Bishop Oliver Sutton gives some further insight into gentry presentation in Lincolnshire. In the archdeaconry of Lincolnshire during his time twenty-one presentations were made to men who shared the surname of their lay patrons.[48] Where the family name of the patron is an eponymous one it is possible, of course, that the new incumbent was not a family member but merely came from the settlement, in which case he would almost certainly

[46] Nicholas Bennett, 'Pastors and Masters: the Beneficed Clergy of North-East Lincolnshire, 1290–1340', in P. Hoskin, C. Brooke and B. Dobson (eds), *The Foundations of Medieval English Ecclesiastical History: Studies Presented to David Smith* (Woodbridge, 2005), 40–62.

[47] Ibid. See also J. H. Denton, 'The Competence of the Parish Clergy in Thirteenth-Century England', in C. M. Barron and J. Stratford (eds), *The Church and Learning in Later Medieval Society: Essays in Honour of Barrie Dobson* (Donington, 2002), 273–85. For ordination lists and numbers of ordinands, see David Robinson, 'Clerical Recruitment in England, 1282–1348', in Nigel Saul (ed.), *Fourteenth Century England* V (Woodbridge, 2008). The earliest substantial ordination lists begin in 1282.

[48] Hill (ed.), *Rolls and Register of Bishop Oliver Sutton*, i, *passim*.

have come from a family who were tenants or were otherwise associated with the lord. Equally, there must be many cases of local association embedded within the institutions of priests by lay patrons but hidden from us by the names. Sometimes, the new incumbent will have come from another manor belonging to the lord. On the other hand, equally hidden from a survey based on the coincidence of surnames are relatives of the patron on the female side. When all the caveats have been made, however, it is at least clear from the evidence that in a minority of cases lay patrons were presenting relatives on the male side.

In some cases they may not have been doing this consistently, as is suggested by the cases of Benniworth, Welesby, and Harrington.[49] In other cases, however, it looks like family policy. At Willoughby in the Marsh, where Sir William de Willoughby appointed Hugh de Willoughby in 1290, the previous incumbent had been Peter de Willoughby. At Manby, where William de Manby appointed Robert de Manby in 1297, the living had previously been held by Master William de Manby. Several cases are of particular interest. At Halton Holgate the living had become vacant through the death of Thomas de Halton, brother of the patron, Sir Richard de Halton. Now, in 1282, Richard presented Ralph de Halton. He was undoubtedly another relative. He had needed a dispensation because of his illegitimate birth. He had to be presented again in 1283 because he had not been ordained priest within a year. At East Barkwith, where Peter de Holywell was presented by Robert de Holywell, we find that Peter had originally been presented while in minor orders and under age. This was in the time of the previous bishop. Other arrangements had had to be made. Now of age, he was ordained subdeacon and instituted. This makes it doubly likely that Peter and his patron were related.

Rand is another example where a tradition was developing of presenting relatives. In 1283 Nicholas Burdet, son and heir of Sir Aimery Burdet, appointed his namesake, Nicholas de Burdet, clerk. Nicholas the clerk must have died (or at least departed from the living) within a few years, for Nicholas Burdet presented again in 1289. On this occasion, however, he chose Alan, vicar of Lissington. But this was opposed by Margery, widow of Sir Aimery Burdet, who presented Robert de Torrington. Nicholas then changed his mind, revoking his original presentation and presenting his own brother, Patrick Burdet. Patrick was at first thought to be a minor but made proof of age. A case ensued in the royal court between Nicholas Burdet and Margery's nominee, by which time Margery had died. The court ruled in favour of Nicholas and the bishop was directed to accept Patrick Burdet. He was duly instituted in June 1289. The right to present to a living was a valuable asset and was sometimes contested even within families. One

---

[49] At Benniworth in 1289 Sir John de Bath presented Master Robert de Necton to the living, vacant by the death of Edmund de Bath; at Welesby in 1290 Sir James Byrun presented James de Welesby to the living, vacant by the death of Master Henry Byrun; at Harrington in 1297 Sir John de Harrington appointed Robert de Cranon, chaplain, to the living, vacant by the death of Master Robert de Harrington.

can imagine that there must have been pressure from relatives of the presenters to secure a living.

That these results are not aberrant is shown by an examination of the archdeaconry of Northampton (covering Northamptonshire and Rutland) over the same period.[50] At Woodford in 1290, Richard du Bois presented his brother, John. The right of presentation alternated here between lords, as was quite often the case. Noticeably, three years earlier, Sir Nicholas de Treyli had also appointed a relative: Robert. Once again, some families were using specific livings to endow family members on a regular basis. We see this in the case of Camoys, Trussel, Paulerspury, and Higham of Helpston. It is also noticeable that some of the new incumbents were very young. At Aston-Le-Walls, where Oliver Sutton was presented by Sir Stephen de Sutton in 1284, we find that Stephen was in fact a canon of York. He was also the guardian of Richard, heir to Sir Robert of Sutton. The new incumbent had been under age when first presented, so that Stephen had had custody of the living for the past four years. Here we have a transparent family arrangement. Similarly, at Titchmarsh, Fulk Lovel had held the living until Gilbert Lovel was of age (in 1288). At Wittering John Ridel, presented by Sir Hugh Ridel in 1292, had made proof of age, as had Richard du Bois at Woodford in 1289 'because he looked very young'. However, lay presentation did not necessarily mean that the men were not educated. On the contrary, in three cases in the archdeaconry of Northampton where the incumbent appears to have been a family member the cleric is called master (*magister*), indicating that he was a university graduate.[51] Younger sons had therefore been prepared for careers in the church.

We see this clearly in the case of the Luttrells, who held the advowson of the church of Bridgeford. When the incumbent died in 1262 the current lord, Sir Andrew Luttrell, presented his third son, Robert, to the living. The fact that he was the third son may be significant. The elder two were perhaps destined for knighthood, although in this case the second son did not live long into adulthood. Robert rose further in the church, becoming a canon of Salisbury Cathedral. Thus, by means of advowsons, gentry families could sometimes find that they had relatives in higher places. Robert lived until 1315. His nephew, Sir Robert Luttrell, father of the Geoffrey who had commissioned the Luttrell Psalter, is most probably the knight whose mutilated effigy remains in the church. He died in 1297. Sir Geoffrey's brother, Andrew, also seems to have been rector there. It causes no surprise, then, to find that Sir Geoffrey left £1 to the church of Bridgeford in his will.[52]

That the appointment of younger sons to benefices was not more systematic in the pre-Reformation church has much to do with the number of advowsons that

[50] Hill (ed.), *Rolls and Register of Bishop Oliver Sutton*, ii. *passim*.
[51] In the archdeaconry of Lincoln there was similarly one case where the new incumbent, and two cases where the previous incumbent, sharing the surname of the patron, was a graduate.
[52] Camille, *Mirror in Parchment*, 128, 132.

had passed into religious hands. An advowson, however, was a significant right and an important means of patronage. Not surprisingly, therefore, it was often a matter of contention not only between religious houses and laymen as a result of past alienation, but also between lay families. In the Multon archive there survives a declaration dated 23 November 1327 by a man describing himself as a public notary of Boston of the proceedings at a ruri-deaconal court held in the parish church at Spilsby. It resulted from a mandate issued by the official of the archdeacon and the bishop of Lincoln to examine the presentation made by Sir Thomas de Multon of Frampton to the church of Miningsby. He had presented Robert de Kirkby, probably from his manor of Kirkby La Thorpe. It was found that the church had become vacant on the Thursday before the feast of All Saints last (29 October) due to the death of Richard de Kelyngwyk, that Thomas was proven by his charters to be the true patron, notwithstanding the fact that the Templars were reported to have made the last presentation, and that the presentee was a person of good life and conversation.[53] It seems likely that the last presentation was made while Thomas was under age.

Much turned on the question of who presented last. Litigation could result. A case came before the court of Common Pleas in 1343 over the presentation to the church of Somercotes. Henry Hillary, on behalf of the Multon family, listed the presentations made by the Multons of Frampton or by those who had custody during wardships going back to the reign of Henry III. The crown had claimed the advowson on the grounds that it was holding the temporalities of the abbot of Langonnet in Brittany of whom the Multons held their property at Somercotes.[54] As the crown defaulted, a writ was issued to the bishop of Lincoln to admit Henry Hillary's clerk. Disputes over presentations are sometimes noted in bishops' registers. In 1283, for example Joan, widow of Alan de Multon, had presented at Somercotes, after winning two suits in royal courts against John de Multon and Thomas son of Lambert de Multon respectively. In 1296 the earl of Lincoln presented at Kirkby La Thorpe as guardian of Thomas, son of Alan de Multon. This was after another candidate had been put forward by John de Grace Dieu by virtue of holding the manor at farm from the late Thomas de Multon.[55]

[53] Multon, 82a.

[54] For the case see W. O. Massingberd, 'Notes on the Pedigree of Multon of Frampton, Co. Lincoln', *The Ancestor* II (1902), 206–7. In fact, the Multons are said here to hold only four acres of land in Somercotes. However, the case had prompted an exemplification of process from 1299 where it had been acknowledged that Thomas de Multon held land in Saltfleetby of the abbey of Langonnet for which he owed £19 1s 4½d per annum: *CPR 1340–3*, 490. This arrangement was undoubtedly an old one. The abbey had been given land in Saltfleetby by Geoffrey, duke of Brittany and earl of Richmond, in 1181–6. The family of Lambert of Multon were involved in this area and this no doubt explains the interest of the Multons Frampton. Alan and Richard de, younger sons of Lambert de Multon, had been courtiers of Duke Geoffrey and of Constance, his widow. Alan's son, Thomas, succeeded to their fee at Somercotes: J. Everard and M. Jones (eds), *The Charters of Constance of Brittany and her Family, 1171–1221* (Woodbridge, 1991), Ge 16, C 67, 190; *Book of Fees*, 1053.

[55] Hill (ed.), *Rolls and Register of Bishop Oliver de Sutton*, i. 37–9, 211.

The relationship between lord and priest was so significant that it could be shown pictorially. Stained glass at Carlton Scroop in Lincolnshire, dating from the early fourteenth century, portrays Sir John de Newmarch as a kneeling figure in armour, displaying his arms both on his shield and on his ailettes. He is shown, however, facing the priest, William de Briddeshall, whom he presented to the living in 1307. William also displays his family's arms (Figure 9.6).[56] Similarly, at Mancetter in Warwickshire there once existed glass showing two knights bearing the arms of Mancetter and Crophull respectively, facing one another. These arms are replicated on their dress. The lord of the manor at this date was Sir Guy de Mancetter and the rector Ralph de Crophull, who was no doubt presented to the living by Sir Guy.[57] Both of these examples probably reflect an interfamilial relationship underlying the presentation, perhaps through marriage. It suggests that it was not unknown for one gentry family to provide a church living for a member of another.

The close relationship that could exist between lord and parish priest when the one was presented by the other helps to explain the church's fear in years to come over the issue of Lollard knights. There certainly were lords who presented clerics who were of the radical persuasion they favoured, although the incidence was undoubtedly small and the dangers to the church open to exaggeration.[58] There is no reason to doubt, moreover, that in the period under consideration the religion of the gentry was not only orthodox but also deeply conformist, conforming that is both to traditional belief and to new church-sponsored trends

Figure 9.6. Newmarch and Briddeshall arms at Carlton Scroop.

[56] For further discussion, see Penny Hebgin-Barnes, *The Medieval Stained Glass of Lincolnshire* (Oxford, 1996), 65–6. The figure of Christ in majesty is a nineteenth-century replacement of a lost figure. It may be St Nicholas, after whom the church is dedicated, or St Edmund whose arms appear below. The priest's head has been restored.

[57] Alexander and Binski (eds), *Age of Chivalry*, no. 227; Coss, *The Knight in Medieval England*, 90.

[58] See Margaret Aston and Colin Richmond (eds), *Lollardy and the Gentry in the Later Middle Ages* (Stroud, 1997).

in religious practice. Their outlook was, as Christine Carpenter has recently written of gentry religion in a subsequent age, 'remorselessly orthodox'.[59]

What, then, can we say in conclusion, of the content of gentry religion? There is hardly need to emphasize any further the belief in Christ's passion, the Virgin and the saints, intercession, prayer, the mass, or heaven, hell and purgatory, or good works. Deep insights are provided by the endowment of chantries, by books of hours, by commemoration, and by devotional images. These can be supplemented as evidence by surviving wills. Wills, as is often pointed out, are problematic in some ways and we cannot necessarily say that we are hearing the testator's own voice. They are bound by their very nature to emphasize piety and, indeed, orthodoxy. Nonetheless, they are arguably the most direct entrée into thought processes that we actually have and they fully conform to the impressions that we gain from elsewhere. They often begin by invoking God, the holy mother, and the saints. This is followed by the stipulation of the chosen place of burial, the granting of the customary mortuary payment and the arrangements for the funeral. Sir Walter de Gloucester, as we have seen, asked to be buried with the Dominicans in London, to whom he gave his best horse. This was to be led before his body 'on the day of my burial with [my] armour and other trappings as shall be fitting and my executors shall appoint'. Sir Geoffrey Luttrell did precisely the same. It was an old custom, and the norm amongst the nobility. In other cases where the horse was given in mortuary, this procession was almost certainly implied.

As far as his funeral expenses were concerned, Walter left 100 marks for distributing to the poor and for other necessary items; this would be increased if deemed necessary (presumably by his executors). Sir Geoffrey Luttrell was more explicit. He left £200 to be distributed to the poor, on the day of his funeral, on the 7th day and the 30th day thereafter. £40 was to be expended on wax (i.e. candles) to be arranged around his body, that is for burning. £2 was to be spent on clerics reciting the psalms. At his wake or 'the gathering of friends' (*convocatio amicorum*), £20 was to be spent on 20 quarters of wheat for bread and 40 quarters of malt for ale, with a further £20 spent on wine, cooked food, spices and other victuals. As we would say today, Sir Geoffrey was to have 'a good send off'. There were of course social considerations in all of this, but much of what was done transcended such concerns and had one very specific purpose: to secure the dead person's release from purgatory as soon as possible, through good works and through intercession. Debts needed to be paid. Sir Walter arranged for the repayment of £240, £200 to the king and £40 to Sir Robert de Chaddeworth, and for any other identified debts to be paid. Mass was to be said daily by twelve chaplains for his soul for the space of a year, at a cost of 60 marks. Again, the pious Sir Geoffrey Luttrell was more extravagant. Mass was to be celebrated for

---

[59] Christine Carpenter, 'Religion', in Raluca Radulescu and Alison Truelove (eds), *Gentry Culture in Late Medieval England* (Manchester, 2005), 138.

him in Irnham church for five years at a cost of 500 marks, and the poor were to receive a further £40 on his anniversary.

These considerations show Sir Geoffrey to have been strongly in tune with the devotional practices of his day, even if he went beyond the norm. Other wills show, for example, that the cult of the holy mother was widespread, not least in the opening evocations. Some gentry wills indicate even wider concerns. Sir Nicholas de Mitton left the money coming from various debts to the subsidy for the Holy Land, while William son of Roger de Clifford left 50 marks to 'a certain man' who was going out there. Sir Nicholas de Mitton, who left legacies to his villeins, exemplified another form of 'good works', in money donated to the upkeep of roads and bridges. He gave 1s for each of the bridges of Nafford, Pershore and the one going from Tewkesbury towards Much, and 6d to each of those at *Salynde, Langford*, and *Wynlade*. These bequests reveal a concern for the welfare of the local community. [60]

We should not think of gentry piety as existing only on the point of death, although of course it is likely to have intensified at the leaving of earthly life. The devotion to altars and images also featured during life. The Multon household accounts record frequent offerings on saints' days, while Sir John de Multon made various offerings as he travelled, at Lincoln for example and at Stow, as well as giving money to the poor.[61] Equally we can perceive a concern for on-going confession, contrition and absolution. Some members of the gentry, like the higher nobility, had their own confessors; often these were friars. Sir Geoffrey Luttrell, as we have seen, left a legacy to his confessor, Brother William de Fotheringay, of 5 marks for clothing.

If we should avoid seeing too strong a dichotomy between the secular and the religious, the same is true of the private and the public. In religious terms these had become, by the thirteenth century at least, two sides of the same coin. Private chapels, devotional books and the obsessive concern with intercession and purgatory all helped to internalize religious experience. The individual was encouraged by the post-Lateran church to take more responsibility for his or her salvation. At the same time the gentry participated, often it seems enthusiastically, in the church's mission to bind the parish community around the patron saint.[62] We see this when it comes to expenditure on the church itself. The official line was that the clergy were responsible for the upkeep of its chancel, the parishioners for its nave. In practice there were a variety of customs, and gentry influence, or at least expenditure, could be found in either or both.[63] The interlinking of

[60] Willis Bund (ed.), *Register of Bishop Godfrey Giffard*, 283, 388.

[61] See also R. N. Swanson, 'Indulgences for Prayers for the Dead in the Diocese of Lincoln in the Early Fourteenth Century', *Journal of Ecclesiastical History*, 52 (2001), 197–219, for an interesting side light on contemporary piety.

[62] On this issue, see Marks, *Image and Devotion*, 77–85: 'The Patronal Image and the Parish'.

[63] For the responsibility of the parishioner, see Emma Mason, 'The Role of the English Parishioner, 1000–1500', *Journal of Ecclesiastical History*, 27 (1976), 17–29.

gentry, parish church and patronal saint is implied by John Mirk in his *Festial*,
written in the early fifteenth century:

> For right as a temporall lord helpyth and defendyth all that byn
> parechons or tenantys, right soo the saynt that ys patron of the
> chyrche helpyth and defendyth all that byn paryschons to hym,
> and don hym worschyp halowyng his day, and offyrne to hym.[64]

It had long been in the interests of the gentry that these two 'defenders' should
be linked, for in this way order and stability were ensured.

[64] Marks, *Image and Devotion*, 81.

10

The Culture of the Cartulary
The Gentry Family and the Protection of Estates

They gentry were acutely law-minded. This was as true in the late thirteenth and early fourteenth centuries as ever it was to be later. At the heart of this law-mindedness was the need and the determination to protect their estates; perhaps one should say to protect their family and their estates, for in their thinking the two were essentially interchangeable. Protection has, of course, a purely physical dimension, and there can hardly have been a secular lord who would not have subscribed to the ethic of the strong, sword-bearing right arm in defence of one's rights. However, as historians have come to recognize, the real knee-jerk reaction if one's property was threatened was to the law, principally and increasingly throughout the thirteenth century and beyond to the courts of the English common law. It is a truism that this was a litigious age and that the gentry were litigious by predilection. Their law-mindedness, however, became so much a part of gentry behaviour as to be more than just a propensity to seek out writs and legal remedies. Rather it became deeply rooted in gentry culture itself.

This aspect of gentry culture has a series of interlocking dimensions and an examination of these will be the subject of this chapter. The first of these, particularly fortunate for the historian, is the emphasis that was placed upon the preservation of written evidence, evidence that could be invoked or at least perused for proof and for ammunition. A second dimension is the proliferation in this period of legal devices used in the protection of estates and family interests, not just to counter attack, as in the past, but also, and increasingly, to anticipate and sidestep future difficulties. These devices, and the mentality that surrounded their utilization, helped to entrench men of law within local society and enhanced the appreciation of their expertise, even if it did not always facilitate their full acceptance within the secular landowning world. The law-mindedness of the gentry carried them into social as well as professional association with lawyers. The new legal devices that were so vital to them also reveal to us the circle of friends, relatives, and associates that were closest of all to these landowners and their families.

Let us begin, then, with the first of these dimensions, the preservation of titles to land and associated records. Over the years considerable numbers of charters, quitclaims, final concords, and the like accumulated in the hands of landed families. For the most part they must have been kept in boxes, chests and cupboards or even in loose sacks. Keeping them in this way both invited loss and reduced their usability. Increasingly, families began to copy them into registers or cartularies, that is books of charters, precisely for ease of reference and to help guard against the loss of originals. Although they were rarely produced in court as evidence, there can be no doubt that the need to preserve evidence was their primary function.[1] The fifteenth-century *Langley Cartulary* makes it plain that prior to its production the documents were kept in deed-boxes and sacks. Sometimes those relating to a specific place were kept together. At others times a family archive was simply kept as one.[2]

As is well known, amongst surviving cartularies those produced by religious houses hugely outnumber secular ones. Famously, G. R. Davis catalogued 1,185 belonging to religious houses compared to only 169 emanating from lay families.[3] The continuity of landholding on the part of the religious stimulated their production, while the post-Reformation activity of antiquaries facilitated their preservation. An unknown number of secular cartularies must have been destroyed or broken up. An example of this is the cartulary of Multon property in and around Frampton and Boston, fragments of which remain in the archive of the Graa family that Bishop Wayneflete passed to Magdalen College.[4] It seems probable though that the compiling of cartularies was never ubiquitous among landowning families as it appears to have been with at least moderately endowed religious institutions. Nevertheless, considerable numbers of lay cartularies were produced, and they were by no means confined to the great lords. In fact, quite a cross-section of landowning families was involved. Examples survive from the early and mid-thirteenth century.[5] However, there is no doubt that they became increasingly popular during the period covered by this book. It is no coincidence, of course, that this mirrors the exponential increase in civil litigation before the central courts. For the most part they were written, in the words of their modern cataloguer, 'with merely business-like competence in ordinary charter-hand, and if they still retain their original covers these consist of limp parchment or of plain wooden boards covered with skin, often with fastening clasps or thongs'.[6]

---

[1] For a recent and very useful discussion of the motivation behind the compilation of secular cartularies, see S. J. O'Connor (ed.), *A Calendar of the Cartularies of John Pyel and Adam Fraunceys*, Camden Society 5th ser., 2 (1993), 75–89. See also Trevor Foulds, 'Medieval Cartularies', *Archives* xviii (1987), 3–35.

[2] Coss (ed.), *The Langley Cartulary*, nos 262 and 293: *Copia de uno pixide tangente diversa tenementa in Coventre* and *Copia de uno saculo de Evidencia de Coventre*. In fact, the contents of the latter were much wider.

[3] G. R. C. Davis, *Medieval Cartularies of Great Britain: A Short Catalogue* (London, 1958).

[4] Multon 140/19.

[5] The *Constable Cartulary*, for example, belongs to the early thirteenth century: Davis, *Medieval Cartularies*, no. 1224.

[6] Ibid. xi.

Lay cartularies of greater elegance do exist, although they are few in number and tend to emanate from the fifteenth century.[7] Like other books they could be the subject of family pride and display. In some cases they include fascinating snippets of family history, as in the case of an estate book belonging to the Hotots of Clapton in Northamptonshire where we hear of a lord returning home with his bride only to find his manor house in flames, a punishment it was said for the house's encroachment on the local churchyard, and of the female ancestor who, back in the reign of King Stephen, had felled a knight with one blow of her spear.[8] For the most part, however, they were utilitarian products, reflecting their predominantly practical purpose.

An example of a secular cartulary produced during the period covered by this book is that of the Huntingfields of Frampton, which is cited on numerous occasions in this book.[9] Its composition is instructive. It consists of two discrete units, one of four folios and another of thirty. Two large sheets of parchment, sewn together, were used to construct a loose binding, with a flap on the right to enclose the whole 'book' and flaps turned inwards at the top and the bottom. These sheets were in fact re-used accounts of sundry purchases by a long list of named individuals. They include, for example, Matilda de Cobeldyke and Ralph de Cobeldyke. It is noted against many of the names that the person concerned 'is quit'. The personal names are on the left side, and the quantities with prices alongside are given in a series of vertical columns. There are columns for sheep, cows and calves, chickens, wool, hay, fruit, bees, and canvas, with far fewer entries in the last three. Sadly, there are no totals, and it is hard to know what proportion of the original account they represent. The accounts are confined to the inside covers, the outer covers being blank.[10] Curiously, this parchment binding is replicated, with a second re-used set of accounts inside the first, presumably to give added strength. The second account is similar in content and form, except that the columns are not ruled. Again, the outer sides are blank. We are dealing, then, with account rolls that were considered ephemeral, with the parchment re-used in a strikingly makeshift way to produce a rather crude binding for the Huntingfield 'book'.

The first and smaller unit of the book consists of only four folios, with writing on five of the eight sides. The contents are miscellaneous. Three charters are followed by a copy of the *Inquisition Post Mortem* of Thomas de Multon who died in Lincolnshire on 26 March 1322. He held 10s annual rent at Miningsby

---

[7] See S. J. O'Connor (ed.), *A Calendar of the Cartularies of John Pyel and Adam Fraunceys*, Camden Society, 5th series 2 (1993), 76–7. The Anlaby Cartulary provides a good example with its miniatures and marginal drawing: M. R. James, 'The Anlaby Cartulary', *Yorkshire Archaeological Journal*, xxxi (1934), 337–47.

[8] *Estate Records of the Hotot Family*, ed. E. King, in *A Northamptonshire Miscellany*, Northamptonshire Record Society, 32 (1983), 3–58.

[9] Lincoln Record Office 3 Anc. 2/1.

[10] Except for a later 'title' on the front, viz. '*Antiquum retoris/ & supervisio del Toft*'.

and the rent of a pair of golden spurs worth 1s to be received annually for 200 acres of land held of him at Sutton. For the latter he owed Roger de Huntingfield 'the service of a clove of gillyflower per annum'. This appears to be the only Huntingfield interest in the matter, and is presumably why the inquisition is included here. On folio two there is a statement in French of the fees held of Sir William de Huntingfield in Holland, which includes the three-quarter fee held by Sir Thomas de Multon, a fee held by the heirs of Walter Maureward and a one-third fee held by the sons of Robert de Kirton. This is followed by an extract from the Book of Fees at the Exchequer relating to Lincolnshire and of the aid paid from Lincolnshire for the marriage of the future Edward I. Then comes the list of the Huntingfield patrons of the priory of Mendham from its founder, William de Huntingfield I to William de Huntingfield IV, whose father died in 1337 and who had livery of his inheritance in 1350.[11] Finally there is a terrier of the lands of William de Huntingfield at Frampton, Toft, and Bicker dated 7 January 1357. This then provides the date by which this, the smaller, unit was completed.

It seems fairly certain that the two units which comprise the cartulary were originally separate and unbound. The larger unit contains very little material after the time of William III, who died in 1313. The items that are later are clearly additions.[12] The bulk of the items were written by a single hand. Perhaps it was constructed for Roger de Huntingfield IV, who had livery of his inheritance, after a minority, on 8 March 1327. Sooner or later after its composition it was bound together with the smaller unit to make one composite, but crudely constructed, cartulary.

The larger unit is a more conventional cartulary. Its charters and related muniments provide details of the Huntingfield interests in Toft, Frampton, Boston, and elsewhere in Holland from the late twelfth century. The core of the property was built up by Roger (I) son of William de Huntingfield, who received the manor of Toft from Maurice de Craon lord of Freiston, who died in 1188.[13] The cartulary records Roger's further acquisitions in the area and those of his successors. The final folios (27r–34v) deal with the Huntingfield interests in Boston. Meanwhile a group of charters reveals Huntingfield dealings in the times of Roger III (1290–1302), William III (1302–1313), and Roger IV (1327–1337). Among the local families who appear as witnesses to their charters are the Kirtons, the Rochfords, the Friskneys, the Rupes, the Pinchbecks, all knightly families, and the Cobeldykes. The Multons, however, are conspicuous by their absence. There were, by contrast, some direct dealings between the

---

[11] *Complete Peerage*, vi. 664–71. For the patrons, see above 150.
[12] A deed relating to Pinchbeck belonging to September 1336 was sewn in, as indeed was an indenture in English belonging to the time of Henry VI, while a deed of Sir William de Huntingfield IV, which concludes the manuscript, is dated 13 October 1350 and is noticeably in a different hand.
[13] Sanders, *English Baronies*, 47.

Huntingfields and the Cobeldykes.[14] We hear of local details, such as the highway which led from Frampton to Wyberton and of the Huntingfields' great park at Frampton. The rector of Toft makes an appearance, as had the rector of Frampton earlier. The *Huntingfield Cartulary* is very much a local record. Notwithstanding the family's wide interests in East Anglia and elsewhere, the manuscript is almost entirely concerned with the Huntingfield interest in Holland. Hence there are no family settlements and no charters relating to their property further south. It is very much an aide memoire compiled to help protect their properties in and around Frampton. Here is one of many indications that such families were conducting not so much a geographically wide enterprise but a series of smaller, more localized ones.

Moving on to the second dimension, what precisely were the new legal devices that, it is argued, were so significant within the history of gentry culture? The short answer is that they comprised the jointure, the entail and enfeoffment to use. They impacted directly upon the gentry principally in terms of the avoidance of wardship, of marriage arrangements and of descent. In other words, they were vital instruments in the move to secure greater control for the family over its destiny and over the destiny of its estates.

In terms of understanding these devices we can take one of two routes. The first is to describe the legal instruments themselves, concentrating upon their genesis and upon their impact within the operation of the law; in other words, the method of the legal historian. The second is to approach them in operation by examining how they functioned in practice within the history of a particular gentry family or families. This is obviously the more appropriate way forward here. However, in order to grasp the impact a little has to be said on the processes themselves and on how they arrived on the scene. Their origins, although not without significance, are not our primary concern. We are interested more in how they functioned and upon how their practice impacted upon gentry culture. In general terms we are dealing with a dialectic between legal developments on the one hand and social demands on the other. One does not determine the other, in either direction.

For convenience, we will begin with spousal jointure. This involved a husband enfeoffing a third party or parties with some or all of his property, and then the couple receiving it back in joint tenure. This procedure was often activated, or at least ratified, by the instrument known as a final concord, the product of what in these instances was a fictitious lawsuit in the court of Common Pleas. Obviously it gave the longer-surviving spouse greater control of the family estates than was hitherto the case. It had, however, one very distinct advantage. Should

---

[14] On 21 July 1311, for example, William de Huntingfield III raised money by conveying to Eleanor de Cobeldyke the place called *Langbrak'* in Frampton. She was to return possession following payment of 41 marks and 10s at Christmas and Easter next in equal proportions. She duly did so.

the husband die, the king—or whoever else was his immediate overlord—could not have wardship of the land during the minority of the heir whilst the lady lived, because she, not the heir, was now the sole tenant.

Wardship, as we have seen, could be debilitating. By 1324, when Thomas de Multon IV succeeded to his estates, the Multons had suffered two long periods of wardship in succession. Thomas III's father had been long dead when he came of age in 1297.[15] (See Figure 2.1.) His mother, Joan, had presented to a Multon living, as his father's widow, as early as 1283.[16] How long she lived thereafter is unknown, but his grandfather's widow, Lucy Pecche, was not very long dead in 1309.[17] In 1300 Thomas III came to an agreement with his uncle John over Multon land.[18] The Multon estates therefore were supporting at least one dowager, and possibly two dowagers, as well as the lord's uncle, whilst they were recovering from wardship. However, Thomas de Multon III was not to enjoy his estates for long. He was dead himself by 1309.[19] There then followed the long wardship of Thomas de Multon IV. Thomas was in the custody of his overlord, Thomas de Multon of Egremont, until the latter's death in 1322. Wardship then passed to the crown and was granted to Hugh le Despenser the Younger. Thomas succeeded to his estates only in 1324.

The Multons of Frampton had therefore suffered two wardships in rapid succession, the second lasting from 1311 to 1324. The effects on the family and its estates can be glimpsed, but the extent of the damage can only be guessed at. It is not surprising that the next generation took steps to limit the chances of this happening again. On 3 February 1326, before the justices at Westminster, the young Thomas de Multon IV acknowledged the manor of Frampton with the advowson of its chapel to be the right of Simon Tuchet and John son of Herbert de Twycross by his gift.[20] They then conveyed the manor to Thomas himself and his wife Elizabeth jointly. Elizabeth was now assured of life tenure. It was further specified, however, that the land should pass after their death to the heirs of their bodies, with reversion to Thomas's own 'right heirs' should the couple fail to leave a bodily heir.[21] This created what was known as a 'fee tail', the

---

[15] In 1296 the earl of Lincoln presented to the church of Kirkby La Thorpe as guardian of Thomas son of Alan de Multon. Thomas presented to the same living in his own right three years later: *The Rolls and Register of Bishop Oliver Sutton 1280–1299* vol. I, ed. Rosalind M. T. Hill, Lincoln Record Society (1948), 211, 245. In 1299, however, Thomas de Multon said that he had been in the wardship of the bishop of Ely: *CPR 1340–3*, 490. Thomas had received a release of some property in 1297 (Multon 97A). In the same year he had seem military service in Flanders.

[16] Hill (ed.), *Rolls and Register of Bishop Oliver Sutton*, i. 37–8.

[17] She was recorded as living in 1303: *Feudal Aids*, iii. 131, 163, 184.

[18] Multon 98A, dated 29 June 1300. John made grants of property to Thomas on 17 March 1301 (Multon 54A and 59A).

[19] Multon 124. His son's wardship is noted on 16 June 1311: *CFR*, ii. 94.

[20] See above 63–4.

[21] Multon 87a. As is well known, three mutually indented copies of a final concord were drawn up, one being held by each of the parties and the other, the foot of the fine, remaining with the court. In this case the foot survives as TNA CP25 1/137/94.

manor of Frampton being now 'entailed' upon the direct heirs of Thomas and Elizabeth. Since the object of the exercise was not only to provide for those heirs, but also to protect the future of the Multon family, it was important that the property should remain in Multon hands should those direct heirs fail, and not pass to Elizabeth's natal family. By such means landed families were increasingly taking control of the descent of their property whilst at the same time ensuring as far as possible that the land did not fall into the hands of an overlord through wardship.

The sort of control that families were increasingly exercising was made feasible by two legal developments. Although jointures can be found as early as the 1270s, their spread was facilitated by two very important statutes. The statute of *Quia Emptores* of 1290 obliged the grantor in any property transaction in fee to drop out of the feudal chain, so that when *B* who held of *A* granted land to *C* the last named would henceforth hold of *A*. This allowed a grantor to use a third party or parties to re-grant property to him and another jointly without the tenurial complications which would previously have ensued. Meanwhile the statute *De Donis Conditionalibus* of 1285 had effectively brought the entail into existence. This statute had arisen out of the need to clarify the law in relation to conditional gifts. Conditional grants to family members who would not normally inherit under the system of primogeniture had quite a long history. The statute *De Donis* was designed to prevent the alienation of such gifts, and the consequent thwarting of the intentions of the grantor to benefit only the grantee and his or her direct heirs, a matter which had clearly been causing some considerable concern. The result of this statute was to protect all parties, but especially the grantor and his own blood line, by forbidding alienation within three generations. By means of an entail, moreover, the grantor could stipulate how the property should descend in default of the grantee or grantees having bodily heirs. In this way a fee tail could be created with remainder, for example, to the grantee's siblings and their issue one by one and ultimate reversion to the original grantor's 'right heirs'. Entails could thus be used for what a recent commentator has called 'estate planning settlements'.[22] As we move into the fourteenth century, jointures and entails become increasingly common among landowning families.

In the case of the Multons, Frampton was not the only property so served. Two years before Thomas de Multon created a spousal jointure at Frampton he had done the same with a group of Multon properties. On 17 June 1324, a final concord was made before the judges at Westminster by which John Pecche conveyed to Thomas de Multon of Frampton and Elizabeth his wife and their heirs the manors of Ingleby and Miningsby, together with 38 messuages, 2 tofts, one carucate, $42\frac{1}{2}$ bovates and 69 acres of land, and £38 1s $2\frac{3}{4}$d rent in Saltfleetby, Somercotes, Hemingby, Bassingham, Wood Enderby, Coningsby,

---

[22] J. Biancalana, *The Fee Tail and the Common Recovery in Medieval England 1176–1502* (Cambridge, 2001), 184.

Stow, Sturton, Bransby, Kirton, and Wyberton, with the advowsons of the churches of Miningsby and Somercotes and the chapel of Ingleby.[23] This was followed, on 24 October, by a private instrument in French by which John Pecche, describing himself as the lord of Hampton in Arden, released to Thomas and Elizabeth and the heirs of their bodies all the properties contained in the fine made between them in the royal court.[24] It was witnessed by Sir Thomas de Willoughby, knight, Sir John Pecche of Lindsey,[25] knight, Alan de Cobeldyke, and John de Stickney.

The can be little doubt that these conveyances were activating part of the marriage settlement arranged by the families of Thomas and Elizabeth. To understand this phenomenon we have to appreciate the shift that occurred during the course of the thirteenth century from one common form of marriage settlement to another. In the traditional form the bride's father gave the groom land in *maritagium* with his daughter while the groom granted his wife dower 'at the church door'. This was one third of his property by common law unless more had been designated. In the new form of marriage settlement, by contrast, the bride's father gave not land but a marriage portion in money, while the groom or his father settled land on the couple in joint fee tail.[26] The entailed land was to provide for them and their children. In its simplest form this would mean that if the issue failed the land would revert to the father or the father's strict heir. The change to the new form of marriage settlement did not occur over night but rather in stages. Marriage portions had begun to replace the *maritagium* from the 1230s onwards, but did not become standard practice until the end of the thirteenth century. Although it can be seen from around 1280, the new form of marriage settlement did not become 'the standard norm' until the second decade of the fourteenth century.[27] Various factors lie behind these changes. Clearly they reflect the increasing monetization of society. They were made possible by precisely those legal devices, the jointure and the entail, that we have previously discussed.

The existence of just such a marriage settlement is clear in the case of Thomas de Multon's son. As soon as it was practicable Thomas de Multon IV set up his own son John and his wife, Anne, with some independent property. The first we hear of this directly in the Multon records is on 23 September 1332 when they received from him four messuages in the town of Boston.[28] On the same day

[23] No original exists in the Multon collection, nor does the foot appear to survive in the National Archives. However, a copy of the final concord was the first of three written onto a single piece of parchment in the Multon collection (Multon 78a). The second of the three is a copy of the 1326 instrument mentioned above (Multon 87a).
[24] Multon 96a.
[25] *de Lindeseye* is interlined, presumably an afterthought to distinguish him from the grantor.
[26] Biancalana, *The Fee Tail and the Common Recovery*, 142.   [27] Ibid. 159.
[28] Multon 110. John is described here as his eldest son (*primogenito filio meo*). This deed has a fine seal. It bears a shield of three bars with a helm and crest alongside on a latticed background. (See Figure 13.1.) According to a genealogy recorded in the court of Common Pleas in 1383 John

Thomas Pecche and John de Twycross received power of attorney from Thomas
de Multon to give seisin to John and Anne of the manor of Heapham, together
with 14 messuages and 17 bovates of land in Hoby, Leicestershire and of 5
messuages, 1 bovate and 90 acres of land, 24 acres of meadow and 1 lb pepper
in Willingham, 'according to the tenor of the charter to them made theron'.[29] It
was some time before these grants were confirmed by final concords. By one of
these, which resulted from a 'plea' begun on 26 November 1332 and completed
on 27 January, Thomas conveyed to the couple the manor of Kirkby La Thorpe
with 9 messuages, 1 bovate and 90 acres of land, 24 acres of meadow, and
the rent of 1lb of pepper in Willingham and Boston and 14 messuages and 17
bovates of land in Hoby. All of this was to be given at once except the manor
of Kirkby which was given in reversion after the death of Andrew atte Gate of
Boston and Alice his wife, who held it for the term of their lives.[30] Once again
there was reversion, failing issue, to the grantor and his heirs. In other words
should the worst happen and they had no surviving children, Anne's family
would be excluded from inheriting. Interestingly, Anne is represented here by
her guardian, John de Kirton, indicating that she is under age. In fact, it seems
unlikely that John de Multon himself can have reached puberty.[31] What we are
witnessing here, then, has all the hallmarks of an arranged marriage between the
Multons and their neighbours, the Kirtons. The 100 marks that were paid over
to Thomas under the terms of the final concord were undoubtedly part of the
marriage portion, the sum paid over by the bride's father. Later, on 27 April
1334, by means of another final concord, Thomas granted the couple the manor
of Heapham, with the same reversion.[32] This property, too, was granted in return
for 100 marks. Jointure and marriage portion seem to have been handed over in
instalments, presumably as the money was raised by John de Kirton.

   The period under discussion in this book is an important one in the development of new strategies for the protection of estates by families.[33] Entails were
often created by means of a final concord, that is by a settlement made in the royal
court to an apparent dispute, a device used most often to convey land in a manner
that made it a matter of record. Biancalana's study of final concords over seven

had an elder brother, Thomas de Multon 'the elder', who died without heir. He had not succeeded
to the estates: Massingberd, 'Pedigree of Multon of Frampton', 206–7.

   [29] The letter of attorney (Multon 37) bears a seal with a shield of three bars and the legend: *S Th
de M'l'ton*.

   [30] Multon 93a.

   [31] Puberty was officially 14 for a boy, and 12 for a girl. Under the Church's rules youngsters
were not supposed to marry before that age, although they could be betrothed from the age of 7.
Marriages made before puberty could be repudiated.

   [32] This is the third of the final concords copied on to Multon 78a. There is no trace of it in
the National Archives. It, too, was begun in an earlier term, Trinity 1333, and completed at Easter
term 1334.

   [33] For what follows, see especially Biancalana, *The Fee Tail and the Common Recovery*, esp.
ch. three, 'Living with Entails'.

counties shows that the zenith in the creation of fee tails by final concord came in the years 1321 to 1340, when about 41 per cent of final concords did so. Some of these were in 'tail male', restricting inheritance to male offspring. There has been some controversy over this issue. In 1993 Eileen Spring argued, from a feminist perspective, that the tail male was being used in this period generally, and quite deliberately, to curtail the amount of property passing into the hands of heiresses. The jointure had itself put more property into women's hands. However, this tended to be temporary and did not greatly affect the transmission of property to men. The tail male was different in that women were being specifically excluded from inheritance.[34] It can be demonstrated, however, that entails of this type, restricting inheritance to male offspring, were very much a minority.[35]

Uncertainty over the validity of tail male may have curtailed their use before the 1340s. One family that did employ this device, however, was that of de la Beche. Their history is instructive. We have encountered them before. The last phases of their story produced the inventory of the possessions of Margery de la Beche and the splendid series of sepulchral effigies in Aldworth church. Meanwhile, however, they had been quite regular employers of the fee tail.

The de la Beche family were originally of sub-knightly stock holding a small estate at Aldworth in Berkshire.[36] Early in the reign of Edward II three of the sons of Philip de la Beche found themselves in the royal household, first as valets and then as knights. They were John, Nicholas, and William.[37] Another brother, Edmund, was a royal clerk.[38] All of them profited from royal service in terms of the acquisition of estates,[39] while Philip and all six of his known sons played a part in the troubled politics of Edward II's reign.[40] In 1330 most of these sons were still alive, while John and his wife, Isabella, had two sons of their own. His

---

[34] E. Spring, *Law, Land and Family* (Chapel Hill, 1993).

[35] On this, see S. J. Payling, 'Social Mobility, Demographic Change, and Landed Society in Late Medieval England', *EcHR* 45 (1992), 57; and Biancalana, *The Fee Tail and the Common Recovery*, 176.

[36] TNA CP25: Berkshire 45 Henry III, no. 45. According to the inquisition post mortem of Sir Nicholas de la Beche in 1345 it consisted, at least at that point in time, of a messuage and a carucate of land in a place called le Beches: *CIPM* viii. no. 574. If this was the extent of the ancestral home of the de la Beches it was indeed meagre.

[37] John appears to have been the first one into the household, although two of his brothers were hard on his heels. John was described as a valet in 1308 and a royal knight in 1311: C. Moor, *Knights of Edward I*, 5 vols, Publications of the Harleian Society 80–5 (London, 1929–32), i. 63–4. He was a trusted royal servant and was associated with the royal favourite, Piers Gaveston. The Ordinances of 1311 included his name among those who were to be removed from office and from the king's service. Nicholas appears in royal service around this time, whereas William had been a king's valet as early as 1309 when he received a royal gift of £5. See also M. Prestwich, 'The Court of Edward II', in G. Dobbs and A. Musson (eds), *The Reign of Edward II* (York, 2006).

[38] From at least 1312: *CCR 1307–13*, 547.

[39] See for example *CPR 1313–17*, 30, 303 (for Edmund); *CCR 1307–13*, 195, 325, 365 (for John) *CPR 1313–17*, 162, 472, *CPR 1317–21*, 59 (for Nicholas); *CPR 1313–17*, 627, 643; *CPR 1317–21*, 139 (for William).

[40] See the entries in *Parliamentary Writs*, ed. F. Palgrave, 2 vols in 4 (London, 1827–34), vol. 2, Division 3, Alphabetical Digest, 505–6. The remaining sons were Robert and Philip.

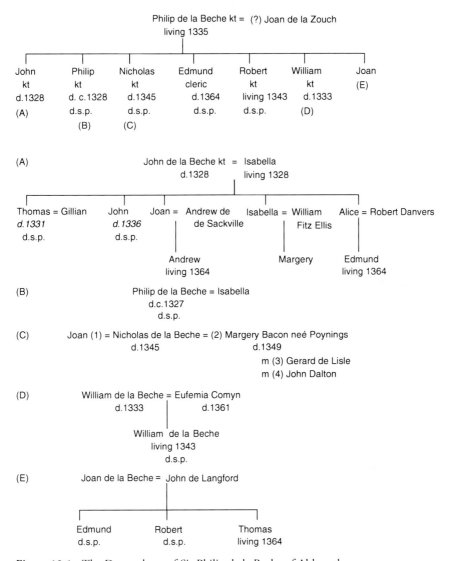

Figure 10.1. The Descendants of Sir Philip de la Beche of Aldworth.

brothers, Nicholas and Edmund, rose even further in the service of Edward III and achieved further enrichment.[41] They proceeded to employ the device of tail male (Figure 10.1).

[41] For their careers under Edward III, see Tout, *Chapters in the Administrative History of Medieval England,* iii. 53 and iv. 81 (for Edmund), and iii. 121 and v. 318–322 (for Nicholas). For the latter's acquisition of land, see *CIPM* viii. no. 574; *CChR 1327–41,* 391, 424, 427, 438.

The earliest instrument which employs this that I have seen is a fine from Easter term 1331 when Philip de la Beche enfeoffed his son, Nicholas de la Beche, of the manor of Haxon in Wiltshire and property at West Compton in Berkshire for the term of his life. After his death, the Berkshire property was to pass to Thomas son of John de la Beche and his wife, Gillian, and their heirs. The manor of Haxon, on the other hand, was to go to John son of John de la Beche, then to Robert son of Philip de la Beche, and then to the male heirs of each of them in turn.[42] Even more revealing is a fine from June 1338 in which Nicholas de la Beche and Margery acquired a jointure of the manor of Whitchurch in Oxfordshire and various properties at Swallowfield and elsewhere in Berkshire, to them and the male heirs of their bodies with successive remainders to Edmund de la Beche, archdeacon of Berkshire, Robert de la Beche, knight, William son of William de la Beche, and Edmund son of John de Langford, and in each case to the male heirs of their bodies before finally passing to any other heirs of Nicholas.[43] Other de la Beche properties were served in like manner, with as many male members as were living included while female heirs, principally the three daughters of John de la Beche, were excluded.[44]

How can we explain this? The obvious point is that there were a considerable number of males and that their interests came first. Moreover, the gentry thought in patrilineal terms and the preservation of the family and the preservation of the name were one and the same. A slightly different way to look at it is to say that it was the number of surviving males in the family that allowed them to do this. There are various indications that the de la Beche males were used to operating as a tightly knit group, aware of their collective interests. The descent of Aldworth itself was rigidly controlled. There can be no doubt that it was in the hands of Philip de la Beche, the father of the six sons, until his death. It then passed to Nicholas as eldest surviving son. On his death it was specifically said to have been held by him and the male heirs of his body. An inquisition held on 3 May 1345 shows that it had now passed to Edmund de la Beche under the terms of a family entail.[45] Other arrangements that they made also suggest a high level of co-operation. Rights such as free warren were jointly acquired. They frequently nominated one another as attorney to act on their behalf.[46] Perhaps this attitude of mind goes back to the beginning of the rise of the de la Beche family. We sometimes hear it said or implied that too many children was a drain on resources. However, a plethora of sons could be used to advantage. It may well be that Philip de la Beche quite deliberately sought to use his fecundity to advance his family, placing his sons in the royal household. Perhaps this governed their thinking from first to last, and perhaps it helps to explain the Aldworth

[42] C. R. Elrington (ed.), *Abstracts of Feet of Fines Relating to Wiltshire for the Reign of Edward II*, Wiltshire Record Society (Devizes, 1974), no. 78.
[43] Ibid. no. 198.   [44] TNA CP25 Berkshire 13 Edward III nos. 1, 11 and 12.
[45] *CIPM* viii. no. 574.
[46] *CPR 1313–17*, 352; *CPR 1317–21*, 421; *CChR 1300–26*, 350.

effigies. It may even explain why two of the sons were on the opposing side in the political struggle of 1321–2.[47] Faced with the prospect of a disastrous civil war which could undermine all they had worked for, the de la Beche men presumably used their numbers to hedge their bets, as aristocratic families had done in the past. If relatively few families employed the tail male could this be because they simply lacked the numbers of male offspring to make this feasible or necessary?

Although entails, let alone tail males, did not constitute a majority among fourteenth-century land grants, granting in fee tail none the less had a cumulative effect in that more and more land became subject to claims to reversion or remainder. As far as the fourteenth century is concerned, the grantees were restrained from alienating the land until the fourth generation. The tendency to settle the same land over and over had the effect of multiplying claims. The land law was becoming increasingly complex. This complexity has been much commented upon by historians and it helps to explain some of the conflict that occurred over the inheritance of estates. Still greater complexity arrived with the development of the enfeoffment to uses, the ultimate in terms of medieval legal devices modifying the operation of the land law. To this we must now turn.

The enfeoffment to uses involved a landowner granting some of his lands to a group of friends, relatives, retainers or clerics, with instructions, verbal or written, to hold them to his use while he lived and dispose of them after his death in accordance with his will or wishes. In this way he could keep his property out of the hands of his overlord, provide for his children, and arrange for the repayment of his debts after his demise. By the 1360s enfeoffment to use was being widely employed.[48] It was once suggested that the gentry were the main instigators in the emergence and spread of the use, and that the barons' petition to parliament in 1339 against enfeoffments which defrauded them of wardships is indicative of this. A detailed study of its usage in Berkshire, on the other hand, showed that enfeoffment to uses did not become common among the gentry until the later fourteenth century, and the evidence suggests that it was diffused first among the greater lords during the reign of Edward III.[49] In this sense it was a facet of the relationship between the higher nobility and the crown. In the technical sense, however, it grew out of pre-existing arrangements in which the gentry, seeking to control the destiny of their lands, played a major part.

Additional insights are provided by the Cobeldykes. When it came to the deployment of legal devices they were by no means novices. The inquisition

---

[47] While Philip de la Beche and four of his sons were among 'the king's enemies', Nicholas and William supported the crown.

[48] Modern study of enfeoffment to uses began with J. L. Barton, 'The Medieval Use', *Law Quarterly Review*, 81 (1965), 562–77, and J. M. W. Bean's major work, *The Decline of English Feudalism* (New York, 1968).

[49] Peggy Jefferies, 'The Medieval Use as Family Law and Custom: the Berkshire Gentry in the Fourteenth and Fifteenth Centuries', *Southern History*, 1 (1979).

following the death of Sir Alexander de Cobeldyke held at Lincoln in January 1335 is quite revealing in this respect. The inquisition found that all his tenements at Wyberton and Frampton had been alienated long before his death to Master John de Wigtoft and Richard de Fordington, parson of the church of Woodhall. Those at Freiston had been similarly alienated to those two, and to Roger de Stickford, chaplain. His tenements at Hagworthingham, Moorby, Coningsby and elsewhere were in the hands of Roger de Stickford and Richard de Fordington. All were held in fee simple, that is to say they were not subject to entail. None of them was held of the king, but by a variety of lords. There can be no doubt that these were being held to the use of the Cobeldyke family, that is to say that their tenure was formal and that the properties in question did not cease to be held by the Cobeldykes on the ground. When Alexander's son, Roger, came of age the legal tenure would be returned to him and his heirs by enfeoffment, and the feudal records of 1346 do indeed record that Wyberton and Freiston were in Roger's hands.[50] The manor of Fordington seems to have been in a different category. Here the *Inquisition Post Mortem* records that Alexander had entailed it three years before his death to Master John de Cobeldyke and the heirs of his body. This would appear to have been a conditional gift of the very traditional type, designed to support a relative but at the same time to prevent as far as possible the alienation of the property outside of the family. The same feudal records show that by 1346 it, too, was back in Roger's hands, almost certainly through lack of such heirs. The Cobeldykes used whatever instruments were appropriate to what they were seeking to achieve in any given instance.

If the Cobeldykes were in the van when it came to the deployment of the various devices, the Multons of Frampton were perhaps equally astute in protecting their interests. Whether the jointures which Sir Thomas de Multon effected in 1324 and 1326 ultimately profited the family is unclear. A jointure was hardly foolproof in avoiding wardship because, of course, the lady might predecease the lord. Thomas and Elizabeth can be seen acting together in property transactions in Kirton and Boston in 1326–7,[51] but she does not seem to appear in the archives thereafter. Moreover, Thomas himself may well have been dead by July 1337 when Sir Henry Hillary makes his first appearance in the Multon archive.[52] As we have seen this man undertook the arrentation of the services of unfree tenants at Frampton some time around 1340 whilst guardian of the young John de Multon. At this point it is necessary to look a little more closely at him and his role because it suggests that the Multons had already moved beyond the reliance upon jointures alone to protect their interests. Early in 1343 Sir Henry Hillary appeared at the court of Common Pleas on behalf

---

[50] *Feudal Aids*, iii. 241–2.   [51] Multon nos 26c, 31a, 92, and 122.
[52] Bond land in Frampton is said to be held of him on 17 July 1337 (Multon no. 21). He leased land at Kirton to John del Meres for a term of ten years at Michealmas 1339 (Multon 23a).

of himself and John de Multon to defend his recent presentation to the church
of Somercotes which the crown was contesting. Sir Henry told the court that
Thomas de Multon of Frampton had granted the advowson of Somercotes and
the land associated with it together with various other properties to Sir Thomas
Pecche and William Hardy, citizen of Lincoln, to hold for the term of their lives.
This looks very much like an enfeoffment to uses to avoid a further minority.
However, Sir Henry further maintained that these two men had conveyed the
entire estate (*status*) to him. Hence he presented to the Multon living. Henry
won his case and the bishop was instructed to admit his clerk to the living.[53]
John de Multon was running his own estates by Michaelmas 1343, when his
household accounts begin. Meanwhile the effects of yet another wardship had
been avoided.

Curiously, there is no trace in the archives of any similar instruments created
by John himself. He may have had other preoccupations. Although we know
from his household accounts that the family lived quite well, there are indications
that he tended to suffer from a shortage of cash since he raised money from
neighbours and others on the security of his land.[54] Be that as it may, one
would have expected the survival of the sorts of conveyances that we have been
discussing. It may well be that existing arrangements were deemed sufficient.
John was dead by 28 September 1358 when his wife, Anne, leased property as his
widow.[55] The jointures created by his father back in the early 1330s presumably
came into effect, providing for Anne and giving her a large measure of control.
Their son, another John, was under age in 1358 and passed into the wardship of
Sir Thomas de Lucy of Cockermouth. Although the jointure probably ensured
that this involved little or no land, it did involve his marriage. By an indenture of
13 June 1365 the young John acquired licence from Thomas de Lucy to marry
whomsoever he wished. For this he undertook to pay Thomas £100, £40 on
the day of his marriage and the rest in two instalments thereafter, following his
coming of age. He made this undertaking in the presence of the Earl of Angus
and Maud his wife and of John de Repynghale and others.[56] Two years later
he decided to join a military expedition to Prussia. As he prepared to go he felt
obliged to put all his affairs in order in case he should not return. He wrote to
his wife, in French, from London on St Clement's day (23 November), 1367[57]
(Figure 10.2). He began as follows:

Very dear and beloved wife know that since our parting I have been in health—thanks
be to God—and my sovereign desire is to hear similar news of you, our daughter and all
our other friends. Dear wife know that Anthony de Lucy and I and all our company make

[53] Massingberd, 'Pedigree of Multon of Frampton', 206–7.   [54] Multon nos. 39, 89, 102.
[55] Multon no. 94. How extensive his debts were is unclear, but he had certainly been withholding
the annual rent of £2 which he owed the prior of Watton from the manor of Frampton. In May
1359 the king authorized the sheriff of Lincoln to raise the £20 representing 10 years' arrears of this
rent charge from the manor now held by John son of John de Frampton (Multon no. 137).
[56] Multon 142.   [57] Multon 71a.

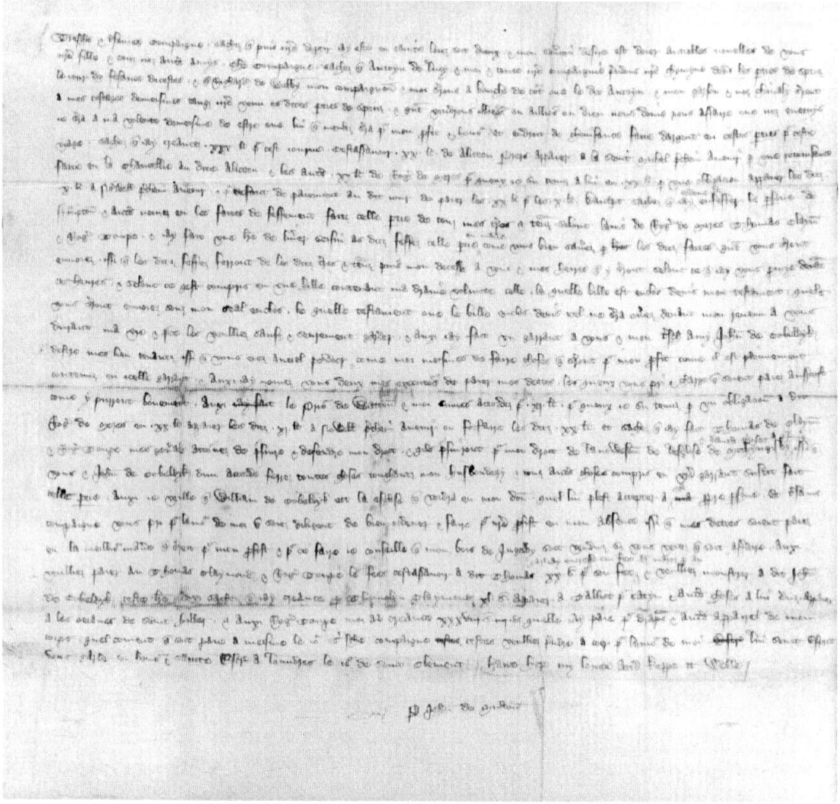

Figure 10.2. Letter of Sir John de Multon III to his wife, Mary (23 November 1367).

our way towards the parts of *Spruz* [i.e. Prussia] the day of the making of these letters and that Richard de Welby my companion and I will be at *bouche a court* with the said Anthony and that my groom and my horses will be at my own cost until we have arrived in those parts, and that when we arrive there or wherever God wills we have anything to do with our enemies it is my wish to be with him, which will be much to my profit and honour.

He proceeded to give details of the money he had borrowed for the journey and then moves on to the item that is of particular interest in the present context, the provisions he had made for the protection of his estates:

Know that I have arranged to enfeoff the parson of Frampton and others named in the deeds of enfeoffment made in this matter of all my lands and tenures according to the advice of Roger de Meres Thomas Claymond and Roger Toupe and I have made a letter to the said feoffees in this matter for the delivery of seisin by hand as you well know so that the feoffees will do towards you and my heirs regarding the said lands and tenures after my death according to that which I promised you before this hour and according to that which is contained in a bill containing my last will, which bill is enclosed within my testament and which will be sent to you enclosed under my seal, which testament with the enclosed bill will not be opened before my return to you during my life to keep my wishes safe and guard them securely.

The feoffees were in fact Thomas de Mappleton, parson of Frampton, Roger de Meres of Kirton, John de Cobeldyke of Frampton, Roger Toupe, Thomas Claymond, and Richard de Welby of Kirton. In the event of John's death they would act according to what his instruction had been. They had been enfeoffed of the manor of Frampton and of all his land in Leicestershire by one deed, and by another of all his lands and tenements held of the earl of Richmond in Holland and of all his property in both Kesteven and Lindsey, including the advowson of Saltfleetby but excluding that of Miningsby. Both documents were drawn up at Frampton and dated 11 November 1367.[58] The enfeoffment was a wise precaution and in practice was needed as John de Multon did not return. According to a later *Inquisition Post Mortem* he died 'in parts beyond the seas' on St Bartholomew's day (18 August) 1368.[59] The king's escheator meanwhile held an immediate inquisition on his death, valuing the manor of Frampton and announcing that his daughter Maud, aged 3 years and more, was his heir and ought to be a royal ward.[60] His lands, however, were in the hands of his feoffees. On 24 February 1371 they formally re-enfeoffed John's widow, Mary (or Marion as she appears in French documents), for her life with reversion to Maud as daughter and heiress and to the heirs of her body. Should these heirs fail the lands would go to John son of Thomas de Multon, late uncle of the deceased, and the heirs of his body, and failing these to the right heirs of the deceased. By this means, then, the feoffees created in effect a belated jointure for Mary, and restricted the descent of the property by entail, excluding all her blood relations and also, implicitly, the family of any second husband. For reasons that are not entirely clear, Frampton was conveyed by a different charter from the other Lincolnshire properties, as it had been to the feoffees.[61] On the same day the same feoffees gave power of attorney to two other men, William Christian of Kirton and Stephen de Redyngs of Wyberton, to give seisin of all the lands, tenements, advowsons, and other items which they had of the gift of John de Multon in Lincolnshire and Leicestershire, except the manor of Frampton, which once again must have been conveyed separately, to Mary.[62]

On some occasions feoffees were given instructions to pay the grantor's debts from his property. Here it is clear, both in the specification of particular debts, and the suggested sale of Ingleby wood, that this was a matter for his executors, that is Mary herself and his 'dear friend' John de Cobeldyke. The wood was to be sold if there were insufficient funds to pay the debts. These included the money he had borrowed for the journey from Alice Perrers, the king's mistress, and from

[58] Multon, 140 and Saltfleetby 25.   [59] *CIPM* xiii. no. 269 (1373).
[60] *CIPM* xii. no. 300.   [61] Multon, nos. 2, 138.   [62] Multon, no. 134.

Roger de Meres, the money he owes the prior of Watton, and two other debts: £2 'to be paid to Talbot for satin' and £1 18s ½d borrowed on his behalf for 'clothes and other apparel for my body'.

Not everything went smoothly, however. The events that followed were the consequences of John de Multon's disastrous decision to go to Prussia. At the same time, however, they illustrate that enfeoffment to uses could be treacherous and that severe complications could ensure.[63] Friction soon occurred between Mary and Richard de Welby of Kirton. Richard was not only the man who had set off for Prussia with John de Multon, and subsequently returned, but also one of the feoffees. The matter went to arbitration before Gilbert count of Angus. An agreement was made, on 22 July 1369, as follows: Marion (the document being in French) and Roger Lyne, chaplain, bound themselves to the payment of £40 by equal portions of 10 marks within the six months following, while Richard released her from all debts to him. Marion also granted him an annual rent of 10 marks for the term of his life out of the lands of which he had been jointly enfeoffed by the said John de Multon. This rent, it says, had been granted to Richard by the said John 'in case he was not loyally served by the said Marion'. Richard now agreed to give up all the obligations and evidences except one instrument, signed before a notary, which witnessed to the same annuity.[64] The mention of a notary suggests that this was an agreement drawn up outside of England after the main enfeoffments. Hence the disagreement which ensued. There were some other contentious matters. For one thing there seems to have been further friction over the rent charge owed to the priory of Watton.[65] Another bone of contention was the rent charge owed to the alien abbey of Langonnet.[66]

There remained the question of the future of the two women. Mary remarried. Her new husband was Sir Ralph Daubeny. However, she was unlucky there, too, for by 24 June 1379 he was also dead.[67] Mary then decided to take a back seat and to hand the running of the estates over to her daughter. Maud had been contracted to marry William son of William Spaigne of Boston when

---

[63] For another example of difficulties caused by the employment of enfeoffment to uses see Peter R. Coss, *The Langley Family and its Cartulary: A Study in Late Medieval 'Gentry'*, Dugdale Society Occasional Papers 22 (Oxford, 1974). That such difficulties played a major part in the development of the equitable justice of the Lord Chancellor is well known.

[64] Multon no. 144.

[65] John de Multon had announced in his letter of 1367 that the question had been resolved by means of a bond. However, in 1377 or 1378 the prior and convent of Watton acknowledged the receipt of £4 due from the manor of Frampton from Sir Ralph Daubeny. As the rent was in fact 40s per annum the rent had clearly been withheld for two years.

[66] On 13 October the sheriff of Lincoln acknowledged the receipt from Mary, widow of John de Multon, by the hand of William son of Walter de Saxilby, of £10 rent which she was accustomed to pay to the abbey, and which no doubt was still going to the crown.

[67] On this day the prior and convent of Watton acknowledged receipt of 40s annual rent due from her, that is to say from Lady Mary de Multon, widow of Sir Ralph Dawbeney, knight, lately deceased: Multon nos. 6, 12.

they were both under age, that is below 7 years. Upon her petition to the commissary of the bishop of Lincoln, this was annulled in view of her subsequent marriage to Thomas Graa of York after she reached marriageable years, but while William was still below them.[68] The marriage had taken place by 18 May 1380, on which day Mary, as widow of Ralph Daubeny of Ingleby, leased to Thomas Graa and Maud, daughter of John de Multon of Frampton, the manors of: Frampton, Miningsby, North Ingleby, Kirkby La Thorpe, Heapham with all lands etc. in Boston, Wyberton, Kirton, Saltfleetby, Somercotes, Wood Enderby, *Maryng*, Coningsby near Tattershall, Willingham, Stow St Mary, Sturton, Bransby, Marton, Bassingham, and Saxilby, Lincolnshire and all lands in Hoby, Leicestershire and all other lands which belonged to John de Multon her late husband. The lands were leased for the lifetime of Maud at an annual rent of 200 marks to be paid quarterly at the church of our Lady Crakepole [*sic*] in Lincoln.[69] On 5 September 1381 Mary acknowledged the first instalment of 200 marks.[70]

Meanwhile, however, on 24 October 1380 Mary and Thomas Graa came to an agreement for her sojourning (*la sojourayne*) with one chaplain, two esquires and two damsels at the rate of 5s per week for herself, and 2s per week for each of the others, *la sojourne* to begin on 29 October. The lady, it seems, drove a hard bargain. How long this King Lear-type situation endured is unknown, but Mary later married Sir John Bussy, the infamous household knight of Richard II. In December 1398 Thomas Graa of York was granted custody of the manor of Multon Hall in Frampton during the minority of his son, John, by which time both Mary and her daughter Maud were dead.[71]

A further group of documents suggests that some of John de Multon's feoffees had never in fact given up the Frampton manor. On December 1382 the sheriff of Lincoln received a royal writ instructing him to order Thomas Claymond and Roger Toupe to give to Thomas Graa and Maud his wife the manor of Multon 'Halle' in Frampton on the basis of the entail created back in 1324 when Simon Tuchet and John son of Herbert de Twycross had enfeoffed Thomas de Multon and his wife, Elizabeth, and the heirs of their bodies. This had precedence over any later enfeoffment and, in any case, the instructions under enfeoffment to uses were difficult to enforce under the common law. On 15 January 1383 Mary gave power of attorney for taking seisin of the manor of Frampton.[72] There follows a deed by which Thomas de Claymond and Roger Toupe conveyed to Mary two parts [*sic*] of the manor of Frampton as in the deed of 24 February 1371, with the entail. It is dated 19 January 1383. Meanwhile the problem with Richard Welby had raised its head again. A document exists in the Multon collection, dated

---

[68] Multon no. 74a.   [69] Multon no. 79.
[70] Multon no. 16.   [71] Multon no. 143.
[72] To Robert de Galway, parson of Kirkby Laythorpe and Stephen de Redyng of Wyberton: Multon nos. 103a, 106a.

13 December 1381, which is an agreement between Thomas Graa of York and Richard Welby of Kirkton to submit the dispute over the former's free tenement in Frampton, the manor of *Multonhalle*, to the arbitration of Thomas Claymond, or in case he dies or is hindered in this before the feast of the Purification next, to Richard Ravener, archdeacon of Lincoln, and William Skipworth or whoever the said Richard may choose. This document appears not to have been sealed and is indeed crossed out and another written on the dorse. This is a bond from Thomas Graa to Elizabeth, widow of Richard de Welby, and her son Thomas for £25 with respect to a payment of £12 10s. If Thomas produces on the specified day two acquittances by which Richard de Welby acknowledged receipt from Mary, widow of Ralph Daubeney, knight, of 5 marks, then for each of the acquittances he shall be released from the payment of £2 10s out of the said sum of £12 10s.[73] Whether the arbitration proposed took effect is unclear, but the matter does seem to have been resolved, even if in a rather uneasy manner. On 29 February 1384 Thomas de Welby of Pinchbeck granted to Mary, widow of John de Multon of Frampton:

whatever could come to him by inheritance from the death of his father, Richard de Welby, one of the feoffees of John de Multon for the manor of Frampton with all other lands, advowsons, etc in Lincolnshire and Leicestershire which formerly belonged to John, to hold for her life, with remainder to Maud, John's daughter, and should those heirs fail to Maud his sister and her issue, and failing them to John's right heirs.[74]

Thomas de Welby gave power of attorney for seisin to be given to Mary.[75]

Having discussed these legal devices and their ramifications in some detail, it is time to move on to examine the relationships involved. The Pecche family figure prominently in these arrangements. The explanation is not hard to find: they were in fact related to the Multons by marriage. The key to unravelling the relationship between the two families is Lucy Pecche. In 1303 Lucy is reported to have held an estate reckoned as one-third knight's fee in Frampton and Kirton, 'which Margaret the wife of Alan de Multon once held'. Lucy was, in fact, a considerable landowner. She held a further one-sixteenth fee in Kirton wapentake, and a whole knight's fee in Freiston, Butterwick, and Boston. This last had passed by 1346 into the hands of John Pecche and Robert Godsfield.[76] This John Pecche held additional estates in Coleby and Althorpe[77] in 1346, and is almost certainly the Sir John Pecche 'of Lindsey', knight, who was among the witnesses to the Multon jointure if 1324. Thomas Pecche, who was given

---

[73] Multon no. 85a.

[74] Multon no. 80a. The witnesses here are the same as in no. 141, viz. William de Spaigne of Boston Ralph de Cobildyk, Thomas de Cobildyk, John Batesone of Frampton, and Stephen de Cobildyk of Frampton.

[75] Multon no. 81a.

[76] *Feudal Aids*, iii. 131–2, 163, 241. In 1346 the same source records a Lucy Pecche holding the one-sixteenth fee 'which Lucy Pecche once held' [*sic*]: ibid. 239.

[77] ? *Obthorp*.

power of attorney (with John Twycross) to enfeoff John de Multon and his wife of Heapham in 1332, was hence also related to the Multons, and was very probably the Suffolk knight of that name.[78] The evidence suggests, then, that a close and intimate relationship had developed between the families of Multon and Pecche.

As we have seen Lucy Pecche was holding property in 1303 which Margaret de Multon once held. Her tenure certainly left its mark on the Frampton estate. The Collector's Account for 1330–1 includes 9s rent from the farm of *Pecchehalle* and 13s 4d from a meadow, with sheepfold, called *Pecchegrove*.[79] The former is probably identical with the *Ladyhalle* itemized in the extent of 1326, which lay beyond the manorial close.[80] The late nineteenth-century OS map tends to confirm this in showing *Ladygarth* immediately to the south of the moated site.[81] Lucy's property in Frampton did not remain, however, in Pecche hands. In 1346 it is recorded as held by John de Multon, and there is no Pecche recorded at Frampton in the subsidies of 1327 and 1332. What we are dealing with is undoubtedly dower land. In August 1297 Lucy made an exchange with Sir Thomas de Multon of Frampton involving some parcels of rent which 'she used to receive in name of dower' from his inheritance.[82] In June 1300 a chirograph in French settled the *divers debatz et demandes* between Sir Thomas de Multon and his uncle, John de Multon over the inheritance of Thomas de Multon and Beatrice his wife. Among the items in contention between them was rent in Boston and Bicker. John was to hold a moiety of these *ausi ben en la vie Dame Luce de Pecche come apres son deses*.[83] Lucy was still living in March 1303 but was dead by August 1309 when William Tuchet leased property in Boston which had previously been leased by Lady Lucy Pecche. It was now in William's custody 'by reason of the minority of the heir of Sir Thomas de Frampton'.[84] A pedigree recorded on the rolls of the court of Common Pleas in 1343 says that Thomas de Multon I of Frampton had a son and heir, named Thomas, the father of Alan.[85] This Thomas must have married Lucy Pecche, for in October 1298, as Lady Lucy Pecche, widow of Sir Thomas de Frampton, she was one of the presenters to the living of Bassingham.[86] The widow of Alan de Multon, whose erstwhile property Lucy was stated to be holding in 1303 by the feudal records, was not therefore Margaret but *Margery*, wife of the Alan de Multon who was progenitor of this line (Figure 2.1, page 142). The one-third fee in question almost certainly represents the property Margery brought to the marriage long ago, that

---

[78] *Feudal Aids*, v. 91, 92.   [79] Multon Adds 9.

[80] The extent also refers to Lady Newland.

[81] There is a map derived from this in the Magdalen archive.

[82] Multon 105a, dated 1 August 1297.   [83] Multon 98a.   [84] Multon 124.

[85] Massingberd, 'Pedigree of Multon of Frampton', 206–7.

[86] *Rolls and Register of Bishop Oliver Sutton*, vol. 1, ed. Hill, 235. Lucy already held land in Holland as early as 1284–5 when she was returned as holding two-and-a-half carucates in Freiston jointly with William de Polebrook and a further carucate in Toft: *Feudal Aids*, iii. 370–1.

is to say her *maritagium* under the old system. It was later used as dower. Lucy Pecche was long supported by the Multon estate. The date of her husband's death is unknown. It is likely that he survived his son Alan, who was dead by 1283, although not perhaps by very much.[87] For two decades Lucy was the most senior member of the Multon family resident at Frampton. Little wonder that she left such a mark on the estate.

What is most significant in all of this, however, is that an enduring relationship between the families of Multon and Pecche was created by marriage, and is reflected in the legal instruments which were employed to protect the Multon interests. We seem to be entering here into a circle of trust. Incidentally, it is noticeable that William Tuchet, who was involved in protecting Multon interests in and before 1309, bears the same surname as Simon Tuchet who was used with John son of Herbert de Twycross to create the jointure of 1326. The Tuchets were, in fact, tenants by military service of the Multons.[88] The Pecches and a few men who were the Multons' own tenants and/or high-ranking servitors provided the core of friends whom the Multons relied on to protect their interests. After these came the men who witnessed the intimate family instruments revolving around the formal final concords. These were in turn one degree closer to the family than the 'mere neighbours' who witnessed the normal run of property transactions.

This first circle of witnesses during the 1320s includes the Multons' close neighbours, the Cobeldykes and Kirtons, as well as knights belonging to the Pecche, Rochford,[89] Willoughby, and Darcy families. Sir Thomas de Multon of Kirton, who figures as a witness for Thomas de Multon of Frampton on a number of occasions during the 1320s, clearly belongs to a related family, although the precise relationship is unclear.[90] It may well have been a blood relationship whose origins lie some way back in time. There may have been some genuine bond between them, although equally one should be wary of exaggerating it. Like the Kirtons and the Cobeldykes, they were also close neighbours.

Other families employed trusted secular clerics for these tasks. On 18 December 1339, for example, William le Forester, parson of Willoughby, and Walter Bronthorp, parson of Spilsby, enfeoffed Roger son of Alexander de Cobeldyke and Maud his wife of the manor of Freiston. It was conveyed to them and to the heirs of their bodies, with remainder to the right heirs of Roger. This was of course a re-enfeoffment. The witness list was headed by five local knights, namely Sir John de Willoughby, lord of Eresby (and patron of Spilsby), Sir William Deincourt, Sir Saer de Rochford, Sir Thomas de Multon de Kirton and

---

[87] During the minority of his grandson people looked back to the time of the late Thomas de Frampton: *Rolls and Register of Bishop Oliver Sutton*, vol. 1, ed. Hill, 211.
[88] On 16 June 1311 the royal escheator for beyond the Trent was ordered to take into the king's hands the land of Nicholas Tuchet, deceased, a tenant by knight service of the heir of Thomas de Multon of Frampton, a minor in the king's wardship: *CFR*, ii. 94.
[89] The Rochefords were near neighbours at Benington and Toft.   [90] Multon 31a, 52a, 92.

Sir Henry de Halton.[91] It is noticeable that this circle overlaps with the one reflected by the Multon instruments of a decade earlier. It is worth suggesting that had they had an adult male living in 1339, the Multons of Frampton would also have figured.

On 19 March 1340 the same parsons, William le Forester and Walter Bronthorp, enfeoffed Roger de Cobeldyke and Maud, his wife, of the manor of Harrington, with the same provisions. Here it is expressly stated that they held the manor through the 'gift and enfeoffment' of the same Roger.[92] The deed conveying the manor to them also survives and is dated 3 February 1340. So, too, does Roger's letter of attorney, written on the same day and addressed to two further clerics, Thomas de Stowe, chaplain, and Gilbert de Burgh, clerk, to deliver seisin to the said parsons.[93]

A further letter of attorney survives, dated 2 March 1342, by which Roger son of Sir Alexander de Cobeldyke authorized the same Gilbert de Burgh, chaplain, to deliver the manor of Wyberton to those parsons. There can be no doubt that this was part of the same sequence of events.[94] All of this took place near the beginning of Roger's tenure of the Cobeldyke lands. He succeeded his father, Alexander, at the age of 18 in 1335.[95] The advantages of using clerics are obvious. There can hardly be any doubt that these clerics will have had other associations with the lord in question, that is to say they were either in his employ or owed their livings to him (or to one of his associates) as patrons.

There was generally one other person who, from the point of view of the male landowner, was within the first circle of trust: that is, of course, his wife. The marital relationship must often have been a genuine partnership, where the lady's interests and the lord's were largely one and the same. In 1367 Sir John de Multon addressed his letter to his wife, and although he expected her to work in concert with John de Cobeldyke, her co-executor, there is no doubt that the directing hand was expected to be hers. The role and competence of ladies in respect of estate and household have been much studied in recent years and there is no need to labour the matter here.[96] The expression of affection, however, is a noticeable feature of John de Multon's letter, both in the address and at the end, and this deserves further comment. 'Very dear wife', he says, as he nears his conclusion, 'you will want to take these things to heart for love of me. The Holy Spirit keep you in honour and in health.' The letter was originally folded and on the exposed surface of the dorse was written: *A me trescher & trebien*

---

[91] *CAD* A 8590. Other witnesses are named but are not given in the printed calendar. Series A (TNA E40) contains a small Cobeldyke archive.

[92] *CAD* A8490.   [93] *CAD* A8633 and A 8640.

[94] *CAD* A 9820.   [95] *CIPM*, vii. no. 597.

[96] See especially, Rowena E. Archer, ' "How ladies . . . who live on their manors ought to manage their households and estates": Women as Landholders and Administrators in the Later Middle Ages', in P. J. P. Goldberg (ed.), *Woman is a Worthy Wight: Women in English Society, c. 1200–1500* (Stroud, 1992). For affective relations within marriage, see Coss, *The Lady in Medieval England*, ch. 4.

amee (ca)mpaigne Mari(on) de Multon.[97] These expressions might be dismissed as conventional but for the fact that the place and date of writing, the substantive end of the letter, is followed by an additional line, in English: *Have here my lovee and keppe it welle.* That the last intimate line of the letter was in English suggests that this, rather than French, the language which they showed the world, was the tongue in which the couple habitually spoke to one another at home. The issue of the vernacular languages is one that will concern us again later. For the moment it is important to note the lady's role. Marion would need all her acquired skill and knowledge in directing affairs when it came to her ensuing widowhood.

The words of the letter, especially the final ones, may have been John's own, but the script was not.[98] It was, however, written by someone who was very close to him. The same hand was responsible for the two documents that were drawn up at Frampton on 11 November transferring legal possession of the Multon estates to trusted feoffees.[99] The writer was therefore both privy to these arrangements and present with Sir John at London later in the month. He was also someone who had access to the Multon archive, for on the dorse of a contemporary copy of a document dated 1350 he penned two Middle English poems.[100] In short, he must have been among his most trusted familiars.

One final dimension needs to be examined before we leave the law: the significance of lawyers themselves within the gentry world, not only as associates and professional advisers, but also in terms of recruitment into gentry ranks. The steady growth of the institutions of the common law led inexorably to a wealthy legal profession whose more successful members graduated to the land and to gentry status. The law was the first of the great professions to provide a major recruiting ground for the gentry. The effect, which in the context of this book we might call 'the Cobeldyke effect', had major cultural consequences. In every generation that follows in the long history of the gentry we can identify the more established families, guardians often of traditional patterns of behaviour, on the one hand, and the nouveaux riches on the other who were sometimes more enterprising, perhaps brasher, but equally predictable in many ways in their aspirations and in their acts. It is to the lawyers that we must now turn.

---

[97] The writing is faded and the letters in brackets have been supplied. A red circle remains indicating that it was sealed. In another hand is written: *Est la volunte John de Mult[on]*.

[98] Below the letter was written *P(ar) Joh(an) de Multon'*, indicating that the letter was authorized, and very likely dictated, by him.

[99] C. M. Woolgar and B. O'Donoghue, 'Two Middle English Poems at Magdalen College, Oxford', *Medium Ævum* LII (1983), 217–22.

[100] Ibid. 218–19, for the texts of the poems.

11

Lawyers and Literacy

The cartulary and the new legal devices were two manifestations of an increasingly litigious society. Another was the prominence of lawyers. In examining this it is useful to begin with the pleaders or serjeants (later known as serjeants-at-law) who operated in the Common Bench at Westminster. Paul Brand, to whom we owe much of our knowledge of the early legal profession, has argued cogently that the serjeants emerged as a professional elite during the reign of Edward I, most particularly during the second half of the reign.[1] His study of the sixty-seven serjeants who have been identified practising in the Common Bench during the reign has produced some interesting results.[2] Very few of them came from substantial families. Exceptions were Edmund de Pashley, whose father took knighthood in 1293 and held lands valued around that time at £40 per year, Robert de Mablethorpe, whose father was returned in that same year as holding £40 land in Lincolnshire but had failed to take on knighthood, and Alan de Walkingham, whose father held the manor of Walkingham and a royal serjeanty at Great Givendale in Yorkshire and whose mother held substantial property in her own right. Details on the background of other serjeants show that they came from free holding families but were poor in relative terms. Henry le Scrope's father was knighted at the battle of Falkirk, but this was seven years after his son became a serjeant and he does not appear to have been a substantial landowner in the North Riding of Yorkshire where he originated. Henry Spigurnel came from a cadet branch of an hereditary family of spigurnels (hereditary sealers of writs) of the royal chancery. Their property, at Dagnal in Buckinghamshire, was valued at £5 per year in 1328. William Inge's father had been coroner of Dunstable and held property at the nearby village of Totternhoe. On the death of William's daughter in 1327 this was valued at 40s. William de Barford (or Bereford) was a younger son of Walter de Barford in north Warwickshire who was not distrained for knighthood in 1257 because his lands were valued at only £5 per year. At least four of the serjeants came from urban backgrounds. These were Alexander de Coventry, Nicholas de Warwick, Ralph de Huntingdon and Robert Norman

---

[1] Paul Brand, *The Origins of the English Legal Profession* (Oxford, 1992), esp. 106–10.

[2] For the details that follow, see Paul Brand, 'The Serjeants of the Common Bench in the Reign of Edward I: An Emerging Professional Elite', in M. Prestwich, R. Britnell and R. Frame (eds), *Thirteenth Century England VII* (Woodbridge, 1999), 81–102. Much of the evidence is drawn from Brand (ed.), *The Earliest English Law Reports*, vol. 2, vii–cxxxix.

of Hedon. The backgrounds of many are obscure but the details that can be gleaned suggest that they tended to be of free holding background, of families that were often fairly substantial in their own communities, but relatively poor on any national or county scale. The fact that most of them carried toponymic surnames is perhaps indicative that they were of some substance in their original communities. Of the twenty-eight serjeants who were practising in or before 1290, for example, no less than twenty-five had surnames derived from places.

What is especially interesting is the counties from which these sixty-seven serjeants were drawn. Overwhelmingly, they came from eastern England. Yorkshire provided ten, Lincolnshire six and Essex five. These were followed by four from Durham, four from Norfolk, and three from Suffolk. Leicestershire, Warwickshire, and Shropshire also provided three. The east Midlands was better represented than the west Midlands. Few came from the south or south-west. What is particularly noticeable is that the great majority came from the old Danelaw, that part of England with a reputation for its preponderance of free tenures and relatively light manorialization. The point is reinforced when we look at the area of origin of those who did not come from eastern England. The Warwickshire men, for example, William de Barford, Alexander de Coventry, and Nicholas de Warwick, all came from the north Warwickshire Arden rather than the more densely settled and more strongly manorialized Feldon area of south Warwickshire. Tenures were freer and the social structure looser in Arden. The well-represented Shropshire exhibits similar characteristics.

With the high and growing demand for practising lawyers and for men knowledgeable in the law during the later thirteenth and early fourteenth centuries, finding the means to give a potential lawyer the requisite schooling was an obvious form of investment for a family with sufficient funds to make this a realistic possibility. It might also result from pressure on income; for example where there were multiple sons to sustain. This may well have been the case with the Kinshams of Kinsham near Presteigne on the Welsh border.[3] Adam and Simon de Kinsham, both serjeants-at-law, were two of the six sons of John de Kinsham, Adam being the eldest. John was probably himself younger son, as Adam de Kinsham the serjeant later claimed property as heir of his uncle, an earlier Adam de Kinsham. Another of the brothers, Henry, was appointed an attorney on a number of occasions before he met a violent death in 1288, and may therefore have been at the beginning of a legal career. A fourth brother, Hugh, was a cleric and held the living of Acton, Herefordshire. One of the others, Walter, was in Gascony in 1297 and may well have been on military service. Equally, the law may have been one of the regular outlets within a culture of enterprise and of upward mobility that was stronger in some social milieu, and hence in some areas, than in others. One immediately recognizes the world around Frampton and Kirton in south Lincolnshire, and the society that the

---

[3] Brand, 'The Serjeants', 83–4.

likes of the early Cobeldykes inhabited. The existence of this sort of social milieu may help to explain why Paul Brand was able to find clusters of lawyers coming from certain localities. One can identify examples where a serjeant came from the same locale as a royal justice, suggesting social and professional patronage of some kind, and examples of where serjeants of successive generations came from the same area, which seems to indicate apprenticeship. Over and above that, however, are situations where two or more coeval serjeants came from the same neighbourhood. This was true of the two Lincolnshire serjeants, Gilbert de Tothby and Robert de Mablethorpe, for example, who became serjeants in 1293 and 1299 respectively. Roger de Higham, William Inge, and Henry Spigurnel came from within ten miles of one another on the Bedfordshire/Buckinghamshire border. John de Lisle, Thomas de Fishburn, and William de Kelloe came from within five miles of one another in county Durham. There must have been close association between them, perhaps even some informal mutual support mechanism.

Concentration on the Westminster serjeants, however, can give a false impression of the reach of the legal profession. Many of them appeared in the counties where the court was on eyre. However, a minority of Brand's serjeants worked in the central courts only for a short period. Around a quarter of them did not establish themselves there. It is possible to consider them as failures, but it is more likely that they had no intention of working there permanently. Rather they were gaining professional experience before moving to more local courts, that is to say before moving back into the community. It is now known that by the beginning of the fourteenth century there were professional serjeants at work in county courts. Up to a dozen or so have been identified operating in the Warwickshire county court, for example, in the year 1303. Among them are John de Heyford, Thomas Boydin of Stretton on Dunsmore, and very probably Robert de Stoke and Adam des Okes of Whitley, also near Coventry.[4]

Even now, however, we have looked at only one branch of the legal profession, the serjeants or pleaders, barristers in modern parlance. There were also the attorneys, who attended court on behalf of their clients. Anyone could be an attorney for another in a particular case. However, there were also professional attorneys active in the central courts, who not only attended for their clients but who provided general knowledge of legal process, acquired writs on behalf of their clients and generally took the burden of litigation away from them. Some of Brand's serjeants can be seen working as professional attorneys in the

---

[4] R. C. Palmer, 'County Year Book Reports: the Professional Lawyers in the Medieval County Court', *EHR*, 91 (1971), 776–81, and the same author's, *The County Courts of Medieval England* (Princeton, 1982), 97–110. Brand, however, recognizes the claims of only six of Palmer's thirteen–fourteen (but includes Heyford and Boydin). The others he rejects on the grounds that there is no evidence that they were speaking as serjeants, and may have been third parties or even litigants: Brand, *The Origins of the English Legal Profession*, 194. There is no doubt, however, that Robert de Stoke and Adam des Okes were lawyers.

national courts before graduating to become pleaders. There was no barrier as yet between one branch of the profession and the other. There were many professional attorneys, however, who specialized in clients from a particular county or counties, so that the client need have little or no contact with Westminster.

Even now we have not exhausted the reach of the legal profession. There were also the professional administrators, many of them with legal knowledge and some, at least, with a degree of professional legal training. Such a man was Robert of Stoke near Coventry. He was named as steward of the prior of Coventry in 1293 and 1300, and was in his service from the 1280s until around 1310. Unlike a number of local contemporaries he does not seem to have been a pleader in the Warwickshire county court. He appeared on at least six occasions, however, as an attorney in the court of Common Pleas between 1302 and 1305 and was appointed as general attorney by two abbots. During the reign of Edward II he was appointed regularly by the crown as a justice of gaol delivery. By this time, too, he was member of peace commissions and was evidently trusted by the central government. He was a justice of assize in Coventry in 1316. By this time he was quite a wealthy and respected figure in his county.[5] Robert's family can be traced back to the reign of Richard I as minor tenants of the earl of Chester. In 1279 Robert held no more than a half carucate of land at Stoke with other dispersed interests in the area. Due largely to the way in which Robert managed his initial advantages, his descendants were able to live in style at Stoke. In the mid-fourteenth century we have a part description of his manor house with its 'knight's chamber', its chamber over the entrance gate and its garden lying between the house and the graveyard of Stoke chapel.[6]

Another local lawyer of this time was Hugh Tyrel of Mannington in north-east Norfolk.[7] In 1287 he inherited from his elder brother a half knight's fee, the family's main holding, in Mannington and the adjacent Itteringham, Oulton, and Little Barningham. There were some additional, minor, properties, but this was their main holding. In 1293 and 1300 he pleaded for clients in three assizes of novel disseisin held at Norwich, and again thereafter. His clients were prominent local landowners and the land at issue substantial. He also gave legal advice to clients, including the choice of available writs, and arranged the writs for them. He was something of a disruptive figure and was involved in the practice of *champerty*, whereby the lawyer paid the client's costs but received a share in the property recovered. But Hugh Tyrel was also a steward. In 1305–6 he held courts for John Engayne at Blickling. Needless to say, Hugh was also active in the courts in his own interests. He moved about in some style, with

---

[5] Coss, *The Origins of the English Gentry*, 191–2.

[6] Coss, *Lordship, Knighthood and Locality*, 313–14.

[7] For what follows, see Paul Brand, 'Stewards, bailiffs and the emerging legal profession in later thirteenth-century England', in Ralph Evans (ed.), *Lordship and Learning: Studies in Memory of Trevor Aston* (Woodbridge, 2004), 139–53.

his own clerk, steward (his kinsman Hugh Tyrel of Itteringham) and even men wearing his livery. He had his own manorial court at Mannington, with free but no unfree tenants. Although he functioned only locally, a good case can be made for regarding Hugh Tyrel and his like as 'part of the fledgling legal profession'.[8]

Needless to say, the law was lucrative, and men could rise much further than Hugh Tyrel. Brand found evidence for forty-four out of his sixty-seven serjeants receiving annual pensions as retainers from their clients, and this takes no account of one-off payments received for their services. Many, as one would expect, invested in land, some of them quite heavily. Among the latter were the Warwickshire men, William de Barford and Nicholas de Warwick. Social elevation tended to follow professional success. Nine of Brand's sixty-seven serjeants, for example, are known to have become knights.

There are many examples of rising lawyers whose stories are securely told. One is Simon Pakeman.[9] The Pakemans came from Kirby Muxloe, a settlement on the western edge of Leicester forest, four miles from Leicester itself. They are documented from the early thirteenth century, and are best described as 'well-to-do freeholders'.[10] Their surviving *Inquisitions Post Mortem* show them holding a demesne of 35–75 acres together with meadow and woodland, free tenants holding four-and-a-half virgates and eight villeins who performed only relatively light labour services. They were entirely local in their interests and their relationships with other prosperous free tenants illustrate this. They did not enjoy a position of dominance at Kirby Muxloe. This fell to the Herle family, who were absentee landlords. These were knighted whereas the Pakemans were sub-knightly. From the early thirteenth century the Pakeman interest was expanding in a piecemeal fashion through acquisitions and by marriage. Into this situation stepped Simon Pakeman III. By 1337 Simon was functioning as an attorney in the court of Common Pleas for local landlords. He probably had some formal legal training and his rise may have been due to Sir William Herle, chief justice of Common Pleas, who acquired his wardship and marriage. Simon was MP for Leicestershire in 1334. In 1340 Henry earl of Lancaster appointed him steward of the honour of Lancaster. He later served John of Gaunt in the same capacity. He now functioned on a wider stage, both at the central courts and on judicial commissions in a string of Midland counties. Notwithstanding his Lancastrian connections, however, he continued to perform for local clients. Economic benefits ensued and the Pakemans became solid members of the Leicestershire gentry.

It is a story that has become familiar to historians. The joint requirements of estate administration and estate protection meant that men with legal training

---

[8] Ibid. 152.

[9] G. G. Astill, 'Social Advancement Through Seigniorial Service? The Case of Simon Pakeman', *Transactions of the Leicestershire Archaeological Society* 54 (1978–9), 14–25.

[10] Ibid. 16.

were much in demand. It is hardly surprising that the law, in its broadest sense, was the most popular means of upward mobility in the period under discussion. From its origins the gentry was permeable to professionals rising through law and administration. In the explosion of royal commissions that took place in the first half of the fourteenth century men of knightly and immediately sub-knightly stock were joined by professionals. In Warwickshire, for example, they include men like Robert de Stoke, John de Heyford, Nicholas de Warwick, Thomas Boydin of Stretton on Dunsmore, and William de Catesby.[11]

Some landowners at least must have become increasingly knowledgeable in the law during this period. Indeed, they could be quite sophisticated in its manipulation and adept in the combination of legal action with tactical use of physical force. A well-documented example is that of Robert Godsfield of Sutton-Le-Marsh in the south riding of Lindsey. Robert was involved in six major disputes between 1298 and 1325.[12] Five of these resulted from his acquisition of the manor of Halstead from Sir Theobald Halstead in the former year. This was not a straightforward purchase, however, for it involved a maintenance agreement by which Robert was to supply Theobald with a variety of provisions plus £10 in cash annually. His apparent failure to honour this agreement led directly to two of his disputes, with Theobald himself and with Stephen Stanham, citizen and former mayor of London. As part of the agreement Robert had undertaken to pay Theobald's debt of £80 to Stephen. The acquisition of Halstead also brought him into a conflict over pasture rights with the prioress of the nearby Cistercian nunnery of Stixwould. In fighting his corner in these battles Robert has been said to have shown 'uncanny knowledge of the law and an ability to use legal technicalities to outwit his opponents'.[13]

Not everything went Robert Godsfield's way, however. A dangerous quarrel with Sir Edmund Deincourt involved his being assaulted and humiliated by Sir Edmund and his supporters by being bound like a prisoner and made to kiss a mare's tail. In 1308 he was in a very tight corner. Facing serious criminal charges, he successfully pleaded benefit of clergy. A later feud with John Toynton of Stixwould, in which a series of lawsuits and counter lawsuits were brought by both parties,[14] became so bitter that it led to Robert's murder on his way to Stixwould church in March 1325.

Robert Godsfield was not altogether typical of the early fourteenth-century gentry. Apart from perhaps being of an unusually violent disposition, he was probably regarded as a social climber and disliked accordingly. Although he was knighted at some point during the years 1313–17, he was not of knightly background. He seems in fact to have been in minor clerical orders in his earlier

---

[11] Coss, *Origins of the English Gentry*, 187–201.
[12] B. McClane, 'A Case Study of Violence and Litigation in the Early Fourteenth Century: the Disputes of Robert Godsfield of Sutton-Le-Marsh', *Nottingham Medieval Studies* 28 (1984), 22–43.
[13] Ibid. 28.   [14] Ibid. 31.

years. He may have been a lawyer, perhaps an attorney. He appears never to have used the services of an attorney in his own disputes and was once employed as a justice of oyer and terminer. It was probably by means of legal employment that he was able to acquire the manor of Halstead, enhancing his family's status above their relatively lowly position at Sutton-Le-Marsh.

But how much knowledge of the law was held within those solid and in many cases ancient landowning families whose members constituted the bedrock of the gentry? Were they solely reliant on their stewards and legal counsel? Or did they take a direct interest in the operation of the law? The question is not an easy one to answer. The very fact that they needed to be vigilant in the protection of their estates suggests a priori that they must have taken such an interest. However, the evidence can hardly be more than indirect. One possible route towards an answer lies in the circulation of legal texts. There was certainly a great deal of legal material in circulation: books of the statutes, registers of writs, treatises and works of instruction, year books containing legal argument around cases and so on. By definition, much of this will have been in the hands of lawyers and law students. However, the fact that a lowly north Warwickshire lawyer like Adam des Okes of Whitley could own a manuscript containing, among other items, two registers of writs suggests the wide availability of such material and the likelihood of it passing into lay hands.[15] We can get closer still in some cases. As we saw in an earlier chapter, John de Longueville, lord of Little Billing near Northampton, owned a manuscript which contained copies of texts on estate management, including the *Seneschaucy* and *Walter of Henley's Husbandry*. The manuscript as a whole has been described, however, as a legal textbook. It contains statutes, a register of writs, and the treatises known as *Bracton* and *Britton*. John de Solers, lord of Dorstone in Herefordshire, also possessed a manuscript containing *Bracton* and *Walter of Henley's Husbandry*. He had in fact bound together two separate books, the second comprising legal reports. John's ownership is shown by the additions and marginalia. They include matters relating to two cases concerning the Dorstone estates (deeds and letters of attorney) as well as a satirical poem on the pope and the king of France and a hostile reference to Piers Gaveston. We know then of a manuscript containing legal material that was owned and used by a gentry family.

It seems likely that some gentry, younger sons in particular, were already receiving a degree of legal training if only for the protection of the family as a whole. The scene was being set for the gentry's later colonization of the Inns of Court. Meanwhile, the need to master legal devices for estate protection, the high and increasing levels of litigation, the requirements of estate administration and the need to work with estate officials, the demand for lawyers and their

---

[15] For Adam de Okes, see Coss, *Lordship, Knighthood and Locality*, 315–16. The book is Lansdowne Manuscript 564. His ownership is suggested by the local material it contains, including items relating to Whitley itself.

ubiquitous and often successful social aspirations all point to the beginnings of the law-mindedness that was for long a characteristic of the gentry.

Both the ownership of books and the practical applications of literacy have been mentioned on a number of occasions during the course of this work. In the next chapter we will look more closely at the impact of literacy upon gentry culture. Before we do so it is necessary to examine the literacy of the gentry themselves and its means of acquisition both by its solid members and those who aspired to join them. In doing this we will need to take account of the status of the three contemporary languages. It is important, however, that we do not treat gentry literacy too narrowly, that is to say solely in terms of individual proficiency. As we have seen, both the gentry household and gentry estates were responsible for the production of documents. The household, and more widely the *curia*, as an estate centre, were communities with their own needs. The household was also a focus for instruction and entertainment. As we have stressed more than once, however, the household was by no means a cultural island sufficient to itself. It belonged, paradoxically, to a wider but still essentially local world. In some respects, moreover, it reached out even more widely still. These wider worlds had a major impact upon what was available for edification and for literary consumption. We need to bear this in mind before we move to examine, in the next chapter, what was actually being read, absorbed, and utilized within the gentry household. We will then be in a stronger position to understand the impact of literacy upon gentry culture.

Let us begin then with literacy. Until relatively recently commentators on the society and literature of medieval England seriously underestimated the true level of literacy. In what was a comprehensive and at the time ground-breaking re-examination of this issue, M. B. Parkes distinguished between three kinds of lay literacy: that of the professional reader (the scholar or professional man of letters), that of the cultivated reader reading for recreation, and that of the pragmatic reader who needs to read or write for business purposes. Confining his discussion to the second and third categories he was able to argue convincingly for a steady expansion of lay literacy under these headings from the twelfth century.[16] Shortly after this the question of the literate knight was specifically re-examined.[17] In arguing that the *miles literatus* (literate or lettered knight) was a rarity even in the thirteenth century, T. F. Tout had been right, but for the wrong reason, for the term referred to the professional and cultivated amateur rather than the pragmatic reader. The *milites literati* may have been comparatively few, but in Ralph Turner's words 'most knights were at least pragmatic readers,

---

[16] M. B. Parkes, 'The Literacy of the Laity', in D. Daiches and A. Thorlby (eds), *Literature and Civilization: The Middle Ages* (London, 1973), 555–77. My remarks here are repeated from P. R. Coss, 'Aspects of Cultural Diffusion in Medieval England: the Early Romances, Local Society and Robin Hood', *Past and Present*, 108 (1985), 49–50.

[17] R. V. Turner, 'The *Miles Literatus* in the Twelfth and Thirteenth Centuries: How Rare a Phenomenon?', *American Historical Review*, 83 (1978), 928–45.

functional literates in today's terms, capable of handling simple Latin as a tool in their many tasks of government'.[18] Much of the reasoning behind this is necessarily deductive. However, there is direct evidence of male literacy at this social level from the end of the thirteenth century. In his ground-breaking book *From Memory to Written Record,* Michael Clanchy cited a particularly pertinent example.[19] In 1297 thirteen knightly and sub-knightly jurors came from Norfolk to the court of King's Bench to attest to the age of a feudal tenant. His birth, twenty-one years before, had been recorded in the chronicle of West Acre Priory. No less than ten of the jurors said that they had read the chronicle entry. One said that he had not done so, although he knew of its contents from the prior. Two others said that they had not read it because they could not read. Thus ten or eleven out of thirteen Norfolk landowners at the end of the thirteenth century could read from a contemporary Latin chronicle. This is not, of course, a statistically valid sample and it is open to various caveats. Nonetheless, it is indicative that the majority of local landowners of any substance could be expected to be able to read. The fact that these men could read, however, does not necessarily mean that they would habitually write. Reading and writing were separate skills, much more so than in our own world.[20] Writing was not only a distinct activity but it was also a chore. Any man, or woman, of distinction would have scribes they could call upon to write for them. Nonetheless the knights probably could write as Latin was taught by writing down vocabulary as well as by reading.[21]

How and where did the gentry acquire their literacy? There can be little doubt that children of the gentry learned their primary education in the household. Mothers seem to have carried the first responsibility. Hence an English poem of around 1300 which states that 'Woman teacheth child on book' and hence the popularity, especially in the fourteenth century, of the image of St Anne teaching the Virgin to read. The impulse to take a direct role in educating their children was no doubt stronger amongst those pious women who were accustomed to read the psalter and lives of the saints.[22] The Essex knight Walter de Bibbesworth who wrote a treatise on language in the mid-thirteenth century to enable a noble lady, Denise de Montchesney, to improve her children's French, assumed as a matter of course that this was part of the mother's role. Walter assumes, too, that both mother and children are already familiar with the Latin primer, the 'book which teaches us *clergie*'.[23] But perhaps the role of mothers has been exaggerated.

---

[18] Ibid. 931.   [19] Clanchy, *From Memory to Written Record*, 224–6.

[20] Ibid. 183. Chapter 7 of this work contains an important discussion of the contemporary significance attached to the words *litteratus* and *illiterattus*, and *clericus* and *laicus*.

[21] I owe this point to the kindness of Michael Clanchy.

[22] Clanchy, *From Memory to Written Record*, 245.

[23] Clanchy's book contains an extensive discussion of Walter's work: ibid. 197–200. For the text, see W. Rothwell (ed.), Walter de Bibbesworth *Le Tretiz*, Anglo-Norman Text Society, plain texts ser. 6 (1990). See also Nicholas Orme, *From Childhood to Chivalry: the Education of the English Kings and Aristocracy 1066–1530* (London and New York, 1984), ch. 1, 'Growing up at Home'.

There must have been many cases where household chaplains participated in teaching the children Latin.

Boys had the option of going on to school. As we have noted, the household account of Sir John de Multon for 1343–4 shows that the lord's brothers were at school in Lincoln, and that they returned to Frampton for the Christmas festivities. Money was given to them periodically and also paid out for their clothing and for their transport to and fro. Around Michaelmas 1343, for example, a sum was allowed to Stephen the Cook for the expenses involved in sending the lord's brothers, William and Thomas, to school at Lincoln, including the hire of a boat. In October 4s 8d was sent to the schoolmaster for their keep.[24] Later we hear of 12s being paid to Thomas de Multon, the lord's brother, 'by commandment of the lord'. It was presumably sent to Lincoln. In the run up to Christmas 1s 6d was paid for the transport (*batilage*) of the brothers and their company, and for their expenses coming to Frampton Dyke from Lincoln. On one occasion cloth was bought for the boys and for Alain Wrangle, presumably a fellow pupil, at a cost of £1 8s 1d. On another occasion 1s 4d was given for the expenses of the brothers and their company coming from Boston to Lincoln. These were considerable sums. Educating boys cannot have been cheap.[25] Boarding schools in the modern sense did not generally exist at this date, and the Multon boys were probably staying with their master. Fees are not directly mentioned in the Multon account and they were perhaps subsumed under the sum for board. No doubt, given the sums expended, the boys were intended to dress, to travel, and to live generally in a manner befitting their status. They will also have required books, tablets, and possibly parchment to write on, as well as quills, ink, and other equipment.[26] We can gain some idea of the age of the boys. If fifteenth-century evidence is anything to go by, boys could go off to grammar school at any age between 7–8 and 12, and perhaps stay until they were 18.[27] As we have seen, John himself seems to have come into his estates only recently in 1343, while his father is not evidenced after 1335 and was dead by July 1337. If John was in his early twenties when we meet him in his account roll his brothers, Thomas and William, were perhaps in their mid- to late teens. Thomas was independent enough to be spending Christmas not at home but in the house of neighbouring landlord, Roger de Cobeldyke.

Why were these boys away at school? The will of Sir Walter de Gloucester of 1311 may be instructive in this respect. To his two eldest sons, Walter and

---

[24] *al mestre des ecoles pur les comuns les freres le seignur.*

[25] In 1277 Merton College, Oxford, paid 4d per boy in the college to attend grammar school, and around the 1380s the university forbade grammar masters from taking more than 8d per term. In 1277 the same college was paying 8d a week per scholar for board, and the identical sum was allowed for scholars of Winchester College in 1400.

[26] For these details, see, in particular, Nicholas Orme, *Medieval Schools from Roman Britain to Renaissance England* (New Haven and London, 2006), 131–5.

[27] Ibid. 29–30.

John, he left all his arms, except those needed for his burial. The two younger sons, Edmund and Thomas, however, received all his books. Where or how they were educated we do not know, but the implication seems clear enough. Two sons were trained as warriors, while two others had need of a literate education, beyond the basics. The latter were almost certainly at school at the time of the will, for Walter the eldest son was only 17. They were most probably destined for the church. The elder sons, one can safely assume, were receiving, or had received, in addition to some *clergie*, a good deal of physical training and education in outdoor pursuits, either in their own home or in the household of a neighbouring or higher lord. Although we should not make too strong a distinction between the education of a warrior–landowner and a cleric, the implied separation in upbringing, however tentative, may well reflect a pattern among the wealthier landowning families. The number of knight-bearing families with two, or more, members figuring in contemporary rolls of arms, especially in the nationwide 'Parliamentary Roll' of *c.*1308, suggests not only that there was a certain cachet in this but also that among the wealthier families this was, if not a normal expectation, at least the ideal.[28] In terms of inheritance it meant of course that there was another layman held in reserve should death overtake the eldest son before he could secure the line. Nonetheless, there must also have been many cases where a cleric unexpectedly inherited and abandoned his clerical career in favour of a secular one. This was the more feasible if his career had not progressed too far and if his own inclinations allowed him to switch. If he were a member of the regular clergy it would probably have been considerably less likely that he would do so. Even if doors were not entirely closed, the sort of pattern of education and career expectation that we are envisaging here is likely to have increased anxiety over the continued production of male heirs. It has been suggested that this sort of anxiety overtook the Luttrells, and even that it is reflected in their psalter. This may be fanciful, but it is nevertheless true that Sir Geoffrey Luttrell had lost three sons by the time the psalter was made, two of them, including the eldest, during childhood and a third as an adult. The elder surviving son, Andrew, though married, had so far failed to produce an heir. The younger, Robert, was a Knight Hospitaller. Sir Geoffrey, at least in his darker moments, might well have been contemplating the end of his line.[29] For a younger son, schooling may also have been an insurance policy, should he be unable to make his way within secular society, via marriage for example. But we would probably be correct to envisage family strategy at work in all of this, as much if not more than personal inclinations and proclivities.

The wars of the Edwardian period must have encouraged soldiering, including the membership of retinues, as a career prospect for younger sons, at least on a temporary basis before they could establish themselves in secular society.

[28] Coss, 'Knighthood, Heraldry and Social Exclusion in Edwardian England', 65.
[29] Camille, *Mirror in Parchment*, 93–5.

Membership of the clergy, on the other hand, was perhaps more recognizable as a career choice in our period. There can be no doubt that the majority who attended the public schools, and those of them who went on to university at Oxford and Cambridge, were intended for clerical careers, even if some of them subsequently dropped out. It is often thought that the gentry and the higher nobility did not begin to penetrate the schools until the fifteenth century, and the universities until after the Reformation. However, that is to take too narrow a view. Sons of the gentry *were* present in public schools from the beginning, but they were not there as yet for primarily secular purposes.[30] Pupils who were the actual heirs to substantial estates were probably very few. There are no extant registers of scholars until those of Winchester College, which began in 1393. The evidence we have, however, suggests that the major schools in the fourteenth century were inhabited by sons of merchants and other substantial townsmen, sons of major freeholders and others of the richer peasantry, and by younger sons of the gentry. The cost in fees, board, books, and writing equipment must have restricted the range of eligible pupils socially and economically.[31]

More specific professional training was available for those who intended a career in the law. Given that we have stressed the significance of lawyers within the ranks of the gentry, it is appropriate that we should briefly consider the legal education that was available. There is no doubt that by 1300 a fully fledged legal profession was in existence. By the late thirteenth century, if not before, 'apprentices of the Bench' were regularly present at the court of Common Pleas at Westminster so that they could learn their craft, and by the turn of the century special accommodation ('the crib') was provided for them. It has become apparent, moreover, that from the second half of the thirteenth century organized education was being provided for them outside of the courtroom.[32] Various legal works of the later thirteenth century which now look like treatises seem to have begun life as lectures given by teachers, perhaps from as far back as the 1250s or 1260s. There are also works of instruction on kinds of action at law which appear to have been aimed at both junior Chancery clerks and law students, and which are probably derived ultimately from spoken texts. The *Register of Writs* may also have been produced for instruction.[33] Furthermore the early year-book reports suggest that by 1300 there was also provision for legal education of a more advanced nature. Manuscripts containing legal arguments or *questiones* of the early to mid-fourteenth century may reflect lectures on

---

[30] On this point, see Orme, *From Childhood to Chivalry*, 66–74.

[31] Orme, *Medieval Schools*, 131–5.

[32] For what follows, see Paul Brand, 'Courtroom and Schoolroom: the Education of Lawyers in England Prior to 1400', *Historical Research*, 60 (1987), 147–65, repr. in his *The Making of the Common Law* (London, 1992).

[33] Many copies contain glosses that appear to be aimed at young lawyers as well as Chancery clerks.

the statutes. What all of this suggests is that the formal education of lawyers long predates the foundation of the Inns of Court during the latter part of the fourteenth century.[34] In the fifteenth century it is clear that the gentry were sending sons to the Inns of Court to acquire the necessary knowledge of the law to allow them to function as property owners as well as providing for younger sons via a professional career in the law.[35] If this lay far into the future, its roots lay in the latter part of the thirteenth century. Although direct evidence is slight, our knowledge of recruitment into the profession in the period under discussion suggests that the young lawyers under direction stemmed largely from the upper ranks of freeholders or urban equivalents, and from sub-knightly local society. Some younger sons of the gentry, however, are likely to have been present, even at this early date.

If grammar schools and universities destined boys primarily for a clerical career and the forerunners of the Inns of Court trained them for the law, they were nevertheless not the only sites of professional training available in early fourteenth-century England. At Oxford, and very probably elsewhere, there were schools where one could learn the practical skills of writing, composition, and accounting. One teacher of the *ars dictandi* of whom details are known is Thomas Sampson, who seems to have taught at Oxford from around 1350 to about 1409.[36] In the words of H. G. Richardson, who first brought Sampson to the scholarly world's attention, pupils went to Oxford for 'intensive cramming in business methods'.[37] Some of the textbooks he used in teaching were widely disseminated. Copies of works were produced for sale, perhaps by Thomas himself. One of them, now in Cambridge University Library, is a particularly apposite example. It exists now in three parts.[38] Part One contains treatises on conveyancing and on wills, a tract on the coroner's office, another on the office of clerk in a noble household, a piece on bills and writs, another on seigniorial courts, and a tract on Latin composition. Part Two contains a treatise on French composition, French vocabularies, verb conjugations, a tract on heraldry and the popular *Orthographia Gallica*. This last is not a learned treatise on the French language but rather a basic work on how to cope with French as it was encountered

[34] These began as communities of lawyers, both established men and apprentices, residing together in London for convenience. Some of them later became the formal Inns of Court: Brand, *Making of the Common Law*, 59.

[35] Orme, *From Childhood to Chivalry*, 47–9. According to Fortescue, writing in the 1460s, knights, barons, and other magnates were putting their sons in the Inns 'although they do not desire them to be trained in the science of the laws, nor to live by its practices, but only by their patrimonies': Fortescue, *De Laudibus Legum Anglie*, ed. S. B. Chrimes (Cambridge, 1942), 116–19.

[36] See H. G. Richardson, 'Business Training in Medieval Oxford', *American Historical Review*, 46 (1941), 259–80.

[37] Ibid. 262.

[38] See Carter Revard, 'Scribe and Provenance', in Susanna Fein (ed.), *Studies in the Harley Manuscript: The Scribes, Contents, and Social Contexts of British Library MS Harley 2253* (Kalamazoo, 2000), 65–6. The manuscript is Cambridge University Library MS Ee.iv.20.

in England around 1400.[39] Part Three of the Cambridge Manuscript contains yet another tract on French composition. We know for certain that Thomas Sampson was not alone in his profession at Oxford, because he complains of his fellow teachers. It seems equally certain that he had forebears going back to the thirteenth century. Around 1280 one John of Oxford wrote tracts on the holding of courts, on accounting, on conveyancing and on the writing of deeds and letters, while similar works survive, again with Oxford connections, from the first quarter of the fourteenth century.[40] A model letter in one of Thomas Sampson's own books tells of a young man who went to Oxford to read for a degree in arts. Having learned of a position in noble service, and taking the advice of his father, he turned to Thomas Sampson instead. By such means many young men must have returned to the localities both literate and highly trained.

The wide dissemination of these works suggests that one did not necessarily need to go to school to acquire the requisite skills. They could be learned independently if one possessed the necessary texts. In this way the stock of literate men was extended even further. Nor, indeed, did one necessarily have to pore alone over formal treatises. There is evidence to suggest that practical business skills might in fact be learned directly within households, including gentry ones. The Multon archive yields some useful insights in this respect. The reeve's account for Wyberton and Cobeldyke for 1327–8 was used at some point not long after its production for a secondary purpose—to improve and practise writing. The three membranes of the account roll, verso and dorse, are festooned with what are generally called pen trials. At times every available space seems to be taken up. The accounts themselves end on the dorse of membrane 2, and the dorse of membrane 3, being left blank, was entirely taken up with such trials[41] (Figures 11.1 and 11.2).

These pen trials are very extensive. Individual letters are practised, sometimes using a variety of forms. Particular words or phrases are written over and over again. Sometimes a capital is written on its own and then with the rest of the word that follows, betraying a certain hesitancy. Abbreviations are also practised. Some Christian names occur repeatedly, often in lists: *Adam, Bernardus, Clemens, Dyonisius, Ennok, Felix, Galfridus, Job, Katerina*, and so on. What is striking is that although the names vary somewhat between lists, they are always in alphabetical order.

Some of the phrases and clauses that reappear are clearly of more than passing significance. One that is given repeatedly, in part or in full, is *fuit homo missus a deo cui nomine erat Johannes*. This is clearly John chapter one, verse 6: 'There was a man sent from God.' Others include: *Amen dico vobis super omnia bona*

[39] See R. C. Johnston, *Orthographia Gallica*, Anglo-Norman Text Society plain texts ser. 5 (London, 1987).

[40] Orme, *Medieval Schools*, 71.

[41] The discussion that follows has been greatly enhanced by the observations of Professor Michael Clanchy.

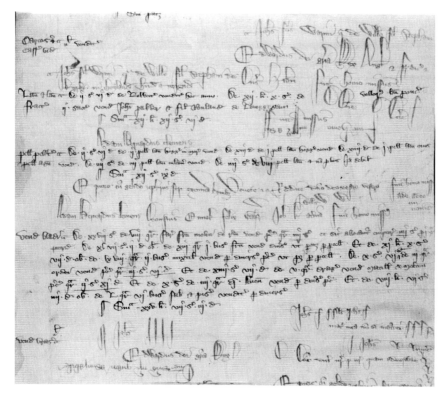

Figure 11.1. Pen trials on the Wyberton account roll of 1327–8.

sua; Equore cum gelido zephirus fert exennia kymbis;[42] and *Domine dominus noster quam admirabile est Nomen tuum.*[43] Yet others are found on just a single occasion. There are also occasional phrases in French.[44] On the final membrane, the writer, by now more efficient and competent, renders the entire *pater noster* and the *ave maria.* Thus far we are witnessing someone learning to write (and read) in the traditional manner: first learning the alphabet (the ABC) and then graduating to the basic prayers.[45]

Soon, however, we begin to understand what the ultimate purpose of this training is. Clauses from legal documents have started to appear. We have, for

---

[42] 'Through the ice-cold field Zephirus bears gifts with *bells* [?]'.

[43] Also *In nomine patris & filio & spiritus sancti amen;* and *Venete* [sic] *& reddite domino deo vestro;* or *Venete domino deo nostro alleluia;* or *Venete & reddite domino deo nostro Alleluya.*

[44] Such as *a deu q' vou garde en honour tot choses q' covent.*

[45] From these two prayers and the Creed the pupils would move to other important texts like the Ten Commandments and the Virtues and Vices and then to the penitential psalms. For a discussion of the process of learning, see especially Nicholas Orme, *Medieval Children* (New Haven and London, 2001), ch. 7: 'Learning to Read'.

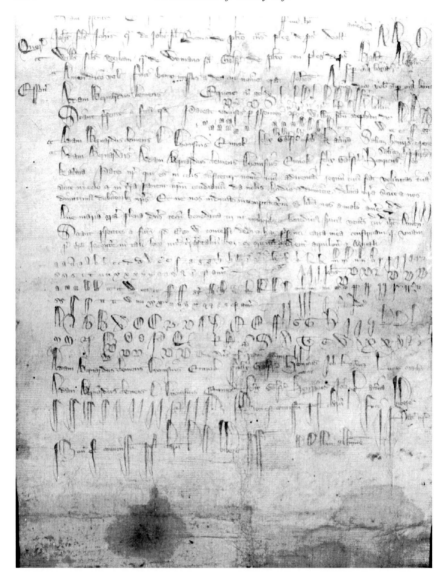

Figure 11.2. Further pen trials on the dorse of the Wyberton account roll.

example, the opening of royal charters: *Edwardus dei gracia Rex Angl[orum] &*
Franc[orum] & Dominus Hib[ernie]. This or parts thereof occurs five times. We
also get the opening words of private charters. For example: *Sciant presentes &*
futuri quod ego Willelmu(s); and *Sciant presentes & futuri quod ego W[illelmus]*
concessi dedi (the normal order *dedi concessi* being inverted here). We also have

what appear to be phrases taken from an actual charter: *Willelmus filius Stephani de Kyrketon' unam placeam terre arabilis; habendum et tenendum.* It may well be that the name William has some special significance, but it is perhaps more likely that it is taken from an exemplar in front of the writer. We also find the (brief) title of an account roll, viz. *Comp[itus] Johannis prepositi* (the account of John the reeve). At one point an item from an actual account roll is included, slightly confusing the underlying text, being itself of course an account roll. More interesting, however, are the extracts from manorial court rolls where plaints (*querele*) are noted. For example: *Johannes filius Warini q(ueritur) de Willelmo filio Stephani de byker in hoyland.* The extracts become fuller on the final dorse, where the category of items from the margin of a court roll are also given, i.e. *Querele* and *Essonie* (essoins or legal excuses).

Whether he is practising from an exemplar is perhaps unclear from this, as the same few names are constantly occurring. It could be that he is writing these items down from dictation. This may be true in other cases too, where an occasional error could be due to mishearing, e.g. *Et quore* for *Equore*. There are also occasions where the form of abbreviation used seems unusual or unorthodox, suggesting that it is not being directly copied.

Intriguingly, a specific court is mentioned, i.e. that of John de Kirton, a lord from the settlement neighbouring Frampton: *Curia domini Johannis de Kyreton; Curia tent' die Veneris proxima post festum sancti martini anno ut supra.* The last very probably represents the title at the head of a membrane on which the record of a court is being continued. All in all, then, it seems fairly certain that the writer did have exemplars in front of him from which he was working. Nevertheless, one gets the distinct feeling, reading through, that this is someone receiving instruction. As to who that someone is it is virtually impossible to guess, other than that he was almost certainly in the Multon household. It is much more likely that he is someone writing at Frampton than at Kirton. As we have seen, these documents were passed around as exemplars, for the sake of good practice, to use a modern idiom. This would explain a Kirton court roll being in the Multon archive. It would be more difficult, on the other hand, to see a reeve's account passing from Wyberton or Cobeldyke to Kirton and then back again, with its pen trials, to Frampton. The practitioner's hand belongs to the mid-fourteenth century. It is up to a generation later than the account roll itself. In fact, it must be later than January 1340 because the opening line of the royal charter which he gives has Edward III as king of England *and France*. It is tempting to think that the trainee is one of the Multon brothers expanding his expertise. It is more likely, however, to have been a young man of less exalted status living in the household but with professional needs and ambitions.

The account roll is not a unique survival in this respect. The 'literary' manuscript, Digby 86, for example, exhibits the same phenomenon. This manuscript was compiled around the early 1280s. However, it was used as a surface for pen trials a couple of generations later, around the 1320s–30s. These

were written at the very top of the manuscript above the text. We find some of
the very same phrases as those encountered on the account roll. We find, for
example, *Equore cum gelido zephirus fert exennia knubis* [recte *kymbis*].[46] This
provides an important clue as to what was going on. As B. D. H. Miller, a student
of this manuscript, has pointed out: 'This (imperfect) hexameter contains all the
23 letters of the Latin alphabet. It was devised to help children learning to write;
being thus familiar, it was employed by scribes as a pen-trial.'[47] *Enoch Ydani*,
which appears on folio 113r, he suggests, 'may be the opening of a similar verse,
actual or projected'. We also find again *Amen dico vobis super omnia bona sua*,[48]
and *Domine dominus meus quam admirabile*.[49]

By contrast there is relatively little practising of individual letters in the pen
trials here, although it does occur.[50] Once again individual Christian names are
also trialed, and there is much practising of the opening of charters. Some of the
charter openings give the name of a grantor. We find William, Robert son of
Robert de Pendock and John lord of Pendock. Most illuminating of all we find
William son of Simon de Underhill, who is also the recipient in an extract from
the will of Robert son of Robert de Pendock. Evidence from elsewhere in the
manuscript indicates that the pen trialer is William de Underhill, son of Simon
and Amice, the manuscript's owners. As we shall see, the Underhills were on
the margins of gentility, of less significance certainly than the owner/compiler,
Richard de Grimhill.[51] The important point here, however, is that within this
milieu William de Underhill, son of its new owners, was learning to write, if
not 'professionally', at least in terms of practical use. Once again he would seem
to have had exemplars in front of him as he did so. Intriguingly, handwriting
experts who have examined the manuscript have detected two contemporary
hands in the pen trials. This gives rise to the intriguing possibility that two boys
were practising here under instruction.

Most of what these pupils were learning to write was of course in Latin. But
they might also be called upon to write in French. It is worth pausing briefly
to explore the role of the respective languages. The role of French in thirteenth-
and fourteenth-century England is now well understood.[52] In the middle of the
thirteenth century Walter de Bibbesworth had written his *Tretiz de langage* for
Lady Denise de Montchesney to enable her to teach her children French, and
this evidence for the formal acquisition of French does not stand alone. William
Rothwell was able to assert with justice that there was not one learned language

[46] On folio 113v and again on 189v, with *Equore* appearing on its own on folio 117v.
[47] B. D. H. Miller, 'The Early History of Bodleian MS Digby 86', *Annuale Medievale*, 4 (1963), 27, and the references given there.
[48] On folios 180v, 193v and again partially on folio 75r.   [49] On 193r.
[50] For example on folio 204v. All is in Latin except *Amours Amours* (folio 90r).
[51] See below 223–4.
[52] See my summary in 'Aspects of Cultural Diffusion', 50–1, from where my comments here are drawn, and see, more especially, Clanchy, *From Memory to Written Record*, ch. 6, and the works cited there.

and two vernaculars but 'two languages requiring formal instruction (Latin and French) and one vernacular (English), only this last tongue being absorbed without conscious effort by the vast majority of children with their mother's milk'.[53] In the thirteenth century, however, French was a widely used language of culture, and the numerous statements by Anglo-Norman writers in support of their choice of medium should be seen in this light. By writing in French they could reach a broader spectrum of people than by writing in Latin or English. Anglo-Norman French had one great advantage over its vernacular rival. It was non-dialectal and hence more generally intelligible. It became, therefore, the language of the common law and a language of administration. The evidence of a vernacular text of Magna Carta suggests that this development may already have been under way by 1215. By mid-century it had reached fruition.

French, we know, was still much in use in the first half of the fourteenth century, both as a spoken and a written language. Indeed, it remained culturally vibrant. Laymen who wrote major works, like Sir Thomas Gray of Heaton who penned the *Scalacronica* and Henry duke of Lancaster, author of a devotional treatise, both wrote in French. Ranulf Higden who produced his *Polychronicon*, his history of the world, during the 1320s reaffirmed that children of gentle families were taught French from the time that they were rocked in their cradles and that those who sought to join their ranks busied themselves of necessity in learning it. He also tells us that in schools Latin was taught through the medium of French.[54] However, when John Trevisa translated the *Polychronicon* into English in 1385 he claimed that since 1349 the language of instruction had switched from French to the native language and that there was now widespread ignorance of the French language. He even named the particular Oxford schoolmaster who had been responsible for the switch. The suddenness of this change has been doubted, however. In all probability it is an Oxford-centred view. It has been suggested recently that English had long been used in schools and that the two vernacular languages were used alongside one another. Given that there was considerable cachet in learning French, it may well be that in many schools the language of instruction shifted from the one language to the other as pupils became older and more proficient. Grammar schools, as a result, tended to be trilingual.[55]

How much French was actually spoken in the established gentry household of the mid-fourteenth century is difficult to know. When John de Multon wrote to his wife from London on 23 November 1367 he wrote, as we have seen, in

[53] W. Rothwell, 'The Role of French in Thirteenth-Century England', *Bulletin of the John Rylands Library*, 58 (1976), 454–5.
[54] *Polychronicon Ranulphi Higden*, ed. C. Babington, vol. II, Rolls Series (London, 1869), 158–61.
[55] Orme, *Medieval Schools*, 87–8, 105–6. See also T. Hunt, *Teaching and Learning Latin in Thirteenth-Century England*, 3 vols (Cambridge, 1991), i. 19–53. School texts in Latin were often glossed in both English and French.

French. He added a personal note to his wife, however, in English, implying that this was the language in which they spoke privately to one another. This is of course late evidence, from a time when spoken French seems to have been in decline. However, the extent of privately spoken French might well be open to exaggeration. As long ago as the reign of Richard I the chronicler Ralph of Coggeshall told the story of a *fantasticus spiritus* appearing in the house of a Suffolk knight. According to the knight's chaplain, from whom Ralph claims to have heard the story, the spirit was accustomed to speak in the Suffolk dialect with the knight's family, but to argue with the priest on theological matters in Latin.[56] Walter of Bibbesworth's treatise makes it clear that English not French was Denise de Montchesney's mother tongue, as it was his own. Both Walter and his readers think in English. There is evidence in plenty to show that the normal tongue of the royal judges in the time of Edward I, if not earlier, was English, despite French being the language of the courts.[57] Nonetheless French was a spoken language in thirteenth- and fourteenth-century England. It was the language of the king's court and of *gentils hommes*. Great prestige was attached to it. 'For unless a man knows French, he is thought of little account', wrote Robert of Gloucester late in the thirteenth century.[58] Although it was learned it was not learned from nothing. Walter of Bibbesworth clearly assumes that Denise de Montchesney can already speak French like the rest of her class. The object of his treatise is to improve on the French learned colloquially.[59] French was traditionally the language of lordship and of management. As we have seen, treatises like the *Seneschaucy*, Walter of Henley's *Husbandry*, and the *Rules of Robert Grosseteste* were written in French, implying at least that it was at certain levels the language of instruction. And, whatever the caveats one needs to make, it was a language of instruction in schools. The relationship between the two vernacular spoken languages in the household is, however, extremely difficult to penetrate. No doubt the situation varied over time, generally away from French and towards English. No doubt it varied from household to household. No doubt, too, it varied according to person and to space. It may have shifted from table to chamber, from chapel to kitchen, from stable to courtyard. In some circumstances and in certain places, however, the languages must have been interchangeable.

Enough has been said for it to be clear that the cultural world of the gentry was affected not only by their own literacy but also by the literacy that was all around them. The number of people who could write (let alone read) in the world of the Multons was far from negligible. We can deduce this both from need and

---

[56] See R. M. Wilson, 'English and French in England, 1100–1300', *History*, 27 (1943), 37–60.

[57] George E. Woodbine, 'The Language of English Law', *Speculum*, 18 (1943), 431–2.

[58] 'Vor bote a man conne frenss. Me telth of him lute': *The Metrical Chronicle of Robert of Gloucester*, ed. W. A. Wright, 2 vols, Rolls Series 76 (London, 1887), ii. 544.

[59] Clanchy, *From Memory to Written Record*, 152–3; Rothwell. 'Role of French in Thirteenth-Century England', 458–60.

from opportunity. In addition to the major schools, legal and business education, there were song schools and the like, and there were village priests who were active teachers. There were household chaplains. There were lawyers and there were estate administrators for whom practical literacy was a near necessity. There were treatises and tracts of many kinds and on many levels encouraging literacy. And there is the evidence of reeves' accounts, extents, manor court rolls, deeds, letters, and wills.

12

Literature and Household Entertainment

What literature, then, was available to be read in the gentry household? At this point the Multons of Frampton finally fail us and we must seek alternative sources. We are fortunate in being able to turn, first of all, to one of the greatest literary manuscripts of the period, the trilingual miscellany known as Harley 2253, for it was the product of precisely the sort of social milieu we have been describing. The scribe who wrote, and probably compiled, the bulk of this book, that is folios 49–140 around the year 1340, has been shown by the extraordinarily meticulous researches of Carter Revard to have been a man who penned forty-one surviving deeds (and no doubt in reality many more) relating to property in and around Ludlow between 1314 and 1349.[1] These are standard legal documents.[2] His penmanship has certain distinctive characteristics, despite some changes over time, making identification possible. In addition to these mundane documents, he was responsible for writing the bulk of three significant manuscripts. They are Harley 273, Royal 12.C.xii, and Harley 2253, all now residing in the British Library.

Harley 273 was the first to be begun, and the first to be finished. However, the evidence suggests that he was working on it at various times between 1314 and 1329. As Carter Revard says, 'a fifteen-year span of use would imply that Harley 273 was his own book or easily accessible in a way suggesting familial ownership if not personal possession by the scribe'.[3] In fact, the 'Harley scribe' wrote only parts of the manuscript himself. He collaborated, for example, with another scribe in writing the *Purgatoire s. Patrice*, a verse romance in French which deals with a knight who observes the torments of purgatory, and completed the *Manuel des péchés*, a handbook designed for priests instructing their parishioners. These were among the earliest items to be copied. The Harley scribe's marginalia against parts that he did not write suggests that he may have been studying the work himself, perhaps as a young cleric. For a decade or more he copied into the

---

[1] For what follows, see especially Revard, 'Scribe and Provenance', in Fein (ed.), *Studies in the Harley Manuscript*, 21–109. With this splendid volume the study of Harley 2253 has entered a new phase. For the manuscript see *Facsimile of British Museum MS. Harley 2253*, introduced by N. R. Ker, EETS o.s. 255 (London, 1965).

[2] Most are grants or quitclaims, although an indenture and a power of attorney are included among them.

[3] Revard, 'Scribe and Provenance', 58.

manuscript devotional and other works and added glosses, treating it, in fact, as his own book. The manuscript also contains an illuminated psalter (in French), the *Benedicite*, *Te Deum*, *Credo*, the Litany, the Office for the Virgin, and the *Placebo*. Other items include charms against fever, wounds, and bleeding, and a copy of Bishop Grosseteste's *Rules*. Here, most interestingly, he completed a line missing in his original, adding that 'this will be 9 quarters', that is the correct amount of grain to be sown, whilst at another point he wrote *xxvii* as a clarifying gloss. Everything suggests that this manuscript was in the hands of a man who was (or at the very least aspired to be) part of a household, probably as its chaplain.[4]

Royal 12.C.xii was begun not long after Harley 273. Our scribe's earliest work in this book is the *Short Metrical Chronicle*, copied around 1316. Not long after this were added, partly in his hand, a doctrinal and devotional piece, the *Merour d'eglise,* and a tract on the mass. During the 1320s (probably 1322–7) he copied the liturgical collection commemorating Thomas of Lancaster (executed 1322) as a saint and the earlier folios of the romance of *Fouke le Fitz Waryn*, which celebrated a local hero. In the same period he copied the commonplace booklet which comprises folios 1–7 and which includes two prophecies, recipes for dyeing linen, a Latin satire on avaricious clerics, verses on phlebotomy, rules for interpreting dreams, hymns to the Virgin Mary, and lines on the death of St Thomas Becket. Another booklet, of similar or slightly later date, deals with prognostications, medical notes, palmistry, and *sortes*. Next probably came the popular romance *Ami et Amile*, following which he copied a hymn to Mary and a poem on the vanity of human life. During the 1330s he copied further prophecies and returned to *Fouke*. Another booklet, which seems to belong to 1335–40, contains not only further prophecies but also mathematical problems, puzzles (in Latin) and recipes for cooking (in French). The conclusion that the component parts of this manuscript belonged to a household seems inescapable.

And so we come to Harley 2253. This was compiled about 1340, at around the time work on Royal 12.C.xii was coming to an end. A text that he copied into Royal 12.C.xii, the Latin *Somnia Danielis*, a work on the interpretation of dreams, was translated into English as *A Bok of Sweueneng*, for Harley 2253. This manuscript contains, among other things, religious pieces in verse and prose, including tracts on pilgrimages and dreams, the Middle English romance, *King Horn*, saints' lives and fabliaux, as well as the political songs and the lyrics for which it is especially famous. It used to be thought that Harley 2253 was written in and for a highly aristocratic household, either that of the Mortimers of Wigmore or that of the bishop of Hereford.[5] Neither proposition can be

---

[4] A calendar containing the dedication date of Ludlow parish church also suggests a man strongly connected with that area.

[5] Part of the evidence lies in the binding leaves of the manuscript. Here we find part of a household account roll from Trim in Ireland for a week in March, which seems to date from 1309.

sustained. They reflect the literary scholars' traditional obsession with noble patronage. In truth we do not know which household Harley 2253 was made in or for; indeed we do not know for certain if it was put together in a major household at all. Assuming that it was, however, there are more likely contenders among the gentry of the Ludlow area, including the family of the great wool merchant, Lawrence de Ludlow, ensconced at Stokesay Castle,[6] the Cheynes of Cheyney Longville, and the Overtons of Overton.[7]

The world in which the Harley scribe moved was a world, then, in which one might read romances and chronicles, saints' lives and political songs, prayers, psalms, and a variety of devotional works, lyrics both secular and religious, and items of a practical and apparently practical nature. We are taken some way towards understanding the variety of literary consumption available to an early fourteenth-century gentry household. We are taken closer still, however, by another manuscript, Digby 86, which can be located securely within just such a household. It is the manuscript in which William son of Simon de Underhill practised his writing. We have encountered some of its contents earlier when examining the devotional texts available for the gentry household. It is time now to look at it more closely. First, however, something must be said of its owner and undoubted compiler, Richard de Grimhill. He wrote the bulk of the manuscript, he tells us, during the years 1282–3, and he died around February 1307. The more that can be revealed about the status of the owner and his household, however, the more valuable the manuscript is going to be to us in our understanding of gentry culture. Richard came, almost certainly, from Grimhill in Hallow, situated to the north-west of Worcester in the bishop of Worcester's hundred of Oswalslow, a settlement now known as Greenhill Farm.[8] In 1315 a Richard de Grimhill, who was probably the son of the compiler, held a quarter of a knight's fee here of the earls of Warwick. This was not all of the land the family held in the settlement, however. In 1208–9 an earlier Richard de Grimhill

---

Hence its putative identification with the Mortimers. The Harley scribe did not write this. In fact he used its dorse on which he wrote part of the Hereford Cathedral Ordinal. This helped to give rise to the idea that it belonged to the bishop's milieu. In reality these fascinating snippets are indicative of its origins within the local society of Ludlow and its surrounding area. They are further insights into its literate and cultural life, in the broadest sense.

[6] According to Revard, 'the political poems of Harley 2253 are compatible with patronage of the Harley scribe and manuscript by the Ludlows of Stokesay, most particularly by Sir Lawrence Ludlow. Nothing in the rest of the manuscript forbids or works against such a view' (ibid. 81). The arguments for patronage derived from the content of the political poems seem to me to be strained. However, the suggestion that the scribe was in the Stokesay household is certainly plausible. It may well be relevant that the Ludlows held the advowson of Wistanstow, some two miles north of Stokesay Castle. Harley 2253 contains the life of St Wistan.

[7] The Harley scribe wrote a dozen or so surviving deeds concerning Overton, including two in which Thomas, lord of Overton was the grantor.

[8] Indicating, of course, a later corruption of the name. Nearby is the village of Grimley, and both were undoubtedly derived from the Saxon personal name, Grim. There was also a *Grimenhull* recorded near Alvechurch in 1244. For these details, see A. Mawer and F. M. Stenton, *The Place-Names of Worcestershire*, English Place-Name Society, vol. IV (1927), 126, 131, 360.

held one hide of land of the bishop of Worcester and this was no doubt the one-fifth of a knight's fee which was said in 1346 to have been held by Richard de Grimhill.[9] The Richard who wrote Digby 86 also held additional land in Worcestershire. Around 1280 he paid several sums to the lay subsidy granted to the king by parliament, viz. 9s at Crown East, half a mark at Berrow and 5s at Lower Sapey.[10] Richard also enjoyed property in Shropshire through his marriage to Agnes, one of the daughters of John de Minton who held the manor of Minton in Church Stretton in serjeanty as a royal forester.[11] He also had some association with the bishop of Worcester, as he occurs among the witnesses of a charter from the bishop to the prior and convent in 1291. He was not a knight, at least not at that point, but six of the eight witnesses were.[12] He was, however, of some consequence in the county, as is indicated by his appearance as one of the three Worcestershire men sent out as justices to examine infringements of Magna Carta.[13] On 28 February 1307 a writ was sent to the escheator to hold an inquisition post mortem with respect to the land he had held in chief in Shropshire. This was a third of the manor of Minton held by courtesy of England, that is by right of his late wife, Agnes, given that he had children by her. The property was now split between his daughters, viz. Isabel, aged 45, Amice, aged 44, and Margery aged 40.[14] Amice was married to Simon Underhill. It was she who inherited the manuscript. His daughters did not succeed to the property at Grimhill, however. As noted above, a Richard de Grimhill held of the earl of Warwick in 1315. He seems to have been a son by another marriage.[15] That the family continued to be of some significance is suggested by the pardon of John de Grimhill in 1321 as one of the followers of Roger Mortimer of Wigmore who were in arms against the Despensers. He may be identical with the John le Young who was holding at Grimhill in 1335.[16]

These details are important because they help to establish the milieu in which the manuscript was produced. One strongly suspects that Richard was yet another local lawyer. He was the sort of man who would later be called an esquire.[17] That Richard belonged to the gentry, albeit at the Cobeldyke rather than the Multon end, is significant because commentators have tended to concentrate rather upon the Underhills to whom the manuscript passed, perhaps

---

[9] J. W. Willis Bund (ed.), *The* Inquisitions Post Mortem *for the County of Worcester, Part 2* (1909), 68; *Book of Fees*, 36; *Feudal Aids*, v. 307. A Robert de Grimhill occurs here in 1220–1 and a Matthew de Grimhill in 1376: *VCH Worcestershire*, iii. 368–9.

[10] A John de Grimenhill, moreover, paid 12d at nearby Worcester: F. J. Eld (ed.), *Lay Subsidy Roll for the County of Worcester, 1 Edward III*, Worcester Historical Society (1895), 2, 57, 63.

[11] His payment of relief and his homage were recorded on 28 March 1263: *Excerpta e Rotulis Finium in Turri Londinensi Asservatis, AD 1216–72*, 2 vols, ed. C. Roberts, Record Commission (London, 1835–6), ii. 394.

[12] Willis Bund (ed.), *Register of Godfrey Giffard*, ii. 393.   [13] *CPR 1292–1301*, 516.

[14] *CIPM*, v. no. 8.

[15] Alternatively, he may have been the heir male, succeeding by grant in fee tail.

[16] *VCH Worcestershire*, iii. 368–9.

[17] Indeed, Grimhill was held by an esquire in the early fifteenth century: *Feudal Aids*, v. 331.

by Richard's will. These are better described as sub-gentry. Simon de Underhill, who married one of Richard's daughters, was a relatively minor figure who came from Underhill in Berrow, in the south-west corner of Worcestershire.[18] His overlords were the probably the Pendocks, a knightly family with much property in the area.[19] There are numerous references to Underhills in the late thirteenth and fourteenth centuries, but few to Simon and none to his son William.[20] Those to Simon show clearly that he was a figure of less significance than his father-in-law. The capacities in which we find him suggest that he was a major freeholder but no more.[21] Although he comes across from the records as a rather insubstantial figure, he clearly had local connections in the area of Redmarley d'Abitot and Pendock, and was not unknown to the Pendocks themselves. That the manuscript functioned for a time in this area on the fringes of gentle society is not insignificant, and most interesting in terms of the downward diffusion of culture, but it tells us less than commentators have suggested about the genesis of the manuscript.[22] We should not be too surprised that Richard de Grimhill's son-in-law was a lesser figure than himself. He was married to the second of three daughters, and these may not even have been Richard's heirs at the time of the marriage. The obit, that is the day of death, of an Alexander de Grimhill appears in the compiler's own hand as an addition to the calendar in the manuscript and he may well have been a son, one perhaps who failed to reach adulthood.[23] Moreover, Richard must still have had the capacity to produce sons when the manuscript was compiled, and one such probably succeeded him. Amice, wife of Simon Underhill, was no doubt brought up in a literate household and may have been enthusiastic about the manuscript; hence it passed to her. What is important in the present context is that Digby 86 was produced within a gentry milieu, and probably by a man whose interests were, at least in part, professional. It helps to explain one of the puzzles of the manuscript. At the bottom of folio 47r

[18] There is still an Underhill farm there.
[19] However, there was also an eponymous family of Berrows with a manor there. In 1377 a manor at Underhill was leased to Robert Underhill by the prior and convent of Worcester: *VCH Worcestershire*, iii. 258–9.
[20] These details, together with the many references to the Pendocks and those to the Grimhills, were collected by Miller in her pioneering study of the manuscript: 'Early history of Bodleian MS Digby 86', 29–42.
[21] He served on juries of inquisitions post mortem, at Redmarley d'Abitot in 1301 and at Pendock in 1322, presumably as a free tenant of the late John de Pendock, subject of the inquiry: Willis Bund (ed.), *The Inquisitions Post Mortem for the County of Worcester, Part I*, 6 and 45. In 1293 he was holding with two other men the messuage and 18 acres of land at Berrow, in the king's hands for a year and a day because the last holder was a convicted felon. This was not his father as is usually suggested. Simon contributed 1s at Underhill to the lay subsidy of 1327: Eld (ed.), *Lay Subsidy Roll 1 Edward III*, 9.
[22] John Hines gives a good description of this milieu in *Voices in the Past: English Literature and Archaeology* (Cambridge, 2004), 80–3. This draws on C. C. Dyer, 'Dispersed Settlements in Medieval England: a Case Study of Pendock, Worcestershire', *Medieval Archaeology*, 34 (1990), 97–121, repr. in his *Everyday Life in Medieval England* (London, 2000), 47–76.
[23] Rather, that is, than Richard's father or brother as is usually suggested.

and again on folio 68 Richard drew heraldic shields: five in all. Without the tinctures it is difficult to say positively to whom the arms belonged. They have no obvious connection with the ownership of the manuscript.[24] However, it has been suggested recently that two of the arms may be connected to the extraneous line at the end of the long debate between two ladies (*L'estrif de ii dames*) on how a lady should live her life, that is to say in virtue and marital fidelity or not. The line, which appears admittedly much later in the manuscript than the arms, reads: *De Aubreie de Basincbourne e Ide de Beauchaunp fu fest.*[25] This line is not present in the continental text and is an obvious addition. The poem is in fact in rhyming quatrains whereas this is a single line occurring at its close. It may reflect a contemporary joke and/or scandal. More than likely it tells us from where the text was acquired. One of the coats of arms on folio 68r is a gyronny, the dartboard effect in which two tinctures alternate, that was borne by very few families. One of these was indeed the Bassingbournes. Moreover, a contemporary Aubrée (Albreda) de Bassingbourne did exist.[26] The other arms were: *quarterly, a bordure* (i.e. border) *vair*. Quarterly arms were commoner. However, the Fitz Johns, a family with Worcestershire property, bore precisely *quarterly or and gules, a bordure vair*. When the last male of this family died in 1297 his heir was his sister Maud, married to William de Beauchamp, earl of Warwick. The link with an Ida de Beauchamp is tenuous, however, and the Beauchamps themselves bore entirely different arms. There is another possibility. Another Beauchamp family, the Beauchamps of Bedford, bore *quarterly or and gules, a bend gules*. The last male of this family, John de Beauchamp, died at the battle of Evesham in 1265. One of his heirs was his niece, Ida.[27] The important point is, of course, that Richard de Grimhill was significant enough to move in circles where heraldry was of great importance, even if he did not bear arms himself; the Underhills, by contrast, were decidedly sub-knightly.

After this rather long but necessary preamble it is time to look more closely at Richard de Grimhill's manuscript and at what it tells us of gentry culture. It has been closely studied in recent years, and understanding of its structure and compilation has been greatly enhanced.[28] It consists essentially of twenty-six

---

[24] See Miller, 'Early History of Bodleian MS Digby 86', 50–5.

[25] For this observation, see Marilyn Corrie, 'Further Information on the Origins of Oxford, Bodleian Library, MS Digby 86', *Notes and Queries*, 244 (1999), 430–3.

[26] She held the manor of Astwick in Hatfield, Herts., in 1277. She may be identical with the Albreda de Bassingbourne who was a substantial landowner in Lincolnshire and Nottinghamshire in 1242–3 and who occurs at Sandon and Kelshall, Hertfordshire, in 1239–40. She occurs in relation to Woodhall, Herts., in 1248: *Book of Fees*, ii. 978, 984, 986, 992, 1034, 1082; *VCH Hertfordshire*, iii. 101, 107, 272. The main line of the Bassingbournes, however, centred on the east Midland counties.

[27] Sanders, *English Baronies*, 11; and Brault, *Rolls of Arms of Edward I*, ii. 40.

[28] See *Facsimile of Oxford, Bodleian Library, MS Digby 86*, introduced by Judith Tschann and M. B. Parkes, EETS (Oxford, 1996). Other important studies include Miller, 'The Early History of Bodleian MS Digby 86', 26–56; John Frankis, 'The Social Context of Vernacular Writing in Thirteenth Century England: the Evidence of the Manuscripts', in P. R. Coss and S. D. Lloyd

quires, two others having been lost from early in the manuscript (original quires i and vi) and three or four later on. The quires were kept unbound for some time, as is shown by the rubbing that can be seen on the front and back of many of the quires. The existing binding dates from 1632–4, although it was bound before then, and probably well before. There are now 207 folios, the last two being additions, but in the main hand of the text. The text is written continuously in this hand, except for a slightly smaller but contemporary hand which was responsible for two quires.[29] The parchment of these quires differs, too. It is slightly smaller than the rest. However, this second writer was working under the direction of the first. The two quires contain the greater part of a single text, *Disciplina Clericalis*, but do not begin it. They are not, therefore, self-contained. Moreover, the bright rubrication is inserted by the first writer throughout, indicating that he was responsible for the book. Both wrote in what is called Anglicana script, of the last quarter of the thirteenth century. The book was written, the compiler tells us, in a year and three months, most probably during 1282–3. Clues as to the identity of the writer are provided by the obits inserted in the calendar which occupies folios 68v–74r: Alexander de Grimhill (18 July), written in the main hand; Amice, wife of Simon Underhill (11 July) and Simon Underhill (23 July) himself, both in a hand that is no later then mid-fourteenth century and could be earlier. It must be after 1327 when Simon was still living. William son of Simon Underhill was responsible, as we have seen, for the pen trials. The date of composition and the obits together indicate that the manuscript began life in the Grimhill household. The compiler and main writer would seem, therefore, to have been Richard de Grimhill, father of Amice, although oddly his name does not appear in the obits. Another possibility that has been canvassed is that it was written by a household chaplain, that is to say in effect by Richard de Grimhill's chaplain. In support of the suggestion that the compiler was a member of the clergy, it has been argued that the manuscript had a dual function: to provide both spiritual guidance and 'book-based entertainment'.[30] The suggestion is a very plausible one. However, as the Luttrell Psalter makes abundantly clear, the tone was set by the head of the household. It could well be that they worked together here, the second hand, writing under direction, being that of the chaplain or other household cleric. Finally, it is worth reciting the conclusions of J. T. Tschann and M. B. Parkes from their analysis of the main hand: that the writer appears to have learned from experience as he went along, and that his rough sketches, his addition of further material in the margins and in vacant spaces and his 'research

(eds), *Thirteenth Century England I* (Woodbridge, 1986), 175–84; Hines, *Voices in the Past*, ch. 2: 'Two Medieval Books'; and Thorlac Turville-Petre, 'Oxford, Bodleian Library, MS Digby 86: a Thirteenth-Century Commonplace Book in its Social Context', in Richard Eales and Shaun Tyas (eds), *Family and Dynasty in Late Medieval England*, Harlaxton Medieval Studies IX (Donington, 2003), 56–66.

[29] Folios 81r–96v.   [30] Frankis, 'The Social Context', 183.

to augment the Kalendar', indicate that he was also the earliest owner of the book.[31]

Richard, as from now on I will hazard to call him, in addition to annotating his texts in the margin, in a serious manner, drew sketches at the foot of the pages, and sometimes in the margins (Figure 12.1). These are in the red ink of the rubrication and are sometimes accompanied by a single word of description. The phenomenon is first encountered by the reader on fol. 4v where we find a hand with sleeve showing a forefinger extended towards the head and shoulders of a tonsured priest followed by the word *presbiter*. Moving to the right we then have a chalice followed by *calyx* and an altar followed by the word *altare*.[32] The texts appearing at this point are ones of religious instruction. In some cases we find a clear association between image or image and word on the one hand and text on the other. On folio 8v, for example, we have a bearded man and the name *ipocras*, the ascribed author of the text which begins on that page. A crescent moon and the word *luna* are again prompted by the text on folio 41r. It is a series of prognostications of lucky and unlucky days according to the moon. The pointed finger appears again from time to time, both in the drawings at the foot and as pointers in the margin to words or items in the text. Head and shoulders 'portraits' of men and women are also found. On fol. 34v there is a man wearing a hood with a goblet at his lips and the word *bibo* (I am drinking). To the right is a crudely drawn coffin with a long cross on the lid and the word *toumba*. Is this a warning against drinking to excess? A series of drawings occur at the foot of folios 79v and 80r. These comprise on the first folio the man with the hood again preceded by what may be a spade or perhaps an arrow, a hand and the word *manus*, which may be pointing to the man or the text, a woman's head and what seems to be a flower with the word *rosa* between them. Perhaps it refers to both. On folio 82v the finger is pointing again to a long-haired woman who is looking grim, either as defiant or as chastized. On folio 84r the finger points to another woman, or perhaps specifically to her headdress. She has painted cheeks.[33] Many of the drawings accompany works of decidedly moral complexion, with women being the greatest object of concern. On folio 102v the woman with the headdress and spotted cheeks occurs again, this time with a man wearing a cap some way to the left of her, looking away and seemingly disconsolate. The man in the cap reappears in the margins on folios 164v and 165r, together with hands and pointed fingers and a truly dreadful attempt at drawing a horse. The text here is the fabliau, *Dame Sirith*. On folio 169r there is a different male figure with three daggers in his tonsure. The man in the cap

---

[31] In short, Richard de Grimhill 'would be a strong candidate for collecting the texts (which are predominantly of a secular or private devotional nature) and copying the manuscript for his own use': Tschann and Parkes, *Facsimile*, lvi–lvii.

[32] There is also some crude decoration in red ink in the margin.

[33] On folio 84v there are two cruder attempts at this drawing, while there is another very poorly drawn head in the margin of folio 83v. These are not in red ink and are in a different hand.

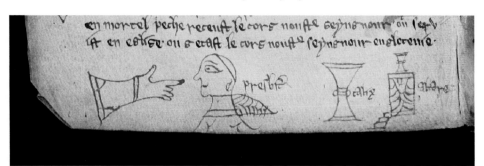

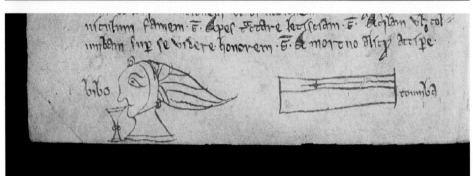

Figure 12.1. Richard de Grimhill's sketches in Digby 86.

appears inside a capital letter *P* on folio 197v and the pointed finger a little earlier in the text. Finally, he appears again at the foot of folio 205v, once the end of the manuscript, alongside the words *scripsi librum in anno et iii mensibus* (I wrote this book in a year and three months). Tschann and Parkes suggest that this may represent Richard himself.[34] If so, he appears to have been a serious and pious man.[35]

What, then, is Digby 86 and what does it contain to edify and entertain the household? Frankis describes it, accurately, as a 'miscellany', similar in content to the 'common-place books' of the later middle ages.[36] It is trilingual, although this does not mean, of course, that all the members of the household were. Roughly half of the contents are in French, with a quarter in Latin and a quarter in English. It is probably significant that most of the actual titles are in French. One commentator has suggested that the family may not have been particularly at ease with the Latin. Most of the Latin pieces are brief and of course the prayers were for recitation rather than for full comprehension.[37] Leaving on one side questions of form and specific genre, in crude terms one can say that the contents of Digby 86 were generally of three kinds: works of devotion or religious instruction; works of a practical or semi-practical nature; and works of entertainment. Although one should not think in terms of hard and fast

---

[34] Tschann and Parkes, *Facsimile*, l.

[35] These drawings may be compared with those found in the plea rolls of the central courts: Andrew H. Hershey, *Drawings and Sketches in the Plea Rolls of the English Royal Courts, c. 1200–1300*, List and Index Society special ser., 31 (London, 2002). These drawings are sometimes accompanied by a pointing hand. Dr Hershey suggests that they were sometimes used as markers or as mnemonics, but they might also be 'the by-product of the depictor's imagination, a vent for artistic freedom' (41). Two of his observations are particularly interesting in the present context. One is that male heads may be representations of the clerk who is writing the roll. The second is that drawings of female faces are comparatively rare in the rolls. On the one hand, then, it suggests that our writer belongs to a clerical tradition. On the other hand his misogynist tendency seems to be confirmed.

[36] Ibid. 182.   [37] Turville-Petre, 'Digby 86', 62.

categories, a crude division of this nature allows us to undertake a general (rather than detailed) analysis.[38]

The first observation to make is that category one—that is, religious and devotional material—predominates. The first (surviving) item is *Distinctio peccatorum* (i.e. distinguishing the sins), a tract on the seven deadly sins. The second concerns confession, i.e. the questions that should be asked. Then follows the ten commandments, the twelve articles of faith, the seven sacraments, and a piece on the other side of confession, i.e. how to make it. After an interval come seven prayers, two in Latin and the others in French. They include *Oremus* (let us pray), a prayer to the Virgin Mary and the five joys of Mary (*Quinque gaudia Marie*). Two further Latin prayers come later on. There are the fifteen Gradual Psalms, the Seven Penitential Psalms, and a French version of the Latin *Veni creator spiritus*, with the first line of each stanza in Latin and in red. There is the long *Disciplina Clericalis*, a French version of a twelfth-century Latin work by Petrus Alphonsus which is essentially a set of moral precepts with *exempla* issued by a father to his son.

Later on in the manuscript we encounter further devotional texts. Some of them are, or contain, dire warnings on how not to live one's life. There is the *Les ounsse peines de enfer* (the eleven pains of Hell)—also known as the Vision of St Paul—describing the torments of the damned, and the dreary *Le regret de Maximian*, in which an old man regrets, at some length, the passing of his youth. Among the shorter pieces is the less dreadful but nonetheless sobering poem on where they are who lived before us:

Vbi sount qui ante nos fuerount

Uuere beth they biforen vs weren
Houndes laden and haukes beren
And hadden feld and wode?
The riche leuedies in hoere bour,
That wereden gold in hoere tressour
With hoere brightte rode;   [complexion]

Eten and drounken and maden henm glad;
Hoere lif was al with gamen I-lad,
Men keneleden hem biforen,   [kneeled]
They beren hem wel swithe heye—   [proudly]
And in a twinkling of on eye
Hoere soules weren forloren.
Were is that lawing and that song,   [laughter]
That trayling and that proude ong, [walking with long trailing garments, gait]
Tho haukes and tho houndes? ll. 1–15

---

[38] For attempts to understand the process of compilation and the principles behind it, see Tschann and Parkes, *Facsimile*, xli–l; and Marilyn Corrie, 'The Compilation of Oxford, Bodleian Library, MS Digby 86', *Medium Ævum*, 66 (1997), 236–49.

The answer is all too obvious:

> Hoere paradis hy nomen here,
> And nou they lien in helle I-fere,
> The fuir hit brennes heuere. ll.19–21   [ever]

Not surprisingly, the manuscript ends, as it began, with various Latin prayers.

Some of the items were of direct practical use in terms of devotion and religious observance. In addition to the prayers and psalms, there is also the calendar itself, a necessary adjunct to religious observance, and a set of directions for calculating moveable feasts. However, the manuscript contains other matters of instruction. There is a version of the Letter of Hippocrates, a medical work, which begins with the exposition of the four humours followed by an extensive discussion of urines. The bulk of the work is a body of medical receipts moving from the head down.[39] A widely known and influential work, its contents vary from manuscript to manuscript. Digby 86 contains numerous receipts not found in other manuscripts.[40] These include no less than seven different remedies for diarrhoea (most of them sounding as unpleasant as the complaint itself) and one for staunching blood. In this case you take the herb called in English *swinekarse* (knotgrass or hog's fennel), hold it in your hand for a long while and watch it attentively. The blood will then stop flowing. As one would expect, numerous plant names appear in these texts. We find, for example, *hundestunge* (houndstongue), *wild tesle* (teasel), *hennebone* (henbane), not to mention lettuce (*letues*) and poppy (*popi*). The medical receipts cover not only a wide range of ailments, but also cosmetic treatments. If you want to have long blonde hair, for instance, you take the fruit growing on a beech, cook it in white wine or in ale and wash your head with it frequently. It is best if you soften the concoction a little before using it. If you want to remove freckles from your face you rub it with oil made from hare's blood. Even more effective is to rub in oil made from black gages and drink plantain. That will remove the freckles and anything else you don't like. If you really want to beautify your face you cook *plectrin* (centaury?) in water with hen's blood, and then oil your face with it. If your face should be *trubluse* you drink a mixture of plantain and fumitory. Naturally people were interested in the welfare of animals and veterinary complaints were also addressed in such medical receipts.[41] Digby 86 also contains a long work on the care of hunting birds.

Medicine and magic overlapped. Medical receipts could contain prayers, invocations and charms. As Tony Hunt puts it: 'The rational has not totally assimilated the prenatural nor neutralized its power and the two co-exist'.[42] It

[39] For what follows, see Tony Hunt, *Popular Medicine in Thirteenth-Century England: Introduction and Texts* (Woodbridge, 1996), 101.
[40] Ibid. 140, where a selection of the additional receipts is given. I have drawn on these, and on Hunt's glossary, for what follows.
[41] Ibid. 16.   [42] Ibid. 78.

is not surprising therefore that we find in the manuscript a series of charms and prognostications. These include a charm for toothache and one for a man who can't speak. There are charms for fevers, for the farcy, for wens, for rankle, for *goutefestre* and for *soriz*. There is also a charm for staunching blood, an alternative—presumably—to the medical receipt. You simply say the following prayer three times:

Nostre Seignur fu pris e en la croys fu mis
Longis i vint a lui e de la launce li feri
Saunc e ewe en issi tret
Ses oilz leve e cler veit
Pur la vertu ki Deus i fist, conjur les veines e la saunc ki ne seine plus avaunt,
Deu veray Pere. Pater Noster

There was also a charm for avoiding being taken to court. Unfortunately, these items are cut short by a missing quire, taking us into another series, this time of experiments, i.e. proofs. Some of the *experimenta* are simply magic. One of them creates the illusion of a river appearing to flow through the house. Another tells you how to make a dead woman sing. After this, those on how to have an abundance of bees and how to get rid of flies seem positively mundane.[43] Then comes a work on the interpretation of dreams, followed by a series of prognostications according to the day of the week on which Christmas falls, and another of lucky and unlucky days according to the moon. This last occurs twice in the manuscript. There are two sets of proverbs, one in French and the other in English. There is a work on Arabic numerals. There is also the *Doctrinal Sauvage*, a continental work of moral and behavioural instruction.

If the above items can be classified loosely as matters for instruction and matters of a practical nature, there are other matters that are more easily described as items of entertainment. Admittedly there is a fine line between the two. Digby 86 contains just a few romances. There is the French romance by Raoul de Houdenc called *Le Songe d'Enfer*. This is very serious in parts but it also contains an arresting portrait of the *cité d'enfer* (city of hell) when the dreamer finally gets there. On his journey he spends the first night in the city of *Covitise* and the next night in the *Inn of Envy* where he meets *Trecherie*, *Rapine*, and *Avarisce*. And so it goes on until he reaches his goal.[44] Just as a romance could be serious, saints' lives, as is well known, could be extremely close to romance. The manuscript contains one such, in the story of St Eustace. Converted after seeing a vision of Christ between a deer's antlers, he goes through various adventures before being martyred in Rome. Lighter in tone is the *Lai du cor*, a romance set in Arthur's court. It tells of a magic horn that spills over if anyone whose wife is unfaithful tries to drink from it. Not surprisingly, it causes many a soaking at court. Also

[43] See Lynn Thorndike, *A History of Magic and Experimental Science*, 2 vols (New York, 1923), i. 801–2.
[44] See Morton W. Bloomfield, *The Seven Deadly Sins* (East Lansing, Michigan, 1952), 132–3.

in French is the letter of Prester John which tells of the marvels of the East,[45] a poem called *Le fable del gelous* (The Fable of the Jealous Man), one called *Un pecheour ki se repenti* (A Sinner who Repented), and another called *un valet qui soutint dames et dammaiseles* (A valet who 'supported' ladies and damsels). There is a satirical poem against the pope called *De roume et de gerusalem* (better known as *Le complainte de Jerusalem*).

And then there are the French fabliaux. These have been famously described as 'contes à rire envers'.[46] They are narrative stories in vernacular verse designed to provoke laughter. They are characterized by deception, followed by a misdeed, and are frequently risqué. The butt of the joke tends to be the person deceived. They are often ironic and often close with a moral, although whether this is to be taken at face value is often unclear. They are frequently antifeminist, dwelling on the cunning and deceit of women. *Les quatre Souhais Saint Martin* (the four wishes of St Martin), for example, which is present in Digby 86, ends with a warning to men against trusting their wives above their own judgement. A peasant, who was especially devoted to St Martin, was rewarded by the saint in being given four wishes. He allowed his wife to make the first one. The outcome is vulgar, involving the multiplication of sexual organs. The couple end up precisely as they were before, with all of the wishes wasted. The fabliaux are similar in many ways to *exempla*, stories used to point up some moral precept. Indeed the same stories can be found in both. An important collection of these was in fact the *Disciplina Clericalis*, a French version of which covers folios 74v–97v in the manuscript. Six of its exempla have recently been published in a collection of Anglo-Norman fabliaux.[47]

In English there is also the fable, *The Fox and the Wolf* (derived from the continental *Le roman de renart*), where the fox entices the wolf down a well and leaves him there. Some items are difficult to classify. One of the most curious is *The Names of a Hare*. Supposedly a charm to give protection from the hare, it consists of around 80 names, mostly abusive, and ends with a greeting to the hare and a wish for such good fortune to befall it as to arrive to the author either in chive sauce (*in cive*) or in bread.[48] As one reader puts it, it gives 'an unparalleled insight into medieval rural superstition'.[49] There is also the nonsense poem *La*

---

[45] For a discussion of the content of this, see Bernard Hamilton, 'Prester John and the Three Kings of Cologne', in Henry Mayr-Harting and R. I. Moore, *Studies in Medieval History presented to R. H. C. Davis* (London, 1985), 177–91.

[46] This phrase, coined by J. Bédier in 1893, has occasioned considerable scholarly debate. There is a very accessible discussion of the nature and content of fabliaux in John Hines, *The Fabliau in English* (London and New York, 1993), ch. 1.

[47] By Ian Short and Roy Pearcy in *Eighteen Anglo-Norman Fabliaux*, Anglo-Norman Text Society, plain texts ser. 14 (London, 2000).

[48] Haue nou godnedai, sire hare (Good day to you, sire hare). See A. S. C. Ross, 'The Middle English Poem on the Names of a Hare', *Proceedings of the Leeds Philosophical and Literary Society* 3 (1935), 347–77.

[49] Frankis, 'Social Context', 182–3.

beitournee (The Upside Down). Among the secular lyrics is a poem on the nature of love:

> Love is soft, love is swet, love is goed sware.
> Love is muche tene love is muchel kare.
> Love is blissene mest, love is bot are   [quick reward]
> Love is wondred and wo, with for to fare. ll. 1–4   [distress]
>
> Love is the softeste thing in herte mai slepe.
> Love is craft, love is goed with kares to kepe.
> Love is les, love is lef, love is longinge.   [false, dear]
> Love is fol, love is fast, love is frowninge.   [foolish, firm]
> Love is sellich an thing, wose shal soth singe. ll. 17–21 [marvellous] . . .
>
> Hit is I-said in an song, soth is I-sene,
> Love comseth with kare and hendeth with tene,   [ends with grief]
> Mid lauedi, mid wive, mid maide, mid quene. ll. 26–8

So far we have concentrated on the content of Digby 86. Can we say anything of the context in which it was deployed within the gentry household? First of all, it is patent that the manuscript, and the greater part at least of what it contains, was for consumption in the chamber rather than the hall.[50] The changes to the construction of manorial complexes during the later twelfth and thirteenth centuries had put increasing emphasis upon private apartments or solars. It was there that the resident family, and their more intimate guests, could enjoy the available comforts of life. The hall, by contrast, is best conceived of in a more public sense. Grand enough to reflect the status of its owner, it was to function as a ceremonial and banqueting hall and to house courts and other assemblies. This was no doubt as true of the gentry as it was of the great lords. One consequence of these architectural changes was that it allowed the lord and lady to dine alone with their guests, apart from their household. As early as the mid thirteenth-century Bishop Grosseteste was warning that no honour could come from eating *hors de sale* (outside of the hall) *en chaumbres*.[51] If the poet William Langland is to be believed, this had become the norm a century later. Another consequence was that it was in the more luxurious *camera* or solar that the family and their guests would be entertained. This could involve communal reading, as one person read to the others or, indeed, members of a group reading in turns. This situation is famously portrayed in literature, by both Chrétien de Troyes and by Geoffrey Chaucer.[52]

---

[50] What follows is taken from Coss, 'Aspects of Cultural Diffusion', 43–6.
[51] Oschinsky (ed.), *Walter of Henley*, 407.
[52] In *Yvain* a 16-year-old daughter of a knight reads a romance to her parents in the garden, while in *Troilus and Criseyde*:

> [Pandarus] *fond two othere ladies sete, and she,*
> *Withinne a paved parlour, and they thre*

In addition to being read to, however, it is likely that people joined in the entertainment in various ways. In some cases at least, it is possible for them to have taken different parts in the dialogues. *The Thrush and the Nightingale*, for example, is a debate poem on the worth of women. The nightingale is for and the thrush against. It is set in the early summer amid blossom and bird song. The poet is disturbed by the commotion of the debate. The nightingale talks of the gentleness and loving nature of women while the *threstelcock* dwells on their falseness and immorality. The debate proceeds by example until the nightingale invokes the Virgin Mary. Given that she was sinless and bore the world's saviour, the thrush could have no answer. The bird debate is a common motif in medieval poetry, no doubt reflecting the closeness of bird life in manorial and similar settings. *The Thrush and the Nightingale* has some affinity with the more sophisticated English poem *The Owl and the Nightingale*, a work of similar date surviving in two late thirteenth-century manuscripts which may also have been household miscellanies.[53] Digby 86 also contains *L'Estrif de deus dames* (The Debate Between Two Ladies) which contains some of the same arguments as found in *The Owl and the Nightingale*.[54] There is so much material on women in the manuscript, the majority—but not all[55]—of it against, that one commentator has been led to suggest that the purpose, both here and in Harley 2253, was 'to provoke outrage and stimulate discussion among the household'.[56] It may be so. It is probably no coincidence that *Des Quatre Files Deu* (The Four Daughters of God) follows the particularly scurrilous *La Vie d'un Vallet Amerous*. A poem of a different sort that could have been read by taking parts is *The Harrowing of Hell*.

Even more interesting is the Anglo-Norman poem *Ragemon le Bon*. The version in Digby 86 was based, loosely, on a continental original called *Les*

> *Herdun a mayden redden hem the geste*
> *Of the siege of Thebes while hem leste.*
> (F. N. Robinson (ed.), *The Works of Geoffrey Chaucer*
> (London, 1957), 402 ll. 81–4).

By way of contrast, the expected entertainment in chamber and hall is demonstrated in the fourteenth-century alliterative poem, *Parlement of the Three Ages*:

> *And then with damsels dere to dawsen in thaire chambirs;*
> *Rich Romance to rede and reken the soothe*
> *Of kempes and of conquerors, of kynges full noblee,*
> *How tha[y] wirchipe and welthe wane in thair lyves;*
> *With renkes in ryotte to revelle in haulle,*
> *With coundythes and carolles and compaynyes sere*
> (M. Y. Offord (ed.), *Parlement of the Three Ages*,
> EETS, ccxlvi (London, 1959), ll. 249–54).

[53] The date of this work has recently been revised. See Neil Cartlidge (ed), *The Owl and the Nightingale: Text and Translation* (Exeter, 2001), esp. xiii–xvi, xl–xlviii. The two manuscripts are BL Caligula A.ix and Jesus College Oxford MS 29 (II).
[54] Ibid. xxxii.   [55] *De dames e dammaiseles*, by contrast, is a poem in praise of women.
[56] Turville-Petre, 'MS Digby 86', 58.

Geus d'Aventure which was a game of chance, played as follows: a series of stanzas (quatrains of two consecutive rhyming couplets) were written on a roll of parchment in haphazard order. At the margin, at the beginning of each stanza was attached, with the aid of string, a seal or a metal or wooden object. Each player then chose one of them. Only when the parchment was unrolled was their chosen stanza revealed. This indicated their character, their fortune, or both. These 'predictions' were described by their early twentieth-century editor, Arthur Långfors, as for the most part 'amiable' but with some misfortunes thrown in, to reflect the realities of the world and to counterbalance the good luck. It was a poem, in short, for 'bonne compagnie'.[57] *Ragemon le Bon*, though longer, shares the basic characteristics of its predecessor. It has been described as 'the text for a parlour-game, a comic fortune-telling by the drawing of lots'.[58] Some of its predictions are of a general type, not very different from those of its precursor: 'You will go into another land to seek your fortune but after a long time you will return with great joy and great nobility.' Or: 'You are very much a man of good intention, you will have money and rent aplenty, you will have rounceys and palfreys and you will be renowned for your feats of arms.' Others, however, will have misfortune: 'You will be rich for a while, but then you will lose your wealth as misfortune and quarrels bring you to poverty.' Misfortune is often linked to moral defect. Some of the stanzas are warnings about conduct: 'Dogs and birds, and pleasure you will have aplenty by day and by night; but there is one thing you need to guard against—don't be too grasping!' Some are calls to repentance, while others give advice. One piece of advice is to know your place: 'God will give you the calling that is appropriate to you, as he pleases, and if you serve him willingly he will keep you from the devil.' However, *Ragemon le Bon* has a harder edge than its continental predecessor. There is scorn, even a touch of malice in it, and its characterizations are sometimes insulting: 'Drunkenness and gluttony, covetousness and lechery: these four will sit firmly in your heart always.' One player is full of anger and greed, another is jealous, yet another proud and cruel. Falseness is a particular target. Some of the stanzas take us straight to the heart of aristocratic values:

> *Prodoume* you will never be,
> Nor preuz, nor sages nor curteis;
> But false and disloyal you will be,
> As long as you live.

There is much talk in fact of courtesy, both positively and negatively. One player has 'courtesy and wisdom, knowledge and education in the ways of the world (*afeitement*), all gifts of nature by the will of the lord'. Of another it is said,

---

[57] It is edited, together with a continental precursor and a fifteenth-century religious version, by A. Långfors, *Un jeu de société du moyen age, Ragemon le Bon* (Helsinki, 1920). His 'Introduction' compares the characteristics of the three versions.
[58] Frankis, 'Social Context of Vernacular Writing', 183.

intriguingly, that courtesy 'fails you in all things; however, this is not a fault of nature but of nurture'.

Another characteristic of *Ragemon le Bon* is its coarseness when it comes to sexual matters.[59] The verb *fotre* is used on four occasions. For example: 'You are gay and amorous, you f . . . much by night and day, there is no woman to be found who is so ugly that you would not f . . . her'. More mildly: 'You will prefer to love a young girl (*pucele*), in a garden or in a meadow, touching her on the breast, than enjoy the pleasure of the lute.' There is more than a little misogyny in *Ragemon le Bon*. One is warned that the damsel who takes him 'will often ridicule him and often f . . . others'. Another is told that the one he will marry is 'ugly and hideous, cruel and full of ire'; consequently he 'will [have to] beat her as her lord (*cume sire*)'.

For the most part the stanzas of *Ragemon le Bon* are couched as if to men, as is the case throughout the continental version. Most if not all, of the last eight, however, are specifically addressed to female players. They begin with the girl who is described as *bloundette*, *doucette*, and *bele* (demur, sweet, and beautiful). Well will he who takes her be able to boast.[60] Another is told that she will have a *prodomme* as her husband but that she will do him a great wrong, for she will f . . . another. One is asked if she knows what her craft (*mester*) is. It is to slander and quarrel so that good friends are turned into mortal enemies. Another damsel is told that she is not at all the little darling she seems but is in reality a shrew.[61] In the final verse the recipient, 'beautiful sister (*bele sere*)', seemingly of bad reputation, is the object of the versifier's vulgar desire.

To some extent, however, these stanzas are counterbalanced by the female players' share in courtesy: 'Courteous you are and well informed, wise in words and deeds, you have the renown and the prize of [above] all those of your country.' Another is told that all the world loves her and that she will be 'praised, exalted and honoured above all'. Yet another is told that she 'will be honoured specifically for her great courtesy'.

According to *Ragemon le Bon* it seems largely a matter of luck when it comes to the type of partner you will have. You may find great joy, or you might find yourself with an undesirable person. Sometimes, it seems, you get what you deserve: one player is told that anyone who does good to him comes to repent of it because he is truly mean; if he does not take care he will end up with a wife who is a 'gaillarde'.[62] With its emphasis upon rectitude and

---

[59] As Långfors writes: 'La petite amusette de société qu'est le poème francais est devenu entre les mains du versificateur anglo-normand . . . une chose singulièrement grossière: outre qu'il semble prendre un plaisir particulier à dire des choses désagréeables, il a du goût pour les imaginations scabreuses, come on le voit surtout dans les strophes destinées aux femmes' (*Ragemon le Bon*, 7).

[60] *Ben se purrad celui vaunter/ Qui une feze (fois) vous poet beiser*. Beiser may mean to kiss or to copulate. Is it perhaps deliberately ambiguous.

[61] She is in fact *forte baudestrope* (?).

[62] A sly or ribald woman? The precise meaning is open to interpretation.

moral failings, one can see why these verses appealed to the compiler of Digby
86. It may well be that he himself put the fifty stanzas together from several
versions in circulation.[63] This seems to be suggested by the fact that some of
the characterizations and predictions are repeated although the words are not
identical. Moreover the many moralistic stanzas fit well with the general content
of much of the manuscript and appear to correspond in tone with some of
Richard de Grimhill's marginal drawings. The seven deadly sins are much in
evidence here, for example, and lechery perhaps above all. Richard was probably
a firm believer in the capacity of women to lead men into sin. It is not altogether
surprising to find that in the fifteenth century another versifier turned *Ragemon
le Bon* into a sermon.

However, important though this aspect is, one should not over emphasize
it to the extent that one misses the other social values that are reflected in
the poem. Courtesy and reputation were equally important. Wisdom and good
manners were praised, falseness, lies, and flattery condemned. Those who get
above themselves are also to be frowned on: 'You are too coarse grained', one
player is told, 'and full of conceit; you believe you are worth all the world, and yet
you are worth nothing.' False presentation is one more object of attack. Another
player is told that although he seems 'most valiant and powerful', when it comes
to action he is in fact 'faint-hearted'. Once again we see that the language of
chivalry had great resonance in the localities.

Ragemon le Bon seems to have acquired its name by analogy between the
dangling objects which connect with the stanzas in the rolled-up parchment and
charters that carry multiple seals. The strips of parchment on which the seal
impressions were fixed produced a jagged or ragged effect: hence ragman. The
royal inquiry of 1274–5, for example, which produced the Hundred Rolls, was
known by contemporaries as the Ragman Quest from the seals hanging from the
returns.[64] For John Frankis, *Ragemon le Bon*, more than any other piece, defines
the owners of Digby 86 as:

requiring entertainment, somewhat naïve and even coarse in taste, rustic rather than
urban, at any rate lacking in the refinement and sophistication that one might expect to
find in an aristocratic court . . . but on the evidence of other texts, fundamentally devout,
responsive to spiritual guidance as well as to fun.[65]

Home-generated entertainment may also have included music. The Multon
accounts themselves indicate the purchase of musical instruments, although
the price suggests that these are unlikely to have been of high quality. Chess,
backgammon and the like must also have been among the possible private
entertainments. The *Disciplina Clericalis* advocates chess as a laudable knightly

[63] The continental version has only thirty-five.
[64] See Helen M. Cam, *The Hundreds and the Hundred Rolls* (London 1930; repr. 1963), 45.
[65] Frankis, 'Social Context of Vernacular Writing', 184.

occupation,[66] while a board game similar to backgammon is depicted in the Luttrell Psalter.

One of the most intriguing pieces of entertainment in Digby 86, however, is *Dame Sirith*, or to give it its full title, *Le fable e la cointise* [trickery] *de dame Sirith*. It is the earliest fabliau in Middle English.[67] It originated in the east Midlands and is in east Midland dialect with some west Midland spellings reflecting its survival (uniquely) in Digby 86.[68] Its plot is a fairly simple one. A clerk, called Wilekin, lusts after a married woman by the name of Margery. She is married to a merchant. One day, when the merchant has departed for the fair at Boston, he makes advances to her. She receives him courteously but when he declares his love for her she quite properly rebuffs him. In a state of some wretchedness he meets a friend who sends him to old Dame Sirith. She refuses to help him at first, protesting her innocence of, and lack of skill in, such matters. She knows nothing, she says of *wicchecrafft*, being a devout woman. She is persuaded, however, after he convinces her that he truly loves Margery and that he will keep the matter secret. The old dame does not want to find herself before the ecclesiastical court. One is left to infer that Wilekin's promise to give her money, a fur coat and shoes was the real deciding factor. He later gave her £20. She then feeds her dog mustard to make its eyes water. After that she visits Margery claiming to be a needy woman. Margery receives her charitably, upon which the old woman tells her 'story'. The dog, she claims, is her daughter who refused the advances of an amorous clerk. This clerk, in revenge, turned her by means of magic into a bitch. This, Dame Sirith adds, is the certain fate of any woman who behaves towards clerks in this way. Margery panics, regrets her action, and begs the old woman to find Wilekin for her. She does precisely this, concluding the fabliau with a vulgar exaltation to Wilekin to go to it and offering her services to any man who finds himself in a similar situation.

Dame Sirith is unlike a French fabliau in the way in which it is presented. Apart from the prologue there is very little narrative, the greater part being dialogue. The narrative sections, moreover, add very little in terms of information, most of the detail being conveyed directly by the 'speakers'. For example Wileken says:

> ʒurstendai Ich herde sai   [Yesterday]
> As Ich wende bi the waie
> Of oure sire;

[66] See Richard Eales, 'The Game of Chess: An Aspect of Medieval Knightly Culture', in C. Harper-Bill and R. Harvey (eds), *The Ideals and Practice of Medieval Knighthood* (Woodbridge, 1986), 12–34.
[67] *Dame Sirith* is edited in J. A. W. Bennett, G. V. Smithers, and N. Davis, *Early Middle English Verse and Prose*, 2nd edition (Oxford, 1968), 96–107, 303–12.
[68] For a recent discussion of *Dame Sirith*, with bibliography, see John Hines, *The Fabliau in English*, ch. 2.

Me tolde me that he was gon
To the feire of Botolfston
In Lincolneschire

The three protagonists are indicated in the margin for a long stretch of the text, with C denoting the clerk, V (presumably for *Uxor*, wife) denoting Margery, and F (*Femina*) for Dame Sirith. It has generally been assumed that *Dame Sirith* would have been performed by a professional entertainer, that is to say a minstrel or *jongleur*, taking the several parts by means of different voices, gestures and perhaps even changes of dress. Such an entertainer would have needed to be very skilled in order to render three parts effectively, though it is by no means impossible. It would have been rendered considerably more difficult, however, by the physical presence of a dog. Since words are spoken directly to the animal, it must actually have been there. It could be done more effectively if people took parts, with the person representing the old lady handling the dog. The marginalia in Digby 86 might suggest that the parts were simply taken by different persons in a joint reading. In this case no professional, or professionals, were necessary at all and the poem could well have been read in chamber rather than performed in hall. Dogs were a visible feature of the gentry household, as indeed is indicated on numerous occasions within the Multon household accounts, and therefore readily available as a visual aid. Lap dogs were, of course, extremely common in the depiction of ladies, on effigies and brasses and in manuscripts. There is no reason why *Dame Sirith* should not have been read together *en famille*, members of the family taking the different parts.

It has been argued, however, that *Dame Sirith* was in fact, a play or rather playlet, with three people actually performing the roles. In this case the pieces of narrative, and perhaps even the prologue, may have resulted from transferring the work to manuscript, helping to keep the reader on track.[69] This argument might also take us back, after all, from the chamber to the hall. The two doors of a hall screen could be used for the different locations, and the dialogues could have been used as interludes between courses. This is rendered more likely perhaps by the existence of a fragmentary work entitled *Interludium de Clerico et Puella*, which survives on a piece of vellum of late thirteenth/early fourteenth-century date.[70] Despite its Latin title it is written in Middle English. It has a very similar plot to *Dame Sirith*, although it concerns a clerk and a maiden rather than a married woman. Here there is only dialogue; there is no narrative, no narrator.

The hall could, and no doubt often was, used for entertainment. Music could have been played in both chamber and hall. There is also the possibility of some sober reading during or after a meal. What, then, of minstrels? Evidence for their

---

[69] For this argument, see Martin M. Walsh, 'Performing Dame Sirith: Farce and Fabliau at the End of the Thirteenth Century', in Ormrod (ed.), *England in the Thirteenth Century*, 149–65.
[70] BL Additional Manuscript 23986. It has been missing since 1971.

existence and their popularity in the medieval world is plentiful enough. The word seems to have referred for the most part to performers of instrumental music, although a variety of others—actors, jugglers, fencers, and the like—are also recorded. Some, no doubt, were storytellers, with or without the accompaniment of music. Minstrels, at least those of quality, perhaps gravitated more towards the royal court and baronial households. The extent to which families like the Multons, let alone the Grimhills, were entertained by travelling minstrels is difficult to say, although in all probability it was seldom. With so few household accounts surviving from the gentry we do not see them often, although a minstrel is once mentioned in the early fifteenth-century household book of Dame Alice de Bryene.[71] This is once across two years, despite the fact that a steady stream of visitors is recorded. Perhaps when minstrels did appear, they approximated to the musicians depicted in the Luttrell Psalter.

Digby 86, then, gives an idea of the sorts of literature that might have been available within a gentry household. Treated uncritically, like any other contemporary manuscript, it can easily give false impressions. For one thing, large manuscripts of this type were atypical of what was in circulation. Digby 86, Harley 2253, and the great compendium of Middle English romances known as the Auchinleck Manuscript, were all unusual in their day. Most written material, outside of bibles and psalters, did not circulate in this way.[72] Our understanding of the way manuscripts tended to be compiled was revolutionized by the study of component booklets published by P. R. Robinson in 1980.[73] A booklet, containing a single work or a number of short works in one or a number of quires, had an existence prior to the manuscript in which it was contained. Medieval readers often assembled a number of booklets to form a composite volume, and could add or subtract items. However, the majority of booklets probably never were bound into larger volumes. No doubt, too, they were often passed from household to household independently.[74] Once lent, they could be copied. Let us take the example of the romance, *King Horn*. This survives in three manuscripts. The earliest of these dates from *c.*1260 and is from the south of England.[75] Another is Harley 2253, from Herefordshire. The third is Bodleian Library Laud 108. None of these three texts is the source of the other two, and all have corrupt passages. Laud 108 is particularly interesting in terms of the

[71] *The Household Book of Dame Alice de Bryene*, ed. M. K. Dale and V. B. Redstone, Suffolk Institute of Archaeological and Natural History (Ipswich, 1931).
[72] What follows is from Coss, 'Aspects of Cultural Diffusion', 61–3.
[73] P. R. Robinson, 'The "Booklet": A Self-Contained Unit in Composite Manuscripts', in A. Gruys and J. P. Gambert (eds), *Codicologica 3, Essais typologiques* (Leiden, 1980), 46–69.
[74] Robinson, 'The "Booklet" ', 57, 66. Among the manuscripts Robinson discusses are two from the Bodleian Library, Douce 137 and 132, which once formed a single composite manuscript of six booklets. At the end of booklet 5 there is a list, in a hand of the second half of the fourteenth century, of books which had been lent to friends.
[75] See *King Horn, Floriz and Blauncheflur, The Assumption of Our Lady*, ed. J. R. Lumby, EETS xiv (London, 1866).

circulation of the work. In a manuscript devoted primarily to saints' lives (*The South English Legendary*), *King Horn* and *Havelok the Dane* are found together in a separate fascicle and in the same hand. Moreover, both were copied from texts which had twenty lines to the page and very probably therefore from the same manuscript. They are markedly different in dialect and the scribe made no attempt to substitute his, any more than did the scribe from whom he copied the texts. *Havelok* is of Lincolnshire provenance. *King Horn* is from the south of England. It found its way to Herefordshire and to the east Midlands. What seems to follow from all of this is not only the wide circulation of some popular texts[76] but also the likelihood of booklet circulation. Items must also have circulated in even less robust form, in loose parchment rolls, for example, or even as single items on parchment sheets.[77]

There are few clues as to how Richard de Grimhill acquired copies of the texts that comprise Digby 86. Although the Digby scribe may have been responsible for a modicum of rearrangement, his collection is basically the result of what he could readily acquire that was broadly of interest to him. This accounts for much of the eclecticism of the volume. Although the tastes of a compiler must undoubtedly have had an impact, much was dependant upon what was available in circulation. Some works undoubtedly travelled far, whilst others circulated more locally. There were bookshops, certainly, in Oxford and in London, but much more was disseminated by the system of loan and copy. Digby 86 gives a strong insight into what was available. In some respects it resembles the later Harley 2253, although there are major differences. The most striking of these is the lack of the overtly political material of Harley 2253. On the other hand, the two manuscripts have many items and many characteristics in common, suggesting that they belong, broadly speaking, to the same cultural milieu. Both tap into older aristocratic tastes, as well as into the relatively new. One obvious feature is the prevalence of works in Middle English. The production of these had steadily expanded from the third quarter of the thirteenth century, with *King Horn* and *Floriz and Blaunchflur*, and the magnificent *The Owl and the Nightingale*, through the *South English Legendary* and the romances produced in the London area at the turn of the century, to the time of Auchinleck and Harley 2253. To these one should add the steady expansion in the composition of lyrics and devotional pieces in English. It may well be that men like Richard de Grimhill, at the lower end of the gentry, the more professional and dynamic of its members, were also among the more forward-looking and appreciative of change when it came to the acquisition and consumption of literature just as they were in terms of enterprise when it came to managing their estates. At the same

[76] *Havelok the Dane*, in contrast, was probably not much known outside of the east Midlands.
[77] On this point see *Thomas Wright's Political Songs of England From the Reign of John to that of Edward II*, with new introduction by Peter Coss (Cambridge, 1996), lxii–lxiii.

time they were equally appreciative of traditional values and of the traditional needs of their households.

There is one further, and quite strong, caveat that must be made. The significance that the modern world—and most particularly of course its academics—attaches to the consumption of 'literature', is likely to cause us to over-emphasize its importance within the gentry household. At least as important, and probably more important, were more physical entertainments. One of these was hawking. That our Lincolnshire gentry indulged in this quintessentially 'aristocratic' pastime is indicated in the household account which plots the itinerary of John de Multon in 1343–4 (Figure 12.2). We are given a glimpse of the preparations made for a party at Ingleby indulging in hawking. Later in the account we find 2s given to the falconer for his expenses. No doubt some of the birds that graced the Multon table—the heron and bitterns, and the ducks, mallards, and teal—appeared there as the by-product of sport.[78] It should not be forgotten that hawks and falcons were most frequently imported into the country through its eastern ports, the most prominent being Boston, King's Lynn, and Yarmouth.[79] Hawking and falconry were expensive and the training of the birds highly skilled and time-consuming. All the indications are that it was taken very seriously in both royal and noble society. Books were written on the subject in general but also on the care of the birds. These appear to have circulated widely. Digby 86 includes a text extending over twenty-seven pages: *Ci commence le medicinal des oiseaus.* These birds could suffer numerous maladies, including parasites, fever, diseases of the digestive and respiratory tracts, infection of the eyes, arthritis, and problems with their feet. And, of course, they might be wounded in action.[80]

Falconry was by no means exclusively a male sport. Women are found hawking both in literature and life, and women as much as men are depicted visually with hawks, not least on personal seals where it is one of the marks of a lady's status.[81] Women are shown hawking in psalters and books of hours. Queen Mary's Psalter of *c.*1320, for example, shows women hawking at duck from horseback, and crane hawking on foot.[82] Lincoln Cathedral boasts a misericord showing a woman hawking and a sculpture of an angel, no less, feeding a falcon.[83] But hawking was not gendered, to use the current idiom, nor was it necessarily segregated. Men and women are found with falcons on luxury tableware and

[78] The subject has been explored most recently in splendid fashion in Robin S. Oggins, *The Kings and Their Hawks: Falconry in Medieval England* (Yale, 2004).
[79] Ibid. 21.   [80] Ibid. 103–4.
[81] Coss, *The Lady in Medieval England*, 38, and figures 12 and 13.
[82] Illustrated in Oggins, *The Kings and their Hawks,* figures 42–4. Seven marginal illustrations of a woman hawking are part of a section in the fourteenth-century Taymouth Hours entitled 'women's games', and a comparable series occurs in the Smithfield Decretals: ibid. 118.
[83] Ibid. 189, note 49 and figure 15.

Figure 12.2. Hawking (from the Luttrell Psalter). Add. MS 42131, fo. 163r. © The British Library Board. All Rights Reserved 2010.

lovers are shown hawking on decorative ivory objects.[84] When they were able, the gentry would also hunt. It is not coincidental that hunting appears with hawking in the very first line of *Ubi sunt*, which deals with the soul-endangering pleasures of this world.

It probably goes without saying that gentry households were more physical than bookish. Few perhaps would have possessed full-blown manuscripts like Digby 86 or Harley 2253, although we cannot know this for certain given the loss of medieval books in succeeding centuries, especially non-illuminated ones which would have had less monetary value.[85] More, no doubt, would have possessed literature, in the widest sense, in booklets or loose quires. These may have been devotional or practical texts from the range we have discussed. In this respect there can have been no such thing as an average household. Tastes and interests varied. Some will have possessed legal texts, including treatises and registers of writs, perhaps in combination with works like the *Seneschaucy* and *Walter of Henley's Husbandry* on the running of estates. It was not entirely unknown for men to write books themselves. The knight, Walter de Bibbesworth, author of the *Tretiz de Langage*, comes immediately to mind, and Thomas Gray of Heaton who wrote the *Scalacronica*. More commonly, or perhaps less uncommonly, they produced books of a more mundane nature. Henry de Bray of Harlestone in Northamptonshire, for example, wrote two books which largely record estate matters. He did, however, notice the deaths of many of his neighbours, and occasionally made reference to startling national events. A minor landowner, a coroner and at some point a steward, his horizons appear from his estate book to

---

[84] See Oggins, *The Kings and their Hawks*, footnote 14, 186–7.
[85] I owe this point to Michael Clanchy.

have been very largely local.[86] Others had their valuable documents transcribed into cartularies and registers, or bound loose quires containing these. In all of these cases we may be dealing with minority activities, but no percentages can ever be guessed at.

The books most commonly encountered were, of course, religious ones: bibles, missals, psalters, primers, and sometimes books of hours. Some gentry found themselves in the presence of graduals and antiphoners. It seems fairly certain that the great majority of houses that had chapels would also have the basic texts for religious observance. These works mattered, even if others did not. John de Multon bought a primer (*premer*) for 7d. More importantly, his account roll for 1343–4 shows the sum of 4s being spent on mending the books in his chapel. Although books appear rather spasmodically in wills in this period, when they do appear they are most likely to be these texts. They were an important resource. The psalter and primer were the books by which children took their first steps in learning to read.

If some gentry encountered books comparatively rarely, at least outside of religious observance, they were nonetheless very much aware of parchment. Household accounts needed to be produced, even by those who paid relatively little direct attention to their estates. Given that the motivation for keeping accounts was chiefly to keep a check on officials, much of the parchment work was treated as ephemeral and therefore disposable after a relatively short time. Some accounts were kept as exemplars, and could be given to other households on that basis. Estate-generated material tended to be kept longer. Here, extents, rentals, terriers, and custumals were useful over a longer period than manorial accounts. In short, documents that constituted valuable evidence were more likely to be kept, and indeed passed on to landowners who succeeded them. These included not only deeds and quitclaims, chirographs and final concords, but also licences and compositions regulating their relationship with the church and extracts from surveys conducted by the central government. Transcripts from court cases might also have been retained. Manor court rolls and memoranda associated with them are likely to have been kept for a time, although they probably had a shorter shelf life.

Chapels must often have stored the more precious items, along with the vestments, chalices, altar cloths, et cetera, that were essential for religious services. Otherwise, books and booklets may have been kept in chambers. Especially where these were constructed in stone, they tended to have built-in cupboards or aumbries. Deeds and such like were also kept in chests, or even in sacks. Manorial court records may well have been kept in the hall, given that this was usually the courthouse, and the same might have been true of estate records. They could also have been held by the officials who ran the estates or held the courts. Practice must have varied.

---

[86] See Coss, *Origins of the Gentry*, 204–5.

Members of gentry families, then, were no strangers to parchment. However, it was expensive. Its purchase was noted on the Multon account roll of 1343–4. A quantity was bought for 3d on one occasion, and four *peles* (i.e. skins) *de parchemein* were purchased for 7d on another. It is little wonder that it was re-used, as binding or stiffening for books for example, or more commonly as seal tags for deeds and the like. The lack of material to write on casually, as it were, is implicit in the use of account rolls, and even the margins of a manuscript, for pen trials. A member of the household of the last John de Multon used the dorse of a document a generation old on which to transcribe the texts of two Middle English poems, incidentally opening up the probability that the members of the Multon household were not entirely without interest in vernacular literature.[87]

The impact of widening literacy upon gentry culture was central: in keeping household and estate records, in religious observance, and in giving access to a variety of practical remedies. We know a good deal about some aspects of this culture because legal manuscripts, for example, and illuminated prayer-books have been deliberately preserved for posterity. Recreational manuscripts, on the other hand, were probably less often kept. All that we can say for certain is that for some gentry families, at least, literacy was also valued for entertainment purposes.[88]

[87] The poems are analysed by Woolgar and O'Donoghue in 'Two Middle English Poems at Magdalen College', 219–21.

[88] I am grateful to Michael Clanchy for his comments on the relative rate of preservation of the several varieties of medieval manuscripts.

13

The Urban Dimension
The Gentry, Towns, and Merchants

In this chapter we will be concerned with two relationships: the relationship between the gentry and towns, and that between the gentry and the elites of urban society. These are among the least explored subjects within gentry studies, yet they are of vital importance in terms of understanding the evolution of the gentry and its culture. In their survey of the early modern gentry, Felicity Heal and Clive Holmes wrote of the ambiguities surrounding the gentle status of merchants and urban oligarchs.[1] These ambiguities go back to the formation of the gentry itself. If we are to understand the nuances involved and their social and cultural implications we must give this relationship some close attention. Before we move to this, however, we need to examine the equally important and multifaceted relationship between the gentry and the towns.

It is well known that landlords, lay and ecclesiastical, were responsible for founding new towns during the twelfth and thirteenth centuries, and that some of the former were not amongst the most elevated of secular lords. We know, for example, that Peter de Birmingham founded the town of Birmingham during the second half of the twelfth century, even though no foundation charter actually survives.[2] Many others founded annual fairs and weekly markets, as they sought to cash in on the commercialization of society in a variety of ways, through rents, tolls, and courts, as well as through the marketing of their own produce. It is also well known that lay landlords held property within urban centres, especially the more important ones, even if a systematic exploration of the phenomenon remains to be undertaken. It was a feature of English society that went back to pre-Conquest times.[3] If the seigniorial borough of Coventry is anything to go by, however, there was a reduction in this urban landholding during the thirteenth century, not least perhaps because the commercial vitality of the times created difficulties in keeping rents at an economic level in the

---

[1] *The Gentry in England and Wales*, 8–9.
[2] Richard Holt, 'The Early History of Birmingham, 1166 to 1600', *Dugdale Society Occasional Papers* 30 (1985).
[3] Robin Fleming, 'Rural Elites and Urban Communities in Late Saxon England', *Past and Present*, 141 (1993), 3–37.

face of constant subletting, unless that is one had a strong and determined local presence. It is not by accident that those lay landowners of some consequence who did maintain a high quantity of urban rents tended to be those with local manors, like the Segraves at Caludon and, quintessentially, the Langleys at Pinley and Shortley, all very close to Coventry.[4] There were, however, social reasons why a relative diminution of urban landowning may have occurred, including a stronger emphasis upon the rural setting of gentility, and a corresponding tendency for town society to become more self-consciously intramural with its own elites.

It was not only established gentry who held urban rents. They were a particular boon to administrators and lawyers who were in the process of actual, or at least attempted, social rise. A number of such figures feature, for example, in late-thirteenth- to mid-fourteenth-century Coventry. There were men like Henry Baker and his son Robert, both bailiffs of the prior of Coventry. Henry had accumulated considerable property in Coventry by 1279. From here the family moved out to Keresley to the north of the city where they came to effectively supplant a decadent lordship. Another prominent bailiff, Robert de Chilton, and his son John, were doing the same but ultimately sold out to the prior who was in process of constructing his park in the area. Some lawyers and lawyer–administrators belonged to established families within the locality of Coventry, substantial freeholders who moved into the profession as the most effective way forward: men like Adam des Okes *alias* Adam de Whitley, the owner of the manuscript BL Lansdowne 564, which contains two registers of writs; Robert de Stoke, the prior's steward; and Richard Ernis and his descendants who had moved out from Coventry to Attoxhall in Sowe.[5] These men belonged to a local elite. Both the Stoke and Erneys family built stylish manor houses in the settlements around Coventry. Robert de Stoke, steward, royal taxer, gaol deliverer and justice of the peace, made himself, by a series of purchases between *c.*1290 and 1309, the lord of Stoke, while William Erneys became royal escheator across five counties during 1332–5 and was MP for Warwickshire four times between 1334 and 1340. Both men were major success stories. An even greater success story is provided by William de Catesby and his son, John. They acquired a string of manors in south-east Warwickshire. Of peasant stock, William was MP for Warwickshire six times from 1339 onwards, not to mention escheator, sheriff, and justice of labourers. The rent roll they built up in Coventry appears to have yielded just over £36 in 1360.[6] There is little doubt that urban rents provided a much-needed avenue of investment for families such as these, the more successful of whom entered at least the lower ranks of the gentry.

    [4] Coss, Lordship, Knighthood and Locality, 88–9, 128–130.
    [5] For what follows, see Coss, *Lordship, Knighthood and Locality*, esp. ch. 9; and Coss, *Origins of the English Gentry*, ch. 7.
    [6] For the Catesby interest in Coventry, see N. W. Alcock, 'The Catesbys in Coventry: a Medieval Estate and its Archives', *Midland History*, 15 (1990).

Nevertheless, even if their urban rents were not as significant as they once were, many lords still retained some urban property in the late thirteenth and fourteenth centuries and they did so for a variety of reasons: rent certainly, but also for ease of sale and purchase, and perhaps for accommodation. We can see this at Boston, where the Multons of Frampton, the Multons of Kirton, the Huntingfields of Frampton, and the Cobeldykes of Wyberton all held urban property, as did some lords whose interests were a little more distant, such as the abbot of Crowland.[7]

Of what did the Multon property in Boston consist? The collector's account of 1330–1 reveals that Thomas de Multon drew £1 2s from a house there that has been put at farm to Emma Stotte 'at will', 13s from a house demised to Robert Litster (*Littest*) and 12s from a messuage put at farm to Thomas Fitzneve, together with £1 13s 4d from the house in Boston called *Haihare* and £1 13s 4d from half of the house in Boston once held by John de Godesone, making a total of £5 13s 8d. Some of these properties can be traced back a little further. The Frampton account roll of 1325–6 shows the collector accounting for Michaelmas farms, including £1 2s from Emma Stotte for a house at Boston, 13s from Robert 'le Luster' for houses in the same, and 12s from Thomas Fitznef[8] for houses there. For one of the houses held by Litster 3s was paid out to the abbot of St Mary's, York. The account roll from the previous year tells us that the collector was pardoned 6s of Emma Stotte's farm because the house unfortunately (sic) burned down.

The history of some of these properties can be ascertained from surviving deeds.[9] The Godesone property was a new acquisition. On 3 April 1326 John Godesone of Boston and his wife Juwetta granted to Thomas de Multon of Frampton and his wife Elizabeth a messuage with buildings in Boston. A month before this the Multons had granted the couple eight acres of land in the territory of Kirton for the term of their lives. In 1322 the same couple had granted to the rector of the chapel of St James at Frampton half of the rent 'issuing in the winter time' from their tenement in Boston. This suggests, obliquely, that summer rents were higher during the period of Boston fair, when they were more likely to be retained directly in the owners' hands. Most interestingly, in 1327 William son of William Godesone, and presumably brother of the said John, granted to Sir Thomas de Multon and Elizabeth the messuage in Boston called *Bayard* in return for a corrody in the Multon household at Frampton.[10] Clearly the Multons were extremely keen to acquire this particular urban property.

The Multon interest in Boston was not new at this time. Indeed, it goes back to the mid-thirteenth century.[11] In 1241 Lady Margery, widow of Sir Alan de

---

[7] Page, *The Estates of Crowland Abbey*, 139.   [8] ? de Thom' Felice nef.
[9] What follows is taken from nos. 31a, 92, 94, 108, 110, 118, 122.   [10] See above 67.
[11] For what follows see Multon nos. 20, 95, 100, 101 (2), 105, 114, 120, 123, 125, 127. There is also a bifolium (Multon 140/19) which seems to be part of a cartulary of the Graa family. It

Multon, leased land in Boston for a period of thirteen years. It is stipulated that if the fair should not be held in any year, through war or fire, then that year will not count as one of the thirteen. The recipient, clearly having taken the land for commercial reasons, needed the full term of fairs to maximize the return on the £2 2s paid. In 1272 Margery and her son, Thomas, jointly received a quitclaim of £2 rent in Boston. At some point Thomas gave his part in all houses in Boston to her. Most of the charters refer to acquisitions but Lady Margery did grant £2 rent (probably the rent referred to above) to the church of St Michael next to Stamford and the nuns there. The charters show a considerable interest in Boston property on her part. On one occasion she granted property in return for a rent of three wooden cups. It was not surprising that she should take an interest in the town, for the charters reveal that she was the daughter of the great Londoner, Reginald de Cornhill. Indeed, on one occasion she calls herself Margery de Cornhill, widow of Sir Alan de Multon knight. She also granted a house in Boston to William de Cornhill, her nephew. Urban rents were perhaps particularly useful for a dowager in that they required a watchful eye but little in the way of management.

They could also be used to give a young son an independent income. In 1332 Thomas de Multon of Frampton gave John, his eldest son, and his wife Anne four messuages in Boston, of which one-and-a-half lay in the street called *Kyrkgate* between the tenements of John de Multon of Kirton and John Stukeneye, one-and-a-half near *Bradlan* and one in John Godstone's lane. In 1358 Anne, now widow of John de Multon of Frampton, granted all her houses at *le Horepytte* in the vill of Boston to two men for a term of five years at an annual rent of 30s. The lessees were to keep the houses and *le Stathe super Ripam* in good repair. This is of considerable significance, for the staithe on the river bank must surely have been used to carry goods, and perhaps people, between Boston and Frampton. Clearly, more was involved than rent when it came to holding Boston property.[12]

What more can we learn of the economic relationship between gentry and towns? What in addition to rent, did they draw from them? Before we use the Multon archive, once again, to enter into this question, it is necessary to take a closer look at Boston's trade.[13] During the twelfth century it had risen spectacularly to become one of the most important ports in England. It was

---

contains, in addition to charters of the family's Yorkshire lands, copies of some Multon deeds dealing with Boston. Many, but not all, survive in the existing collection.

[12] The surviving account roll for the Cobeldykes shows that they, too, held property in Boston in 1328, namely 12s in farm from William Bayard for the small hall and chamber once of Alan son of Sarra (*Sarr*), 5s from John ad Grene for a house next to the hall on the east, 5s from Hernis house (*del hernis hous*) demised to Simon Page, and 3s from Stephen son of Guy Alkok for a small house: Multon Adds 24.

[13] For what follows I have drawn upon Stephen Rigby's invaluable doctoral thesis: S. H. Rigby, 'Boston and Grimsby in the Middle Ages' (University of London Ph.D. thesis, 1978).

the outport for Lincoln, situated thirty miles upstream. When the Roman Foss Dyke was reopened in 1121, linking the River Witham at Lincoln with the River Trent at Torksey, Boston became the port of entry for that entire system of inland waterways. Although the surviving records for the thirteenth and fourteenth century are slight from the point of view of social history, they do enable us to reconstruct Boston's trade. The earliest customs accounts for wool, from 1272 onwards, show that Boston was the leading wool exporter in the thirteenth century, well ahead of London, Southampton, and Hull. Its wool was coming from as far away as the Welsh border, as well as from the West Midlands, Leicestershire, and of course Lincolnshire. The summer and autumn fair made it well-placed to receive the wool clip. It exported cloth from the east coast and from the Midlands. It was a distribution centre for a wide range of imports, including cloths, wine from Gascony and Anjou, and wax and furs from north-eastern Europe. Among Scandinavian imports were hawks. Significantly, Hacconby, on the edge of the Fens, was held of the king by the Hauvill family by the service of receiving hawks from Boston fair. These were gerfalcons, goshawks, and sparrowhawks. Lead came in through Boston, as did spices including sugar, ginger, cinnamon, and nutmeg together with almonds. Cloth of gold, samite and silk were bought there, as was canvas from Brittany. Monastic houses sold their arable produce at the fair, while meat, dairy produce, and stockfish were sold both at the fair and at Boston's weekly markets. Given its local importance, Boston became the pre-eminent port for the export of salt. Merchants from far and wide attended the fairs. Internally Boston's reach extended from Newcastle to London and East Anglia and, most significantly of all, into the Midlands. Not surprisingly, Boston was chosen under the statutes of 1283 and 1285 as one of the towns where debts were to be registered.

Boston was in steady decline, however, during the first half of the fourteenth century. In 1334 it was said that foreigners did not come like they used to do. From the same date the start of the fair was delayed until 4 August. The rise of London was certainly one factor in the decline. Others included the decline in cloth-making at York, Leicester, and Northampton. Wool exports from Boston fell, as did the import of wine and of wax. Nonetheless, Boston remained an important port throughout the timespan of this study. Nor should we neglect the importance of local trade to Boston's economy, both before and after the onset of decline. Much of this was predicated upon the explosion of the Fenland population.

It is within this general context that we need to examine the Multon evidence. The household roll of John de Multon, running from Michaelmas 1343 to Lent 1344 contains some important clues to the economic relationship between gentry and towns. It gives us an indication of the range of purchases that the household made and sometimes, helpfully, the location of the purchase. Clearly nearby Boston was the locus of many purchases. Here the lord and his household seem to have bought most of their supplies. They had dealings with a Thomas

Marchaunt, William le Clerc, a shearman (i.e. a cloth-cutter) and an equally unnamed pelterer, all of Boston. John Driffeld of Boston supplied them with ermine, while Roger de Farnham, who supplied shoes, and Roger le Drapur who, as his name suggests, supplied cloth also seem to have been from there. We hear of expense on horses when the lord was at Boston to buy his livery. It is clearly where the Multons bought much of their cloth. A goldsmith at Boston was paid £1 17s for the lord's belt or girdle and small sums on various occasions 'for the lord's work'.[14] The reeve's account of 1325–6 records among foreign expenses 3s 2d spent on the carriage of a tun of wine from Gascoigne Row, Boston, to Frampton and of 1s spent on a man with a horse carrying one kympe of herrings and sixty dried fish from Boston to the Multon manor of Miningsby at the beginning of Lent. The household accounts are unlikely to reveal the full range of purchases that were made at Boston, but what they do tell us is consistent with what we know of Boston's trade. In other instances we may suspect that commodities came from there, including, for example, the canvas for the Frampton windmill. The seven bushels of London salt purchased in 1347–8 in all probability also came from Boston.

The accounts also reveal that the Multons needed (or preferred) to go further afield for some items. Lincoln was where Sir John went to have his seals mended, and presumably where he had acquired them in the first instance (Figure 13.1). Parchment was also purchased there, as was timber which had to be transported to Boston. Armour, by contrast, was purchased at King's Lynn. On one occasion 10s was paid to a John le Armourer and on another 7s to the armourer of Lynn for a *pisaine*, a neck defence in chain mail. Later again a further 1s was paid to the armourer of Lynn, while two pairs of spurs were purchased, almost certainly at King's Lynn. It would be a reasonable assumption that all of these items were bought from the same John who was, in effect, the lord's armourer. There were other services, too, that a major town could offer. As we have seen, John de Multon's two younger brothers were at school in Lincoln. Expenses of 1s 7d were noted on Wednesday after the feast of St Hillary for doing business at Boston with the king's bailiff, although it does not say who precisely conducted the business. The large towns like Boston, Lincoln and King's Lynn were probably convenient meeting places, perhaps at inns and taverns as well as at private dwellings. We hear in the accounts of 4d paid to John de Lodlow for a dinner at Boston, and of another 1s 3d paid for a dinner there for the lord and his 'company' (*compainie*).

On the other hand, some purchases were made more locally. The household account speaks of shoes purchased from the *corveyser* of Kirton and ermine from the pelterer of Kirton. These were probably purchased at the market and were not necessarily manufactured there. In recent years economic historians

---

[14] See above, Ch. 4 for the details of some of these transactions.

Figure 13.1. The Multon seal (Sir Thomas de Multon IV).

have been paying some attention to the activities of the medieval consumer.[15] Families like the Multons belonged to what C. C. Dyer calls the 'second tier of consumers', as opposed to the great households which constituted the first tier. In general these second-tier households appear to have made greater use of smaller towns than the great lords who tended to confine themselves to the great fairs and ports. All households, however, needed to purchase consumables locally, both as they itinerated and when they were resident in one place for

[15] See, in particular, Harvey, 'The Aristocratic Consumer', 17–37; and for the later middle ages, C. Dyer, 'The Consumer and the Market in the Later Middle Ages', *EcHR* 2nd series 42 (1989), 305–26; repr. in his *Everyday Life in Medieval England*, 257–81.

an extended period of time. Officials also needed to make purchases while on the move. In addition, stewards and others were required to open up houses in advance of the lord's arrival, which involved 'some baking, brewing and cooking in preparation . . . and perhaps some shopping too'.[16] Such purchases were often, no doubt, made at local markets. But they could also be made *in patria*, that is to say directly from producers outside of formal institutions. The Multon household accounts of 1343–4 specify on occasions that purchases of fish and meat were made at Frampton, while bread was bought at Kirkby and bread, meat, candles, wine, and fish at Ingleby as Sir John itinerated. Expenses, such as those paid to John de Bassingham at Heapham, were perhaps in anticipation of the lord's arrival.

The same features are found in the le Strange household accounts. One or two of them are worthy of further comment. On Christmas day 1347 we hear that the lord himself had bought two gallons of wine at Heacham, probably at Heacham market. This does not necessarily mean that he physically bought them himself but rather that they were paid for from his privy purse. Lynn was clearly for the Hunstanton household the major source of spices.[17] As regards regular foodstuffs we learn more often who the supplier was than their place of operation. In 1328–9, for example, meat was regularly supplied to the le Strange family by Robert Spink. As far as purchases for the household are concerned there is every reason to suppose that most of the face-to-face contact was between the lord's servants and tradesmen of varying status. In this respect horizons were decidedly local.

So much for gentry purchases. What of sales? An essay by Richard Britnell on the Langenhoe estate in Essex is particularly informative in this respect.[18] As we have seen in an earlier chapter, there are five early account rolls for this estate, between 1324–5 and 1347–8. Lionel de Bradenham's account rolls have a special quality. Every year the serjeant recorded the names of a large number of people who bought grain from the manor, whatever the quantity they bought. Some grain never left the village and was sold to customary tenants and the landless. On the other hand, at least half of the sixty people who bought grain between 1324 and 1348 were townsfolk. The number of small sales involved indicates that the serjeant went regularly to Colchester market. However, he rarely carted the grain to town. Only twice are tolls recorded. The townsmen bought the grain on the market but came for it themselves. The roll of 1344–5 is outstanding for the number of large sales recorded. All except two of the buyers were prosperous townsmen who were active in satisfying urban needs.

The nearest sizeable town was often therefore the destiny of marketable produce. In certain circumstances, however, landlords could also directly involve themselves in trade. Pamela Nightingale has recently reviewed the participation

---

[16] Harvey, 'The Aristocratic Consumer', 32.   [17] See above 69.
[18] Britnell, 'Production for the Market'.

of knights and other lay landlords in the wool trade of the late thirteenth and fourteenth centuries with some interesting results.[19] Her evidence comes from the certificates of debt produced under the Statute of Acton Burnell of 1283 and the Statute Merchant which amended it in 1285. The aim was to assist merchants by the swift enforcement of debt. In order to achieve this it ordered the registration of recognizances in a number of towns. The resulting certificates reveal the debts that were unpaid. Between 1284 and 1311 there are eighty-seven certificates showing that knights were debtors for wool. The geographical spread suggests that they were most active where professional English merchants were least established and where urban influences were weakest. Some were selling only their own demesne clip but the quantities involved show that others must have been selling far more. In 1304, two Yorkshire knights owed 24 sacks worth 240 marks and another Yorkshire knight, with two partners, owed twenty sacks. This, Nightingale points out, was equivalent to the clip of 5,650 sheep owned by the Bishop of Winchester in 1290. Twenty of the contracts made between 1304 and 1311, when wool export was booming, were for between five and twenty-four sacks. It was not unusual for knights to lead joint enterprises. Clearly they were selling the wool of several flocks. In the majority of cases, Nightingale tells us, the creditors were townsmen, raising the possibility that the knights were acting as agents for professional urban merchants. Sometimes they were extremely active. The Bulmer family of North Riding dealt in 1294 with three separate merchants, and on later occasions with four other merchants of York, and also a Luccan merchant. The same pattern is found in other counties, indicating that the knights were actively seeking out those merchants who would give them the best prices. The merchants were clearly paying for the wool clip in advance.

However, it seems to be the case that professional merchants with more capital at their disposal were already extending their control over the trade. From 1311 to 1322 only merchants were allowed to register their debts under the Statute Merchant, in accordance with the Ordinances of 1311. By the time the landowners were allowed back in, the economic situation had changed and knights played a smaller role. Wool prices fell considerably during the 1330s. However, in the south-west, where London capital did not penetrate and where the port of Bristol had not brought the region's wool trade under control, the landowners had more scope and continued to trade. Moreover, many of them had large flocks. A curious feature of the certificates of Statute Merchant from 1331 is that knights and other landowners of the south-west began to describe themselves as merchants. Between then and 1353 Bristol issued thirty-five certificates of unpaid debt in which six knights, eight sons of knights and twenty-one lords of manors described themselves as merchants, where they were usually debtors. The

[19] Pamela Nightingale, 'Knights and Merchants: Trade, Politics and the Gentry in Late Medieval England', *Past and Present* 169 (2000), 36–62.

largest number (nineteen) came from Somerset, but Gloucestershire, Wiltshire, Dorset, Hampshire, Devon, Cornwall, and (in one case) Warwickshire also figured. The designation 'merchant' was presumably a formal one here to comply with the terms of statutes, but it can also be used to suggest that within gentry circles there was no stigma attached to the term itself.

Members of the gentry bought and sold in towns and in some instances engaged directly in the wool trade. There was no disgrace attached to gentry engagement in trade, given the level at which they operated. But what in general was the relationship between gentry and professional merchants? This is not an easy relationship to grapple with because, as we have indicated, it is heavily nuanced. We need to be wary of sweeping generalizations and the impact of spectacular careers needs to be tempered by an appreciation of broader social and cultural realities. A great deal of weight has been attached to the figure of Lawrence de Ludlow. His career is indeed instructive, but it does have to be understood in its full context.

In a recent compilation of essays on the subject of town and country in the middle ages, Oliver H. Creighton has pointed to the 'glaring absence' of fortified private dwellings in English towns apart, that is, from castles and episcopal palaces.[20] The 'elite urban classes' simply did not construct defensible dwellings within the towns. Neither did members of the gentry. This was in contrast not only to southern Europe but also to other areas of Britain, such as Ireland, where urban tower houses were fairly common features. Stokesay Castle, he suggests, provides an extremely rare example of 'a private residence built not for a landed aristocrat but for a member of the urban classes'. The wealthy wool merchant Lawrence de Ludlow adapted it from an existing building after purchase and received a licence to crenellate it in 1291.[21] On the basis of this Christopher Dyer states that

No insuperable barrier separated the wealthier townsmen and the aristocracy, as is demonstrated by the building of Stokesay Castle as the centre of a country estate by the wool merchant Lawrence de Ludlow, one of many examples of the acquisition by merchants of the high status and stable income associated with land.[22]

There was no insuperable barrier, it is true, but the implications of this statement may be misleading if it is taken to suggest a degree of porosity into the gentry that was not the case in practice. Lawrence de Ludlow's career has been examined recently in some detail by Henry Summerson.[23] His father, Nicholas

---

[20] Oliver H. Creighton, 'Castles and Castle Building in Town and Country', in K. Giles and C. Dyer (eds), *Town and Country in the Middle Ages* (Leeds, 2005), 281–2.

[21] Citing R. A. Cordingly, in *Art Bulletin* 45 (1963), 91–108: 'Stokesay Castle, Shropshire: the Chronology of its Buildings'; and *VCH Shropshire*, 60. See also above, Ch. 2.

[22] Christopher Dyer, 'Making Sense of Town and Country', in Giles and Dyer (eds), *Town and Country in the Middle Ages* (Leeds, 2005), 316.

[23] For what follows, see Henry Summerson, ' "Most Renowned of Merchants": The Life and Occupations of Laurence of Ludlow (d. 1294)', *Midland History* xxx (2005), 20–36.

de Ludlow, was a successful merchant dealing in the fine wools of Herefordshire and Shropshire by the early 1260s. In 1272 he was described as 'merchant of Edward the king's son'. In 1262 and 1263 he sent large quantities of foreign silver to the London mint. Lawrence himself first appears in 1272 and was probably born in the late 1240s. He, too, was soon dealing in wool. The chief source for his commercial activities, the recognizances of debts made under the Statute Merchant of 1285, show that like the Italian merchants operating in England at the time he was buying up wool clips in advance of shearing and receiving delivery later.

Although the Welsh marches were the centre of his operations, Lawrence also traded in eastern England. All the surviving evidence suggests that he bought wool in England for sale overseas, specifically in the Low Countries. In Flanders he operated in the opposite way from how he conducted operations in England, handing over the wool on the promise of future payment. He was clearly involved in an international network that centred on the Low Countries. He was also a moneylender. By 1290 he was lending money to the king. Real estate provided another outlet for his money. His most important acquisition was the manor of Stokesay, the purchase of which is recorded by a fine of 21 January 1281. It fitted well with his commercial needs for it is sited on the north–south road between Ludlow and Shrewsbury with connections to Hereford, Gloucester, and the Severn. As Summerson points out, however, he immediately showed that he had seigniorial ambitions in that he obtained a charter of free warren on his demesne at Stokesay and nearby Newington and Whettleton. His eldest son, William, took his place among the Shropshire gentry when he married Matilda, daughter and heir of William de Hodnet, lord of Hodnet and four other Shropshire manors.[24]

It is important to remember, however, that in his day Lawrence de Ludlow was wholly exceptional. He was very far from being a run of the mill merchant, and both his career and his 'castle' can easily convey a misleading impression. Rather he was a merchant financier, of a kind that was to become less unusual in years to come but, even then, was far from being the norm. Although Lawrence lived like a member of the gentry—indeed in greater style than most of them—and he no doubt quite intentionally founded a landed family, he can hardly be taken as a typical example to illustrate the porosity of the gentry to men of merchant stock.

Merchant financiers were a special category, in terms of their wealth, their contacts and sometimes their aspirations. They could gentrify if they wished, in the sense of founding country-based dynasties. Even so, however, it was by no means automatic for them to do so. Moving forward to the latter part of our period, when English merchant financiers were more numerous, we

[24] None of Lawrence's sons is recorded as trading in wool, and his descendants lived instead as gentry in Shropshire, where they continued in the direct line until 1497.

come to Adam Fraunceys and John Pyel, both of whom—as we have already noted—produced cartularies recording their acquisitions of property. Their histories, thanks to the work of S. J. O'Connor, have a great deal to tell us about the activities of merchant financiers and their aspirations.[25] Adam Fraunceys, who was most probably from Yorkshire, had become a London citizen by December 1339. Throughout his career he dealt in wool. He was mayor of the Staple of Westminster in 1357 and was appointed collector of the customs on several occasions in the late 1350s and 1360s. Most of his loans were to Londoners or men from the home counties, the east Midlands or East Anglia. He also had dealings with religious houses and loaned to the crown. Between 1352 when he was elected an alderman and then mayor until his death in 1375 he played a major part in London affairs and appears to have been devoted to the city.

John Pyel came from Irthlingborough in Northamptonshire. The family appears to have been of villein descent and to have been bettering itself in the late thirteenth century by taking on leases. John's father had probably been able to get him at least an elementary education. John himself was well established in the capital by the mid 1340s. Like Fraunceys he was a mercer. He was involved in exporting with the wealthy merchant of King's Lynn, John de Wesenham, who had moved his base from Norfolk to London. John Pyel had business interests in Northamptonshire and in the east Midlands more generally. Once again, however, it was the advancing of credit that brought him the greatest rewards. He made loans to religious houses, to fellow Londoners, and to members of the gentry in straightened circumstances. He was somewhat less involved in civic government than Adam Fraunceys. In the 1370s he became associated with members of the court party, especially Richard Lyons, and in making loans to the crown. He died in 1379.

Both men acquired property outside of London. In Adam's case these centred on north Middlesex and south-west Essex. John Pyel's purchases seem more resolute and were more extensive. In the same year as he inherited a holding at Irthlingborough he began making purchases in neighbouring parishes together with the manor of Cransley which he purchased from Elizabeth Wake widow of Sir Thomas Wake, a man previously indebted to him.[26] Thereafter he purchased manors both at Irthlingborough, and at Woodford, Cranford, and Sudborough.[27]

The ambitions of the two men differed somewhat. Adam Fraunceys never left London. He was buried in the church of the convent of St Helen's Bishopsgate

---

[25] O'Connor (ed.), *A Calendar of the Cartularies of John Pyel and Adam Fraunceys*. For what follows I am indebted to his full introduction and to his preliminary essay, 'Adam Fraunceys and John Pyel: Perceptions of Status Among Merchants in Fourteenth-Century London', in D. J. Clayton, R. G. Davies, and P. McNiven (eds), *Trade, Devotion and Governance* (Stroud, 1994).

[26] Adam Fraunceys was also involved in this enterprise.

[27] One of his acquisitions, Woodford, was the estate of Thomas Bozoun, part of whose household account of 1348 survives: O'Connor, *Cartularies of John Pyel and Adam Fraunceys*, Pyel's Cartulary, no. 218.

and left property to the nuns. He established two chantries for himself and his family in London. His property outside London would seem to have been built up for the social benefit of his family. O'Connor has reconstructed his social circle. His business colleagues included Simon Fraunceys, who was probably a relative, John Pyel and Thomas de Brandon who was for some years his regular business partner. As a senior alderman by the late 1360s, he rubbed shoulders with the likes of William Walworth, John Philpot, and John Pecche, merchant financiers to the core, as well as the notorious Richard Lyons and Thomas Latimer. How many of these were his actual friends is unknown, although John Pyel and Simon Fraunceys probably were. He had, it would seem, few friends among the gentry.[28] Although he did not turn his back on London, his children did. Adam junior played little part in its life, remaining for the most part on his estates and living the life of a country gentleman.

That John Pyel's aim was social advancement seems abundantly clear. Outwardly, at least, he succeeded. He left a monument to himself in the transformation of the parish church of St Peter at Irthlingborough into a college for secular canons. The Pyel arms—a bend separating two mullets—are found on the tower and on either side of the west door, 'which gave the church a distinctly proprietorial air'.[29] John Pyel acquired his estate, but how far he succeeded in joining the ranks of the established landowners is debateable. His will and his witness lists include many men from Irthlingborough but none who appear to have been of any consequence outside the immediate locality. In fact, as O'Connor points out, his neighbouring lords, men from whom in some instances he bought land, seem remarkably distant. Simon de Drayton of Lowick, the Wakes of Blisworth, the Mallorys at Sudborough, and the Seymour family, from whom Pyel bought one of the Irthlingborough fees, rarely if at all appear as attestors to his deeds. In some cases, like the Seymours, this may have been because those families no longer lived on their lands in the area. But this was not the case with Simon de Drayton and deeper reasons may have been in play. At county level, the families and men who dominated local society, like the Zouches of Harringworth, seem to have had little to do with Pyel, and Pyel himself held no important local office in the county. It seems that John Pyel had difficulty in finding acceptance among the upper levels of Northamptonshire society. Set against this is his apparent relationship with Thomas Bozoun, whose estate he acquired. Preparing to go on pilgrimage, and aware that he might not return, Thomas assigned his half of the advowson of the church of Woodford to his 'dear and beloved friend' John Pyel, citizen of London, as his attorney and procurator. However, Thomas Bozoun was not a particularly elevated figure, at

---

[28] He was, however, close to members of the higher nobility. He was appointed as trustee for the young earl of Pembroke. He was close to Humphrey de Bohun, earl of Hereford. He acted as one of his feoffees and supervised his will. His daughter, Maud, took as her third husband John Montagu, earl of Salisbury. Nonetheless, his own circle consisted almost entirely of Londoners.

[29] O'Connor, 'Adam Fraunceys and John Pyel', 29.

least in landowning terms. John Pyel's will allows us to see the names of some
of his actual friends. His provision for prayers included not only his relatives
but also Adam Fraunceys, John de Wesenham, William Halden, and John Holt.
The last-named was a lawyer and estate official of John of Gaunt at Higham
Ferrers in Northamptonshire, close to Irthlingborough. The others were London
colleagues. In short his closest relationships were formed with men he had met
in the city.

John Pyel was not alone, of course, in his acquisitions and in his evident
desire to join landed society. Other examples include John Pulteney, the London
draper who was knighted by Edward III in 1337 and who built impressive
holdings in the home counties and the Midlands and the mansion at Penshurst
in Kent.[30] However, many others were content with town life and preferred to
invest in commercial enterprises rather than land. It may well be true that as
one moves away from London to provincial cities the degree of investment in
rural estates lessens, although the phenomena described above can all be found.
In a study of the cities of York, Beverley and Hull across the later middle ages,
Jenny Kermode makes a number of pertinent statements.[31] Real property, she
points out was a more versatile asset than has often been supposed. It could be
used for a variety of commercial, legal, and personal purposes. It could ensure
spiritual security through investment in prayers and charity. It provided physical
security for children. It could also be used to build up estates for reasons of
social ambition. However, it still tended to be regarded as capital tied up in land.
Consequently, most Yorkshire merchants held scattered properties, both urban
and rural, and few acquired large estates outright. Rural property, of varying
size, came into their hands primarily because real estate was used as security
for cash loans or for credit. There are, admittedly, some examples of property
accumulation and social success, the most spectacular being William de la Pole
of Hull.[32] However, generally, there seem to have been very few merchants who
accumulated sufficient land or rents to found gentry families, or for whom 'the
accumulation of property was an end in itself'.[33]

The extent to which merchants became landed gentry, as Sylvia Thrupp
stressed long ago, is difficult to pin down.[34] We can find examples everywhere
of merchants turning into rural lords. They were always, however, a minority.
There were 'no insuperable barriers', it is true, but the transition may not always
have been as easy as the bald history of property transactions might lead us

[30] W. M. Ormrod, *The Reign of Edward III: Crown and Political Society in England* (New Haven and London, 1990), 172 and references given there.
[31] Jenny Kermode, *Medieval Merchants: York, Beverley and Hull in the Later Middle Ages* (Cambridge, 1998), ch 9.
[32] See R. Horrox, *The de la Poles of Hull*, East Yorkshire Local History Series 38 (Hull, 1983); E. B. Fryde, *William de la Pole. Merchant and King's Banker* (London, 1988).
[33] Kermode, *Medieval Merchants*, 291.
[34] Sylvia L. Thrupp, *The Merchant Class of Medieval London* (Michigan 1948, repr. 1962), 279.

to suppose. Moreover, it was not only a matter of resistance to full social and cultural intercourse on the part of rural lords. In many cases successful merchants and financiers, even if they looked to the country estate as the summit of social achievement, must often have felt happier in the milieu to which they were used and in which they had functioned very effectively for so long. Perhaps the best way to tackle the issue of social relations between gentry and merchants is by an in-depth examination of the merchants of one urban community. Ideally, given the emphasis here on the Multons of Frampton, one would take Boston. However, its records are deficient. A more than adequate substitute is provided, however, by Coventry. It was connected with Boston, most especially in terms of the wool trade and, like Boston, it was a highly successful seigniorial borough. Moreover, the wool merchants of fourteenth-century Coventry were among the wealthiest of the time. If merchants were becoming gentry in sizeable numbers it is arguably there that we are most likely to encounter them. In a famous essay published as long ago as 1944, R. A. Pelham drew attention to the activities of the Warwickshire wool merchants of the period, the majority of whom came from Coventry.[35] He listed those who were summoned to attend the Council at York in 1322 to discuss the establishment of wool staples and those who attended the various assemblies concerned with the operation of the export monopoly held between 1337 and 1356. The 1322 list contains nineteen names, of whom thirteen were Coventry merchants. The second list contains twenty-five names, twenty of whom were from Coventry, three from Warwick, one from Birmingham and one who appears to be entered under the wrong county. From these it is possible to construct a composite list of significant Coventry wool merchants.

There are thirty-five names. The list does not contain every Coventry wool merchant who was active in 1322 or in 1337–56. Pelham himself listed forty-five names of wool merchants contributing to the 1327 and 1332 subsidies at Coventry. However, there is no doubt that the list contains the most significant and wealthiest figures. It should be noted that in a number of cases the wool trade was a family enterprise. This was true of the Botoners, the Meringtons, and the Shepeys, for example. This was the time when Coventry's prosperity was at its height and when the townsmen were in conflict with the prior of Coventry for control of the city. A merchant oligarchy was established in power in 1345. The commercial activities of these merchants show that London was the pre-eminent port of exit but that their trade via Boston was not inconsiderable.[36]

We are dealing therefore with substantial, in some cases very substantial, merchants. The interests of these families, however, appear to have remained overwhelmingly intramural. Warwickshire's feet of fines record some of their

---

[35] R. A. Pelham, 'The Early Wool Trade in Warwickshire and the Rise of the Merchant Middle Class', *Transactions of the Birmingham Archaeological Society*, 63 (1944).
[36] Ibid. 48.

property transactions in the city, but little activity elsewhere. There is little evidence of landholding ambitions in rural Warwickshire. The major exception is the Meringtons.[37] Hugh de Merington and other members of the family arrived in Coventry during the 1290s and made the city the centre of their operations. In 1321 his son, John de Merington, with other members of his family—his brother Henry and their parents Hugh and Agnes—leased the grange belonging to the monks of Pipewell Abbey at Newbold-on-Avon in east Warwickshire for the term of their lives. This was probably a considerable property.[38] John de Merington was the largest taxpayer in Newbold in 1332, paying the substantial sum of 18s. The family remained substantially involved in the wool trade. Alice, now widowed, figured in 1338 and John in 1347. Nicholas and Henry de Merington were operating in Bruges in 1332. John loaned money to John de Hastings, to Lawrence de Hastings, earl of Pembroke, and to the abbot of Combe. We find him involved in property transactions at Long Itchington and Little Lawford as well as in Coventry. There can be no doubt that we should classify him as a merchant financier. There is no doubt either that he had ambitions to join the gentry. In 1360 John had licence for an oratory for two years at his manor of Little Lawford. By 1367 he had been succeeded by his son, Thomas, who was granted the same on four occasions. Moreover, the Meringtons appear to have been successful in their aim of joining the gentry. John was appointed a collector of royal subsidies in Warwickshire in 1338, 1340, and 1341 and justice of the peace in 1345. He was a justice of labourers for Coventry in 1354 and for Warwickshire in 1355. Thomas, his son, was classed as an esquire in the poll tax returns of 1379.

The Meringtons, however, appear to have been an exception among Coventry merchants in this respect. Of course, it is possible that some of the families may have had social ambitions further afield, the Tolthams and the Shepeys for example. However, the houses which Lawrence de Shepey had at Coventry, at Warwick and elsewhere in the county seem to have been essentially storage centres and are unlikely to reflect an attempt to become gentry.[39] All the indications are that the Coventry wool merchants were an oligarchy with a powerful commercial interest in exporting wool but with a strong social and political commitment to their city. Adam Botoner, William Botoner, Henry Clerke, William Horn, William Luffe, Nicholas Michel, John Papenham, Jordan de Shepey, and Richard de Stoke were all mayors of the city, most of them more than once. In 1353 Nicholas Michel and Richard de Stoke were its MPs, just as Lawrence de Shepey, Ralph Tuwe, and John Russel had been at the very beginning of the century.

[37] For what follows, see Coss, *Origins of the English Gentry*, 190, 200, and references given there.
[38] *VCH Warwickshire*, vi. 188.
[39] In a series of commissions of oyer and terminer issued in 1346, 1347, and 1350 he alleged that they had been broken into and ten sacks of wool valued at £60 taken. His father, Robert, moreover, said that he had been robbed of nineteen sacks worth £110 in the same places.

At least five wool merchants are among the twelve men who are said to have purchased the city's charter of incorporation. It may well have been the strength and perhaps social self-sufficiency of the merchant community in Coventry that kept their ambitions within the city.

The Clodeshales of Birmingham may have been closer to the Meringtons in outlook. Walter de Clodeshale was summoned to the council of wool merchants in 1322. In 1341 he was one of the collectors of wool in Warwickshire, having been nominated by the county's two MPs. By 1329 Walter had acquired property at Water Orton.[40] In 1333 Walter and his son Richard acquired a lease of the manor of Saltley from Sir John Gobaut and his wife, Annabel. Ten years later, in widowhood, she sold the manor to them. They also acquired property in Worcestershire.[41] In 1360 Richard de Clodeshale was appointed to levy the subsidy in Warwickshire. Meanwhile, in 1356, he had been returned under distraint of knighthood as a man who with £40+ of land ought to be a knight.[42] In 1360, 1371, and 1373 members of the family received licences for an oratory at Saltley. It would seem that they had successfully made the transition from merchant to gentry. However, there remained an attachment to Birmingham, for both Walter (in 1330) and Richard (in 1347) had founded chantries in St Martin's church there.[43] Another Birmingham wool merchant, John atte Holte, acquired the manor of Aston in 1366. It passed to Walter atte Holte who, in 1377, was escheator for Warwickshire.[44]

This phenomenon is replicated elsewhere. At Southampton, for example, where there was a small and cohesive 'ruling caste', Henry Fleming removed himself in the late thirteenth century 'from the urban environment which had suited his father so well' and 'joined the ranks of the gentry'.[45] In short, the evidence of such land acquisitions tells us not about merchants in general in this period but rather about merchant financiers, and even then only about those who *sought* to become members of gentry society. There is some evidence, moreover, that the transition was not necessarily easy and that often it was only in the second generation that such families became wholly accepted.

Let us approach the question from the opposite direction. That gentry had commercial relationships with merchants, of varying levels, is obvious enough from what has gone before. But how close to them were they socially? One possible avenue of approach might be through membership of merchant guilds. Interesting in this respect is the register of the Guild of Holy Trinity, St Mary,

[40] *VCH Warwickshire*, iv. 262; E. Stokes and L. Drucker (eds), *Feet of Fines Warwickshire for the County of Warwickshire*, Vol. II, Dugdale Society (London, 1939), no. 1663.
[41] At Woodcote in Bromsgrove, at Pedmore, and at Stockton on Teme: *VCH Worcestershire*, iii. 25, 201; and iv. 346.
[42] TNA C47/15.
[43] *VCH Warwickshire*, vii. 65, 366; *Warwickshire Feet of Fines*, nos. 1754, 1928.
[44] *VCH Warwickshire*, vii. 60, 80.
[45] Colin Platt, *Medieval Southampton* (London, 1973), 60–3.

St John the Baptist, and St Katherine of Coventry.[46] This guild represents the amalgamation of earlier guilds, the earliest being the guild of St Mary's (the Guild Merchant) founded in 1340. Its editor, Mary Dormer Harris, described the manuscript as written in a fine book hand of the later fourteenth and early fifteenth centuries. It comprises columns of names (alphabetically, by first name) of those who entered the guild. Some of the names seem to have been taken from earlier registers, for it includes those of the merchant oligarchs who came to power in 1345, preserving the membership of the first merchant guild. Needless to say, it includes the names of numerous Coventry merchants of succeeding generations. However, the membership was not confined to those whose lives were bound by craft and trade. Lawyers, gentry, higher nobility, and even princes were among those who found it expedient to belong to the fraternity. The gentry included figures like John de Charlton, lord of Pinley, William de Catesby, and Joan his wife of Ladbroke who was MP for Warwickshire and who died in 1370. However, we should be careful not to read too much into such membership. The fact that the royal family, members of the highest nobility, and courtiers like Sir Thomas Erpingham were also in the guild should give us pause in thinking that they or the gentry members belonged to it socially. The reason they were there must have been primarily economic. Franklins, farmers, dealers, and craftsmen with wool or cloth to sell from across the county would further their interests by joining, and this would have been no less true of interested gentry.

Membership reflects the chief ports and centres of trade with which Coventry was connected—London, Bristol, Chester, Newcastle, Boston, and the staple town of Calais. Naturally we find Cotswold merchants, pre-eminently William Greville of Chipping Campden. It was undoubtedly within the world of the merchants themselves that membership of the guild brought social and cultural contacts alongside economic ones. John Onley, twice mayor of Coventry, was also mayor of Calais and was said to be the first Englishman born in Calais after the occupation by Edward III. Richard Whittington figures in the stained glass in St Mary's Hall, indicative of the fact that relations between Coventry and London were always close. John Pultney, four times mayor of London, built the church of Whitefriars in Coventry and the arms of many London mayors were found on its misericords. Among the London guildsmen may be noted the names of John of Coventry, Simon Francis, and William Holys, who built the famous Coventry cross. In cannot be doubted that commercial contacts had cultural implications.

The question of social relations between gentry and merchant financiers and the like is certainly problematic. Some social contacts there must surely have been, if only because of the incidence of intermarriage. A few merchants were of gentry stock. John de Langley, merchant of Coventry in the late thirteenth and

---

[46] *Register of the Guild of Holy Trinity, St Mary, St John the Baptist and St Katherine of Coventry*, volume I, edited by M. Dormer Harris, Dugdale Society (1935).

early fourteenth centuries, undoubtedly belonged to the gentry family of that name, although the precise relationship remains obscure.[47] John Pecche, the fourteenth-century London alderman and fishmonger, was most likely derived from the gentry family of that name. Despite the interdependence of town and country, however, and the commercial interests of gentry, it remains highly likely that many gentry retained a sense of social superiority. Paradoxically, merchant financiers probably had easier relations with higher lords. Adam Fraunceys, the London financier, apparently 'moved with relative ease in aristocratic circles'.[48] If the question is problematic at the merchant financier level, it is even more so as we move down the merchant scale. As far as general purchases for the household and sales from the estates are concerned there is every reason to suppose that most of the face-to-face contact with tradesmen was undertaken not by the lords but by their servants at one level or another. But what actually happened when Sir John de Multon, for example, was at Boston to buy his livery? And did he have direct dealings with the goldsmith of Lincoln or the armourer of Lynn? When in June 1302 Sir John de Segrave granted 11s rent in Coventry to William 'his tailor' and Margery his wife, what relationship did this imply?[49] How much contact was there between them? Such questions are extremely difficult to answer.

It is observable that in some respects gentry and merchants inhabited the same cultural world. Where they did so it tended to be the gentry who set the pace. One clear example of convergence is in religious practice and religious preoccupations. An important expression of religious preference in the later thirteenth and fourteenth centuries was the desire to be buried with the Franciscan friars. As we have seen, members of the gentry increasingly chose to be buried at the Franciscan Friary in Coventry during the later thirteenth and early fourteenth centuries. The merchants were there too. What was the chronology of merchant interest in burial in the friary, and how did it relate to that of the gentry? A number of burials were of people who contributed to the 1327 and 1332 lay subsidies. One was Robert de Stone who, with his wife Margaret, was buried as we have seen on the steps of the chancel. Others include the wool merchants Adam Botoner and William Horne, and John Warde who was Coventry's first mayor in 1345. There are a number of burials of people who figure in 1327 but not in 1332, indicating that they may have died between the two subsidies.[50] Buried there were Richard de Weston, who was an MP for Coventry in 1295, and Thomas Ballard who was MP in 1301. To these we should add John de Langley, who was an MP in 1314. There are many other members of wool merchant families of the early to mid-fourteenth century who

---

[47] *The Langley Family and its Cartulary*, 10.   [48] See above, note 28.

[49] *The Early Records of Medieval Coventry*, ed. P. R. Coss, British Academy Records of Social and Economic History, n. s. 11 (Oxford, 1968) no. 712.

[50] Or, of course, that they were omitted from the rolls. Most of these are identifiable as merchants.

were buried at Grey Friars. In fact, of the greatest wool merchant families, only the Meringtons are missing.

By 1330, then, merchant families were choosing Grey Friars as their site of burial. How much earlier were they there? One of the earliest is likely to have been Guy de la Grene who was buried on the steps of the chancel. Some of the names of those buried are coincident with names that occur in the Hundred Rolls of 1280 and in the published Coventry records before 1307.[51] It seems to be the case, however, that the first burials of Coventry citizens in Grey Friars occurred in the early decades of the fourteenth century, growing thereafter and coming to include members of the most prominent merchant families. They continued into the third quarter of the century. The important point is that their arrival there *followed* that of the gentry.

Of course, there were other considerations. A large section of the urban elite of Coventry were in serious contention with the prior of Coventry, who had amalgamated the lay and ecclesiastical lordships in his own hands, from the very beginning of the fourteenth century. By the 1320s and 1330s the resultant struggle for power had become bitter and at times violent. It was the wealth and power of the wool merchants who, in alliance with Queen Isabella, holder of the residual rights of the earls of Chester and their successors, finally wrested power from the prior in 1345. It seems that burial in the friary was one symbol of solidarity and opposition to the prior. This would explain its increasing popularity during the 1320s to 1350s.

If Grey Friars had a rival in respect of burials it was the parish church of St Michael, itself associated with the earl of Chester's erstwhile lordship. Here the earliest recorded chantry was that founded by Hugh de Merington for himself and his wife Agnes. This, of course, explains the lack of Merington burials in the friary, at least from that date. Lawrence de Shepey followed suit in 1330 for the souls of himself, of several members of his family and of Adam Standylf and Alice, his wife. The Shepeys clearly switched their attention from the friary. This foundation was augmented for other members of the family, in 1344, 1383, and 1390. In the second half of the century some other families began to follow suit.[52] This was the time when the old church was subject to a major rebuilding, one of the many expressions with which the merchant oligarchs were physically transforming their town. Famously, two brothers belonging to a third great merchant dynasty, William and Adam Botoner, paid for the building of its tower.[53] Both were mayors of the city. There is a contrast here between this more collective patronage of an urban church and the more isolated patronage by individual gentry families of rural parish churches, although it should not be pushed too far. Commemoration of specific urban oligarchs was also based on the individual family.

---

[51] Pride of place goes to Simon de Shepey and his wife Margaret. Simon himself occurs in 1270s and 1280s.

[52] *VCH Warwickshire*, viii. 348.   [53] Ibid. 353; the evidence is from the city annals.

The same cultural lag occurs, in fact, in the case of sepulchral monuments, especially brasses and incised slabs, as we saw with burial at friaries. The merchants were slower than the gentry in responding to fashion in this area. There is no evidence of burgess patronage of brasses in the first quarter of the fourteenth century. The earliest extant is that to John de Balgidone and his wife at East Wickham, Kent, which belongs to around 1325. The most likely explanation for this late arrival is that brasses were regarded at first as 'an elite form of commemoration'.[54] There tended to be special dimensions to merchant commemoration. For example the effigial slabs of fourteenth-century Boston and other east coast ports (King's Lynn and Yarmouth) tend to be of Flemish design and workmanship. At Boston, F. A. Greenhill noted fifteen which he dated to *c*.1325 and another from the early fourteenth century, but which may be a little later. The great majority are of civilians and their wives. In addition there is the famous slab to Wessel, called Smallborough, citizen and merchant of Munster and his wife, of 1340, and five others dating from *c*.1350 to *c*.1370.[55]

On the other hand there were aspects of urban culture to which the gentry were peripheral. They were perforce absent from much routine civic life. The level of merchant participation in chivalric culture also reveals a high degree of divergence. The issue has recently been explored by Caroline Barron, with respect to London.[56] Unlike the situation in cities across the Channel, the mayor and aldermen of London do not seem to have organized civic jousts or tournaments and the city did not pay for the services of a herald. Although tournaments took place frequently within the city in the fourteenth century, they were not 'of the City'. They were organized by the crown for the amusement of the court, and Londoners did not take part. No Londoner of this period became a member of the Order of the Garter. At the first of Edward III's London tournaments, held in Cheapside in September 1331, three days' jousting was proceeded by a solemn procession through the city in which ladies dressed in red velvet tunics and white hoods were led on silver chains by knights dressed as tartars. Similarly, in 1375, towards the end of his reign, the king's mistress, Alice Perrers, dressed as the 'lady of the Sunne', rode in a procession from the Tower to Smithfield accompanied by a large number of ladies, each one 'leading a lord by his horse bridle'. Again, the jousting lasted for three days. Londoners took no part, other than as guests and spectators. Pertinently Barron adds, 'It may well be that they chose to be excluded and were perfectly content with their own, distinct, urban culture.'[57]

The books bequeathed by London citizens in their wills show little taste in chivalric literature. Susan Cavanagh's analysis of books bequeathed in wills by

[54] N. Saul, 'Bold as Brass', 173.

[55] F. A. Greenhill, *Monumental Incised Slabs in the County of Lincoln* (Newport Pagnell, 1986), 21–8. There is another collection, though not quite so extensive, at Barton on Humber.

[56] Caroline Barron, 'Chivalry, Pageantry and Merchant Culture in Medieval London', in P. Coss and M. Keen (eds), *Heraldry, Pageantry and Social Display* (Woodbridge, 2002).

[57] Ibid. 222.

men and women across the whole of society between 1300 and 1450 includes sixty-one cases where the testators may be described, broadly speaking, as Londoners. Almost all the books are religious: primers, missals, bibles, and saints' legends. Only three wills contain chivalric books, two of them being fourteenth century. Henry Graspays, fishmonger, who died in the Black Death in 1348, left his 'book of romanse' to his son, while William Kyng, draper, left his 'cronicles' in French to St Osyth's priory in Essex. All his other books, however, were religious and these he left to London parish churches.[58] For various reasons one cannot take the evidence from wills entirely at face value. However, the results are suggestive. Of course, chivalric books and other artefacts did pass through the hands of London merchants. In 1382 William Walworth recovered a debt from a merchant of Bruges by taking possession of 'a book of Romance of king Alexander in verse, well and curiously illuminated', valued at £10, together with a large Arras showing the coronation of Arthur worth £6. However, he does not appear to have held it for long, as it does not figure among the twenty-one books in his will three years later.[59] Few Londoners were knighted in this period.[60] Many fourteenth-century Londoners were, however, using armorial seals.[61] One was the famous Richard Whittington. In his case, however, this no doubt reflects the fact that he came from knightly stock, that is to say the Whittingtons of Pauntley in Gloucestershire.[62] Sometimes, however, their coats of arms did not conform to heraldic practice. They might fail to be divided symmetrically, for example, or carry the owner's initials as charges.[63]

Contact between wealthy and powerful Londoners on the one hand and great lords, on the other, was made possible by the festivities surrounding tournaments, but was also facilitated by the fact that many had town houses where they stayed with their households and where they entertained on a lavish scale.[64] On a lesser level some of the gentry, no doubt, had town houses too. Many others must already have been staying in London inns. This practice can only have increased the more the business of the central courts at Westminster grew and the

[58] Susan H. Cavanagh, 'A Study of Books Privately Owned in England 1300–1450' (Unpublished University of Pennsylvania Ph.D. thesis, 1980); cited by Barron, 'Chivalry, Pageantry and Merchant Culture', 224.
[59] Barron, 'Chivalry, Pageantry and Merchant Culture', 224–5. This is not to suggest that Londoners were ignorant of chivalric culture. After all, they were relied on to supply armour, costumes, pavilions, and all the necessary furnishings.
[60] Richard de Refham was knighted c.1312 and John Pulteney in 1337. Few, in fact, were knighted before the Yorkist period: ibid. 236–7.
[61] Ibid. 232. An analysis of 54 London seals (all but six being fourteenth-century) shows that 56 per cent were armorial.
[62] Caroline Barron, 'Richard Whittington: The Man behind the Myth', in A. Hollaender and W. Kellaway (eds), *Studies in London History Presented to P. E. Jones* (London, 1969), 197–248.
[63] Barron, 'Chivalry, Pageantry and Merchant Culture', 232–3, citing Thrupp, *Merchant Class*, 252–3.
[64] Caroline Barron, 'Centres of Conspicuous Consumption: The Aristocratic Town House in London 1200–1500', *London Journal*, 20 (1995), 1–16.

Commons became an increasingly important forum in national politics. Just as these factors increased the commercial contacts between gentry and Londoners, they are likely to have facilitated social contacts too. London, as is well known, was becoming an increasingly important consumption centre with a growing national reach.

For these and other reasons it may well have been the case that relations between gentry and merchants grew stronger from the second half of the fourteenth century. They certainly became closer politically. From 1343 county knights and the burgesses from the towns began to meet together in parliament in the painted chamber at Westminster. A committee of merchants had generally spoken at parliament for the mercantile community. In 1348 it was the parliamentary assembly itself which spoke for it. Now, too, they began to be named in the common petitions. In 1373 the merchants asserted that it was parliament which represented their will. In 1376 they joined in the celebrations of the earl of March after the overthrow of the court clique at the Good Parliament.[65] As Mark Ormrod has said:

In social terms the burgesses may still have been regarded as inferior to the knights of the shire; but the successful political alliance between these two groups had allowed the commons to emerge as a major force in English politics.[66]

Change was no doubt slower in the provinces. Even there, however, the social contacts between successful merchants and families like the Multons are likely to have grown stronger in the course of time. As we have seen in the last chapter, the Multon heiress was later to marry Thomas Graa, great merchant of York. Thomas was a member of one of the richest and most high profile of mercantile families in fourteenth-century York.[67] He was mayor of York for the year 1375–6 and was a member of the town council for the next twenty years. He was heavily involved in the wool trade and he and a group of associates lent money to the crown. He served on a dozen occasions as an MP for York and was appointed to a parliamentary committee for reform of the royal household and of royal finances in general alongside the London financiers William Walworth and John Philipot. He played a full part in staffing royal commissions for the county of York. He became a royal escheator and a JP. He was also employed as an ambassador overseas.[68] From early on in his career, Thomas was interested in property accumulation outside of York. He married three times, Maud, daughter

---

[65] See Ormrod, *The Reign of Edward III*, 190, 194–6. See also Nightingale, 'Knights and Merchants', 36–7.

[66] Ormrod, *The Reign of Edward III*, 196.

[67] For Thomas Graa, see J. S. Roskell, Linda Clark, and Carole Rawcliffe, *History of Parliament: The House of Commons 1386–1421*, 4 vols (Stroud, 1992), iii. 218–20; and Christian P. Liddy, *War, Politics and Finance in Late Medieval English Towns: Bristol, York and the Crown, 1350–1400* (Woodbridge, 2005), 131–2, 137–8, 175–7, 207, and appendix, table 2.

[68] This was in 1388 when he was sent to Prussia to negotiate with the Grand Master of the Teutonic Order over trade disputes between English merchants and the Hanse.

of Sir John de Multon, being his second wife. All three wives brought him substantial property. Thomas's interests straddled county and city. Despite this, his primary attachment seems to have remained with York. For a time at least he lived with Maud and their servants at Castlegate. This was an 'urban manor' with a very long history. It lay outside York Castle and was coincident with the parish of St Mary, Castlegate.[69] He was buried in the parish church, of which he was patron, alongside Maud. He left £5 for a stone tomb bearing their effigies and provided for a chantry.

In short, Thomas Graa exemplifies the type of urban figure we have been examining. He was rich merchant and financier, a man of affairs who sought association with the established gentry. He aspired, successfully it seems, to belong to their world, but without letting go of the milieu from which he came and in which he, no doubt, remained most comfortable. London, exceptionally, had been producing this type of figure consistently for several centuries. After all, as we saw earlier, Margery, the wife of Sir Alan de Multon, the probable founder of the Frampton branch of the family, was herself a daughter of Reginald de Cornhill. This was Reginald de Cornhill the younger who paid King John 10,000 marks to succeed his father as sheriff of Kent.[70] The Cornhills were a long-standing London dynasty, from before 1100 until well into the thirteenth century.[71] Like the Graas, they had wide interests straddling county and city. During the fourteenth century this type of figure became more common in other major cities. They remained, however, a distinct minority among merchants as a whole.

The Multons' major contacts in Boston appear to have been men like Roger de Meres and Roger Toupe, who functioned as members of the last John de Multon's counsel in 1367. These were successively John of Gaunt's stewards at Boston, representing the honour of Richmond. They were the type of men whom Rosemary Horrox, looking at succeeding generations, has famously described as 'urban gentry'.[72] Nevertheless, ambiguities remained. To be accepted as fully fledged gentry but without a rural estate was ultimately possible, but it seems to have taken centuries to achieve.[73]

These developments take us into the future. The die had been cast, however, in the period under scrutiny. No insuperable barriers existed, for sure, but the

---

[69] Sarah Rees Jones, 'Building Domesticity in the City: English Urban Housing Before the Black Death', in Kowaleski and Goldberg, *Medieval Domesticity*, 80–2.

[70] Owen, *Oxford Dictionary of National Biography*, 13. 456.

[71] Reginald's father, a son of Gervase de Cornhill, was not only a wool merchant and financier, but also an agent for buying cloth for the royal household, a collector of scutage and tallage and an itinerant justice. He died in 1209–10 having built up a substantial landed estate. For the Cornhills, see Derek Keene, 'London from the Post Roman Period to 1300', in D. M. Palliser (ed.), *The Cambridge Urban History of Britain vol. I 600–1540* (Cambridge, 2000), 206. See also W. Page, *London: Its Origins and Early Development* (London, 1923), 242–4; and J. H. Round, *Geoffrey de Mandeville* (London, 1892), 304–12.

[72] Rosemary Horrox, 'The Urban Gentry in the Fifteenth Century', 22–44.

[73] Heal and Holmes, *The Gentry in England and Wales*, 8–9.

gentry nevertheless remained distinct. Contacts were stronger and easier between the gentry and financiers and other major urban figures than they were with the run of the mill merchants. The social stock of a wider sector of the urban elite seems to have been growing during the fourteenth century and after, with an increase in both intermarriage between merchants and gentry and translocation. There must certainly have been tensions, although these seem to have been experienced on an individual level. That the relationship was peaceable was very largely due to the accepted social superiority of the gentry, to a degree that was palpable but was neither aggressive nor overwhelming. That this was so was an achievement of the thirteenth and fourteenth centuries.

14

Cultural Horizons

Virtually all of the directions in which we have looked have revealed the gentry's cultural horizons to have been intensely local. This is most obviously the case when it comes to the exploitation of resources, to the relationship between the gentry and their tenants, and to the functioning of their households. It is also true, however, when we examine the protection of their interests. Legal support was largely predicated upon local relationships. Interaction with the church, too, had a series of local dimensions; indeed, the relationships involved here became increasingly localized in the period under discussion. Patterns of consumption also show the gentry to have been rooted in large measure within a local economy. The nearest large town provided goods and services that were not available within their own resources or through the network of local markets.

We can rarely, of course, fix precise geographical boundaries within which gentry operated, except in respect to specific considerations. 'Local' and 'locality' are naturally elastic terms.[1] As we saw when examining the visitors to the gentry household, most recreational guests came from the locality in the broadest sense, reinforcing further the impression of a geographically restricted life. This is largely what one would expect given the physical conditions of the age. However, we have also seen that the greater gentry were to some degree at least mobile, in a broadly regional sense. They looked outwards when and as required. The Multons had some dealings, as we have seen, with both Lincoln and King's Lynn in addition to Boston. Both goods and services required additional and wider contacts. The Multon boys, for example, went to school in Lincoln. It is often said that the greater gentry, with numerous estates—families like the Multons—transcended county boundaries and operated on a regional basis, this being revealed by their marriage patterns, for example, where they sought partners among those of their own greater, and broader, status. That there were status levels is undeniable, although they were not rigid ones. However, the 'regionality' of these families is open to some exaggeration. In many respects it may be more accurate to think of them functioning within a series of localities. We saw this clearly in relation to their religious loyalties and associations. Very

---

[1] Indeed, contemporary terminology itself reflects this, with words like *patria* and *visnetum*, whose usage depends rather upon the context. For a discussion of these terms see Coss, *Lordship, Knighthood and Locality*, 8–10.

often one, or perhaps two, localities took precedence over the others. This could lead them into a preferential association with one county rather than another.[2]

The themes explored in this book allow us to understand the foundations of gentry culture, that is to say a series of important components that underpinned the whole of gentry life. It would be wrong, however, to treat the political and chivalric dimensions to gentry culture as secondary. This is certainly not how contemporaries would have understood things, and we should be wary of falling into the trap which sees such matters as 'superstructural', for as we now know well models that rely on such terminology do violence to the complexity of real life and to the myriad interactions which characterize human existence. The action of the young Sir John de Multon when he set out for Prussia in 1367 to meet his untimely death must give us pause. Even though he made careful provision for his wife and daughter, for the paying of his debts and hence for his salvation, for the running of his estates and for the legal protection of the family property, his actions can nonetheless seem to us spectacularly rash and even irrational when seen from the perspective of the material interests of his family. What possessed him to do this? To put it another way, what pressures and what influences was he under that prompted him to make this choice?

It is here that we must confront directly the military dimension to gentry life. Although there had always been a military component to the lives of the English nobility the period from the middle years of Edward I through the reigns of Edward II and Edward III saw what has been described as 'the "re-militarisation" of the "gentle-born" '.[3] The result was a very powerful and wide-ranging military dimension to English culture that deeply permeated the counties. Not surprisingly heads of gentry houses and many other male members of the gentry families tended to see themselves in military terms. Sir Geoffrey Luttrell, for example, whose psalter allows us spectacular insight into how he viewed his household and his estates, defined himself primarily as a knight and from within chivalric culture. In his psalter he is shown mounted on his warhorse below the words: *Dominus Galfridus louterell me fieri fecit* (Sir Geoffrey Luttrell had me made). It is an image with multiple and interlocking dimensions. First of all, it proclaims Geoffrey's status as a knight. The Luttrell arms—*azure a bend between six martlets argent*—are everywhere in the image. Secondly, the arming of the knight by his lady injects an element drawn straight from romance. Thirdly, it is linked in the text with psalms 108 and 109 with their military overtones and with King David, the putative founder of the knightly order. It evokes, then, the duties of the Christian knight and validates knighthood within the faith.

---

[2] Coss, *Origins of the Gentry*, ch. 8: 'Identity and the Gentry'.

[3] Andrew Ayton, 'English Armies in the Fourteenth Century', in A. Curry and M. Hughes (eds), *Arms, Armies and Fortifications in the Hundred Years War* (Woodbridge, 1994), 29. The significance of the reign of Edward I in this development has recently been strongly reaffirmed by David Simpkin, *The English Aristocracy at War from the Welsh Wars of Edward I to the Battle of Bannockburn* (Woodbridge, 2008).

Fourthly, it proclaims Geoffrey's lineage through the medium of chivalry. And, finally, the inclusion of his wife and daughter-in-law and their respective coats of arms within the image proclaims his affiliation with two other prominent families. Thus, within the space of a single image Geoffrey Luttrell conveys his social standing, his lineage, and his earthly affinity with other wealthy and powerful families.[4] These feelings were replicated assuredly in the sepulchral monuments and other expressions of martial and heraldic culture that we have encountered on numerous occasions during the course of this book.

One who speaks to us directly in terms of his preoccupations and values is Sir Thomas Gray, lord of Heaton in Northumberland, who wrote a prose history, the *Scalacronica*, in the late 1350s and early 1360s.[5] Like his father and namesake he was constable of Norham Castle, a northern fortress belonging to the bishop of Durham. In writing his history Thomas drew on extant chronicles[6] but also on his own experiences and the recollections and eyewitness accounts of his father and others. The name *Scalacronica* comes from a scaling ladder which appears to have been a family device. It much befits Thomas's father, Thomas Gray *le piere*, who was a fierce soldier, fighting consistently in the Scottish wars of Edward I and Edward II.

The elder Thomas knew a great deal about life in noble retinues from the 1290s onwards. He fought with John de Warenne, earl of Surrey, Robert fitz Roger, lord of Warkworth, Patrick of Dunbar, earl of March, Hugh de Audley, the earl of Arundel, and most especially with the émigré, Henry de Beaumont. Thomas Gray *le fitz* seems to have lived a slightly more balanced life than his father, although he too was a keen warrior. As a trusted landowner he received numerous judicial commissions from the crown, including those of oyer and terminer, and served as a justice in the bishop's court at Durham. Thus the author of the *Scalacronica* enjoyed an active life both as a soldier and as an agent of the crown. He was well placed to participate in the shared value system of the landowning class.

The *Scalacronica* has much to say, as one would expect, of military prowess, of courage, and of feats of arms. We find honour and we find fear of shame.[7] All of these are of course traditional aristocratic values. We also find some passages which reflect a society steeped in romance. One of these is justly famous; it is

---

[4] This is a précis of my discussion in Coss and Keen (eds), *Heraldry, Pageantry and Social Display*, 41–3, 64–5.

[5] It was begun after his capture by the Scots in October 1355 and extends to 1363. Thomas died in 1369. It seems, however, that the greater part was compiled between November 1356 and October 1359. On these points see the excellent introduction to *Sir Thomas Gray: Scalacronica 1272–1363* (Surtees Society, 2005), edited and translated by Andy King, which also contains details of the lives of the two Thomas Grays.

[6] Most particularly the 'golden chronicle' (*Historia aurea*) of John of Tynemouth.

[7] For example: 'We should think of our great duty to prove that we are descended from good knights, and of the great honour and profit that God has destined for us, and the great shame which will befall us if we do not boldly prove ourselves in this great affair' (*Scalacronica*, 109).

the story of how William Marmion earned fame for his battle helm in the most perilous place in England (Norham Castle), under instruction from his lady.[8] This incident, moreover, does not stand alone in the chronicle. Thomas tells us of another one which parallels an episode in the *Perceval, le Conte du Graal*, of Chrétien de Troyes:[9]

At Fresnay, an English fortress on the march of Beauce, a French knight, who took the name 'The White Knight', requested the constable of the place for a personal combat of two English against two French. The combat was granted at a place agreed, and the knight, with his squire, was defeated by the two English, who were dressed all in arms of vermilion; and they were taken into the foresaid English fortress as prisoners.

Such men, it has become fashionable to say, belonged to 'the military community' of Edwardian England. What is becoming increasingly clear from modern research is the extent to which military service reflected the social connections that pre-existed within the counties of England. This was essentially because military forces tended to be recruited in terms of retinues and sub-retinues. It meant not only that men often fought with captains with whom they had particular associations but also that retinues often consisted of clusters of knights, esquires, and other men at arms from particular localities who regularly served together, although not necessarily with the same captain.[10] Needless to say, these features strongly reinforced the martial component of gentry culture. They go a long way towards explaining or at least contextualizing the action of Sir John de Multon.

In his case two relationships are particularly significant. The first is that with Anthony de Lucy, the greater lord whose retinue he had joined and to whom he expressed great loyalty and eagerness to follow. In this case, the lord was distantly related. Anthony was the last of the Lucy barons of Cockermouth, descendants of Sir Thomas de Multon (d.1240), the progenitor of the Multon clan, through his son Alan. As the Multons of Egremont were extinct, Anthony was probably also Sir John's current overlord for his manor of Frampton. Moreover they were both young men of about the same age. Custom would dictate that Sir John de Multon should make his military mark as soon as possible, and preferably in such company. Needless to say his family had a history of military service. Thomas de Multon II fought for Edward I in Wales, in Flanders and in Scotland.[11] Thomas IV fought in Scotland in 1333 and 1335, while John's own father, John de

---

[8] Ibid. 80–3.   [9] Ibid. 176–7, and 251 note 23.

[10] See, most recently, Andrew Ayton, 'Armies and Military Communities in Fourteenth-Century England', in Peter Coss and Christopher Tyerman, *Soldiers, Nobles and Gentlemen: Essays in Honour of Maurice Keen* (Woodbridge, 2009). See also Philip Morgan, *War and Society in Medieval Cheshire 1277–1403* (Manchester, 1987).

[11] The number of Thomas de Multons who fought in the wars of Edward is large and it is difficult to separate them. I have taken as definite references only those to men who are specifically described as of Frampton. Thus Thomas de Multon of Frampton received letters of protection for the Welsh campaign of 1277. He was probably the Thomas de Multon who fought there in the service of the earl of Lincoln. He may also be the Thomas de Multon 'of Hoyland' who fought

Multon II, was at the battle of Crécy in 1346 in the retinue of Thomas Hatfield, bishop of Durham.[12] As one would imagine, the holders of the several Multon baronies had regularly fought in the king's wars. So, too, did the Multons of Kirton, and some additional male members of the Frampton family.[13] By the time of John de Multon II the need for a young lord to achieve a reputation for active participation in war was very heavily entrenched in terms of both personal and social expectation.

The second relationship involved was that between Sir John de Multon and his tenant, Richard de Welby, who went to Prussia with him, as his friend and companion. This relationship, too, seems to be derived, in part at least, from tradition and expectation. In 1305 an earlier Richard de Welby had gone to Ireland in the retinue of Thomas de Multon, probably Thomas III of Egremont, as had Alan de Multon (almost certainly a member of the Frampton family) and Alan de Cobeldyke.[14] It looks as though the Multons had shared their military experiences with at least one family of Frampton tenants. The institutional arrangements involved in going to war have rightly been given much attention by historians. We must never forget, however, that these were underpinned by social relationships, which may sometimes have been familial and tenurial ones. They were also underpinned by a complex of inherited values and pressures. These values and pressures were moulded and re-moulded across time but revolved perennially around a persistent core belief in the worth of military service.

Soldiering was a unique profession among the gentry in the sense that it alone descended from the ethos of the nobility from whom they were derived. Service had long lain at the heart of the military calling. Although it had a crown or state-orientated dimension, it was for long mediated through the higher nobility. It was this duality of service that gave rise to the military community, or more aptly military communities, to which historians have drawn attention. The ethos of the proud and haughty higher nobility was disseminated through the retinue. From the Edwardian era onwards, however, military service became more and more obviously service to the state. The upper echelons of the nobility long retained the role of military commanders. For the gentry, however, it became increasingly a profession, like the church and the law. For family tradition of

in the campaign against Rhys ap Maredudd in 1287. He certainly fought in Flanders in 1297–8 and was described as captain in the latter year. He was in Scotland in that capacity in 1298 and 1301: *CPR 1272–81*, 190, 221; *CPR 1281–92*, 272; TNA C67/12 m7, C67/13 m 5d; BL Add MS 7966a f 96r. I owe these references to the kindness of Dr David Simpkin.

[12] TNA C71/13 m.31, C71/14 m2, C76/22 m.26. I owe these references to the kindness of Dr Andrew Ayton.

[13] Thomas de Multon of Kirton fought in Scotland, for example, in 1333: TNA C71/14 m.2. An Alan de Multon was a commissioner of array in Holland in 1322: *Parliamentary Writs II*, ii. 573–5, 578–9. A John de Multon of Frampton served in Scotland in 1335: C71/14 m.2. Once again I am indebted to Dr Ayton for these notices.

[14] *CPR 1301–7*, 337, 340.

association with great lords was substituted, far in the future, association with particular regiments.

It is not only the military and chivalric components of gentry life which interlocked with the dimensions we have explored in this book. The same is surely true of political culture. Much flows from the role of the gentry as agents of the crown in the localities. This involved a good deal of social intercourse in which views and attitudes were disseminated. The same is true of local gatherings. Crown servants, as we have seen, might stay over with a household, and there was a steady stream of guests of one sort or another. Moreover, all those meetings around matters of trust among members of gentry networks, which we discussed earlier, were also points of contact where opinions were shared and viewpoints reinforced. How we would love to know something of what was said between the Multons, Pecches, Cobeldykes, and others on such occasions. Some of it must certainly have been political in one sense or another.

Sir Thomas Gray, whose chronicle says so much about military events and military values, was equally able to reflect on national politics. Following his account of the deposition of Edward II and an assessment of his character, he adds an observation which was probably shared by many and an opinion that seems to have been essentially his own:[15]

some men like to argue that the diversity of temperaments in the English is the cause that provokes amongst them upheavals of society, which is more unstable in Great Britain than in other countries, for foreigners of all nations have been greatly advanced there in the time of every king since Vortiger. These were of diverse condition, and so their estate was disunited in its aims, each one wanting to be a lord, because lordships there came not from nature, but fortune; therefore they long for change, each supposing that the lot will fall to him. It is always said that running water is the strongest thing that can be, for although it is gentle and soft by nature, because all of the particles take their part pushing equally in the flow, therefore it pierces hard stone. It is just so with a nation that with one mind, turns its hand to maintaining the estate of its lords, who do not desire anything save the good of the community, nor individually strive for any other aim. Amongst such a people an upheaval of society is seen very rarely, at least as regarding changes in the estate of their lords, which is the greatest dishonour to the people.

It is hard to believe that when the likes of Sir Thomas Gray went to meetings of England's parliament at Westminster, 'maintaining the estate of its lords' was not uppermost in their minds and that this, above all else, governed their political culture. Nor can we doubt that when they arrived there they came with attitudes, opinions, values and hopes that had been forged through a multiplicity of experiences in dealing with the economy of the household and estate, with neighbours and associates, with the church and with clergy, with towns, with commerce and with the law as it directly affected them. These matters concerned them at least as much as did military matters, more general questions of law and

---

[15] *Scalacronica*, 95–7, and 234 note 67.

social order and configurations of political power. The recent publication of a full edition of the extant parliament rolls will allow this aspect of gentry culture to be put more confidently under the microscope. This needs to be done, however, with an ear to contemporary literature, including the so-called political songs, and an eye on the material foundations and social relationships that we have discussed in this book. There is the opportunity for a thorough re-examination of the dawn of political culture among the gentry. Shortage of space means that it cannot be covered more thoroughly here, but will have to wait for another occasion. In the meantime enough has been done, one hopes, to uncover and explain the foundations upon which gentry culture rested, and to make a valuable contribution towards understanding the evolution of the gentry.

Bibliography

MANUSCRIPT SOURCES

Bodleian Library, Oxford
Digby 86

British Library
Harley 273
Harley 2253
Harley 6033 (*Book of Robert Treswell*)
Royal 12.C.xii
Luttrell Psalter

Lincoln Record Office
Episcopal Register V (Henry Burghersh)
Episcopal Register VII (Thomas Bek)
Huntingfield Cartulary 3 Anc. 2/1
Map of Frampton (Frampton Parish 23/2–3)

Magdalen College, Oxford
Multon Hall Archive
Deeds 1241–1398, plus:
Booklet containing rentals and arrentation of *c.*1340 (165/30)
Cartulary (Adds 36 and 140/19)
Collector's Account (Adds 9)
Court Rolls (84/2)
Extent (Adds 11)
Household Accounts (160 and Estate Paper 85/2)
Letter of Sir John de Multon, 1367 (71a)
Manorial Account Rolls (Adds 5, 12, 13, 24)
Memoranda on exchanges of land and services (128/11)
Rental (Adds 7)

The National Archives
C47 Chancery Miscellanea
C67 Supplementary Patent Rolls
C71 Scottish Rolls
C76 Treaty Rolls
C133 and 134 Inquisitions Post Mortem
C145 Miscellaneous Inquisitions

CP25 Feet of Fines
E40 Ancient Deeds (Series A)
E179 Lay Subsidy Rolls

National Monuments Record
Aerial photographs (17879/17; MAL_ 62558_ 106175; OS_68059_179 91968)
Site Report (TF33NW9)

Norfolk Record Office
LEST/NH 1–12 Household Accounts of the Le Strange Family of Hunstanton

PRINTED SOURCES

Abstracts of Feet of Fines Relating to Wiltshire for the Reign of Edward II, ed. C. R.
    Elrington, Wiltshire Record Society (Devizes, 1974)
The Book of Fees, Commonly Called Testa de Nevill, 1198–1293, 3 vols (London,
    1920–31)
Britton, ed. F. M. Nichols, 2 vols (Oxford, 1865, repr. Holmes Beach, 1983)
Calendar of Ancient Deeds, 6 vols (London, 1890–1915)
A Calendar of the Cartularies of John Pyel and Adam Fraunceys, ed. S. J. O'Connor,
    Camden Society, 5th series 2 (1993)
Calendar of Charter Rolls, 6 vols (London, 1903–27)
Calendar of Close Rolls (London, 1900–)
Calendar of Fine Rolls (London, 1911–)
Calendar of Inquisitions Miscellaneous (London, 1916–)
Calendar of Inquisitions Post Mortem (London, 1904–)
Calendar of Patent Rolls (London, 1906–)
Cartae Nativorum, ed. C. N. L. Brooke and M. M. Postan, Northamptonshire Record
    Society 20 (1960)
The Cartulary of Cirencester Abbey, vol. 2, ed. C. D. Ross (London, 1964)
The Charters of Constance of Brittany and her Family, 1171–1221, ed. J. Everard and
    M. Jones (Woodbridge, 1991)
Complete Peerage of England, Scotland, Ireland, Great Britain and the United Kingdom,
    13 vols in 14, ed. Vicary Gibbs *et al.* (London, 1910–59)
The Court Rolls of Walsham le Willows 1303–50, ed. R. Lock, 2 vols (Woodbridge, 1998,
    2002)
The Earliest English Law Reports, ed. P. A. Brand, vols 1 and 2, Selden Society (London,
    1996)
Early Middle English Verse and Prose, ed. J. A. W. Bennett, G. V. Smithers, and N. Davis,
    2nd edition (Oxford, 1968)
The Early Records of Medieval Coventry, ed. P. R. Coss, British Academy Records of Social
    and Economic History, n. s. 11 (Oxford, 1986)
Eighteen Anglo-Norman Fabliaux, ed. I. Short and R. Pearcy, Anglo-Norman Text Society,
    plain texts series 14 (London, 2000)

Estate Records of the Hotot Family, in. E. King (ed.), *A Northamptonshire Miscellany* Northamptonshire Record Society 32 (1983)

Excerpta e Rotulis Finium in Turri Londinensi Asservatis, AD 1216–72, 2 vols, ed. C. Roberts, Record Commission (London, 1835–6)

Facsimile of British Museum MS Harley 2253, introduced by N. R. Ker, EETS o. s. 255 (London, 1965)

Facsimile of Oxford, Bodleian Library, MS Digby 86, introduced by Judith Tschann and M. B. Parkes, EETS (Oxford, 1996)

Feet of Fines for the County of Warwickshire, ed. E. Stokes and L. Drucker, II, Dugdale Society (London, 1939)

Feudal Aids, 6 vols (London, 1899–1920)

Fortescue, *De Laudibus Legum Anglie*, ed. S. B. Chrimes (Cambridge, 1942)

Hieatt, C. B. and Butler, S., *Curye on Inglysh: English Culinary Manuscripts of the Fourteenth Century*, EETS (1985)

Holly, G. H., 'The Earliest Roll of Household Accounts in the Muniment Room at Hunstanton for the Second Year of Edward II [1328]', *Norfolk Archaeology* 21 (1920–2)

Household Accounts of Medieval England, ed. C. M. Woolgar, 2 vols, British Academy Records of Social and Economic History, n. s. 18 (Oxford, 1993)

The Household Book of Dame Alice de Bryene, ed. M. K. Dale and V. B. Redstone, Suffolk Institute of Archaeology and Natural History (Ipswich, 1931)

The Inquisitions Post Mortem *for the County of Worcester*, Part 2, ed. J. W. Willis Bund (Worcester Historical Society, 1909)

Un jeu de société du moyen age, Ragemon le Bon, ed. A. Långfors (Helsinki, 1920)

King Horn, Floriz and Blauncheflur, The Assumption of Our Lady, ed. J. R. Lumby, EETS xiv (London, 1866)

Kingsford's Stonor Letters and Papers 1290–1483, ed. C. Carpenter (Cambridge, 1996)

The Langley Cartulary, ed. P. R. Coss, Dugdale Society, main series 32 (Oxford, 1980)

Lay Subsidy Roll for the County of Worcester, 1 Edward III, ed. F. J. Eld, Worcester Historical Society (1895)

A Lincolnshire Assize Roll, ed. Walter Sinclair Thomson, Lincolnshire Record Society cvi (1944)

Lincolnshire Church Notes made by Gervase Holles A.D. 1634 to 1642, ed. R. Cole, Lincoln Record Society (1910)

Lordship and landscape in Norfolk 1250–1350: the Early Records of Holkham, ed. W. Hassall and J. Beauroy, British Academy Records of Social and Economic History, n. s. 20 (Oxford, 1993)

The Luttrell Psalter: A Facsimile, introduced by Michelle P. Brown (British Library, London, 2006)

Macray, W. D., *Catalogue of Magdalen College Deeds, Lincolnshire* (typescript in Magdalen College, n.d.)

The Making of King's Lynn, ed. D. M. Owen, British Academy Records of Social and Economic History, n. s. 9 (London, 1984)

Manorial Records of Cuxham, Oxfordshire, circa 1200–1359, ed. P. D. A. Harvey (London, 1976)

The Metrical Chronicle of Robert of Gloucester, ed. W. A. Wright, 2 vols, Rolls Series 76 (London, 1987)

Middle English Dictionary

Monasticon VI–3, ed. J. Caley, H. Ellis and B. Badinel (London, 1830)

Orthographia Gallica, ed. R. C. Johnston, Anglo-Norman Text Society, plain texts series 5 (London, 1987)

The Owl and the Nightingale: Text and Translation, ed. N. Cartlidge (Exeter, 2001)

The Parlement of the Thre Ages, ed. M. Y. Offord, EETS, ccxlvi (London, 1959)

Parliamentary Writs, ed. F. Palgrave, 2 vols in 4 (London, 1827–34)

Paston Letters and Papers of the Fifteenth Century, ed. N. Davis, vol. 1 (Oxford, 1971)

Polychronicon Ranulphi Higden, ed. C. Babington, vol. II, Rolls Series (1869)

Register of Godfrey Giffard, ed. J. W. Willis Bund, 2 vols, Worcestershire Historical Society (1898–1902)

Register of the Guild of Holy Trinity, St Mary, St John the Baptist and St Katherine of Coventry, Vol. 1, ed. M. Dormer Harris, Dugdale Society (1935)

The Register of Walter Reynolds, Bishop of Worcester, 1308–13, Dugdale Society (1928)

Robinson, J. A., 'Household Roll of Bishop Ralph of Shrewsbury (1337–8)', in T. F. Palmer (ed.), *Collectanea I*, Somerset Record Society 39 (1924)

The Rolls and Register of Bishop Oliver Sutton, 1280–99, ed. R. M. T. Hill, 7 vols, Lincoln Record Society (1948–75)

Rotuli Hundredorum, ed. W. Illingworth, 2 vols, Record Commission (London, 1812–18)

Rotuli Ricardi Gravesend Episcopi Lincolniensis, 1258–1279, ed. F. N. Davis, Lincoln Record Society (1925)

Sir Thomas Gray: Scalacronica 1272–1363, ed. A. King, Surtees Society (2005)

Thomas Wright's Political Songs of England From the Reign of John to that of Edward II, introduced by Peter Coss, Royal Historical Society (Cambridge, 1996)

The Vision of Piers Plowman: An Edition of the 'B' Text, ed. A. V. C. Schmidt (London, 1978)

Walter de Bibbesworth, *Le Tretiz*, ed. W. Rothwell, Anglo-Norman Text Society, plain texts series 6 (1990)

Walter of Henley and Other Treatises on Estate Management and Accounting, ed. D. Oschinsky (Oxford, 1971)

Woolgar, C. M., *A Catalogue of the Estate Archives of St Mary Magdalen College, Oxford* (typescript, 1981)

The Works of Geoffrey Chaucer, ed. F. N. Robinson (London, 1957)

SECONDARY SOURCES

Alcock, N. W., 'The Catesbys in Coventry: A Medieval Estate and its Archives', *Midland History* 15 (1990)

Alexander J. and Binski, P., *Age of Chivalry: Art in Plantagenet England 1200–1400* (London, 1987)

Archer, R. E., ' "How ladies ... who live on their manors ought to manage their households and estates": Women as Landholders and Administrators in the Later

Middle Ages', in P. J. P. Goldberg (ed.), *Woman is a Worthy Wight: Women in English Society, c.1200–1500* (Stroud, 1992)

Astill, G. G., 'An Early Inventory of a Leicestershire Knight', *Midland History* 2 (1974) 'Social Advancement through Seigniorial Service? The Case of Simon Pakeman', *Transactions of the Leicestershire Archaeological Society* 54 (1978–9)

Aston, M. and Richmond, C. (eds), *Lollardy and the Gentry in the Later Middle Ages* (Stroud, 1997)

Ayton, A., 'Armies and Military Communities in Fourteenth-Century England', in P. Coss and C. Tyerman (eds), *Soldiers, Nobles and Gentlemen: Essays in Honour of Maurice Keen* (Woodbridge, 2009)

—— 'English Armies in the Fourteenth Century', in A. Curry and M. Hughes (eds), *Arms, Armies and Fortifications in the Hundred Years War* (Woodbridge, 1994)

Badham, S., '*A new feire peynted stone*: Medieval English Incised Slabs', *Church Monuments*, XIX (2004)

Badham, S. and Norris, M., *Early Incised Slabs and Brasses from the London Marblers* (Society of Antiquaries of London, 1999)

Bailey, M. (ed.), *The English Manor c.1200–c.1500* (Manchester, 2002)

Bardsley, S., 'Women's Work Reconsidered: Gender and Wage Differentiation in Late Medieval England', *Past and Present* 165 (1999)

Barg, M. A., 'The Social Structure of Manorial Freeholders: An Analysis of the Hundred Rolls of 1279', *AgHR* 39 (1991)

Barron, C., 'Centres of Conspicuous Consumption: The Aristocratic Town House in London 1200–1500', *London Journal* 20 (1995)

—— 'Chivalry, Pageantry and Merchant Culture in Medieval London', in P. Coss and M. Keen (eds), *Heraldry, Pageantry and Social Display* (Woodbridge, 2002)

—— 'Richard Whittington: the Man Behind the Myth', in A. Hollaender and W. Kellaway (eds), *Studies in London History Presented to P. E. Jones* (London, 1969)

Barton, J. L., 'The Medieval Use', *Law Quarterly Review* 81 (1965)

Bean, J. M. W., *The Decline of English Feudalism* (New York, 1968)

Beckerman, J. S., 'Procedural Innovation and Institutional Change in Medieval English Manorial Courts', *Law and History Review* 10 (1992)

Bennett, H. S., *Life on the English Manor* (Cambridge, 1937, repr. 1969)

Bennett, N., 'Pastors and Masters: the Beneficed Clergy of North-East Lincolnshire', in P. Hoskin, C. Brooke, and B. Dobson (eds), *The Foundations of Medieval English Ecclesiastical History: Studies Presented to David Smith* (Woodbridge, 2005)

Beresford, G., 'The Medieval Manor of Penhallam, Jacobstow, Cornwall', *Medieval Archeaology* 18 (1974)

Biancalana, J., *The Fee Tail and the Common Recovery in Medieval England 1176–1502* (Cambridge, 2001)

Biddick, K., *The Other Economy: Pastoral Husbandry on a Medieval Estate* (California and London, 1989)

Binski, P., *Medieval Death: Ritual and Representation* (London, 1966)

—— *Westminster Abbey and the Plantagenets: Kingship and the Representation of Power 1200–1400* (New Haven and London, 1996)

Birrell, Jean, 'Confrontation and Negotiation in a Medieval Village', in Richard Goddard, John Langdon, and Miriam Müller (eds), *Survival and Discord in Medieval Society: Essays in Honour of Christopher Dyer* (Turnhout: Brepols, 2009)

Blair, J., 'Hall and Chamber: English Domestic Planning 1000–1250', in G. Meirion-Jones and M. Jones (eds), *Manorial Domestic Buildings in England and Northern France* (London, 1993)

Bloomfield, M. W., *The Seven Deadly Sins* (East Lansing, Mich., 1952)

Brand, P., 'Courtroom and Schoolroom: The Education of Lawyers in England prior to 1400', *Historical Research* 60 (1987) repr. in his *The Making of the Common Law* (London, 1992)

—— *The Origins of the English Legal Profession* (Oxford, 1992)

—— 'The Serjeants of the Common Bench in the Reign of Edward I: An Emerging Elite', in M. Prestwich, R. Britnell, and R. Frame (eds), *Thirteenth Century England VII* (Woobridge, 1999)

—— 'Stewards, Bailiffs and the Emerging Legal Profession in Later Thirteenth-Century England', in Ralph Evans (ed.), *Lordship and Learning: Studies in Memory of Trevor Aston* (Woodbridge, 2004)

Brandon, P. F., 'Cereal Yields on the Sussex Estates of Battle Abbey during the Later Middle Ages', *EcHR* 2nd ser. 25 (1972)

Brault, G. J., *The Rolls of Arms of Edward I*, 2 vols, Society of Antiquaries (London, 1997)

Brears, P., *Cooking and Dining in Medieval England* (Totnes, 2008)

Britnell, R. H., *The Commercialisation of English Society 1000–1500* (Cambridge, 1993)

—— 'Feudal Reaction After the Black Death in the Palatinate of Durham', *Past and Present* 128 (1990)

—— 'Minor Lords in England and Medieval Agrarian Capitalism', *Past and Present* 89 (1980) repr. in *Landlords, Peasants and Politics in Medieval England*, ed. T. H. Aston *et al.* (Cambridge, 1987)

—— 'Production for the Market on a Small Fourteeth-Century Estate', *EcHR* (1966)

Burton, J., *The Monastic Order in Yorkshire, 1069–1215* (Cambridge, 1999)

Cam, H. M., *The Hundreds and the Hundred Rolls* (London, 1930: repr. 1963)

Camille, M., *Mirror in Parchment: The Luttrell Psalter and the Making of Medieval England* (London, 1998)

Campbell, B. M. S., 'Arable Productivity in Medieval England: Some Evidence from Norfolk', *Journal of Economic History*, 43 no. 2 (1983) repr. in his *The Medieval Antecedents of English Agricultural Progress* (Aldershot, 2007)

—— 'The Complexity of Manorial Structure in Medieval Norfolk: a Case Study', *Norfolk Archaeology* 39 (1986), repr. in his *English Seigniorial Agriculture 1250–1450*

—— *English Seigniorial Agriculture 1250–1450* (Cambridge, 2000)

Campbell, B. M. S. and Bartley, K., *England on the Eve of the Black Death: An Atlas of Lay Lordship, Land and Wealth, 1300–49* (Manchester, 2006)

Carpenter, C., 'Religion', in R. Radulescu and A. Truelove (eds), *Gentry Culture in Late Medieval England* (Manchester, 2005)

Cherry, J., 'Pottery and Tile', in J. Blair and N. Ramsay (eds), *English Medieval Industries* (London, 1991)

Clanchy, M. T., *From Memory to Written Record: England 1066–1307* (London, 1979)

Conway Davies, J., *Baronial Opposition to Edward II* (Cambridge, 1918)

Cordingly, R. A., 'Stokesay Castle, Shropshire: the Chronology of its Buildings', *Art Bulletin* 45 (1963)

Corrie, M., 'The Compilation of Oxford, Bodleian Library, MS Digby 86', *Medium Ævum* 66 (1997)

—— 'Further Information on the Origins of Oxford, Bodleian Library, MS Digby 86', *Notes and Queries* 244 (1999)

Coss, P. R., 'An Age of Deference', in R. Horrox and W. M. Ormrod (eds), *A Social History of England, 1200–1500* (Cambridge, 2006)

—— 'Aspects of Cultural Diffusion: The Early Romances, Local Society and Robin Hood', *Past and Present* 108 (1985)

—— *The Lady in Medieval England 1000–1500* (Stroud, 1998)

—— *The Langley Family and its Cartulary: A Study in Late Medieval 'Gentry'*, Dugdale Society Occasional Papers 22 (Oxford, 1974)

—— *Lordship, Knighthood and Locality: A Study in English Society c. 1180–1280* (Cambridge, 1991)

—— *The Knight In Medieval England 1000–1400* (Stroud, 1993)

—— 'Knighthood, Heraldry and Social Exclusion in Edwardian England' in P. R. Coss and M. Keen (eds), *Heraldry, Pageantry and Social Display in Medieval England*

—— *The Origins of the English Gentry* (Cambridge, 2003)

—— 'Sir Geoffrey de Langley and the Crisis of the Knightly Class in Thirteenth-Century England', *Past and Present* 68 (1975), repr. in T. H. Aston (ed.), *Landlords, Peasants and Politics in Medieval England* (Cambridge, 1987)

Coss, P. R. and Keen, M. (eds), *Heraldry, Pageantry and Social Display in Medieval England* (Woodbridge, 2002)

Cownie, E., *Religious Patronage in Anglo-Norman England, 1066–1135* (Woodbridge, 1998)

Creighton, O. H., 'Castles and Castle Building in Town and Country', in K. Giles and C. Dyer (eds), *Town and Country in the Middle Ages* (Leeds, 2005)

Darby, H. C., *The Medieval Fenland* (Cambridge, 1940; repr. 1974)

—— *The Changing Fenland* (Cambridge, 1983)

Davis, G. R. C., *Medieval Cartularies of Great Britain: A Short Catalogue* (London, 1958)

Denholm-Young, N., *Seigniorial Administration in England* (Oxford, 1937; repr. 1963)

Denton, J. H., 'The Competence of the Parish Clergy in Thirteenth-Century England', in C. M. Barron and J. Stratford (eds), *The Church and Learning in Later Medieval Society: Essays in Honour of Barrie Dobson* (Donington, 2002)

Dodwell, B., 'The Free Tenantry of the Hundred Rolls', *EcHR* 14 (1944)

Donovan, C., *The de Brailes Hours* (British Library, 1991)

Duffy, E., *Marking the Hours: English People and their Prayers 1240–1570* (New Haven and London, 2006)

—— *The Stripping of the Altars* (New Haven and London, 1992)

Dugdale, W., *The Antiquities of Warwickshire* (London, 1656); rev. W. Thomas (London, 1730)

Dyer, C. C., 'The Consumer and the Market in the Later Middle Ages', *EcHR* 2nd Series 42 (1989); repr. in his *Everyday Life in Medieval England* (London, 1994)

—— 'The Consumption of Freshwater Fish in Medieval England', in his *Everyday Life in Medieval England*

—— 'Dispersed Settlements in Medieval England: a Case Study of Pendock, Worcestershire', *Medieval Archaeology* 34 (1990) repr. in his *Everyday Life in Medieval England*

—— *Everyday Life in Medieval England* (London, 2000)

Dyer, C. C., 'The Ineffectiveness of Lordship in England, 1200–1400' in C. Dyer, P. Coss and C. Wickham (eds), *Rodney Hilton's Middle Ages: An Exploration of Historical Themes* (Oxford, 2007)
—— *Making a Living in the Middle Ages: The People of Britain 850–1520* (New Haven and London, 2002)
—— 'Making Sense of Town and Country', in K. Giles and C. Dyer (eds), *Town and Country in the Middle Ages* (Leeds, 2005)
—— 'The Social and Economic Background to the Rural Revolt of 1381', in R. H. Hilton and T. H. Aston (eds), *The English Rising of 1381* (Cambridge, 1984); repr. in his *Everyday Life in Medieval England*
—— Standards of Living in the Later Middle Ages: Social Change in England *c.1200–1520* (Cambridge, 1989)
Eales, R., 'The Game of Chess: An Aspect of Medieval Knightly Culture', in C. Harper-Bill and R. Harvey, *The Ideals and Practice of Medieval Knighthood* (Woodbridge, 1986)
Emery, A., *Discovering Medieval Houses* (Princes Risborough, 2007)
—— *Greater Medieval Houses of England and Wales: 1300–1500*, 3 vols, Cambridge, 1996–2006)
Fleming, R., 'Rural Elites and Urban Communities in Late Saxon England', *Past and Present* 141 (1993)
Foulds, T., 'Medieval Cartularies', *Archives* xviii (1987)
Fowler, G. H., 'A Household Expense Roll, 1328', EHR 55 (1940)
Frankis, J., 'The Social Context of Vernacular Writing in Thirteenth Century England: the Evidence of the Manuscripts' in P. R. Coss and S. D. Lloyd (eds), *Thirteenth Century England I* (Woodbridge, 1986)
Fretton, W. G., 'Memorials of the Franciscans or Grey Friars Coventry', *Transactions of the Midland Institute, Archaeological Section* (Birmingham, 1882)
Fryde, E. B., *William de la Pole. Merchant and King's Banker* (London, 1988)
Gardiner, M., 'Buttery and Pantry and Their Antecedents: Idea and Architecture in the English Medieval House', in Kowaleski and Goldberg (eds), *Medieval Domesticity*
Gibbons, A., *Early Lincoln Wills* (Lincoln, 1888)
Gittos, B. and Gittos, M., 'Motivation and Choice: The Selection of Medieval Secular Effigies', in Coss and Keen, *Heraldry, Pageantry and Social Display in Medieval England*
—— 'A Survey of East Riding Sepulchral Monuments before 1500', in C. Wilson (ed.), *Medieval Art and Architecture in the East Riding of Yorkshire*, British Archaeological Association (1989)
Giuseppi, M. S., 'The Wardrobe and Household Accounts of Bogo de Clare, A.D. 1284–6', *Archaeologia* 70 (1918–20)
Goldberg, P. J. P., 'The Fashioning of Bourgeois Domesticity in Later Medieval England: a Material Culture Perspective', in Kowaleski and Goldberg (eds), *Medieval Domesticity*.
Golding, B., 'Burials and Benefactions: An Aspect of Monastic Patronage in Thirteenth-Century England', in W. M. Ormrod (ed.), *England in the Thirteenth Century* (Harlaxton, 1984)
Goodman, A., *The Loyal Conspiracy: The Lords Appellant under Richard II* (London, 1971)
Greenhill, F. A., *Monumental Incised Slabs in the County of Lincoln* (Newport Pagnell, 1986)

Hall, D. and Coles, J., *Fenland Survey: An Essay in Landscape and Persistence* (London, 1994)

Hallam, H. E., 'Farming Techniques (Eastern England)' and 'Population Movements in England, 1086–1350 (Eastern England)', in H. E. Hallam (ed.), *The Agrarian History of England and Wales Volume II 1042–1350* (Cambridge, 1988)

—— *Settlement and Society: A Study of the Early Agrarian History of South Lincolnshire* (Cambridge, 1965)

Hamilton, B., 'Prester John and the Three Kings of Cologne', in H. Mayr-Harting and R. I. Moore (eds), *Studies in Medieval History presented to R. H. C. Davis* (London, 1985)

Hammond, P., *Food and Feast in Medieval England* (Stroud, 1993)

Hanawalt, B., *The Ties That Bound: Peasant Families in Medieval England* (Oxford, 1986)

Harriss, G., 'William Wayneflete and the Foundation of the College, 1448–1486', in L. W. B. Brockliss (ed.), *Madgalen College: A History* (Oxford 2008)

Harvey, B., 'The Aristocratic Consumer in the Long Thirteenth Century', in R. Britnell, M. Prestwich, and R. Frame (eds), *Thirteenth Century England VI* (Woodbridge, 1997)

—— *Living and Dying in England 1100–1540: The Monastic Experience* (Oxford, 1993)

Harvey, P. D. A., 'Agricultural Treatises and Manorial Accounting in Medieval England', *AgHR* (1972)

—— *A Medieval Oxfordshire Village: Cuxham 1240–1400* (Oxford, 1965)

—— *The Peasant Land Market in Medieval England* (Oxford, 1984)

Hatcher, J., 'England in the Aftermath of the Black Death', *Past and Present* 144 (1994)

—— 'English Serfdom and Villeinage: Towards a Reassessment', *Past and Present* 90 (1981)

Hatcher, J. and Bardsley, S., 'Debate', *Past and Present* 173 (2001)

Hebgin-Barnes, P., *The Medieval Stained Glass of Lincolnshire* (Oxford, 1996)

Heal, F. and Holmes, C., *The Gentry in England and Wales 1500–1700* (London, 1994)

Hershey, A. H., *Drawings and Sketches in the Plea Rolls of the English Royal Courts, c.1200–1300*, List and Index Society, special series 31 (London, 2002)

Hesse, C., 'The New Empiricism', *Cultural and Social History* vol. 1, no. 2 (2004)

Hilton, R. H., *Bondmen Made Free: Medieval Peasant Movements and the English Rising of 1381* (London, 1973)

—— 'Peasant Movements in England before 1381', *EcHR* 2nd ser. II (1940)

—— '*The Social Structure of Rural Warwickshire*', Dugdale Society Occasional Papers 9 (1950), repr. in his *The English Peasantry in the Later Middle Ages* (Oxford, 1975)

Hines, J., *The Fabliau in English* (London and New York, 1993)

—— *Voices in the Past: English Literature and Archaeology* (Woodbridge, 2004)

Holt, R., '*The Early History of Birmingham, 1166 to 1600*', Dugdale Society Occasional Papers 30 (1985)

Horrox, R., *The de la Poles of Hull*, East Yorkshire Local History Series 38 (Hull, 1983)

—— 'The Urban Gentry in the Fifteenth Century', in J. A. F. Thomson (ed.), *Towns and Townspeople in the Fifteenth Century* (Gloucester, 1988)

Hunnisett, R. F., 'The Reliability of Inquisitions as Historical Evidence', in D. A. Bullough and R. L. Storey (eds), *The Study of Medieval Records* (Oxford, 1971)

Hunt, A., *Governance of the Consuming Passions: A History of Sumptuary Law* (London, 1996)

Hunt, L., *The New Cultural History* (Berkeley, 1999)

Hunt, T., *Popular Medicine in Thirteenth Century England: Introduction and Texts* (Woodbridge, 1996)

—— *Teaching and Learning Latin in Thirteenth Century England*, 3 vols (Cambridge, 1991)

Hyams, P. R. *King, Lords and Peasants in Medieval England* (Oxford, 1980)

James, M. R., 'The Anlaby Cartulary', *Yorkshire Archaeological Journal* xxxi (1934)

Jefferies, P., 'The Medieval Use as Family Law and Custom: The Berkshire Gentry in the Fourteenth and Fifteenth Centuries', *Southern History* I (1979)

Keene, D., 'London from the Post Roman Period up to 1300', in D. M. Palliser (ed.), *The Cambridge Urban History of Britain*, vol. I, 600–1540.

Kermode, J., *Medieval Merchants: York, Beverley and Hull in the Later Middle Ages* (Cambridge, 1998)

Kosminsky, E. A., *Studies in the Agrarian History of England in the Thirteenth Century*, ed. R. H. Hilton (Oxford, 1956)

Kowaleski, M. and Goldberg P. J. P. (eds), *Medieval Domesticity: Home, Housing and Household in Medieval England* (Cambridge, 2008)

Kuper, A., *Culture: The Anthropologists' Account* (Cambridge, Mass., and London, 1994)

Lachaud, F., 'An Aristocratic Wardrobe of the Late Thirteenth Century: the Confiscation of the Goods of Osbert de Spaldingham in 1298', *Historical Research*, 67 (1994)

—— 'Dress and Social Status in England before the Sumptuary Laws', in Coss and Keen (eds), *Heraldry, Pageantry and Social Display in Medieval England*

—— *Mills in the Medieval Economy* (Oxford, 2004)

Langdon, J., *Horses, Oxen and Technological Innovation* (Cambridge, 1986)

—— Mills in the Medieval Economy (Oxford, 2004)

Le Strange, H., 'A Roll of Household Accounts of Sir Hamon Le Strange of Hunstanton, Norfolk, 1347–8', *Archaeologia* 69 (1920)

Liddy, Christian P., *War, Politics and Finance in Late Medieval English Towns: Bristol, York and the Crown, 1350–1400* (Woodbridge, 2005)

Lord, J., 'Repairing and Cleaning of the Said Burying Places', *Church Monuments*, vol. IX (1994)

McClane, B., 'A Case Study of Violence and Litigation in the Early Fourteenth Century: the Disputes of Robert Godsfield of Sutton-Le-Marsh', *Nottingham Medieval Studies* 28 (1984)

Maddern, P., 'Honour among the Pastons: Gender and Integrity in Fifteenth-Century Provincial Society', *Journal of Medieval History* 14 (1998)

Manchester Guardian (1906) 'The Days of the Squire have Passed Away', 11 August 1906.

Marks, R., *Image and Devotion in late Medieval England* (Stroud, 2004)

—— *Stained Glass in England during the Middle Ages* (London, 1993)

Martindale, A., 'Patrons and Minders: the Intrusion of the Secular into Sacred Spaces in the Late Middle Ages', in D. Wood (ed.), *The Church and the Arts*, Studies in Church History 28 (1992)

Mason, E., 'The Role of the English Parishioner, 1000–1500', *Journal of Ecclesiastical History* 27 (1976)

—— 'Timeo barones et dona ferentes', in D. Baker (ed.), *Religious Motivation: Biographical and Sociological Problems for the Church Historian,* Studies in Church History 15 (1978)

Massingberd, W. O., 'Notes on the Pedigree of Multon of Frampton, co. Lincoln', *The Ancestor* II (1902)

Mawer A. and Stenton, F. M., *The Place-Names of Worcestershire*, English Place-Name Society vol. IV (1927)

Mead, W. E., *The English Medieval Feast* (London, 1931 repr.1967)

Mertes, K., *The English Household 1250–1600: Good Governance and Politic Rule* (Oxford, 1988)

Millar, E. G., *The Luttrell Psalter* (London, 1930)

Miller, B. D. H. 'The Early History of Bodleian MS Digby 86', *Annuale Medievale* 4 (1963)

Miller, D. and Tilley C., 'Editorial', *Journal of Material Culture* 1 (1996)

Miller, E., *The Abbey and Bishopric of Ely* (Cambridge, 1951)

Miller, E. and Hatcher, J., *Medieval England: Rural Society and Economic Change 1086–1348* (London, 1978)

Moor, *Knights of Edward I*, 5 vols, Publications of the Harleian Society 80–5 (London, 1929–32)

Morgan, M., *English Lands of the Abbey of Bec* (Oxford, 1946)

Morgan, P., *War and Society in Medieval Cheshire 1277–1403* (Manchester, 1987)

Myers, A. R., 'The Wealth of Richard Lyons', in T. A. Sandquist and M. R. Powicke (eds), *Essays in Medieval History Presented to Bertie Wilkinson* (Toronto, 1969)

Netherton, R., 'The Tippet: Accessory after the Fact?' in R. Netherton and G. R. Owen-Crocker (eds), *Medieval Clothing and Textiles* I (Woodbridge, 2005)

Newton, S. M., *Fashion in the Age of the Black Prince: A Study of the Years 1340–1365* (Woodbridge, 1980)

Nicholls, J., *The Matter of Courtesy: Medieval Courtesy Books and the Gawain Poet* (Woodbridge, 1985)

Nightingale, P., 'Knights and Merchants: Trade, Politics and the Gentry in Late Medieval England', *Past and Present* 169 (2000)

O'Connor, S. J., 'Adam Frrunceys and John Pyel: Perceptions of Status Among Merchants in Fourteenth-Century London', in D. J. Clayton *et al.* (eds), *Trade, Devotion and Governance* (Stroud, 1994)

Oggins, R. S., *The Kings and their Hawks: Falconry in Medieval England* (Yale, 2004)

Orme, N., *From Childhood to Chivalry: The Education of the English Kings and Aristocracy 1066–1530* (London and New York, 1984)

—— *Medieval Children* (New Haven and London, 2001)

—— *Medieval Schools from Roman Britain to Renaissance England* (New Haven and London, 2006)

Ormrod, W. M., *The Reign of Edward III: Crown and Political Society in England* (New Haven and London, 1990)

Owen, D., *Church and Society in Medieval Lincolnshire* (Lincoln, 1971)

Oxford Dictionary of National Biography, ed. H. C. G. Matthew and B. Harrison, 60 vols (2004)

Page, F. M., *The Estates of Crowland Abbey* (Cambridge, 1934)

Page, W., *London: Its Origins and Early Development* (London, 1923)

Palliser, D. M. (ed.), *The Cambridge Urban History of Britain Vol. 1, 600–1540* (Cambridge, 2000)

Palmer, R. C., *The County Courts of Medieval England* (Princeton, 1982)

Palmer, R. C., 'County Year Book Reports: the Professional Lawyers in the Medieval County Court', *EHR* 91 (1971)

Parkes, M. B., 'The Literacy of the Laity', in D. Daiches and A. Thorlby (eds), *Literature and Civilization: The Middle Ages* (London, 1973)

Payling, S. J., 'Social Mobility, Demographic Change and Landed Society in Late Medieval England', *EcHR* 45 (1992)

Pelham, R. A., 'The Early Wool Trade in Warwickshire and the Rise of the Merchant Middle Class', *Transactions of the Birmingham Archaeological Society* 63 (1944)

Pevsner, N., *The Buildings of England: South and West Somerset* (London, 1958)

—— *The Buildings of England: Herefordshire* (London, 1963)

Piponnier, F. and Mane, P., *Dress in the Middle Ages*, trans. C. Beamish (New Haven and London, 1997); first published as *Se Vêtir au Moyen Age* (Paris, 1995)

Platt, C., *Medieval England: A Social History and Archaeology from the Conquest to 1600* (London, 1978)

—— *Medieval Southampton* (London, 1973)

Platts, G., *Land and People in Medieval Lincolnshire* (Lincoln, 1985)

Pollock, F. and Maitland, F. W., *The History of English Law*, 2 vols (Cambridge, 1895; repr. 1968)

Poole, B., *Antiquities of Coventry* (1888)

Postan, M. M., *The Famulus: The Estate Labourer in the XIIth and XIIIth Centuries*, *EcHR* Supplements 2 (1954)

Postles, D., 'The Perception of Profit before the Leasing of Demesnes', *AgHR* 34 (1986)

Pounds, N. J. G., *Hearth and Home: A History of Material Culture* (Bloomington, 1969)

Prestwich, M., 'The Court of Edward II', in G. Dobbs and A. Musson (eds), *The Reign of Edward II* (York, 2006)

Raban, S., *A Second Domesday? The Hundred Rolls of 1279–80* (Oxford, 2004)

Razi, Z. and Smith, R., 'The Origins of the English Manorial Court Rolls as a Written Record: a Puzzle', in Z. Razi and R. Smith (eds), *Medieval Society and the Manor Court* (Oxford, 1996)

Rees Jones, S., 'Building Domesticity in the City: English Urban Housing Before the Black Death', in Kowaleski and Goldberg, *Medieval Domesticity*

Revard, C., 'Scribes and Provenance', in S. Fein (ed.), *Studies in the Harley Manuscript: The Scribes, Contents, and Social Contexts of British Library MS Harley 2253* (Kalamazoo, 2000)

Rickard, J., *The Castle Community: The Personnel of English and Welsh Castles, 1272–1422* (Woodbridge, 2002)

Richardson, H. G., 'Business Training in Medieval Oxford', *American Historical Review* 46 (1941)

Richmond, C., 'Landlord and Tenant: the Paston Evidence', in J. Kermode (ed.), *Enterprise and Individuals in Fifteenth-Century England* (Stroud, 1991)

—— *John Hopton: A Fifteenth-Century Suffolk Gentleman* (Cambridge, 1981)

Riddy, F., '"Burgeis" Domesticity in Late-Medieval England', in Kowaleski and Goldberg, *Medieval Domesticity*

Rigold, S. E., 'Structures Within English Moated Sites', in F. A. Aberg (ed.), *CBA Research Report No. 17: Medieval Moated Sites* (London, 1978)

Roberts, M., 'Sickles and Scythes: Women's Work and Men's Work at Harvest Time', *History Workshop* VII (1979)

Robinson, D., 'Clerical Recruitment in England, 1282–1348', in N. Saul (ed.), *Fourteenth Century England V* (Woodbridge, 2008)

Robinson, J. A., 'Household Roll of Bishop Ralph of Shrewsbury (1337–8)', in T. F. Palmer (ed.), *Collectanea I*, Somerset Record Society 39 (1924)

Robinson, P. R., ' "The Booklet": a Self-Contained Unit in Composite Manuscripts', in A. Gruys and J. P. Gambert (eds), *Codicologica 3, Essais typologiques* (Leiden, 1980)

Rosenthal, J. T., *The Purchase of Paradise* (London, 1972)

Rosewell, R., *Medieval Wall Paintings* (Woodbridge, 2008)

Roskell, J. S., Clark, L., and Rawcliffe, C., *History of Parliament: The House of Commons 1386–1421*, 4 vols (Stroud, 1992)

Ross, A. S. C., 'The Middle English Poem on the Names of a Hare', *Proceedings of the Leeds Philosophical and Literary Society* 3 (1935)

Rothwell, W., 'The Role of French in Thirteenth-Century England', *Bulletin of the John Rylands Library* 58 (1976)

Round, J. H., *Geoffrey de Mandeville* (London, 1892)

Rubin, M., 'What is Cultural History Now?', in D. Cannadine (ed.), *What is History Now?* (London, 2002)

Sanders, I. J., *English Baronies: A Study of their Origin and Descent 1086–1327* (Oxford, 1960)

Saul, N., 'Bold as Brass', in P. Coss and M. Keen (eds), *Heraldry, Pageantry and Social Display in Medieval England*

—— *Death, Art and Memory in Medieval England* (Oxford, 2001)

—— *English Church Monuments in the Middle Ages: History and Representation* (Oxford, 2009)

—— 'The Religious Sympathies of the Gentry in Gloucestershire, 1200–1500', *Transactions of the Bristol and Gloucestershire Archaeological Society* (1980)

Schofield, P. R., 'Access to Credit in the Early Fourteenth-Century English Countryside', in P. R. Schofield and N. J. Mayhew (eds), *Credit and Debt in Medieval England* (Oxford, 2002)

—— 'Dearth, Debt and the Local Land Market in a Late Thirteenth-Century Village', *AgHR* 45 (1997)

—— *Peasant and Community in Medieval England 1200–1500* (Basingstoke, 2003)

Scott, M., *Medieval Dress and Fashion* (London, n.d.)

Scott-Stokes, C., *Women's Books of Hours in Medieval England* (Woodbridge, 2006)

Scully, T., *The Art of Cooking in the Middle Ages* (Woodbridge, 1995)

Serjeantson, D., 'Birds: Food as a Mark of Status', in Woolgar, Serjeantson, and Waldron (eds), *Food in Medieval England: Diet and Nutrition*

Serjeantson, D. and Woolgar, C. M., 'Fish Consumption in Medieval England', in Woolgar, Serjeantson, and Waldron (eds) *Food in Medieval England: Diet and Nutrition*

Sewell, W. H., 'The Concept(s) of Culture', in V. E. Bonnell and L. Hunt (eds), *Beyond the Cultural Turn: New Directions in the Study of Society and Culture* (Berkeley, 1999)

Sherwood, J. and Pevsner, N., *The Buildings of England: Oxfordshire* (London, 1974)

Simpkin, D., *The English Aristocracy at War from the Welsh Wars of Edward I to the Battle of Bannockburn* (Woodbridge, 2008)

Smith, K. A., *Art, Identity and Devotion in Fourteenth-Century England: Three Women and Their Books of Hours* (London, 2003)

Soden, I., *Coventry: The Hidden History* (2005)

Spring, E., *Law, Land and Family* (Chapel Hill, 1993)

Stone, D., *Decision-Making in Medieval Agriculture* (Oxford, 2005)

Stone, E., 'Profit and Loss Accountancy at Norwich Cathedral Priory', *TRHS* 5th ser., 12 (1962)

Summerson, H., ' "Most Renowned of Merchants": the Life and Occupation of Laurence of Ludlow (d.1294)', *Midland History* xxx (2005)

Swanson, R. N., 'Indulgences for Prayers for the Dead in the Diocese of Lincoln in the Early Fourteenth Century', *Journal of Ecclesiastical History* 52 (2001)

Thompson, B., 'From Alms to Spiritual Services: the Function and Spiritual Status of Monastic Property in Medieval England', in J. Loades (ed.), *Monastic Studies* II (Gwynnedd, 1991)

Thompson, M., *The Medieval Hall: The Basis of Secular Domestic Life, 600–1600 AD* (Aldershot, 1995)

Thorndike, L., *A History of Magic and Experimental Science*, 2 vols (New York, 1923)

Thornton, C. C., 'The Level of Arable Productivity on the Bishopric of Winchester's Manor of Taunton, 1283–1348', in R. Britnell (ed.), *The Winchester Pipe Rolls and Medieval English Society* (Woodbridge, 2003)

Thrupp, S. L., *The Merchant Class of Medieval London* (Michigan, 1948; repr. 1962)

Titow, J. Z., *English Rural Society 1299–1350* (London, 1969)

Tout, T. F., *Chapters in the Administrative History of Medieval England* (Manchester, 1920; repr. with minor additions and corrections, 1937)

Tummers, H. A., *Early Secular Effigies in England in the Thirteenth Century* (Leiden, 1980)

Turner, R. V., 'The *Miles Literatus* in the Twelfth and Thirteenth Centuries: How Rare a Phenomenon?', *American Historical Review* 83 (1978)

Turville-Petre, T., 'Oxford, Bodleian Library, MS Digby 86: a Thirteenth-Century Commonplace Book in its Social Context', in Richard Eales and Shaun Tyas (eds), *Family and Dynasty in Late Medieval England*, Harlaxton Medieval Studies IX (Donington, 2003)

Victoria County Histories: Berkshire, Bedfordshire, Hertfordshire, Huntingdonshire, Lincolnshire, Northamptonshire, Shropshire, Suffolk, Warwickshire, Worcestershire, Yorkshire

Wade Labarge, M., *A Baronial Household in the Thirteenth Century* (London, 1965)

Walsh, M. M., 'Performing Dame Sirith: Farce and Fabliau at the End of the Thirteenth Century', in W. M. Ormrod (ed.), *England in the Thirteenth Century* (Harlaxton, 1985)

Ward, J. C., 'Fashions in Monastic Endowment: the Foundations of the Clare Family, 1066–1314', *Journal of Ecclesiastical History* xxxii (1981)

Wilson, R. M., 'English and French in England, 1100–1300', *History* 27 (1943)

Wood, M., *The English Medieval House* (London, 1965)

Woodbine, G. E., 'The Language of English Law', *Speculum* 18 (1943)

Wood-Leigh, K. L., *Perpetual Chantries in Britain* (Cambridge, 1965)

Woolgar, C. M., 'Diet and Consumption in Gentry and Noble Households: a Case Study from Around the Wash', in R. E. Archer and S. Walker (eds), *Rulers and Ruled in Late Medieval England: Essays Presented to Gerald Harriss* (London, 1995)

—— *The Great Household in Late Medieval England* (New Haven and London, 1999)

—— 'Meat and Dairy Products in Late Medieval England', in Woolgar, Serjeantson, and Waldron (eds), *Food in Medieval England: Diet and Nutrition*

C. M. Woolgar and B. O'Donoghue, 'Two Middle English Poems at Magdalen College, Oxford', *Medium Ævum* III (1983)

Woolgar, C. M., Serjeantson, D., and Waldron, T. (eds), *Food in Medieval England: Diet and Nutrition* (Oxford, 2006)

UNPUBLISHED THESES

Cavanagh, S. H., 'A Study of Books Privately Owned in England 1300–1450' (University of Pennsylvania Ph.D. thesis, 1980)

Rigby, S. H., 'Boston and Grimsby in the Middle Ages' (University of London Ph.D. thesis, 1978)

Index

Bryene, Dame Alice de, 251
Buckle, Reginald, 122
Budbrooke, Warwicks., 160
Bulmer family, North Riding, 265
Burdet, Sir Aimery, 178, Margery his widow, 178, Nicholas his son, 178, Patrick his brother, 178; Nicholas (another), 178
Burgh, Norfolk, 72
Burgh, Gilbert de, clerk, 207
Burgh by Sands, barony of, 11
Burghersh, Henry, bishop, 177
burials, 140, 151, 154–63, 159–60, 167, 173, 182, 219, 268, 275–7
(Burnham) Thorpe, Norfolk, 73
Burwell, Robert de, chaplain, 144
business training, 221–2
Bussy, Sir John, 203
Butler (Boteler) family, of Warrington, 161–2
Thomas son of william, 161
Butterwick, Lincs., 204
buttery, 25, 35, 58–9
Byford, Sir Hugh de, chaplain, 60

Calais, 35, 274; siege of, 57
Caludon, nr. Coventry, 158
Cambridge University, 220–1
Camille, Michael, 33, 37, 115–16, 126–7
Camoys family, 73, 172, 179
John de, 40, 56–7, 71–2, his wife, 57
Ralph de, 71
Campbell, Bruce, 78, 83, 90
candles, 39–40, 69, 98, 264
Cantelupe family, 161; Sir William de, 156; Thomas de, bishop of Hereford, 156
Canterbury, 153
Carlaverock, siege of, 168–9
Carlton Scroop, Lincs., 181
Carmelite friars (White Friars) *see* friars and friaries
Carpenter, Christine, 182
cash
    cash crop, 102
    cash surplus, 105
    income, 86
    liveries of, 104
Casterton, Sir Richard de, 93
Castleford, Hugh de, 108, 131, 137
Caston, Norfolk, 72
Cat, Henry le, 83
Catesby, William de, of Ladbroke, 214, 258
    and Joan his wife, 274, his son John, 258
cathedrals, 176 *see also* Exeter, Lincoln, St Paul's, Salisbury, Wells
Cavanagh, Susan, 277
Cayley, John de, 70–1
Chacombe Priory, Northants., 158, 160

Chaddeworth, Sir Robert de, 181
chambers, 20, 24–5, 35, 46, 212, 228, 244, 255
    entertainment in 46–9, 54, 244, 251, 256
champerty, 212
Chancery 209; Chancery Rolls, 35
chantries, 137, 141–4, 147, 167, 182, 269, 273; licence for, 141
chapels, 32, 35, 135, 153, 156–9, 162, 168, 192, 212, 228, 255
    household chapel, 141–2, 149, 151, 183, 259
chaplains, 167, 198, 202–3, 207, 228, 236
    household chaplain, 141–3, 229
    parish chaplain, 153
Charlton, John de, lord of Pinley, 274
Chaucer, Geoffrey, 24, 244, his Franklin, 24, 46, 52
Chaunceus, Lady Joan de, 160
Chaworth, Thomas de, of Osberton, 59
    Lambert, his son, 59
    William de, chamberlain, 58
Chelreye, Henry de, 60–1
Chertsey, Surrey, 152
Chester, 274; St Werburg's at, 155
    earl(s) of, 212, 276 *see also* Ranulf (III) *and* the Montalts
Cheylesmore, Coventry, 154–5
Cheyneys of Cheyney Longville, 232
Chilton, Robert de and his son John, 258
chivalry, 1, 284, 287–8
    chivalric/courtly literature, 2, 77, 118
Christchurch Priory, 151
Christian, William, of Kirton, 201
Christmas festivities, 218
church livings, 141, 177–81, 199
church services, 143, 147, 168, 176, 182, 231
churches, 152–3, 162, 167, 203, 260, 269, 276, 280, 287
    altars, 153, 162–4
    apse, 165
    chancel/presbytery, 159–60, 162, 164–5, 174, 275–6
    choir, 155, 160, 162, 168
    nave, 164–5
    tower, 174
Cirencester Abbey, 151
Cirencester, Laurence de, rector, 152
Cistercian order, 150
Clanchy, Michael, *From Memory to Written Record*, 217
Clare, Suffolk, 150; family of, 150
Claymond, Thomas, 200–1, 203–4
clergy, clerics 143, 152, 172, 177–9, 183, 207, 210, 219–20, 229, 236, 287
    archdeacons, 196, 204
    official of, 144, 180

Wykes in Donington, Lincs., 16
Wynceby, Geoffrey de, steward, 64, 87

Yarmouth, Norfolk, 253, 277
Yeldon, Beds., 56

York, 153, 261, 265, 270–1, 279–80; Castle,
280; St Mary's, abbot of, 259; St Mary's,
parish of, Castlegate, 280

Zouche family of Harringworth, 269